Logics and Languages

Logics and Languages

M. J. CRESSWELL
READER IN PHILOSOPHY
VICTORIA UNIVERSITY OF WELLINGTON

METHUEN & CO LTD
11 NEW FETTER LANE LONDON EC4P 4EE

First published 1973
by Methuen & Co Ltd
11 New Fetter Lane London EC4

Printed in Great Britain by
William Clowes & Sons Limited
London, Colchester and Beccles

SBN 416 76950 0

Distributed in the U.S.A. by
HARPER & ROW PUBLISHERS INC
BARNES & NOBLE IMPORT DIVISION

Contents

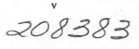

Preface

Among the most central issues in philosophy seem to me to be questions about the relation between language and the world. This book attempts to tackle some of these questions by providing a formal model within which to define notions which play a crucial role in the study of language: notions like 'sentence', 'meaning' and 'truth'.

Parts I and II set out a class of formal languages and their semantics, while Parts III and IV try to shew that these formal languages are rich enough to be used in the precise description of natural languages.

It seems to me that the aim of Parts III and IV is best achieved by trying to give a formal analysis of a particular natural language; and, for obvious reasons, I have chosen English. While I have tried to be as accurate as I could in my treatment of English I would not be worried, or surprised, if a great deal of what I have said needs to be amended in the light of further linguistic evidence. I shall be satisfied if I have been able to make plausible the applicability of the approach to semantics outlined in the earlier part of the book.

The inspiration for this book arose as a result of spending three months of my sabbatical leave at UCLA in 1970 and attending lectures by Richard Montague on the philosophy of language. Latterly I have benefited from discussions with a number of people: Dr G. D. Kennedy, who taught the only linguistics course I ever attended, members of our logic seminar here in Wellington, and, most particularly, Professor G. E. Hughes, who read the whole manuscript and made many valuable comments. I am also grateful to the publications committee of the Victoria University of Wellington for a grant towards the cost of the book's production. My wife, Mary, helped to prepare the manuscript and Helen Fleming did the typing.

Wellington, New Zealand M. J. CRESSWELL
August 1972

Note on references

All references to the literature are given in footnotes, and in abbreviated form, by name of author and date of publication. Full details will be found in the Bibliography on pp. 250–62 which is arranged in alphabetical order of authors and chronologically under each author's name. In not a few cases articles have been cited in collections of reprints because they are usually more accessible in that form.

Introduction

There are at least two ways of approaching the study of language. One approach is to regard language as an existent human phenomenon and to jump right in and study what occurs. Another approach is to study artificial languages, which can be kept under tight control by means of the stipulative definitions with which they are introduced, and try to incorporate into them more and more of the features possessed by the natural languages we use in our everyday lives.

The present book will attempt an exposition of this second approach, i.e. I shall introduce a series of formal languages, modelled on the languages of symbolic logic, which gradually increase in complexity until they reach a point at which they can profitably be thought of as models for natural languages.

In this century the prevailing attitude of philosophers to language appears to have been that the languages of formal logic have only a rough correspondence with natural languages. Some philosophers have therefore said so much the worse for formal languages and have concentrated on describing natural languages. Other philosophers have said so much the worse for natural languages and have concentrated on using formal languages for the task of precise description in such areas as the physical sciences.[1]

It will be one of the contentions of this book that the reason for the common attitude of philosophers of both persuasions to the relation between formal and natural languages is a result of nothing more than the structural poverty of the only formal languages which have been in wide use, viz. the languages of first-order predicate logic, and that a consideration of a wider class of formal languages, of the kind we shall be undertaking, lends support to the view that formal languages have

[1] This point is made at length in the early part of Katz [1966].

a connection with natural languages which is as revealing of the structure of the latter as any more direct form of description.[2]

A consequence of undertaking linguistic analysis with the aid of formal languages requires that we be very clear about how we use the term 'language'. Leonard Bloomfield[3] has described language as 'the noise you make with your face'. A definition of this kind immediately puts him (as it should put a linguist) in the camp of those who plunge in and study the language which is actually in use 'out there' in the world. A logician on the other hand may well choose to define a language as an abstract system of a certain kind, without going on to ask whether this system is used by any group of people for communication.[4]

We might mark this distinction by the terms *a-language* and *u-language* (for an abstract language and a used language respectively).[5] The distinction enables us to keep apart certain questions which have often been regarded as inseparable. Given merely an a-language $\mathscr{L}$ we might define a further abstract system which we could call a *semantics* for $\mathscr{L}$. I.e. we might describe those interrelations between the abstract system $\mathscr{L}$ and aspects of reality, which look like the kinds of interrelation we think of as having to do with meaning. In this

[2] Though, curiously enough, those linguists who are most enamoured of a base language in the style of symbolic logic appear to have in mind some version of first-order logic. *Vide* e.g. McCawley [1971] and G. Lakoff [1970a]. The point of course is that one can use a simple base language with a large number of transformational steps or a complicated base language with a few steps. It is not surprising that a linguist should be more inclined to the former while a logician might well prefer the latter (though many logicians too like a first-order base language). I would hope that this book might give a glimpse into the riches of the more complex formal languages and tempt some linguists to think of making use of them.

[3] Bloomfield [1936], p. 139.

[4] Or whatever other purpose language may be used for. I say a bit, but not much, about this in Chapter 14. Chomsky [1957], p. 13, is clearly talking about a-languages so that the two senses both occur in the work of linguists. Cf. Carnap's distinction [1942], pp. 11–15 between pure and applied semantics; and Harman [1971].

[5] We shall not use the terms 'a-language' and 'u-language' in the text of the book. Most of the time we shall be talking about a-languages in general or about the a-language or family of a-languages which comes closest to English but we shall rely on the context, and the remarks I have just made about the importance of the distinction, to make clear the sense of 'language' we are, at any particular stage, assuming. In view of the fact that most recent work in the philosophy of language has been concerned with theories of language use I am taking it that no apology is needed for refusing to venture into this area. I would of course like to think that what I have written may help to put some of this work into focus. I shall not attempt to refer to the literature here except to mention Grice [1968], on the philosophical side, and Halliday [1970], on the linguistic side, as good examples of what is being done.

sense therefore we can divorce a *theory of meaning* for an a-language from a *theory of use* for an a-language. A theory of use for an a-language will be a theory which tells us when a certain a-language together with its semantics can provide a model for a certain u-language. Philosophers such as John Searle who take the 'speech act' as primary, and therefore begin by studying u-languages, quite rightly insist that they cannot divorce use and meaning. This is because a theory of meaning for a u-language will, in our terms, be explicated[6] by providing a theory of meaning for some a-language which is a model of that u-language, and although we do not require a theory of use to study the semantics of the a-language we do require a theory of use to tell us which a-language is a model of the u-language in which we are interested. (And indeed to tell us what 'being a model of' amounts to in this area.)

The view that formal languages might help us in understanding such notions as meaning and truth is part of a philosophical tradition which goes back at least as far as Frege.[7] The more immediate origin of the present book is in the semantical study of systems of modal logic, and in particular the idea used there of a *possible world* or *state of affairs*. The notion of a possible world is even older than Frege and can be traced to Leibniz if not further. Its use in defining meaning was seen by Wittgenstein who in the *Tractatus*[8] claimed that to understand a proposition is to know what is the case if it is true. From the sort of logical atomism presented in the *Tractatus* comes some of our metaphysical analysis though the philosophy of language associated with atomism finds little place in the present work.

One of the earliest attempts to apply modal logic to an analysis of meaning was Carnap's *Meaning and Necessity*, and a comparison of that work with our own will be instructive for those with an historical interest in our subject. Carnap recognizes his debt to Wittgenstein for the notion of a possible world and introduces the notion of a *state-description*.[9] If we assume that there are a set of atomic sentences

[6] 'Explication' is Carnap's word for the task of 'making more exact a vague or not quite exact concept used in everyday life or in an earlier stage of scientific or logical development' (Carnap [1947], p. 7). A fuller account is given in Carnap [1950], pp. 3–8.

[7] A good defence of the approach to language study via formal languages is found in Martin [1971]. For a more purely philosophical approach *vide* Wiggins [1971] and some of the other articles in that collection.

[8] Wittgenstein [1922], 4.024 but *vide* also 4.41, 4.431.

[9] Carnap [1947], p. 9 f.

which may be either true or false without prejudice to the truth or falsity of any other atomic sentences then a state-description is a class which contains for every atomic sentence either that sentence or its negation.

The big advance in the semantical study of modal logic after Carnap was to remove possible worlds from the dependence on language which they have in Carnap's work and treat them as primitive entities in their own right, in terms of which the semantical notions required by the modal systems can be defined. Possible-world semantics for modal logic have become best known through the work of Saul Kripke in the late fifties and early sixties though others were active at the same time as well. The conviction which has been growing in recent years on a number of philosophers as a result of these developments is that the semantical insights gained from this work in modal logic and in particular the notion of a possible world have a much wider application than the extraordinarily intensive, but very restricted, studies of particular intensional logics would indicate. Ideas closest in spirit to those of this book will be found in the work of, among others, David Lewis and Richard Montague.[10] At the time of his death Montague was planning a monograph on the analysis of language and the present book owes much to his work. Although I shall be giving what is primarily an exposition of my own views on the formal analysis of natural languages I would hope that what I have written may also serve as an introduction to the kind of work which is currently being pursued by those who share similar convictions about the study of language.

The first two parts of the book set out the class of formal languages which are to be put forward in Parts III and IV as models for natural language. I have called these languages *categorial languages*, adapting the name from an idea of Leśniewski in the early thirties.[11] The idea behind them is that the syntactic category of a symbol or complex expression is either basic or is determined by the kind of expression it makes when combined with other expressions. Part I tries to accustom the reader gradually to the idea by presenting what I have called *propositional languages*.[12] These have sentences as their only basic

[10] Lewis [1970], Montague [1970a].

[11] Expounded and developed in Adjukiewicz [1935]; though Adjukiewicz apparently called them 'semantic' categories.

[12] The name is chosen because the notion of a propositional language is a generalization of the languages of what is frequently called 'propositional logic'.

category and for each natural number n a class of n-place propositional functors or connectives which when placed before n other sentences (called the *arguments* of the functor) form a new complex sentence. As an example consider the Latin word ***amat*** (he loves) and the adverb ***non*** (not). We can regard ***amat*** as a simple sentence symbol and ***non*** as a one-place functor. This means that the sequence ⟨***non, amat***⟩ would be a complex sentence of a propositional language because ***non*** makes a sentence, (⟨***non, amat***⟩), out of a sentence, (***amat***). Live examples of propositional languages are found in the many systems of propositional logic. Propositional languages enable the discussion of quite a number of points which arise in the study of language. Most important among these is the development of a semantical analysis in which the meaning of a sentence is defined as the set of possible worlds in which it is true and in which the notion of a proposition as a set of possible worlds makes its appearance.

Categorial languages are particularly amenable to semantical treatment, using the idea which is due to Frege of taking the values of the functors as functions which operate on the values of the expressions which follow the functor to give a value for the whole expression. The languages of Part II are generalizations of propositional languages to languages involving symbols and expressions in many syntactical categories and enriched with an abstraction operator (written as λ) to bind variables. Variables in a λ-categorial language, as such languages are called, play only a structural role in the evaluation of sentences and may thus be termed *logical* symbols. We allow a slight relaxation of the rules which allows that in unambiguous cases the order of a functor relative to its arguments may be varied so that, e.g., a functor may follow its arguments or may be placed between them. This allows a sequence like

⟨***amat, et, currit***⟩

to be a well-formed sentence even though the functor ***et*** stands between the two sentences which are its arguments and not in front of them.

From time to time, in Parts I and II, I have exercised the philosopher's prerogative of indulging in a little speculative metaphysics.[13] I have indicated in these passages that the metaphysics is for the purposes of illustration only but the illustrations are seriously

[13] I hope it is descriptive metaphysics rather than revisionary (*vide* Strawson [1959], pp. 9–11). Though, in view of footnote 6 *supra*, it might be better to call it *explicatory* metaphysics.

intended. The price for sticking one's neck out in such areas is undoubtedly to have it chopped off but the alternative is to leave the reader completely in the dark about the nature of the entities required for the semantical analysis of language.

Part III tries to exhibit English as an example of a categorial language of the kind defined in Part II. Basically the idea is that a sentence of a categorial language is a rather complicated thing, looking like, say:[14]

$$\langle \textbf{\textit{John}}, \langle \lambda, x, \langle\langle \lambda, y, \langle \textbf{\textit{loves}}, x, y \rangle\rangle, \textbf{\textit{someone}} \rangle\rangle\rangle$$

but that ordinary English can be got by simply deleting all the 'logical' words like the λ, x, y, and so on to get

$$\langle \textbf{\textit{John, loves, someone}} \rangle$$

The original sentence, with its λ's, x's and so on can be thought of as akin to a structural description of the sentence which results from the deletions. Where two different sentences in a categorial language give the same result after deletion we can sometimes get a case of structural ambiguity, as when we derive

$$\langle \textbf{\textit{everyone, loves, someone}} \rangle$$

from

$$\langle \textbf{\textit{everyone}}, \langle \lambda, x, \langle\langle \lambda, y, \langle \textbf{\textit{loves}}, x, y \rangle\rangle, \textbf{\textit{someone}} \rangle\rangle\rangle$$

or

$$\langle\langle \lambda, y, \langle \textbf{\textit{everyone}}, \langle \lambda, x, \langle \textbf{\textit{loves}}, x, y \rangle\rangle\rangle\rangle, \textbf{\textit{someone}} \rangle$$

Part III is built on the general theoretical framework defined in detail in Part II, and what I have tried to shew here is how much of English can be fitted in to that framework. Any discussion of English as a formal language which is compressed into about half the length of a book the size of the present one is of course bound to be fragmentary and incomplete, and at the present stage of linguistic knowledge is also bound to be very tentative. As with the metaphysics, this part may sound far more dogmatic than the facts warrant but I would rather err on the side of overstating my case than understating it.

Part IV takes up some of the many remaining problems in obtaining a natural language from a categorial language. Chief among these are

[14] It does not matter at the moment just what these hieroglyphics really mean. All is explained in Part II.

first the relation of the symbols of categorial languages to the words and their tokens in the languages we use and second the problem of specifying which sentences in the categorial base are acceptable in English when the logical symbols have been deleted and which are not. A final chapter attempts to say something about the relation between meaning and use.

A word should be said here about the relation between Parts III and IV and current work in linguistics. I have noted some differences between the approach to language adopted in this book and the approach via transformational grammar, and have tried to explain why I have chosen to exhibit ordinary English sentences as obtainable directly from λ-categorial sentences rather than by a series of transformations operating on phrase-markers.[15] This does not mean that the present work is quite independent of linguistics. Extensive reference is made to recent work in this area and such results as seemed appropriate have been discussed. But the purpose of the book is not to describe a natural language in detail but rather to argue for a certain view of the nature of the entities required in semantic analysis and to attempt to give a philosophically adequate theory of meaning. I had hoped to be able to say something more in Chapter 13 about the principles which generate those sentences in the categorial base language which result in acceptable surface sentences when the logical symbols are deleted. I still think there is a role here for a transformational component, though, as my remarks on pp. 224–7 indicate, I have had little success in formulating it. Whether linguists will take this up will depend on whether a base in a λ-categorial language and the semantics that go with it are considered helpful tools in the study of natural languages.

The attitude to analysis adopted in this book is that set theory provides the most adequate framework known for precise description. This does not mean that the theory of sets is above philosophical examination; indeed the discovery of Russell's and other paradoxes ensures that no one can feel quite certain of its foundations. But it does mean that any alternative framework must be shewn to be at least as comprehensive and as well-founded. As far as its consistency goes it is probably fair to say that axiomatic systems of set theory have been

[15] The most important early work in transformational grammar is Chomsky [1957]. A good general introduction is Lyons [1969], pp. 247–69. Lewis [1970] is an excellent account of how to base transformational grammar on categorial languages.

subject to far more rigorous testing than any other formal theory. For the purposes of this book at any rate, we may safely assume that if its set-theoretical foundations should crumble a great deal more will be destroyed than the structures here defined.

Set theory is held to be extensional. The word 'extensional' seems to mean just about all things to all men. It has also become a value-loaded word which marks philosophers and logicians into two camps. I have tried not to use it much, nor its companion, 'intensional'. In a few cases I have used 'extensional' to describe the two-valued propositional and predicate calculi and 'intensional' to describe such systems as the modal systems, particularly their semantics. These uses amount to mere descriptions to single out certain well-studied areas of logic and have only an historical connection with the original meanings of the terms. I have occasionally used the words *intension* or *intensional* in roughly Carnap's sense, but in each case the context should make clear exactly what is meant. From one point of view a language can be said to be extensional if it can be formulated in first-order predicate logic. In this sense set theory is extensional and insofar as the formal development of the philosophy of language presented in this book is expressed in set theory then our philosophy of language could be described as an extensional one. But since it is known that any system of logic can be 'translated', in a precisely definable sense, into an 'extensional' one,[16] a claim on this ground that one's work is extensional means so little as to be virtually worthless.

Appendix I sets out all the set theory which is needed for understanding what is going on in just about every section of the book. I have recommended a couple of texts which might be helpful to those who have had no prior acquaintance with it at all but the book is intended to be, for the most part, self-contained. Similar remarks apply to an acquaintance with symbolic logic. No knowledge of logic is presupposed but some of the definitions in the early part of the book will obviously be more immediately intuitive to those who have seen their counterparts in logical systems. Any justification, though, which the book may have is to be measured by the success with which it assists our understanding of natural languages, in particular of

[16] E.g. *vide* Cresswell [1968]. This is not as startling as it sounds. For first-order logics the analysis simply takes the intensional entities used in the semantics for non-extensional languages as the domain of values for the individual variables in an extensional lower predicate calculus. This method involves no commitment to any view about the nature of these entities, such as the view that propositions are sentences.

English, and not by any connection it may have with recognized branches of symbolic logic.

The technical vocabulary used in the book is roughly of two kinds. In the formal development and whenever I am being precise I have used the notions of set theory together with any others I have defined. Words from traditional philosophical jargon, like 'symbol', 'proposition', 'world', 'property', and so on, will all be given precise set-theoretical definitions and when we use them in any context in which precision is required they will be used *in precisely the sense in which they have been defined.* Of course I shall have my off moments when I shall speak rather loosely in order to get an idea across with the minimum of pain, and of course too I have chosen the terms I define because of their pre-definitional suggestions but there ought to be no question of vagueness or unclarity in places where this could be disturbing.

Examples are given by numbers enclosed in parentheses and these mostly begin anew with each section. Rules, theorems, definitions and important points are given by chapter number followed by a decimal point and a number in a series which is consecutive throughout the chapter. All cross-referencing is done by page numbers and so no sections within chapters have been numbered. Reference by page number seems to me unquestionably the most efficient. Various devices have been used to enrich the (English) metalanguage in which the book is written. Particularly several different type styles have been used for variables of one sort or another. While I have tried to maintain a certain consistency here, I have also explained in each context what kind of thing a variable is a variable for and so the type style is merely a reader's aid. Prominent among these metavariables is the use of English words printed in bold-face italic type (as *supra* p. 6). These are metavariables for the symbols of a formal language but so chosen because they suggest the English words which the formal language is trying to represent.

Certain chapters and sections can be omitted without loss of continuity and these have been so marked. In addition, of course, such passages as the proofs of theorems in Parts I and II can be omitted by those who are prepared to take them on trust. In the main however the book is intended as a unified whole and frequent use will be made at later stages of material introduced earlier.

PART ONE

Propositional Languages

CHAPTER ONE

Syntax and Semantics of Propositional Languages

Our aim in this book will be to set out and discuss artificial languages which can exhibit many if not all of the semantical features of natural languages. Such an aim will necessitate a very general definition of a wide class of languages. Part I of the book will prepare the way by studying the general form of the languages of propositional logic, particularly the languages of intensional logic.

Syntax

By a *propositional language* $\mathscr{L}$ we mean an ordered pair $\langle \Delta, S \rangle$ where $\Delta = \langle \Delta_0, \ldots, \Delta_k \rangle$ is a finite sequence of pairwise disjoint, possibly empty, finite sets, and S is the smallest set such that:

1.1 $\Delta_0 \subseteq S$.

1.2 If $\delta \in \Delta_n$ $(1 \leqslant n \leqslant k)$ and $\alpha_1, \ldots, \alpha_n \in S$ then $\langle \delta, \alpha_1, \ldots, \alpha_n \rangle \in S$.[17]

What the definition comes to is this. The union of all the sets in Δ, denoted by Δ^+, is the set of *symbols*[18] or *words* of $\mathscr{L}$ and S is the set

[17] My exposition, both in this chapter and throughout the book, will frequently make use of set theory. An appendix (pp. 241–5) has been included to explain the terminology for those who may not be familiar with it. That there is a smallest set S satisfying these conditions is proved on p. 9.

[18] 'Symbols' is the term we shall use throughout this book but it can be a little confusing in that the symbols of the written versions of a natural language like English can equally be thought of as letters. Perhaps the linguists' word 'morpheme' would be better. (*Vide* e.g. Lyons [1969] pp. 180–94.) On the use of the notation 'Δ^+', *vide* p. 245. A symbol is only defined in relation to a language. When we speak of symbols as being 'simple' we do not mean that they may not have a complex internal structure but only that this structure is irrelevant to the syntax of the language.

of sentences or (well-formed) formulae. Δ_0 is the set of simple sentence symbols (for by 1.1 any member of Δ_0 is a member of S, i.e., a sentence) and Δ_n ($1 \leqq n \leqq k$) is the set of n-place *propositional functors*. An n-place propositional functor is a symbol which when placed before n sentences forms another (complex) sentence. This is what 1.2 says. Those familiar with propositional logic, who may be finding all this rather too abstract, should think of the propositional calculus as a propositional language. Δ_0 is the set of 'propositional variables', Δ_1 contains one member, the symbol $\sim$, Δ_2 may contain the symbols $\supset$, $\vee$, ., $\equiv$ and perhaps a few others.[19] In this case $k = 2$; and indeed most versions of the propositional calculus contain at most 2-place functors.

Other propositional logics (modal logics, e.g., with the symbols L and M, or $\Box$ and $\Diamond$; in Δ_1) also fall under our definition. There is however one important restriction, that is that Δ_0 is finite. In most propositional logics the simple sentence symbols are denumerably infinite and in some, e.g. PC itself, it is crucial that this should be so. There are not too complicated ways of achieving an infinite number of simple sentence symbols out of a finite alphabet (e.g. p, p', p'', p''', p'''', etc.) but they take us a little beyond the definition we have given.

The only restriction we have placed on the members of Δ^+ is that they be finite and have no common members. This does not rule out the possibility that a complex sentence might also be a symbol. Suppose for instance that $\Delta_0 = \{\alpha\}$ and $\Delta_1 = \{\delta, \langle\delta, \alpha\rangle\}$. Then Δ_0 and Δ_1 are disjoint but $\langle\delta, \alpha\rangle$ is both a functor and a complex sentence. Since this is undesirable for all sorts of reasons we shall say that a propositional language is *grounded* iff for no $\delta \in \Delta_n$ and $\alpha_1, \ldots, \alpha_n \in$ S is $\langle\delta, \alpha_1, \ldots, \alpha_n\rangle \in \Delta^+$. We shall assume that all the propositional languages we discuss are grounded.

Apart from these restrictions the members of Δ^+ may be anything we please. At first this may seem a little strange. Since we speak about them as symbols shouldn't we say what symbols are? And since we talk about functors making complex sentences out of simpler ones shouldn't we say something about how the putting together is done? The answer is that, fortunately, for the semantical analysis of a language we do not, at this stage at least, have to answer these questions. When we actually use a language of course the members of Δ^+ can't be just any old things. E.g., suppose Big Ben is a member of Δ_0 and Walter Scott a member of Δ_1, then the sequence (ordered pair)

[19] Thus if α and $\beta \in$ S, so is $\langle\supset, \alpha, \beta\rangle$. Most propositional languages also include brackets among their symbols. The reason for this is discussed *infra* p. 78n.

whose first member is Walter Scott and whose second Big Ben is a sentence of our language, and it is a little difficult to see how such a language would be any good in practice. For languages actually in use the symbols can perhaps be regarded as classes of utterances.[20] We shall have a little more to say on this problem later: for the moment we simply repeat that symbols can be anything we like and that sentences are set-theoretical entities (sequences) made up out of the symbols according to 1.1 and 1.2.

The rules 1.1 and 1.2 may be regarded as specifying the *syntax* of propositional languages, for they determine the class of grammatically well-formed sentences of these languages. Before we proceed to semantics we shall describe these rules in a slightly different way which will lend itself to fairly easy generalization when we come to more elaborate languages. In describing a propositional language we make use of the notion of a *syntactic category*.[21] In propositional languages one of these is the category of *sentence*, while the others are all categories of *functors*.

A functor is a symbol which, occurring as the first member of a sequence of symbols of certain syntactical kinds, makes a sequence of the same or another syntactical kind. If $\delta \in \Delta_n$ then δ placed before n members of the category *sentence* forms another sequence of the category *sentence*.

In Chapter Five we shall use 'F' to denote a class of functors and use a subscript to indicate the kind of functor. We shall be using 0 to indicate the category of sentence. Since an n-place propositional functor forms a sentence, i.e. a thing of category 0, out of n other things of category 0 we can represent the class of n-place functors as

$$\mathrm{F}_{\overbrace{\langle 0, \ldots, 0 \rangle}^{n+1 \text{ times}}}$$

Here the ordered $n+1$-tuple of 0's may be said to be the *category index* of n-place propositional functors. The first member of the $n+1$-tuple tells us that what is formed by the functor is a thing of category 0 and the last n members tell us that this is formed out of n other things of category 0. Thus Δ_0 would be F_0, Δ_1 would be $\mathrm{F}_{\langle 0, 0 \rangle}$

[20] Cf. Quine [1960], pp. 191–5, and pp. 111–15 *infra*.

[21] Adjukiewicz [1935]. It has more recently been used by Bar Hillel [1964], Lewis [1970], Geach [1970], Montague [1970a] and no doubt by others. The possibility of applying it in linguistics is developed in Lyons [1966] and [1969], pp. 227–31. *Vide* also Keenan [1971]. For phrase-structure grammars *vide* Bar Hillel [op. cit.], pp. 99–150, Chomsky [1957], pp. 26–33 and McCawley [1968b].

and so on. 0 is called the *basic* category and the others are called *functor* categories or *derived* categories.

There are alternative ways of indexing syntactic categories. We prefer the one we have just mentioned because of its simple set-theoretical construction out of numbers. Frequently s is used instead of 0 and the notation[22]

$$s/(\overbrace{s,\ldots,s}^{n\text{-times}})$$

instead of

$$\langle\overbrace{0,\ldots,0}^{n+1\text{ times}}\rangle$$

Yet another way of describing this syntax is available to us from linguistic theory in terms of a set of context-free phrase-structure rules. For each n we assume a rule of the form

1.3 $s \to \langle s/(\overbrace{s,\ldots,s}^{n\text{-times}}), \overbrace{s,\ldots,s}^{n\text{-times}}\rangle$

What this means is that s can be rewritten as a sequence consisting of $s/(\overbrace{s,\ldots,s}^{n\text{-times}})$ followed by n s's. Δ then supplies the *lexicon* which allows us to put actual symbols for the s's. Given $\Delta = \langle \Delta_0, \ldots, \Delta_k \rangle$ we would have for each $\alpha \in \Delta_0$

1.4 $s \to \alpha$

and for each $\delta \in \Delta_n$ $(1 \leqslant n \leqslant k)$

1.5 $s/(\overbrace{s,\ldots,s}^{n\text{-times}}) \to \delta$

By this means we could derive all the well-formed sentences. E.g. suppose $\delta \in \Delta_3$, $\zeta \in \Delta_1$, and α and β are both in Δ_0. Obviously by our formation rules

1.6 $\langle \delta, \alpha, \langle \zeta, \beta \rangle, \langle \zeta, \langle \delta, \alpha, \beta, \alpha \rangle\rangle\rangle$

is in S.

By **1.4** and **1.5** we have: $s \to \alpha$, $s \to \beta$, $s/(s) \to \zeta$, $s/(s, s, s) \to \delta$.

[22] As is done e.g., Bar Hillel [1964], pp. 61–74. Our preferred notation is very like that of Church [1940]. Church has two basic categories 0 and ι.

To derive 1.6 according to phrase-structure rules we should do the following:

1.7 s

$\langle s/(s,s,s), s, s, s\rangle$	by 1.3
$\langle s/(s,s,s), s, \langle s/(s), s\rangle, s\rangle$	by 1.3
$\langle s/(s,s,s), s, \langle s/(s), s\rangle, \langle s/(s), s\rangle\rangle$	by 1.3
$\langle s/(s,s,s), s, \langle s/(s), s\rangle, \langle s/(s), \langle s/(s,s,s), s, s, s\rangle\rangle$	by 1.3
$\langle \delta, \alpha, \langle \zeta, \beta\rangle, \langle \zeta, \langle \delta, \alpha, \beta, \alpha\rangle\rangle\rangle$	by 1.4, 1.5

Corresponding to this derivation we have the 'tree' or 'phrase-marker':

1.8

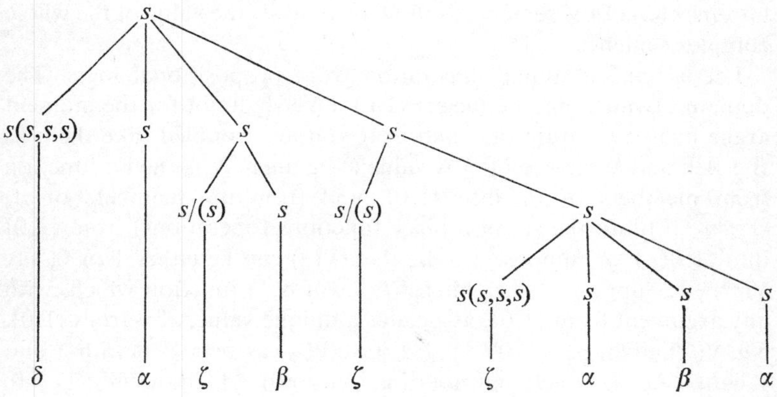

In dealing with propositional logics, 1.1 and 1.2 are obviously much simpler to handle than the methods we have just indicated, and indeed their analogues are perhaps clearer for many of the languages we discuss, but the notion of a syntactic category is certainly very helpful in the general case, and the description of it in terms of phrase-structure grammar does give it a link with linguistic theory.

Semantics

Semantics, for us, is going to be the study of the relation between words and the world. More specifically, its goal will be the explication of the notion of a true sentence under a given interpretation.[23] We have seen

[23] This puts us in the tradition dating from Tarski [1935]. *Vide* also Davidson [1967]. The closest work to this is that of Montague [1970a] and [1970b]; *vide* also Lewis [1970].

that syntactically the members of the Δ_n ($1 \leqq n \leqq k$) are functors which operate on things of a certain kind to give other things of a certain kind. In propositional languages these other things are always sentences. An interpretation for a language like this consists of an assignment of values to the symbols from which values can be calculated for the sentences. (In propositional languages sentences are the only kind of well-formed complex expressions; we have no complex one-place functors, for example.) If we have a set of things which are the values of the sentences then the kinds of things the values of the functors will be will be fixed too. Remember that an n-place functor put before n sentences makes a sentence out of them. So the value or interpretation (or perhaps even meaning or intension) of a functor should be a function[24] which, when applied to the values (or interpretations, etc.) of the sentences following it, gives the value of the whole complex sentence.

Let us take a simple illustration from propositional logic. The domain of values can be the set $\{1,0\}$. (We shall not for the moment argue over the nature of 1 and 0. If you are troubled take them as Big Ben and Walter Scott.) A value assignment V is then a function from members of Δ_0 into $\{1,0\}$, and from the members of Δ_n ($1 \leqq n \leqq k$) into the set of n-place functions (operations) from $\{1,0\}$ into $\{1,0\}$. E.g., suppose $\alpha \in \Delta_0$, then $V(\alpha)$ can be either 1 or 0, say $V(\alpha) = 1$. Suppose $\sim \in \Delta_1$, then $V(\sim)$ will be a function which, with any argument from $\{1,0\}$, associates a unique value, also from $\{1,0\}$, e.g. $V(\sim)$ might be $\{\langle 1,0\rangle, \langle 0,1\rangle\}$, i.e., $V(\sim)$ associates 0 with 1 and 1 with 0, i.e., in functional notation $(V(\sim))(0) = 1$ and $(V(\sim))(1) = 0$. The rule for evaluating complex sentences will require that the value of $\langle \sim,\alpha\rangle$ is $(V(\sim))(V(\alpha)) = (V(\sim))(1) = 0$.

More generally we shall say that an *interpretation* for a propositional

[24] *Vide* Appendix I, p. 242 f. There is a sense in which we are talking about functions of three different kinds here and only confusion will result if we mix them up. Firstly, the functor itself is a sort of function (though *vide* p. 54), for we may regard the sentences which follow it as its arguments and the complex formula it forms as its value for those arguments. Secondly, the value assignment is a function whose argument is a linguistic expression and whose value is a certain kind of entity depending on the category of the expression. Thirdly, the value of the assignment function for a particular expression, i.e. the meaning of that expression, may itself be a function; as here the value of an n-place functor is an n-place function which can have as its own arguments and values things which are also the values of the assignment function. To avoid confusion, 'δ' is normally used to refer to functors, 'V' to the valuation or assignment function and 'ω' for the functions which are the values of the functor symbols.

language $\mathscr{L}$ is an ordered pair $\langle \mathbf{P}, V \rangle$ in which $\mathbf{P}$ is a set and V a function such that

1.9 If $\alpha \in \Delta_0$ then $V(\alpha) \in \mathbf{P}$
1.10 If $\delta \in \Delta_n$ then $V(\delta) \in \mathbf{P}^{\mathbf{P}^n}$.

What 1.10 means is that if δ is an n-place functor then $V(\delta)$ is an n-place operation on $\mathbf{P}$.[25]

V is thus a value assignment to the symbols. On the basis of $\langle \mathbf{P}, V \rangle$ we can work out meanings for all the complex expressions (i.e. sentences) of $\mathscr{L}$. The meaning assignment induced by V is that unique[26] function V^+ from S into $\mathbf{P}$ such that

1.11 If $\alpha \in \Delta_0$ then $V^+(\alpha) = V(\alpha)$
1.12 If $\delta \in \Delta_n$ $(1 \leqq n \leqq k)$ and $\alpha_1, \ldots, \alpha_n \in S$ then $V^+(\langle \delta, \alpha_1, \ldots, \alpha_n \rangle) = (V(\delta))(V^+(\alpha_1), \ldots, V^+(\alpha_n))$.

Sometimes, when there is no ambiguity about different V's, we write $V(\delta)$ as ω_δ. Thus

$$V^+(\langle \delta, \alpha_1, \ldots, \alpha_n \rangle) = \omega_\delta(V^+(\alpha_1), \ldots, V^+(\alpha_n)).$$

These rules reflect an important general principle which we shall discuss later under the name *Frege's principle*, that the meaning of the whole sentence is a function of the meanings of its parts. The reason for distinguishing between V and V^+ is to make quite clear that what an interpretation does is give a meaning to the symbols from which *follows* the meaning of the complex expressions. This property of language, that a speaker on the basis of knowing the meanings of a finite number of words can recognize the meanings of infinitely many sentences, most of which he has never heard before, is one of the most crucial things to be captured in any analysis of its nature. The arguments of V (as opposed to V^+) are finite in number. This is why V^+ must depend on V.

We remarked above that semantics must lead to a definition of truth. To obtain a definition of truth we must add to our interpretation a subset of $\mathbf{P}$ as the 'designated' set of 'true' values. When we do this we convert an interpretation into what may be called a *model*.

[25] *Vide* Appendix I, p. 244.
[26] That V^+ is unique is easily seen provided $\mathscr{L}$ is grounded. Obviously V^+ is uniquely defined for $\alpha \in \Delta_0$. If $\alpha \in S$ but $\alpha \notin \Delta_0$ then α is $\langle \delta, \alpha_1, \ldots, \alpha_n \rangle$ for some $\delta \in \Delta_n$ for some n. Since each of the $\alpha_1, \ldots, \alpha_n$ is shorter than α we may assume the result to hold for them, and since ω_δ is a function then $V^+(\alpha)$ is unique.

1.13 A model for a propositional language $\mathscr{L}$ is an ordered triple $\langle \mathbf{P}, \mathbf{T}, \mathrm{V} \rangle$ in which $\langle \mathbf{P}, \mathrm{V} \rangle$ is an interpretation for $\mathscr{L}$ and **T** is a proper subset of **P**. We shall say that a sentence α of $\mathscr{L}$ is *true* in $\langle \mathbf{P}, \mathbf{T}, \mathrm{V} \rangle$ iff $\mathrm{V}^{+}(\alpha) \in \mathbf{T}$.

Sometimes we want to make reference to **P** and **T** without involving the language and its interpretation. We call $\langle \mathbf{P}, \mathbf{T} \rangle$ a *model structure*. At this point the notion of a model structure is so wide as perhaps to appear useless. For where **P** is any set and **T** is a proper subset of **P** then $\langle \mathbf{P}, \mathbf{T} \rangle$ is a model structure. There is however a reason for this generality, for we want to provide a semantic framework which is broad enough to provide for any possible assignment of meanings to any symbol in a propositional language.

Most treatments of propositional languages are interested in studying them as logics. This means that they pick out one or two symbols as 'constants' or 'logical words' and only consider interpretations which fit in with the intended meaning of these words. We are interested in propositional languages as languages and do not want our semantical framework to impose any particular meaning on any symbol. We can formulate this criterion of semantic generality as follows. Suppose that we have a set **P** of propositions with a designated subset **T**. We want to shew that for any set A of sentences of $\mathscr{L}$ there is an assignment V to the symbols of $\mathscr{L}$ which makes precisely the members of A true. This would shew that our meaning assignments do not impose restrictions which would prevent a sentence (like say $\alpha \vee \sim\alpha$) from being false. Under the assumption that **T** and $\mathbf{P} - \mathbf{T}$ are both infinite we can prove that our semantical framework is sufficiently general.

THEOREM **1.14** *If* **P** *is an infinite set and* **T** *an infinite subset of* **P** *and* $\mathbf{P} - \mathbf{T}$ *also infinite, then for any set* $\mathrm{A} \subseteq \mathrm{S}$ *there is a model* $\langle \mathbf{P}, \mathbf{T}, \mathrm{V} \rangle$ *such that for every* $\alpha \in \mathrm{S}$, α *is true in* $\langle \mathbf{P}, \mathbf{T}, \mathrm{V} \rangle$ *iff* $\alpha \in \mathrm{A}$.

PROOF: Since **P** and **T** and $\mathbf{P} - \mathbf{T}$ are all infinite and since S, A, and $\mathrm{S} - \mathrm{A}$ are at most denumerable there is a $1-1$ mapping[27] π of S into **P** such that $\alpha \in \mathrm{A}$ iff $\pi(\alpha) \in \mathbf{T}$. We use this mapping to define V:

1.15 If $\beta \in \Delta_0$ then $\mathrm{V}(\beta) = \pi(\beta)$.

[27] *Vide* Appendix I, p. 244.

1.16 If $\delta \in \Delta_n$ ($n \geq 1$) then V(δ) (i.e., ω_δ) is defined as follows: If $a_1, \ldots, a_n \in \mathbf{P}$ are respectively $\pi(\alpha_1), \ldots, \pi(\alpha_n)$ for some $\alpha_1, \ldots, \alpha_n \in$ S then $\omega_\delta(a_1,\ldots,a_n) = \pi(\langle\delta,\alpha_1,\ldots,\alpha_n\rangle)$. Since π is 1 – 1 there will be at most one set $\langle\alpha_1,\ldots,\alpha_n\rangle$ such that $\langle a_1,\ldots,a_n\rangle = \langle\pi(\alpha_1),\ldots,\pi(\alpha_n)\rangle$, thus $\omega_\delta(a_1,\ldots,a_n)$ will be unique. If there is no such set $\langle\alpha_1,\ldots,\alpha_n\rangle$ then we may let $\omega_\delta(a_1,\ldots,a_n)$ be defined arbitrarily. If this is worrisome we could suppose ourselves to have nominated some member of **P** in advance as the value of ω_δ for arguments of this kind. (Note that $\mathscr{L}$ must be grounded to ensure that π can be consistently defined.)

LEMMA **1.17** *For any* $\alpha \in$ S, $V^+(\alpha) = \pi(\alpha)$.

The proof is by induction on the construction of α. If $\alpha \in \Delta_0$ then the lemma holds by definition. If α is $\langle\delta,\alpha_1,\ldots,\alpha_n\rangle$ then we suppose $V^+(\alpha_1) = \pi(\alpha_1), \ldots, V^+(\alpha_n) = \pi(\alpha_n)$. So by 1.16 V($\delta$) is that function ω_δ such that

$$\omega_\delta(V^+(\alpha_1),\ldots,V^+(\alpha_n)) = \pi(\langle\delta,\alpha_1,\ldots,\alpha_n\rangle)$$

i.e.,

$$V^+(\delta(\alpha_1,\ldots,\alpha_n)) = \pi(\langle\delta,\alpha_1,\ldots,\alpha_n\rangle)$$

whence the lemma is proved.

So since $\alpha \in$ A iff $\pi(\alpha) \in \mathbf{T}$, then $\alpha \in$ A iff $V^+(\alpha) \in \mathbf{T}$. **Q.E.D.**

We could have devised an easier, though less powerful, theorem by proving merely that for any set A of wff of $\mathscr{L}$ there is some model in which all and only members of A are true. For such a case we could let $\mathbf{P}$ = S and A = $\mathbf{T}$. For $\alpha \in \Delta_0$ V(α) would be α itself and V(δ) would be that function ω_δ such that for any $\alpha_1,\ldots,\alpha_n \in \mathbf{P}$ (= S), $\omega_\delta(\alpha_1,\ldots,\alpha_n) = \langle\delta,\alpha_1,\ldots,\alpha_n\rangle$. Such a theorem has the advantage of exhibiting a particular model but is not nearly as general as the one we proved and is an obvious corollary of it.

One thing to notice is that the nature of **P** and **T** does not matter in the least. Provided only that they are infinite then we can build up a model which is characteristic for A. This is going to be a feature of all the languages we study. Quite generally, wherever we have a semantics based on entities of a certain type and where we have another set which is at least as large as the first then we can build up a structure isomorphic (in the algebraic sense) to the original semantics but using entities from the new set. The only thing that is important is the size.

Since **T** has to be a proper subset of **P** in any model for $\mathscr{L}$ the smallest semantics is a two-membered **P** and a one-membered **T**. Say $\mathbf{P} = \{1,0\}$ and $\mathbf{T} = \{1\}$. From what we have just now observed the nature of 1

2

and 0 does not matter; for the purposes of semantic analysis any two-membered **P** is as good as any other. Where **P** has only two members we shall say that ⟨**P**, **T**⟩ is a *truth-functional* model structure and when V is any assignment, ⟨**P**, **T**, V⟩ is a truth-functional model. We have already used truth-functional models by way of illustration. We shall now prove that they do not have the semantic generality we have demanded. I.e., we prove the following:

THEOREM **1.18** *There is a propositional language* $\mathscr{L} = \langle \Delta, \mathrm{S} \rangle$ *such that for some* $\mathrm{A} \subseteq \mathrm{S}$ *there is no truth-functional model* ⟨**P**, **T**, V⟩ *in which for any* $\alpha \in \mathrm{S}$, $\mathrm{V}^+(\alpha) = 1$ *iff* $\alpha \in \mathrm{A}$.

PROOF: Let $\mathscr{L}$ be the unique language based on $\Delta = \langle \Delta_0, \Delta_1 \rangle$ where $\Delta_0 = \{p,q\}$ and $\Delta_1 = \{\delta\}$. Let $\mathrm{A} = \{\langle \delta, p \rangle\}$.

We claim there is no assignment V of truth-values to Δ_0 and truth functions to Δ_1 such that $\mathrm{V}^+(\alpha) = 1$ iff $\alpha \in \mathrm{A}$. We suppose, for reductio ad absurdum, that there is such a V. Now $p \notin \mathrm{A}$ so $\mathrm{V}^+(p) = 0$ and $\langle \delta, p \rangle \in \mathrm{A}$ so $\mathrm{V}^+(\langle \delta, p \rangle) = 1$. Further, by 1.12, $\omega_\delta(\mathrm{V}^+(p)) = \mathrm{V}^+(\langle \delta, p \rangle)$ so $\omega_\delta(0) = 1$.

But $\mathrm{V}^+(q) = 0$ since $q \notin \mathrm{A}$, and therefore $\omega_\delta(\mathrm{V}(q)) = \omega_\delta(0) = 1$. Therefore, by 1.12, $\mathrm{V}^+(\langle \delta, q \rangle) = 1$.
But $\langle \delta, q \rangle \notin \mathrm{A}$, which contradicts the reductio hypothesis and so the theorem is proved.

Note that $\mathscr{L}$ need only have one functor and only a one-place one at that. The reason why truth-functional semantics, though inadequate for the general study of propositional languages, are so well known is simply that they *are* adequate when we want to restrict ourselves to languages in which the propositional functors are all to be interpreted as 'not', 'and', 'or', 'if' and so on.

We have defined 'interpretation' and 'model' as widely as possible and have proved they are general enough. We are now discussing particular kinds of models. One kind is truth-functional models. This class we have shewn to be not semantically general. A class **K** of models for a propositional language $\mathscr{L}$ is semantically general iff for any set A of sentences of $\mathscr{L}$ there is some model in **K** which is *characteristic* for A. I.e., there is some ⟨**P**, **T**, V⟩ ∈ **K** such that for all $\alpha \in \mathrm{S}$, $\alpha \in \mathrm{A}$ iff $\mathrm{V}(\alpha) \in$ **T**. Our earlier theorem (1.14) shewed that the class of models for $\mathscr{L}$ based on any sufficiently large **P** and **T** is semantically general.

What we are going to be interested in now is some more restricted classes of models which also turn out to be semantically general.

Indexical semantics

From a purely formal point of view there is no need to ask what kinds of things the members of **P** and **T** might be. But if our task is real semantics we can only regard it as so far half fulfilled. Provided any set **P** is sufficiently large we have shewn it can do all that is required by way of explaining how any given set of sentences can be regarded as the true ones. But we might ask what **P** is supposed to be under its intended interpretations. According to one philosophical tradition the answer is *propositions*. A proposition is something which can be true or false. **T** will be the set of those which are true.[28] But this does not really get us much further than putting a name to the members of **P**. If it is to be helpful we must at least be able to say something about what propositions are.

There are a number of disadvantages in taking propositions as primitive notions. Principally they are that propositions can have certain properties and enter into certain logical relations which seem difficult to explain. E.g. we want to divide propositions into those which are logically necessary or impossible and those which are contingent, we want to speak of relations of compatibility and incompatibility and most important of all, we want an analysis of the notion of entailment. (Indeed, Richard Montague has made this requirement, along with a definition of truth, one of the defining aims of semantics.[29]) All of these particular notions are interdefinable, but there seems no way of analysing them without giving an analysis of propositions themselves.

The key notion which has seemed to open most doors in this area is that of a *possible world*.[30] If we think for a moment of the job a proposition has to do we see that it must be something which can be true or false, not only in the actual world but in each possible world. Suppose for the moment that we could 'shew' a person all possible worlds in turn. This is of course impossible, but try to imagine it

[28] Semantics based on domains of propositions have been developed for various kinds of intensional logics in Cresswell [1966b] and [1967]. However these treatments are all subject to the disadvantages of interpretation noted in the text.

[29] Montague [1970a], p. 373 f and also [1970b].

[30] For some historical remarks on the notion of the role of possible worlds in metaphysics and logic, *vide* the introduction, *supra* pp. 3–5. An introductory account of their use in modal logic is found in Hughes and Cresswell [1968], pp. 75–80.

anyway. We want to know whether two people are thinking of the same proposition. So we ask them, as we shew them each (complete) possible world, 'Would the proposition you are thinking of be true if that was the way things were?' If their answers agree for every possible world there is at least the temptation to suppose that they have the same proposition in mind.[31] Or to put it another way, if the set of worlds to which A says 'yes' is the same as the set of worlds to which B says 'yes' we can say that A and B have the same proposition in mind. So why not simply identify the proposition with the set of worlds in question? As a first approximation therefore we shall say that a proposition is a set of possible worlds. A proposition p then will be true in a possible world w iff $w \in p$.

Armed with this definition we can give an analysis of the logical relations between propositions. A proposition will be *logically necessary* if it is true in (contains as members) all possible worlds, *impossible* if true in none; i.e., the impossible proposition is the null set.[32] One proposition will *entail* another iff it is a subset of the other. Two propositions will be *incompatible* iff they contain no common world. Corresponding to our set **T** of true propositions we can now designate one of the possible worlds as the 'real' world. A proposition, set of worlds, will be in **T** iff it is true in the real world, i.e. iff it contains the real world as a member.

We want then to define a new kind of interpretation based on a set **W** of possible worlds. From a formal point of view of course the nature of the members of **W** is just as irrelevant as was the nature of the members of **P** in our earlier modelling. And indeed there are plausible alternatives to possible worlds. If we think of propositions, as Arthur Prior did,[33] as things which can change their truth value

[31] To know which worlds a proposition is true in and which it is false in does not involve knowing everything, since to know everything is to know which world is the real one. The ability we are speaking of is of a rather different kind. We would say a person had it if we could say of him that *if* he knew all the facts about a world w then he would know whether his proposition was true or false in w, cf. Tichý [1972], p. 92 f. Note that we are not putting forward this procedure as a model for language learning (and cf. pp. 49–51).

[32] In Chapter Three we shall refine this notion of a proposition in order to avoid the rather embarrassing consequence of our present definition that there is only one necessary and one impossible proposition, and that all logically equivalent propositions are the same. This means that our present discussion is provisional. It should be stressed however that the development up to this point, especially theorem 1.14 (p. 20), is independent of any particular analysis of **P**.

[33] In many articles, stemming principally from Prior [1957], p. 8 f. Some of these are collected in Prior [1968], and a survey of the history of tense logic is found in Prior [1967].

from time to time, then we shall want the members of **W** to be instants of time (or perhaps, if we want to combine the two approaches, combinations in the form of ordered pairs of a world and a time). If we think that the sentence 'I am hungry' expresses the same proposition when *A* says it as when *B* says it then we will want **W** to include people, for 'I am hungry' may be true of *A* but false of *B*. All this has made some logicians look for a more neutral description of the things in **W**. Some have called them 'points of reference', others 'indices'. Any interpretation which analyses the semantics of sentences in this way can then be called an *indexical*[34] interpretation.

We shall continue to talk of possible worlds and later try to shew how all these other indices can be manufactured out of them, but all the formal work we do in the rest of this chapter and in the next will be just as true for indices of whatever kind.

We shall say that $\langle \mathbf{W}, w \rangle$ is an *indexical model structure* iff **W** is a set and $w \in \mathbf{W}$. We frequently write w_1 for the designated member of **W** in an indexical model structure. Obviously if $\langle \mathbf{W}, w_1 \rangle$ is an indexical model structure then $\langle \mathscr{P}\mathbf{W}, \{a \subseteq \mathbf{W} : w_1 \in a\} \rangle$ is a model structure in the sense of p. 20. $\langle \mathbf{W}, w_1, \mathrm{V} \rangle$ is an *indexical model* for a propositional language $\mathscr{L}$ iff $\langle \mathscr{P}\mathbf{W}, \{a \subseteq \mathbf{W} : w_1 \in a\}, \mathrm{V} \rangle$ is a model for $\mathscr{L}$.

LEMMA **1.19** *If $\langle \mathbf{W}, w_1, \mathrm{V} \rangle$ is an indexical model for a propositional language $\mathscr{L}$ then if $\alpha \in \mathrm{S}$, α is true in $\langle \mathbf{W}, w_1, \mathrm{V} \rangle$ iff $w_1 \in \mathrm{V}^+(\alpha)$.*
PROOF: By definition 1.13, α is true in $\langle \mathscr{P}\mathbf{W}, \{a \subseteq \mathbf{W} : w_1 \in a\}, \mathrm{V} \rangle$ iff $\mathrm{V}^+(\alpha) \in \{a \subseteq \mathbf{W} : w_1 \in a\}$, i.e., iff $w_1 \in \mathrm{V}^+(\alpha)$. **Q.E.D.**

THEOREM **1.20** *If $\mathscr{L}$ is a propositional language and **W** is an infinite set and $w_1 \in \mathbf{W}$, then where $\mathrm{A} \subseteq \mathrm{S}$ there is an indexical model $\langle \mathbf{W}, w_1, \mathrm{V} \rangle$ such that for $\alpha \in \mathrm{S}$, α is true in $\langle \mathbf{W}, w_1, \mathrm{V} \rangle$ iff $\alpha \in \mathrm{A}$.*
PROOF: Since **W** is infinite then so are $\mathbf{P} = \mathscr{P}\mathbf{W}$, $\mathbf{T} = \{a \subseteq \mathbf{W} : w_1 \in a\}$ and $\mathbf{P} - \mathbf{T} = \{a \subseteq \mathbf{W} : w_1 \notin a\}$. Thus by Theorem 1.14 there is a model $\langle \mathbf{P}, \mathbf{T}, \mathrm{V} \rangle$ such that $\alpha \in \mathrm{A}$ iff $\mathrm{V}^+(\alpha) \in \mathbf{T}$. Whence by Lemma 1.19, $\alpha \in \mathrm{A}$ iff $w_1 \in \mathrm{V}^+(\alpha)$. **Q.E.D.**

LEMMA **1.21** *An indexical model structure $\langle \mathbf{W}, w_1 \rangle$ is truth-functional iff $\mathbf{W} = \{w_1\}$.*
The proof is immediate.

This lemma shews that the theory of truth-functions can be thought of, in indexical terms, as defined by one-world model structures.

[34] Montague [1970a], p. 379 f, treats worlds and times together and separates them from all the other contextual features. We discuss contexts in Chapter Eight, pp. 109–11.

In an indexical model a sentence α is assigned a set of worlds. I.e., $V^+(\alpha) \subseteq \mathbf{W}$. Since a proposition is true in a world iff it contains that world as a member we can say that $V^+(\alpha)$ is true in world w iff $w \in V^+(\alpha)$. Sometimes it is convenient to express this as a function from formulae and worlds to truth values. I.e., we write $V^+(\alpha, w) = 1$ to mean α is true in w (by assignment V). 1 and 0 are not now propositions but truth values (though again their nature need not concern us when we are interested only in formal manoeuvrings). This relies on the fairly obvious set-theoretical fact that if we have a set A and a pair of objects, say 1 and 0, then for any subset B of A we have a set of pairs $\langle x, y\rangle$ such that y is 1 if $x \in$ B and 0 if $x \notin$ B. In a sense this set of pairs can represent B. We can call it the *characteristic function* for B and write it as C_B thus

1.22 $C_B(x) = 1$ iff $x \in$ B; and $B = \{x \in A : C_B(x) = 1\}$.

We shall call a function from sentences of $\mathscr{L}$ and members of **W** to $\{1,0\}$ a truth assignment. Given an indexical model $\langle \mathbf{W}, w_1, V\rangle$ we shall say that V *induces* the *truth assignment* V^t iff

1.23 If $\alpha \in \Delta_0$ and $w \in \mathbf{W}$ then $V^t(\alpha, w) = 1$ iff $w \in V(\alpha)$.

1.24 If $\alpha = \langle \delta, \alpha_1, \ldots, \alpha_n\rangle$ and $w \in \mathbf{W}$ then $V^t(\langle \delta, \alpha_1, \ldots, \alpha_n\rangle, w) = 1$ iff $w \in \omega_\delta(\{w \in \mathbf{W} : V^t(\alpha_1, w) = 1\}, \ldots, \{w \in \mathbf{W} : V^t(\alpha_n, w) = 1\})$.

Let $\langle \mathbf{W}, w_1, V\rangle$ be an indexical model and V^+ and V^t be the induced assignments and truth assignments, respectively.

LEMMA **1.25** *For any* $\alpha \in$ S, $w \in \mathbf{W}$, $V^t(\alpha, w) = 1$ *iff* $w \in V^+(\alpha)$.
PROOF: By induction on the construction of α. We first note that the induction hypothesis is equivalent to $V^+(\alpha) = \{w \in \mathbf{W} : V^t(\alpha, w) = 1\}$. The result follows by definition for $\alpha \in \Delta_0$. Suppose α is $\langle \delta, \alpha_1, \ldots, \alpha_n\rangle$. Then $V^t(\alpha, w) = 1$ iff $w \in \omega_\delta(\{w \in \mathbf{W} : V^t(\alpha_1, w) = 1\}, \ldots, \{w \in \mathbf{W} : V^t(\alpha_n, w) = 1\})$, (induction hypothesis) iff $w \in \omega_\delta(V^+(\alpha_1, \ldots, V^+(\alpha_n))$ iff $w \in V^+(\alpha)$.

Q.E.D.

COROLLARY **1.26** $V^+(\alpha) = \{w \in \mathbf{W} : V^t(\alpha, w) = 1\}$.

The truth-assignment semantics suggest an alternative way of looking at the assignment to the symbols. Both V^+ and V^t in Lemma 1.25 depend on an assignment to Δ as defined in 1.9 and 1.10. But of course there is no reason why we should not give the assignment to Δ_0

by saying that for any $w \in \mathbf{W}$ and $\alpha \in \Delta_0$, $V(\alpha, w) = 1$ or $V(\alpha, w)$ $\boldsymbol{w}$ 0.[35] For Δ_n $(1 \leqq n \leqq k)$ we could keep the assignment as in 1.10 but even here there is an alternative. After all if $\omega_\delta(a_1,\ldots,a_n)$ (where $a_1,\ldots,a_n$ are sets of worlds) is a set of worlds and if $V^t(\langle\delta,\alpha_1,\ldots,\alpha_n\rangle, w) = 1$ iff $w \in \omega_\delta(a_1,\ldots,a_n)$ why not have a relation R_δ so that $wR_\delta(a_1,\ldots,a_n)$ holds iff $w \in \omega_\delta(a_1,\ldots,a_n)$? (Conversely, given such a relation we could define $\omega_\delta(a_1,\ldots,a_n)$ as $\{w \in \mathbf{W} : wR_\delta(a_1,\ldots,a_n)\}$.)

Where $\delta \in \Delta_1$ we have simply a relation R_δ between a world and a set of worlds. Where $wR_\delta a$ holds, a is sometimes said to be a *neighbourhood* of w and semantics of this kind called 'neighbourhood semantics'.[36] By contrast one might call the semantics of 1.9–1.12 operator semantics. Operator semantics prove to be more convenient than neighbourhood semantics when the values of the operator are other than sets of possible worlds and so we shall be mainly using them. What we have said above should shew the interchangeability of each kind of semantics.

[35] As, e.g., in Hughes and Cresswell [1968], p. 73. But note that there no distinction was made between V and V^+. So long as it is recognized that the assignment to complex formulae depends on the assignment to the symbols, there is no harm in not separating these. Cf. Kripke [1963a] and [1963b].

[36] The term 'neighbourhood' seems to have been introduced by Scott [1970], p. 160. It is used in Segerberg [1972]. Montague claims in [1968], p. 105, to have developed this type of semantics jointly with Charles Howard in 1965. It is also found in Cresswell [1970] and [1972a].

CHAPTER TWO

Propositional Logics

The purpose of this chapter is to relate what was said in the last to propositional logics. It can be omitted by those who want to get on with the analysis of language.

Validity

The word 'logic' has so many different shades of meaning that a definition would be confusing. We have already (p. 24) met the notion of a logically necessary proposition and various logical relations which may hold between propositions. We now want to examine a slightly different, though allied, notion of logical truth, the logical truth of a sentence. With respect to a particular meaning assignment a sentence α of a propositional language $\mathscr{L}$ may be logically true in the sense that $V^+(\alpha)$ is a logically necessary proposition. Such a sentence is sometimes called *conceptually necessary* or *analytic*. In an indexical model a logically true sentence will remain true whichever world is the real one since its value, a logically necessary proposition, contains all worlds. Thus its truth may be said to depend only on the meanings of words.[37]

There is however a narrower use of the phrase 'truth of logic'. A truth of logic in this narrower sense is a sentence which is true by its form alone and not by its content. Now one thing this cannot mean in the case of sentences of a propositional language is that the sentence is true independently of the meaning of its symbols. For theorem 1.14

[37] The necessity of the proposition $V(\alpha)$ has of course nothing to do with the meanings of words, and is not a fact about language. What is a fact about language is that α means that proposition under V.

(p. 20) guarantees that any sentence (or set of sentences) can be made true, and therefore can be made false, by giving appropriate meanings to its symbols. In order to see what the distinction between a *logically valid* sentence, as we shall call this restricted sense of 'logical truth', and a conceptually necessary or analytic sentence, comes to we shall examine an example of each kind.

(1) If Jones is a bachelor Jones is unmarried.
(2) If Jones is unmarried Jones is unmarried.

These are not of course sentences of a propositional language but if we suppose α to be a member of Δ_0 which we are to interpret as 'Jones is a bachelor' and β as 'Jones is unmarried' then with $\supset$ to represent 'If' we get

(1′) $\langle \supset, \alpha, \beta \rangle$
(2′) $\langle \supset, \beta, \beta \rangle$

Now if a meaning assignment V is to reflect normal English usage it is probable that both (1′) and (2′) will be conceptually necessary. Yet in the narrow sense (2) is frequently held to be logically valid while (1) is not.[38] The reason for this is that the truth of (1) and therefore of (1′) depends on the assignment to α and β as well as on the assignment to $\supset$. In the case of (2) and (2′) however this need not be so. For suppose $\supset$ has the following meaning in a model based upon a set **W** of worlds:

[V$\supset$] V($\supset$) is that function ω such that for any $a, b \subseteq \mathbf{W}$, and $w \in \mathbf{W}$ $w \in \omega(a,b)$ iff either $w \notin a$ or $w \in b$.

I.e. for γ and $\delta \in \Delta_0$, $w \in V(\langle \supset, \gamma, \delta \rangle)$ iff $w \notin V(\gamma)$ or $w \in V(\delta)$. This is in fact the normal rule for material implication. Whether the rule for material implication really does reflect the English 'if then' is a question we need not go into. Let us suppose it does in this case. It is easy to see that $\langle \supset, \beta, \beta \rangle$ will be true and furthermore true no matter what value is assigned to β. Or to put the matter more correctly $\langle \supset, \beta, \beta \rangle$ will be true in all models which satisfy [V$\supset$] whatever values they may assign to α and β. (2′) then will be a truth of logic because it is not only true in the model which represents its ordinary language meaning but also in the class of models which agree only on [V$\supset$].

Thus the idea of a truth of logic emerges as a sentence true in a class of models which are alike in interpretation of some of the symbols but differ in interpretation of others. Where **K** is a class of models for $\mathscr{L}$

[38] *Vide* e.g. Quine [1953], especially p. 22 f, and Montague [1970a], pp. 380–2 The points made in the text are amplified in Cresswell [1972a], pp. 5–7.

we shall say that a sentence α is **K**-*valid* iff α is true in every member of **K**. If A is a set of sentences of $\mathscr{L}$ then **K** is *characteristic* for A (cf. p. 22) iff for any sentence α of $\mathscr{L}$, $\alpha \in$ A iff α is **K**-valid.

What usually happens when we study a logic is that we are interested in a small number of symbols which we regard as particularly important for some purpose and we want to consider all interpretations which give these symbols a fixed meaning but vary as widely as they please on the meanings given to the other symbols. I.e. the class of models treats a few symbols as constants and regards the rest as variables. In propositional languages the distinction between variables and constants cannot be made within a single model but only with respect to a class of models. We shall say that a class **K** of models treats a symbol $\alpha \in \Delta^+$ as a variable iff the following holds:

If $\langle \mathbf{W}, w_1, \mathrm{V} \rangle \in \mathbf{K}$ and $\langle \mathbf{W}, w_1, \mathrm{V}' \rangle$ is like $\langle \mathbf{W}, w_1, \mathrm{V} \rangle$ except in assignment to α, then $\langle \mathbf{W}, w_1, \mathrm{V}' \rangle \in \mathbf{K}$. Otherwise α is a constant with respect to **K**.

When we have variables in the system we sometimes find it convenient to abandon the requirement that the number of symbols in the language be finite. Frequently, in the case of propositional languages, we want the functors to be treated as constants and so retain only a finite number of them but we want (some or all) of the simple sentence symbols to be variables. We shall say that $\mathscr{L}$ is 0-*arily extended* iff Δ_0 is infinite. (We could restrict this definition in various ways, e.g. by requiring Δ_0 to be at most denumerable and to be effectively specifiable. The idea that a language might contain infinitely many words is not such a departure from natural language as one might have thought. If Arabic numerals, e.g. '937', are regarded as words of English then English has infinitely many words.) A set A of sentences of a 0-arily extended propositional language $\mathscr{L}$ we call a *propositional logic* iff there is some class **K** of models which is characteristic for A and treats all but finitely many of the symbols of $\mathscr{L}$ as variables. If **K** treats all the members of Δ_0 as variables and all the functors as constants then A is a *pure propositional logic*.

Truth-functional logic

The simplest kind of propositional logic is what has come to be known as the *propositional calculus* or *truth-functional logic*. Indeed there are, apparently, philosophers who would claim that this is the only genuine propositional logic.[39] Part of the reason is that, as we noted on p. 25,

[39] E.g. Quine [1940], p. 11.

truth-functional logic can be characterized by one-world models and therefore the propositional functors have a simple semantics. The other reason is that certain key words in deductive arguments like 'and', 'or' and 'if' have all been given an analysis in terms of the two values of truth and falsity.

Truth functions can be introduced into models with more than one possible world. We shall say that a functor $\delta \in \Delta_n$ is *truth-functional* in a model $\langle \mathbf{W}, w_1, V \rangle$ iff the following holds for any w, $w' \in \mathbf{W}$ and $a_1, \ldots, a_n, b_1, \ldots, b_n \subseteq \mathbf{W}$:

Where $w \in a_i$ iff $w' \in b_i$ $(1 \leqslant i \leqslant n)$
then

$$w \in \omega_\delta(a_1, \ldots, a_n) \text{ iff } w' \in \omega_\delta(b_1, \ldots, b_n).$$

Such an operator determines a unique truth table in the following way. Let a be $\{w_1\}$ and b be $\{\mathbf{W} - w_1\}$. For each row of the table let 1 in an argument place be replaced by a and 0 by b. This will give an n-tuple $c_1, \ldots, c_n$ each member of which is either a or b. Let the value of the function for that row be 1 if $w_1 \in \omega_\delta(c_1, \ldots, c_n)$ and 0 if $w_1 \notin \omega_\delta(c_1, \ldots, c_n)$. It is easy to check that any such truth functor evaluated in each world according to its truth table will yield exactly the same value as according to the standard rules of p. 19. Further, if a formula α contains, with respect to a model $\langle \mathbf{W}, w_1, V \rangle$, only truth functors then the value of α in w_1 will depend only on the assignment to its proposition symbols in w_1. And if we consider the 'truncated' model $\langle \{w_1\}, w_1, V' \rangle$ where V' is V but restricted to w_1, we shall get a one-world model which treats α exactly as $\langle \mathbf{W}, w_1, V \rangle$ does. This is why, when only truth functors are involved, no more than one world is needed.

Where a class of models is involved it is often important to know that an operator is assigned the same truth function by each member of the class. E.g. if $\supset$ is defined by the rule $[V\supset]$ in one model we want to make sure it is defined by this rule in all the models. We call a set of models of this kind *truth-functionally similar* and call a system characterized by a set of this kind a *propositional calculus*.[40] We shall frequently want, in our metalanguage, to talk about a member of Δ_1 which is being interpreted as negation and members of Δ_2 which are interpreted as conjunction, disjunction, material implication and material equivalence. We shall always use the same signs for these to avoid repeating a lengthy preamble. We shall use

[40] Introductions to truth-functional logic abound, since the propositional calculus is the basis of almost all modern logic. A standard work is Church [1956].

'$\sim$', '&', 'v', '$\supset$' and '$\equiv$' respectively. It must be stressed though that these are simply metalinguistic names for entities which may turn out to be anything we please (cf. p. 14 f). To claim that a functor is being interpreted in one of these ways is to claim that it satisfies the following rules:

For any model $\langle \mathbf{W}, w_1, V\rangle$ in $\mathbf{K}$ and any $w \in \mathbf{W}$ and $a, b \subseteq \mathbf{W}$

[V$\sim$]	$w \in \omega_{\sim}(a)$	iff	$w \notin a$			
[V&]	$w \in \omega\ (a,b)$	iff	$w \in a$	and	$w \in b$	
[V$_{\text{v}}$]	$w \in \omega_{\text{v}}(a,b)$	iff	$w \in a$	or	$w \in b$	
[V$\supset$]	$w \in \omega_{\supset}(a,b)$	iff	$w \notin a$	or	$w \in b$	
[V$\equiv$]	$w \in \omega_{\equiv}(a,b)$	iff	$w \in a$	iff	$w \in b.$	

Modal logic

We mentioned earlier the importance of truth functors as an analysis of certain 'logical words' which appear in deductive reasoning. We also suggested that they have been singled out for study not so much for this reason as because of their simple structure. When we move on to functors which are non-truth-functional we come across some more which have a simple structure, in particular the ones which give rise to modal logic. Among these the simplest is the necessity operator, or as Dana Scott calls it, the *universal necessity* operator.[41] We refer to this functor as '*L*'.

In any given model it is unique since ω_L is that operation such that:

[V*L*] For any $a \subseteq \mathbf{W}$, $\omega_L(a) = \mathbf{W}$ if $a = \mathbf{W}$ and $\varnothing$ if $a \neq \mathbf{W}$.

Any truth-functionally similar class of models for a 0-arily extended propositional language whose only functors are truth functors and a necessity operator and which treats all members of Δ_0 as variables determines a class of formulae which we can call a *modal logic*, more specifically an *S*5-*modal logic*.[42] Where **K** contains at least one infinite model (i.e. model in which **W** is infinite) or where there is no largest **W** among the (possibly all finite) models in **K**, we say that the set of formulae is a *proper S*5-*modal logic*.

[41] Scott [1970], p. 157. For an account of modal logic *vide* Hughes and Cresswell [1968] and Segerberg [1972].

[42] S5 is only one among many systems of modal logic (*vide* Hughes and Cresswell, op. cit.) but it seems to be the one which most closely captures the notion of logical necessity. Note that *L* cannot be interpreted as 'it is logically valid that', for logical validity on the 'narrow' view of logical necessity is a property of sentences not propositions. And it is a property which is not preserved by substitution of sentences with the same value. In the intended model of English both (1) and (2) are true in the same worlds and so express the same proposition but only (2) is logically valid. In fact 'it is logically valid that' does not make sense, for 'that' is a word which introduces a proposition.

In models which contain a full set of truth functors we can use the necessity operator to define two other rather important 'logical' notions. Let us write $\alpha \strictif \beta$ for $\langle L, \langle \supset, \alpha, \beta \rangle \rangle$. Then $\strictif$ determines an operation $\omega_{\strictif}$ as follows:

$$\omega_{\strictif}(a, b) = \omega_L(\omega_{\supset}(a, b))$$

Now $\omega_{\supset}(a, b) = \mathbf{W}$ iff $a \subseteq b$, so $\omega_{\strictif}(a, b) \neq \varnothing$ iff $a \subseteq b$, i.e. for any $w \in \mathbf{W}$, $w \in \omega_{\strictif}(a, b)$ iff $a \subseteq b$, i.e. $\mathrm{V}^t(\alpha \strictif \beta, w) = 1$ iff $\mathrm{V}^+(\alpha) \subseteq \mathrm{V}^+(\beta)$.

Thus $\strictif$ represents logical entailment in the sense that in any world $\alpha \strictif \beta$ is true iff the set of worlds assigned to α is included in the set of worlds assigned to β, i.e. in any possible situation in which α is true so is β.

Secondly, consider the complex sentence $\langle \&, \langle \alpha \strictif \beta, \beta \strictif \alpha \rangle \rangle$. We can refer to this as $\alpha = \beta$ since for any $w \in \mathbf{W}$, if $w \in \mathrm{V}^+(\alpha \strictif \beta)$ then $\mathrm{V}^+(\alpha) \subseteq \mathrm{V}^+(\beta)$, and if $w \in \mathrm{V}^+(\beta \strictif \alpha)$ then $\mathrm{V}^+(\beta) \subseteq \mathrm{V}^+(\alpha)$; so if $w \in \mathrm{V}^+(\langle \&, \alpha \strictif \beta, \beta \strictif \alpha \rangle)$ then $\mathrm{V}^+(\alpha) = \mathrm{V}^+(\beta)$. Obviously the converse holds too.

There may be other operators which would qualify as 'logical' in propositional languages but of those which have been proposed these are the only ones which have much plausibility. Note that any formula beginning with a necessity operator will be true in all worlds in a model or false in them all. I.e., for any given interpretation the formula will be true whatever world is designated as the real one or false whatever world is designated as the real one. It will be a logical truth in the sense of p. 28. Any formula in any model is necessary iff it is assigned the set of all worlds in the model. **W** itself then might be thought of as the one necessary proposition. Logical necessity, which is a property of a formula within a given model (or interpretation), should not therefore be confused with validity in a class of models though, as we have seen, the phrase 'logical truth' can refer to sentences valid in the class of models which is regarded as treating all but the 'logical words' as variables.

We shall later (pp. 39–44) go into the question of how to have more than one necessary proposition (so as to allow e.g. the possibility of the increase of mathematical knowledge) and shall have a little to say about logics in which logically equivalent formulae are not intersubstitutable in all contexts *salva veritate*.[43] In systems whose only

[43] Such logics are discussed in detail in Cresswell [1970] and [1972a].

functors are truth functors and the necessity operator the distinction does not arise but if we allow functors which are to be interpreted as, say, 'mathematicians have discovered that', the question becomes crucial.

Axiomatic systems

One reason why 'truths of logic' have been historically thought of in the narrow sense we have called 'logical validity' is undoubtedly that the logically valid principles which result from treating only a small number of symbols as constants allow of reasonably simple formulation. It is even often possible to formulate them without any reference to interpretation at all, a fact which is no doubt partly responsible for the idea that they are true independently of content. Such formulations are usually presented as axiomatic systems. Given a propositional language $\mathscr{L}$ (whether 0-arily extended or not), by an *axiomatic system* in $\mathscr{L}$ shall be meant a pair $\langle\mathfrak{A},\mathfrak{R}\rangle$ where $\mathfrak{A}$ is an effectively specifiable subset of S and $\mathfrak{R}$ a function from natural numbers $n \geqslant 2$ such that $\mathfrak{R}_n$ is an effectively specifiable subset of S^n. I.e., we have an effective procedure[44] for deciding whether or not any sentence of $\mathscr{L}$ is a member of $\mathfrak{A}$ and whether any n-membered sequence of sentences is a member of $\mathfrak{R}_n$. The members of $\mathfrak{A}$ are called the *axioms* of the system and the members of $\mathfrak{R}$ the *transformation rules*.

A *proof* in $\langle\mathfrak{A},\mathfrak{R}\rangle$ is a finite sequence $\mathfrak{C}$ of members of S such that for any $\alpha \in \mathfrak{C}$ either $\alpha \in \mathfrak{A}$ or for some $\beta_1, \ldots, \beta_n$ preceding α in $\mathfrak{C}$, $\langle\beta_1,\ldots,\beta_n,\alpha\rangle \in \mathfrak{R}_{n+1}$. A sentence α is a *theorem* of $\langle\mathfrak{A},\mathfrak{R}\rangle$ iff there is a sequence $\mathfrak{C}$ of which α is the last member and $\mathfrak{C}$ is a proof in $\langle\mathfrak{A},\mathfrak{R}\rangle$. From this definition it clearly follows that given any sequence of members of S we can effectively tell whether or not that sequence is a proof in $\langle\mathfrak{A},\mathfrak{R}\rangle$, though given merely some $\alpha \in S$ we may not be able to tell effectively whether or not α is a theorem, for that involves deciding whether or not there is some sequence which is a proof of α, and without some finite upper limit on the length of sequences there is not in general a procedure for making such a decision.[45]

[44] An *effective* procedure is one which will, in a finite number of mechanically determined steps, give an answer to the question whether something is a member of a set or not. The theory of effective computability is an ever-growing branch of mathematics, *vide* Hermes [1965]. Under certain very general conditions (which means conditions under which we may establish a symbol of the language as a conjunction symbol, and one as an implication symbol) it can be proved that we can dispense with all but one transformation rule; and that one of the form $\langle\alpha,\langle\supset,\alpha,\beta\rangle,\beta\rangle$, where α and β are any sentences. For the details *vide* Craig [1953].

[45] For the strategy of undecidability proofs, *vide* Hermes, op. cit., Chapter Six.

THEOREM **2.1** *If* $\langle\mathfrak{A},\mathfrak{R}\rangle$ *is an axiomatic system and* **K** *a class of models and every* $\alpha \in \mathfrak{A}$ *is* **K**-*valid and if* $\langle\alpha_1,\ldots,\alpha_n\rangle \in \mathfrak{R}_n$, *and* α_n *is* **K**-*valid if* $\alpha_1, \ldots, \alpha_{n-1}$ *are (for every* $\alpha_1, \ldots, \alpha_n$*), then every theorem of* $\langle\mathfrak{A},\mathfrak{R}\rangle$ *is* **K**-*valid.*

The proof is immediate.

We shall say that **K** is characteristic for $\langle\mathfrak{A},\mathfrak{R}\rangle$ iff **K** is characteristic (p. 30) for the class of theorems of $\langle\mathfrak{A},\mathfrak{R}\rangle$. By 1.14 (p. 20) we have that there is a single model characteristic for any set of sentences, in particular for the set of theorems of $\langle\mathfrak{A},\mathfrak{R}\rangle$. From this we have:

THEOREM **2.2** *If* α *is not a theorem of* $\langle\mathfrak{A},\mathfrak{R}\rangle$ *then there is a model for* $\langle\mathfrak{A},\mathfrak{R}\rangle$ *in which* α *is false.*

Viz. the characteristic model for $\langle\mathfrak{A},\mathfrak{R}\rangle$.

COROLLARY **2.3** α *is true in all models of* $\langle\mathfrak{A},\mathfrak{R}\rangle$ *iff* $\langle\mathfrak{A},\mathfrak{R}\rangle \vdash \alpha$.

This is a kind of extended completeness theorem but in view of the generality of the notion of a model it is rather trivial.

Where $\langle\mathfrak{A},\mathfrak{R}\rangle$ is an axiomatic system we let $\mathfrak{T}_{\langle\mathfrak{A},\mathfrak{R}\rangle}$ be the set of theorems of $\langle\mathfrak{A},\mathfrak{R}\rangle$. r is said to be a *derived rule* of $\langle\mathfrak{A},\mathfrak{R}\rangle$ iff the following holds; $\langle\alpha_1,\ldots,\alpha_n\rangle \in r$ iff if $\alpha_1, \ldots, \alpha_{n-1} \in \mathfrak{T}_{\langle\mathfrak{A},\mathfrak{R}\rangle}$ then $\alpha_n \in \mathfrak{T}_{\langle\mathfrak{A},\mathfrak{R}\rangle}$.

THEOREM **2.4** *If* r *is a derived rule of* $\langle\mathfrak{A},\mathfrak{R}\rangle$ *then* $\mathfrak{T}_{\langle\mathfrak{A},\mathfrak{R}\rangle} = \mathfrak{T}_{\langle\mathfrak{A},\mathfrak{R}\cup r\rangle}$.

In most axiomatic systems the axioms and rules will treat most symbols as variables in the sense that all substitution instances of theorems with respect to these symbols will also be theorems. Where $p_1, \ldots, p_n \in \Delta_0$ we use the notation $\alpha[\alpha_1/p_1,\ldots,\alpha_n/p_n]$ to indicate the result of replacing p_1 by α_1 uniformly throughout α, p_2 by α_2, ... and so on. We want to link rules of uniform substitution with our earlier (p. 30) semantical definition of a variable.

We recall that a symbol α (of Δ^+) is said to be a *variable* in (with respect to) a class **K** of models for $\mathscr{L}$ iff if $\langle\mathbf{W},w_1,\mathrm{V}\rangle \in \mathbf{K}$ and if $\langle\mathbf{W},w_1,\mathrm{V}'\rangle$ is like $\langle\mathbf{W},w_1,\mathrm{V}\rangle$ except in assignment to α then $\langle\mathbf{W},w_1,\mathrm{V}'\rangle \in \mathbf{K}$. Otherwise α is a constant in **K**.

We prove a very general theorem involving the validity-preservingness of the rules of uniform substitution.

THEOREM **2.5** *If* **K** *is a class of models in which* $p_1, \ldots, p_n$ *are variables then for any wff* $\alpha, \alpha_1, \ldots, \alpha_n$ *if* α is **K**-*valid so is* $\alpha[\alpha_1/p_1,\ldots, \alpha_n/p_n]$ *(call this* α'*).*

PROOF: Suppose $\alpha[\alpha_1/p_1, \ldots, \alpha_n/p_n]$ were not **K**-valid. I.e. for some model $\langle \mathbf{W}, w_1, \mathrm{V} \rangle \in \mathbf{K}$, $w_1 \notin \mathrm{V}(\alpha')$.

Let $\langle \mathbf{W}, w_1, \mathrm{V}' \rangle$ be exactly like V except that

$$\mathrm{V}'(p_k) = \mathrm{V}(\alpha_k) \qquad (1 \leqslant k \leqslant n).$$

It is easy to shew by induction on the construction of α and α' that $\mathrm{V}'(\alpha) = \mathrm{V}(\alpha')$.

So $w_1 \notin \mathrm{V}'(\alpha)$; i.e. α is false in $\langle \mathbf{W}, w_1, \mathrm{V} \rangle$, but $p_1, \ldots, p_n$ are variables with respect to **K**, hence $\langle \mathbf{W}, w_1, \mathrm{V}' \rangle \in \mathbf{K}$ and so α is not **K**-valid.

Q.E.D.

An analogous theorem can be proved for variable functors but the substitution rule involved is very complicated to state and the theorem involves no new principles of interest.

Other results about the relations between validity and axiomatizations concern particular axiomatic systems, e.g. the propositional and modal calculi referred to earlier in this chapter. As results about particular systems they are too well-known to bear repetition here and as examples of our general definition enough ought to have been said to see how they might be accommodated. In future chapters we shall be studying richer languages. In these cases too we can if we wish select certain words to be 'logical constants' and confine attention to them. Words like 'all' and 'some' are cases in point. Enough ought to have been said in this chapter however to shew the sort of things which could be done and we shall not, in the rest of the book, be concerned, except incidentally, with looking at logical constants.

CHAPTER THREE

The Metaphysics of Propositions

Basic particular situations

Our theory of meaning has so far depended on an initially given set of 'possible worlds'. The aim of this chapter is to look at the question of what these things are and try thereby to gain a slightly clearer notion of the relation between language and the world.

Of course we might well have stopped with possible worlds as primitive, as most authors do.[46] Two justifications (at least) can be given for this. The first is that we are doing logic (or philosophy of language) and therefore should not wish to prejudge the metaphysical issue by dogmatizing on the nature of the entities we assume. This is the attitude which, taken to extremes, results in the so-called 'truth-value' semantics[47] in which truth-values are assigned directly to formulae without the trouble of having domains of values, and possible worlds are thought of as (certain kinds of) sets of formulae. This is thought to 'free' the logician from any possibly embarrassing 'ontological commitment' (as if there were a virtue in not having to believe in the existence of anything but languages). One reason for the title of this chapter is to make it clear to those who have a more sure idea than I about just what ought to be the logician's business that I am quite happy to regard myself in this chapter as doing not logic but meta-

[46] *Vide* e.g. Montague [1969], Lewis [1970] and Stalnaker [1970]. (Also the whole tradition of possible-worlds semantics for modal logic.)

[47] E.g. Leblanc and Meyer [1970]. Allied with this type of semantics is what is called the 'substitution interpretation' of quantification popularized by Barcan Marcus [1962] and others. For a criticism of substitutional quantification, *vide* Quine [1969], pp. 104–7.

physics. It seems to me that it ought to be someone's business to ask what possible worlds are.

The second justification for not considering the nature of possible worlds, a justification which David Lewis has put forward,[48] is that the possible worlds are defined in terms of the role they play in linguistic analysis. In this they are like, say, the ultimate particles of physics and it might be thought inappropriate to ask for a definition. There is much truth in this, but perhaps the parallel with physics may help to see just what more we can do. Just as the use of the word 'particle', even if we don't define it, can suggest what may be fruitful ways of looking at these entities by suggesting further questions to ask about their behaviour, so an attempt to say what a possible world is may lead to further insight into the nature of language.

The analysis I shall give of possible worlds will be an atomistic one.[49] We are to suppose that we are given a set **B** of 'basic particular situations'.[50] The idea is that any subset w of **B** determines a possible world. The elements of **B** which are members of w might be thought of as the 'atomic facts' of the world w.

We can give a very easy illustration of how this might work. We suppose that **B** is the set of all space-time points. For the present we are not making any assumptions about the structure of space and time but we have in mind physical theories whose ultimate entities are conceived of as things whose properties can all be expressed in terms of the space-time points they occupy.[51] I.e., we are thinking of a theory such that if we know of any spatial point s and time t whether or not there is something occupying s at t then we know the complete state of the world. One might wonder whether a member of **B** should be not

[48] In conversational comment on Cresswell [1972b].

[49] Carnapian state-descriptions as in [1947], p. 9, are atomistically made up but they are linguistic entities. The 'atomic facts' of the logical atomists, *vide* Urmson [1956], pp. 60–2, also have some affinities with the members of our **B** but the difference between the atomists' philosophy of language and the one developed in his book should be obvious.

[50] 'Basic' of course in the role they play in the theory. We do not mean that they have any epistemological primacy. The nature of the members of **B** can only be discovered by a mammoth operation of philosophical analysis of the whole of a language. That is why we can do no more than illustrate.

[51] Quine [1969], pp. 144–56, appears to have come round to such a view of possible worlds. A useful discussion of the kind of spatial structure they might fit into is found on pp. 147–52. Quine, though, only appears to bring them in when he is forced to, as objects of certain manifestly non-linguistic propositional attitudes, and does not seem inclined to base an entire philosophy of language on them. Yet if they can be used in the analysis of 'the cat is afraid the dog will hurt him' there seems no reason why they might not be used more widely.

a space-time point but rather the occupation of a space-time point. Luckily for the analysis of language it makes no difference; and indeed it might plausibly be said that the possible occupation of a space-time point is no different from the notion of that space-time point itself. A set of space-time points at least *determines* a world (the world in which those and only those points are occupied) and in the absence of a more plausible candidate one might just as well say it *is* a world.

This illustration is of course a materialistic one, though the general theory is not in that **B** may contain, if there are such things, non-material basic particular situations. But no harm is lost in restricting ourselves for the moment to the case where **B** is the set of all space-time points, since it seems plausible to suppose that there are at least as many possible worlds as there are sets of space-time points. I lay some stress on the possibility of such a materialistic analysis of **B** since one important problem in the philosophy of language is how to reconcile the idea that one can give a complete physical description of the world with the idea that not everything we say can be analysed in purely physical terms. What I have to say in this chapter and in Chapter Seven is intended to contribute to a solution to this problem. There is also some point to a materialistic illustration since those philosophers who are prepared to accept points of space, together with some set theory, will find that they can help themselves to all the entities required for a highly intensional theory of meaning without needing to lose the least sleep.[52]

We then define a possible world as a set of basic particular situations, i.e., as a subset of **B.** We have already noted (p. 24) that using the notion of a possible world enables us to define logical properties of and relations between propositions in a language-independent way.

Propositions

In Chapter One we defined a proposition as a set of possible worlds. We could proceed in this manner now but it would have some intuitively inconvenient consequences. If a proposition is thought of as a set of possible worlds then two propositions are identical iff they are the same set of worlds. But also two propositions would seem to be logically equivalent iff they are the same set of worlds. Thus, propositions will be identical iff logically equivalent.

This is the intuitively inconvenient consequence of our earlier definition, since there are many cases in which we are not happy to

[52] Thus Quine, op. cit.

identify logically equivalent propositions. Propositional attitudes e.g., provide one case; there is no reason why someone should not take a different propositional attitude (belief, say) to two propositions which are logically equivalent. And when a mathematician discovers the truth of a mathematical principle he does not thereby discover the truth of all mathematical principles.

One way out is to divide the worlds into those we may call 'classical'[53] and those we can call 'non-classical'. Two propositions are logically equivalent iff they contain the same *classical* worlds, though they may differ in the presence or absence of certain non-classical worlds. There is nothing formally wrong with this proposal, and its consequences have been studied in a number of places.[54] Further, if possible worlds are taken as primitive then there is nothing to prevent us from taking a subset and saying that these are the ones which are the genuinely possible worlds; the others are in some sense impossible. And to one who asks what it is about a world which makes it a possible or an impossible one we answer as before that this is determined by the role the world plays in the theory.

This answer seems a little less satisfactory here because we *are* attempting to analyse the notion of a world. The whole idea of the points-of-space-time analysis was to make no one world any more logically possible than any other. If we are going to have impossible worlds they cannot be sets of space-time points. Before we look at what they might be we shall briefly consider how the formal analysis in terms of non-classical worlds works. This is necessary because we have in Chapter One proved a theorem to the effect that a possible-worlds analysis is sufficiently general to take care of the semantics of any propositional language and so it may be wondered why all this talk of impossible worlds is necessary. Part of the answer has already been given by saying that it is only when we come to analyse the notion of a possible world that we have to be bothered by the distinction between kinds of worlds, but this needs spelling out a little.

[53] This usage was coined in Cresswell [1970], p. 354. Montague [1970a], p. 382, speaks of 'designated points of reference'.

[54] Cresswell, op. cit. and [1972a]. Similar work, most of it as yet unpublished, is being done by logicians influenced by the 'Pittsburgh' school. I know of such work by Routley, Meyer, Dunn, Urquhart; and there are no doubt others. Their approaches however are a little different in several ways. E.g., Routley [1971], p. 606 f, distinguishes between worlds and 'set ups', worlds being what we have called classical worlds. However Routley thinks of set ups and therefore of worlds as sets of formulae.

Consider two examples. In most propositional logics, if α is a sentence and $\sim \in \Delta_1$ then α and $\langle \sim, \langle \sim, \alpha \rangle \rangle$ are, under any assignment, the same proposition. I.e., α and $\langle \sim, \langle \sim, \alpha \rangle \rangle$ are true in precisely the same set of worlds. This is because the meaning rule for $\sim$ has the consequence that for any sentence α and world w, $V(\alpha)$ is true in w ($w \in V(\alpha)$) iff $V(\langle \sim, \alpha \rangle)$ is false in w ($w \notin V(\langle \sim, \alpha \rangle)$). With this rule it is easy to see that for any α and any w, $V(\langle \sim, \langle \sim, \alpha \rangle \rangle)$ is true in w iff $V(\alpha)$ is true in w, i.e., $V(\alpha) = V(\langle \sim, \langle \sim, \alpha \rangle \rangle)$. So what we do if we want to avoid a replacement rule for tautologous equivalents,[55] is require that it is only in the set **C** of classical worlds that the ordinary truth-table rule for $\sim$ holds. I.e., if $w \in \mathbf{C}$ then $w \in V(\langle \sim, \alpha \rangle)$ iff $w \notin V(\alpha)$. Since we say nothing about what happens when $w \notin \mathbf{C}$ it follows that although $V(\alpha) \cap \mathbf{C} = V(\langle \sim, \langle \sim, \alpha \rangle \rangle) \cap \mathbf{C}$ we need not have $V(\alpha) = V(\langle \sim, \langle \sim, \alpha \rangle \rangle)$.

Now certainly one way of construing this is to take **C** as the set of possible worlds and the others as impossible ones, but another way of construing it is to say that **C** is the set of worlds in which $\sim$ behaves as negation and $\mathbf{W} - \mathbf{C}$ the worlds in which it need not. We may then say that although $\sim$ is a kind of negation it is only a partial kind, much as intuitionistic negation is a special kind of negation; when we know what kind we see that laws like $\sim\sim p \supset p$ fail not because they are not true of classical negation but because they are not true of intuitionistic negation. But if $\sim$ is not a true negation then when we claim that $p = \sim\sim p$ fails we do not mean that the double negation rule fails but merely that $\sim$ here does not represent true negation.

Our second example is $\langle \&, \alpha, \langle \sim, \alpha \rangle \rangle$. If in a non-classical world either $\sim$ or & does not obey its truth-table then in that world $\langle \&, \alpha, \langle \sim, \alpha \rangle \rangle$ may be true, but this will be only because either & is not a true conjunction or because $\sim$ is not a true negation. I.e., $\langle \&, \alpha, \langle \sim, \alpha \rangle \rangle$ will be true in w because it is not a real contradiction. If it were, then the possible worlds in $V(\langle \sim, \alpha \rangle)$ would have to be precisely the worlds not in $V(\alpha)$ and the worlds in $V(\langle \&, \alpha, \langle \sim, \alpha \rangle \rangle)$ would have to be precisely the worlds in both. But such a set is empty. The fact that we can reinterpret & and $\sim$ so that $\langle \&, \alpha, \langle \sim, \alpha \rangle \rangle$ is true in a possible world no more shews us how a contradiction could ever be true than calling birds 'pigs' shews us how pigs could fly.

For these reasons we shall not define a proposition as a set of possible worlds.[56] But since we shall need sets of possible worlds to do

[55] Cresswell [1970], p. 354 f.

[56] The analysis which follows arises largely from a conversation with David Lewis in September of 1971.

some of the jobs we use propositions for (e.g. defining logical equivalence, necessity, entailment, etc.), we shall define what we shall call a *proto-proposition*:

DEFINITION **3.1** A *proto-proposition* is a set of possible worlds.

We have seen why proto-propositions are not fit subjects for propositional attitudes. This is in part because when somebody imagines or conceives a 'state of affairs' it may turn out not to be a consistent one. Suppose someone is thinking of a world in which there is a round square dinner plate on the dining-room table. Now there is no such world in which this is so (provided we really do mean round and square by those words and are not thinking of, say, mathematical definitions of them in terms of which it would be possible to devise a world in which the structure of space was such that 'round' and 'square' were not contraries) but the person in question thinks there is. I.e., his belief 'world' contains both the proto-proposition that there is a round plate on the table and the proto-proposition that there is a square plate on the dinner table. Since such a 'world' would never be a world it seems better to call it a *heaven*.

DEFINITION **3.2** A *heaven* is a set of proto-propositions.

Now no heavens will be worlds but some heavens will correspond to worlds in that the proto-propositions in them will jointly characterize one and only one world.

DEFINITION **3.3** A *world-heaven* is a set h of proto-propositions for which there is some world w such that for any proto-proposition a, $a \in h$ iff $w \in a$.

DEFINITION **3.4** A proposition is a set of heavens.

At this point some questions of nomenclature arise. The most sensible procedure would appear to be to define some such series as this:

We begin with **B** as the set of basic particular situations. We then define:

3.5 **W**, the set of possible worlds, as $\mathscr{P}$**B**,
3.6 **PP**, the set of proto-propositions, as $\mathscr{P}$**W**,
3.7 **H**, the set of heavens, as $\mathscr{P}$(**PP**),
3.8 **P**, the set of propositions, as $\mathscr{P}$**H**,

(Note that since **B** is supposed to be a set, then so are **W**, **PP**, **H**, and **P**.)

As far as the intuitive discussion goes, this captures what we have just been saying. As far as our formal development goes it is now heavens which play the role previously played by worlds and a good many of the theorems, such as 1.14 (p. 20), need reinterpreting with **H** replacing **W**. Further, when we spoke earlier of propositions, although we were thinking of them as sets of worlds yet the things we said in many cases applied to the things we still call propositions but which are now not sets of worlds but sets of heavens.

But we shall stick to the definitions of 3.5–3.8. We can offer two justifications. First, an historical one: Kripke's articles on modal logic all use **H** for the set of possible worlds. Second, a more compelling one: We wish to speak of a proposition (not just a proto-proposition) as being true or false in a world (not just a heaven).

Obviously if h is a world-heaven then there is some unique world w such that $\bigcap h = \{w\}$ (i.e., the set of things which are in every member of h is the set whose only member is w). Further, for each world w there is a unique h such that $\{h = a \in \mathbf{PP} : w \in a\}$. (The proof of these results is an easy exercise in set theory and is anyhow intuitively obvious.) Since **W** and **H** are disjoint then there is a 1–1 function $\eta \subseteq (\mathbf{W} \cup \mathbf{H})^2$ such that

3.9 if $w \in \mathbf{W}$, $\eta(w) = \{a \in \mathbf{PP} : w \in a\}$.

3.10 if $h \in \mathbf{H}$ and for some $w \in \mathbf{W}$, $\bigcap h = \{w\}$; then $\eta(h) = w$.

(I.e., η is the 1–1 function connecting each world with the corresponding world-heaven and vice versa.)

3.11 If $p \in \mathbf{P}$ then p is true in w iff $\eta(w) \in p$.

Remember **P** is the set of all propositions and any $p \in \mathbf{P}$ is a set of heavens. What 3.11 says is that p is true in a world iff it contains the world-heaven corresponding to that world.

Now two propositions will be logically equivalent iff they are true in exactly the same worlds. Let us use **C** for the set of world-heavens; then p and $q \in \mathbf{P}$ will be logically equivalent iff $p \cap \mathbf{C} = q \cap \mathbf{C}$, p will be logically necessary iff $\mathbf{C} \subseteq p$, p will entail q iff $p \cap \mathbf{C} \subseteq q \cap \mathbf{C}$ and so on. Obviously there is no reason why we may not have $p \cap \mathbf{C} = q \cap \mathbf{C}$ but $p \neq q$. Two propositions will be identical if they contain the same heavens but not necessarily if they contain merely the same world-heavens. Propositional functors take propositional arguments and give propositional values. Of these some do and some do not obey the rule

3.12 If $p_1 \cap \mathbf{C} = q_1 \cap \mathbf{C}, \ldots, p_n \cap \mathbf{C} = q_n \cap \mathbf{C}$ then $\omega(p_1,\ldots,p_n) \cap \mathbf{C} = \omega(q_1,\ldots,q_n) \cap \mathbf{C}$.

The advance of mathematical and logical knowledge can be seen as the discovery of more and more propositions which contain **C**. Of course the real world (the set of space-time points which are actually occupied) determines a world-heaven and so what is necessarily true is indeed true.

Note that all this makes no reference to language. For all we have said so far in this chapter there might be no such thing as language at all. This is rather important since even philosophers who are prepared to accept a notion of logical equivalence which is non-linguistic may well wonder whether any stricter notion of propositional identity can be analysed without reference to language.

Synonymy

Given a set **B** of basic particular situations, of which some subset w is designated as the 'real world', we define the model structure based on $\langle \mathbf{B}, w \rangle$ to be the structure $\langle \mathbf{P}, \mathbf{T} \rangle$ in which **P** is defined as in 3.5–3.8 on p. 42 and $\mathbf{T} \subseteq \mathbf{P}$ is the set of all propositions p such that $\eta(w) \in p$ (i.e. all propositions true in the real world). Any model $\langle \mathbf{P}, \mathbf{T}, \mathrm{V} \rangle$, where V is defined as on pp. 18–20 will be said to be a model based on $\langle \mathbf{B}, w \rangle$. Obviously theorem 1.14 still applies to a **P** and **T** so defined since provided **B** is infinite so are **P**, **T** and **P**–**T**.

We shall say that two sentences α and β are *synonymous* in a model iff $\mathrm{V}^+(\alpha) = \mathrm{V}^+(\beta)$. It is possible to have models based on some $\langle \mathbf{B}, w \rangle$ in which no two distinct sentences are synonymous. The model used in the proof of theorem 1.14 on p. 20 shews how such models may be constructed. At the other extreme we can have models in which every sentence has the same value, and of course there will be models in between in which some but not all the sentences are synonymous. Two sentences α and β are *logically equivalent* in a model iff $\mathrm{V}^+(\alpha) \cap \mathbf{C} = \mathrm{V}^+(\beta) \cap \mathbf{C}$ (where **C** is defined as on p. 43). Obviously if $\mathrm{V}^+(\alpha) = \mathrm{V}^+(\beta)$ then $\mathrm{V}^+(\alpha) \cap \mathbf{C} = \mathrm{V}^+(\beta) \cap \mathbf{C}$ and so synonymous sentences will be logically equivalent. The converse however will not in general hold though it will in some models.

The point of this last paragraph is merely to stress that the discussion of the present chapter has had nothing to say on the question of synonymy conditions for sentences. It is important to say this because it is very easy to confuse two radically different questions; viz:

(i) What are the conditions for propositional identity?
(ii) What are the conditions for sentence synonymy?

The first question, in our view, is a language-independent metaphysical question whose answer demands an analysis, of the kind we have tried to give in this chapter, of the notion of a proposition. The second is a question whose general answer is simply that α and β are synonymous in an interpretation $\langle \mathbf{P}, \mathrm{V} \rangle$ iff $\mathrm{V}^+(\alpha) = \mathrm{V}^+(\beta)$ and whose answer in particular cases depends on the interpretation of the language under consideration.

Not all philosophers would be content to leave the question of synonymy entirely up to the meaning-assignment to the language. Some would want to insist that certain sentences could never have the same meaning. E.g. that $\langle \sim, \langle \sim, \alpha \rangle \rangle$ could never mean the same as α (no matter what $\sim$ means) because it is a more complex sentence than α and therefore has a more complex meaning. One such is David Lewis,[57] and we shall give a brief account of his theory of meaning as a representative of this tradition.

Lewis distinguishes between a 'meaning' and an 'intension'. Suppose in a propositional language $\mathscr{L}$, $\alpha \in \Delta_0$ and $\sim \in \Delta_1$. (We have in mind that $\sim$ is a negation functor but this is not necessary for the illustration.) The intension of α with respect to some value assignment will be a set of possible worlds[58] and the intension of $\sim$ will be an operation from sets of possible worlds into sets of possible worlds. This is just like our procedure in Chapter One. Let us refer to the intensions of α and $\sim$ (with respect to the value-assignment in question) as $I(\alpha)$ and $I(\sim)$. Since α is a single symbol the meaning of α is identified with its intension. The meaning of $\langle \sim, \alpha \rangle$ however is thought of as the ordered pair $\langle I(\sim), I(\alpha) \rangle$ and the meaning of $\langle \sim, \langle \sim, \alpha \rangle \rangle$ as $\langle I(\sim), \langle I(\sim), I(\alpha) \rangle \rangle$.[59] It must be noted that this analysis is, in common with ours, independent of language, for although $\langle I(\sim), \langle I(\sim), I(\alpha) \rangle \rangle$

[57] Lewis [1970], pp. 31–5. Lewis' theory is in fact an adaptation of Carnap's notion of 'intensional isomorphism' though dealt with in a language-independent way. *Vide* Carnap [1947], pp. 56–9.

[58] Actually, as well as possible worlds Lewis has other indices which reflect aspects of the 'context of use' of the sentence (cf. *infra* p. 111). We shall be discussing these later, and ignoring them for the present does not affect the argument here.

[59] This is not entirely fair to Lewis. His definition is somewhat more complicated a nd he is using 'meanings' to do the kind of jobs we discuss on pp. 211 ff *infra*.

mirrors the structure of $\langle\sim,\langle\sim,\alpha\rangle\rangle$ it is a complex set whose members are not parts of the language $\mathscr{L}$ but parts of the interpretation of $\mathscr{L}$.

As it stands this proposal is in need of some adjustment since it does not allow for functors within whose scope a difference in meaning unaccompanied by a difference in intension might cause a difference in intension. E.g., if $\delta \in \Delta_1$ is a belief functor it may well happen that two logically equivalent but non-synonymous sentences α and β are such that $\langle\delta,\alpha\rangle$ and $\langle\delta,\beta\rangle$ differ in intension. To repair this deficiency the propositional operators cannot simply take intensions into intensions, they must take meanings into meanings. Since Lewis' definition of meaning involves operations taking intensions from intensions some rather complicated technical manoeuvres would be necessary but the idea could certainly be made to work. As we have noted, this approach on the one hand prohibits a model from giving α and $\langle\sim,\langle\sim,\alpha\rangle\rangle$ the same meaning (since obviously $I(\alpha)$ and $\langle I(\sim), \langle I(\sim), I(\alpha)\rangle\rangle$ are not the same) and on the other hand requires that sentences which have the same form (say two members of Δ_0) have the same meaning if they have the same intension. Lewis does not mind this[60] for he regards himself as able to help himself to either intensions or meanings, whichever suits him. Also the philosophy of language which he seems to favour is one in which structured meanings play a rather important role. In the next chapter we shall have something to say about how analyses of meaning like Lewis' can be accommodated in the more general framework we outlined earlier.

Postscript

A rather sweeping objection to what we have been doing in this chapter is the following – that propositions, whatever they are, cannot be sets, because there have been philosophers who were undoubtedly talking about propositions but who knew no set theory and would have answered 'no' to the question of whether the entities they were talking about were sets. This objection is a rather general one about the nature of analysis and we shall make a pretty standard reply.

The present chapter is not addressed to those who already have a clear idea of what propositions are and who know they are not sets,

[60] Lewis [1970], p. 31 f. It may be that Lewis has forgotten here the existence of functors such as belief functors. He gives the impression that he is happy to deal with only intensions if he is interested in truth conditions, and meanings when interested in more grammatical enterprises. The existence of belief functors shews that these two cannot be divorced and that even if we are only interested in truth conditions we still need something finer than intensions.

it is addressed to those who like myself feel the need to postulate entities which behave in certain ways and who would like a set-theoretical analysis of these entities. The choice of set-theoretical analyses is discussed in the introduction (p. 7); all we shall say here is that set theory seems to be the best-understood and most comprehensive language for precise description. Those who do not share this view will find a great deal in this book uncongenial but the burden will be on them to provide a substitute metalanguage.

It would perhaps have been nicer to remain with propositions as sets of possible worlds. From time to time in later chapters we shall forget our more sophisticated analysis and speak of sets of possible worlds. The more complex analysis seems needed only when we have functors which represent 'propositional attitudes', functors like 'know', 'believe' etc. A full justification of our procedure would need a far deeper semantical analysis of these notions than has yet been given.[61] All that we shall say here is that when we are interested in propositional attitudes, and perhaps only then, we are interested in 'worlds' which are not really worlds at all but are the sort of things a person may build up in his mind from bits of experience. These bits of experience can be thought of as common features of genuine worlds and may therefore be represented by sets of worlds, viz. the sets of worlds which have the common feature in question, and that is what proto-propositions are.

At any rate whatever detailed philosophical work on the language of propositional attitudes will ultimately shew, we have at least produced a semantical framework which does the job of distinguishing between logically equivalent propositions in a language-independent way and is quite open on the question of synonymy conditions for sentences.

[61] The fullest work in this area has been done by Hintikka in [1962] and elsewhere. However, Hintikka has confined himself to cases of what might be called 'rational belief' where all logically equivalent propositions are regarded as identical. A brief examination of belief logic in which substitution of logical equivalents is not always truth-preserving is given in Cresswell [1972a], pp. 10–14, but the picture given there is rather a gloomy one.

CHAPTER FOUR

The Structure of Propositions

This chapter is like Chapter Two in that it is not strictly necessary for later developments. Its purpose is to shew how certain alternative approaches to semantics can be accommodated in the framework we have developed. That they can be so accommodated means that we are not obliged to defend our own approach against them. This should not be taken to mean that we either agree or disagree with these other approaches but only that we can, if we wish, remain neutral. In this chapter, more than any other so far, we shall be using propositional languages primarily as illustrations for the richer languages we shall consider in Part II.

Language learning and innate ideas

Our metaphysical account of the entities required for the semantics of propositional languages contains no reference to any 'mental' entities on the one hand or 'behaviour dispositions' on the other since in our view these entities figure in theories of language use rather than in semantics proper. David Lewis[62] has protested at the confusion which comes of failing to distinguish between 'the description of possible languages or grammars as abstract semantic systems whereby symbols are associated with aspects of the world' and 'the description of the psychological and sociological facts whereby a particular one of these abstract semantic systems is the one used by a person or population'. This book is primarily concerned with the first of these and the present chapter is one of the few places where we have any-

[62] Lewis [1970], p. 19, and *supra*, p. 2 f.

thing to say about the second. Even here we shall concern ourselves merely with the formal structure of the semantical theories we discuss.

A theory of language use must be able to shew how it is that the meanings of the symbols and expressions of a language can be learnt by human beings, or, what comes to the same thing, how one person can test whether another person has the same meaning in mind. The semantics we have so far been presenting have had little to say on this problem. E.g., consider the motivation given on pp. 23–5 for thinking of a proposition as a set of possible worlds. The impression left by that passage might seem to be that if one person wishes to tell another what proposition he has in mind he must in some sense shew that other person each possible world in turn and tell him whether the proposition is true in that other world or not. Our purpose in Chapter One was of course to give a preliminary account of what a proposition might be, and nothing in the present chapter is intended to affect the ontological status of these entities, but it would be very implausible to suppose that the procedure described above is the way we go about teaching the meanings of words.

What has just been said illustrates a very general problem about the learning of general terms. We shall illustrate this difficulty by using the more familiar example of a class or property word. Consider, for example, knowledge of the concept of redness. Knowledge of the concept of redness is, or at least involves, the ability to separate things which are red from those which are not. How can we test whether a person has this ability? If we try to do it by observing whether he correctly distinguishes between red things and non-red things we can never be certain that he has the ability since we shall have observed only a very small proportion (only a finite number) of the total possible cases in which the ability could be tested. Yet we frequently do know that another person has learnt the concept of redness.

One solution to this problem says that the reason we can know that another person is operating with the same concept as we are is that all humanly graspable concepts or ideas are made up in certain specifiable ways from simple ideas which are either innate in us or derived from experience. Thus when we observe another person distinguishing red things from non-red things we can know (perhaps not infallibly but with a high probability) that he is operating with the concept of redness because there is no other of the humanly graspable properties which things can have which marks off just that class of things which he has so far considered to be red. Redness could be called a *natural kind*, and language learning becomes possible because although a finite number of discriminations between red and non-red things could be continued in infinitely many ways which would have no connection with the concept of redness, yet of the ways of continuing in accordance with some natural kind perhaps redness is the only one; or if there are others they can be eliminated one by one by further testing. Even philosophers who would be unhappy with innate ideas frequently feel forced to accept some doctrine of natural kinds.[63]

The same point can perhaps be made in another way. We have spoken as if knowledge of the concept redness were the very same as the ability to distinguish between red and non-red things. But it could well be maintained that this is a *result* of knowing the concept of redness. This objection can be used against the very definition of things like properties and propositions. As applied to propositions (which is all that we have so far attempted to give a strict account of) it would go somewhat as follows:

You have spoken of propositions as sets of possible worlds but your reasons were bad. Suppose that you wanted to shew another person that the proposition you had in mind was the proposition that some people in Wellington do Scottish country dancing. Suppose also for the moment that you are not interested in any stricter identity criterion than logical equivalence. We may grant that you can shew him each possible world in turn and say 'yes' or 'no' according as the proposition is true or false in it. But surely you have selected the worlds in which to say 'yes' *because* the proposition, which must therefore be something else, is true in them. And if all your pupil has learnt is a set of worlds, how can he have grasped the same proposition as you?

This objection is both good and bad. It is a bad objection to the notion of a proposition as a set of possible worlds since whatever it is the pupil has learnt it is something which is logically equivalent to the original proposition. It is a good objection to the idea that the sorts of propositions we can have in mind (and these are the only sorts of propositions we can ever give as examples) might be just arbitrary sets or worlds. Some sort of natural kinds doctrine is at work here too

[63] In some ways the problem of deciding which predicates are 'projectible' in the sense of Goodman [1954], p. 89, is a parallel one though Goodman attempts to find a basis for such a distinction in experience. *Vide* also Quine [1969], essay 5 (pp. 114–38). Papers from a symposium between Chomsky, Putnam and Goodman on innate ideas are reprinted in Searle [1971], pp. 121–44.

which ensures that the set of worlds in which some people in Wellington do Scottish country dancing is humanly graspable.

If we go back to the rather sophisticated analysis of propositions we gave in Chapter Three and consider the remarks we made on p. 42 we can think of a humanly graspable proto-proposition as representing some aspect of experience which enables us to pick out a set of worlds. Presumably by reflection on experience, or some such process, the details of which it will not be our task to investigate, certain sets of proto-propositions represent ways we can imagine the world to be. Some of these ways are inconsistent and could not represent a world, and we have called them heavens; they too can be put together in humanly graspable ways to give us propositions. Thus when we give an example of a proposition, say that the capital city of New Zealand is not its largest, we are able to grasp it in our mind because we build it up ultimately from certain aspects of our experience. This does not mean that its ontological status is different from what it was said to be on pp. 41–4 but only that we never get to understand a proposition by an enumeration of its members and its members' members and so on.

We shall now look at the formal structure of the innate-idea doctrine as applied to propositional languages. Later in the book we shall try to give explications (in the Carnapian sense) of things like properties and concepts (our talk about them has been a little loose but we hope not unilluminating) and most of what is said in this chapter will either carry over or can be extended to all the entities required for the semantics of richer languages than propositional ones. The extensions needed are complicated but fairly routine and shed little new light on what we say here.

Meaning algebras

The innate-idea doctrine is basically that language-learning is possible because the entities required for semantics can all be built up out of certain initially given entities by a number of operations. In this they are rather like the sentences of language itself, and it is thought to be no accident that languages are also built up in this way.

Suppose that we have a domain **P** of propositions. We are of course ultimately interested in thinking of a **P** defined as on pp. 41–4 but the formal development will apply where **P** is any set at all and some of our examples will use sets of other kinds. We next assume a subset $\mathbf{I}_0$ of **P**. $\mathbf{I}_0$ is to be thought of as the set of all those propositions which are initially given, or graspable, the propositions which the human mind can understand immediately. What sort of propositions they are is not our concern, nor is the question of what it means to say that something is immediately graspable by the human mind. As far as formal structure is concerned all we require is that $\mathbf{I}_0$ be a subset of **P**. Parallel to the initially-given propositions we assume for each $n > 0$ a set $\mathbf{I}_n$ of initially given n-place functions whose arguments and values are all in **P**. (For some n, $\mathbf{I}_n$ may be empty.)

Our formal definition is as follows:

A meaning algebra $\langle \mathbf{P}, \mathbf{I}, \mathbf{G} \rangle$ is an ordered triple in which **P** is a set, **I** a sequence $\langle \mathbf{I}_0, \mathbf{I}_1, \ldots \rangle$ etc. such that $\mathbf{I}_0 \subseteq \mathbf{P}$ and $\mathbf{I}_n$ $(1 \leqslant n)$ is a set of n-place operations on **P**. **G** is the (unique) smallest set such that:

4.1 $\mathbf{I}_0 \subseteq \mathbf{G}$

4.2 If $a_1, \ldots, a_n \in \mathbf{G}$ and $\omega \in \mathbf{I}_n$ then $\omega(a_1, \ldots, a_n) \in \mathbf{G}$

G of course is supposed to be the set of 'graspable' propositions, and the idea behind these rules is that any proposition made up out of initially given propositions by means of graspable functions is itself to count as graspable. The members of **G** all have the property that they can be expressed (possibly in many different ways) as the result of a finite number of operations on the members of the initial functions. Given a member of **G** we can express its meaning by saying how it is made up out of **I**. Our definition of model remains as described in Chapter One (pp. 18–20) and Chapter Three (p. 44) except that we now restrict the assignments so that where $\alpha \in \Delta_0$ then $V(\alpha) \in \mathbf{G}$ and where $\delta \in \Delta_n$ $(1 \leqslant n)$ then $\omega_\delta \in \mathbf{I}_n$.[64]

Since **G** satisfies 4.1 and 4.2 every sentence will have a graspable meaning. Sometimes this last requirement is dispensed with. Some philosophers would want to say that it is possible to have sentences which are made up from perfectly meaningful parts yet do not make sensible wholes. Arthur Prior[65] once considered a propositional operator meaning 'It was with a knife that'. When put before 'Brutus killed Caesar' we get a meaningful and true sentence. Yet

[64] The restriction of $V(\delta)$ to $\mathbf{I}_n$ (for $\delta \in \Delta_n$, $n \geqslant 1$) is more severe than it need be but is made so for technical reasons. E.g., suppose we wanted to define $\omega_{\supset}(a,b)$ as $\omega_{\vee}(\omega_{\sim}(a),b)$, where $\omega_{\vee}$ and $\omega_{\sim}$ are in $\mathbf{I}_2$ and $\mathbf{I}_1$ respectively. There is no reason why $\omega_{\subset}$, being so made up from graspable functions, should not itself be graspable. For a statement of a plausible set of rules for generating new graspable functions, *vide* Cresswell [1972c], p. 309 f.

[65] I have a vivid recollection of reading this somewhere in his writings but I am now unable to find it. It is certainly Priorian in spirit and makes the required point very well.

(1) It was with a knife that $2+2=4$

hardly seems susceptible of a sensible interpretation. In terms of propositional languages the meaning of 'It was with a knife that' could be a member of $\mathbf{I}_1$ and the meaning of '$2+2=4$' a member of **G**, and yet the whole sentence (1) might not be graspable.

We define an incomplete or partial meaning algebra as a quadruple $\langle \mathbf{P}, \mathbf{I}, \mathbf{G}, \mathbf{J} \rangle$ in which $\langle \mathbf{P}, \mathbf{I}, \mathbf{G} \rangle$ is a meaning algebra (as on p. 52) and **J** is a set such that:

4.3 $\mathbf{I}_0 \subseteq \mathbf{J} \subseteq \mathbf{G}$

It is now **J** which represents the set of graspable propositions and condition 4.3 ensures that all initial propositions are graspable and that only propositions made up by graspable functions are themselves graspable but that not all need be. We shall now of course require that in any model where $\alpha \in \Delta_0$ then $V(\alpha) \in \mathbf{J}$.

There are now two ways we can deal with complex sentences. Suppose α is $\langle \delta, \alpha_1, \ldots, \alpha_n \rangle$. Under the rules of Chapter One on p. 19 in any interpretation $\langle \mathbf{P}, V \rangle$, $V^+(\alpha) = \omega_\delta(V^+(\alpha_1), \ldots, V^+(\alpha_n))$. Now if $\omega_\delta \in \mathbf{I}_n$ and $V^+(\alpha_1), \ldots, V^+(\alpha_n) \in \mathbf{G}$ then by 4.2 $V^+(\alpha) \in \mathbf{G}$ but we have no guarantee that $V^+(\alpha) \in \mathbf{J}$. We can either say that $V^+(\alpha)$, although a proposition, is not a 'graspable' one, or modify our definition of value assignment and leave $V^+(\alpha)$ undefined in these circumstances. The choice is between whether there are 'absurd' propositions or whether certain combinations do not yield a proposition at all. Yet a third approach would be to allow the functions assigned by V to the symbols to be partial functions which do not always give a value even when applied to arguments of the right kind.

The logical structure of propositions

Each member of **G** in a meaning algebra can be built up by composition from members of **I**. So far there is nothing to prevent a proposition from being built up in many different ways. Perhaps there is nothing wrong in this. Consider a case from arithmetic. Suppose that **P** is the set of all natural numbers. Let $\mathbf{I}_0$ contain only 0, $\mathbf{I}_1$ contain the successor operation S of adding one, $\mathbf{I}_2$ the operators $+$ and $\times$ (addition and multiplication). Consider, say, the number 4. This number can be shewn to be a member of **G** in several different ways:

$4 = S(S(S(S(0))))$

$4 = ((S(0) + S(0)) + (S(0) + S(0)))$

$4 = (S(0) + S(0)) \times (S(0) + S(0))$

and there are many other ways still. Even the number 0 which is the only initially given member of **P** can be expressed as the value of a complex function, e.g. $0 = 0 \times (S(S(0)) + S(0))$. In this arithmetical situation there is nothing objectionable about the fact that 0 is the value of a complex function. What it does mean though is that if we were to ask whether a member of **P** is simple or complex there would not be a sensible answer, at least not if by 'simple' we mean 'not the value of a function of (the same or other) members of **P**'.

Let us now look at a case in which this talk of simple and complex members of **P** does make sense. Consider how we might make an algebra out of a propositional language itself.[66] For simplicity let us take the language $\mathscr{L}_{\langle \sim, \vee \rangle}$ of a version of the propositional calculus in which Δ_0 contains (say) just the letters p, q, r, Δ_1 contains only $\sim$ and Δ_2, $\vee$. We define an algebra $\langle \mathbf{P}, \mathbf{I}, \mathbf{G} \rangle$ as follows:

4.4 **P** is S (i.e. the set of sentences of $\mathscr{L}_{\langle \sim, \vee \rangle}$)

4.5 $\mathbf{I}_0$ is $\{p, q, r\}$

4.6 $\mathbf{I}_1$ contains the operation $\omega_\sim$ defined as: for any $\alpha \in \mathbf{P}$ (=S), $\omega_\sim(\alpha) = \langle \sim, \alpha \rangle$ (remember since $\alpha \in$ S and $\sim \in \Delta_1$ then $\langle \sim, \alpha \rangle \in$ S and so is in **P**).

4.7 $\mathbf{I}_2$ contains the operation $\omega_\vee$ defined as, for any α, $\beta \in \mathbf{P}$, $\omega_\vee(\alpha, \beta) = \langle \vee, \alpha, \beta \rangle$.

G is determined by **P** and **I** according to the definition on p. 52.

In an algebra of this kind (sometimes called a word-algebra[67]) we can distinguish between those elements of **G** which are simple and those which are complex. The members of $\mathbf{I}_0$ are simple in that no member of $\mathbf{I}_0$ is the value of any function in **I**. Further, every member of **P** has a unique decomposition into the members of **I**, for there is just one way a sentence can be written; if it is written differently it is a different sentence, i.e., a different member of **P**. Let us call a meaning algebra which has the property that each member of **G** may be finitely decomposed into members of **I** in a unique way a *free* meaning algebra.[68] The first point to note is that although the set **P** on which the free meaning algebra was constructed was of a special kind, viz. a set

[66] An extended study of the algebraic structure of formal systems is found in Rasiowa and Sikorski [1963] (2nd ed. 1968).

[67] Cohn [1965], p. 117.

[68] Of course we shall always be able to define non-graspable functions so that some $a \in I_0$ is the value of them for some argument; e.g. the ω such that for any $a \in \mathbf{P}$, $\omega(a) = \alpha$ if a begins with $\sim$, and β otherwise. This is a well-defined operation on **P** which has simple propositions as its values but is not a member of $\mathbf{I}_1$.

of sentences, this fact is immaterial. It is a very general property of algebraic systems that given any algebra based on a set **P**, and given any set **P**′ of the same size as **P**, we can construct an algebra based on **P**′ which is isomorphic with (has the same structure as) the algebra based on **P**. The proof, which we shall not give here, is very like the proof of theorem 1.14 on p. 20. For reasons such as these there will be many free algebras whose set **P** is a set of propositions as defined on pp. 41–4.[69]

We now recall David Lewis' definition of meaning referred to on p. 45 and shew how to express it in terms of a free meaning algebra. Suppose **P** is a set of propositions based on a set of basic particular situations, as in Chapter Three, and $\langle \mathbf{P}, \mathbf{I}, \mathbf{G} \rangle$ is a free meaning algebra which has an additional property which ensures that no distinct members of **I** have the same intension:

4.8 For $a, b \in \mathbf{I}_0$ if a and b are true in precisely the same worlds (i.e. if $a \cap \mathbf{C} = b \cap \mathbf{C}$) then $a = b$; and for ω, $\omega' \in \mathbf{I}_n$, if for every $a_1, \ldots, a_n, \in \mathbf{P}$, $\omega(a_1,\ldots,a_n) \cap \mathbf{C} = \omega'(a_1,\ldots,a_n) \cap \mathbf{C}$ then $\omega = \omega'$.

We can now obtain the meaning, in Lewis' sense, of a sentence of a propositional language by requiring that each symbol in Δ_0 be assigned a member of $\mathbf{I}_0$ (not merely of **G** as before). This means that each symbol of a sentence will be assigned a simple proposition or function and the form of the meaning will reflect the form of the sentence and vice versa. Whether or not this requirement is thought to be too restrictive in semantics it can certainly be expressed in our framework.[70]

The idea of an algebra of meanings may prove helpful on the allied question of the role of certain logical (or other) words in models based on some $\langle \mathbf{B}, w \rangle$. Take negation. Where a proposition is simply a set of worlds as in Chapters One and Two it is very easy to state the semantic rule for negation, viz.,

[V~] $w \in \omega_{\sim}(a)$ iff $w \notin a$.

[69] And, by contrast, the example of p. 53 f shews that there will also be many meaning algebras based on **P** which are *not* free. The fact that a propositional language can be regarded as a free algebra must not delude us into thinking that its intended interpretation must therefore be a free algebra. Theories such as Lewis' in which it is, must be independently supported.

[70] In the context of Lewis' essay his theory of meaning is more plausible than the impression given here may have suggested. Lewis in fact puts a very heavy load on 'transformation rules' which take the expressions of ordinary language and transform them into a base language which is in fact a meaning algebra. I prefer to put the heavy load on the meaning assignment though, on pp. 211–15, I go some way towards a theory of the kind Lewis has in mind.

This defines a unique $\omega_\sim$. But take a model structure based on $\langle \mathbf{B}, w \rangle$ as on p. 44. We certainly have that $\omega_\sim(a)$ is true in w iff a is false in w; and this means that $\eta(w) \in \omega_\sim(a)$ iff $\eta(w) \notin a$, so that we know which world-heavens are in $\omega_\sim(a)$ but beyond that we have no way of telling what $\omega_\sim(a)$ is. In other terminology, although we know whether $\omega_\sim(a)$ is true or not in a particular classical world (given that we know which worlds a is true in) we do not know whether it is true or not in a particular non-classical world.

If we decide to call all operations satisfying [V~] negation operations we must abandon talking about 'the' negation operation. In languages whose meaning assignments have only one or a small number of functors whose values are negation operations, we can talk about which particular negation is meant but we would still be unable to do this in a language-independent way. If, however, the algebra of meanings (which is supposed in some sense to be a universal feature of all humanly learnable languages) contains only one or a small number of negations then such talk can be reinstated. Similarly with the other 'logical' operators mentioned in Chapter Two (p. 32).[71]

Semantic information

Suppose for the moment that there does exist an 'algebra of meanings' of the kind just described. Suppose further that we have a language in which this algebra of meanings can be expressed. Since this algebra is universal, it means that we have a metalanguage in which we can give a complete semantic specification for any propositional language $\mathscr{L}$. Such a specification can be called a *dictionary*.

Whether there is a universal algebra of meanings in the sense that all human language-users have the same set of primitive concepts or whether certain key concepts are universal and others are, say, culturally or otherwise conditioned, we leave to others to decide.[72] If there is such an algebra then the possibility of compiling, in a

[71] It is only if some kind of meaning algebra is accepted that one can sensibly ask questions such as whether a proposition is the same as its double negation. Philosophers who claim to know the answers to questions of this kind seem to have access to intuitions about the nature of this meaning algebra which some of us do not share. E.g., Arthur Prior used to maintain (*vide* e.g. Prior [1963], p. 191 f) that no proposition can be a logical complication of itself.

[72] The attempt to find the 'simples' out of which all meanings can be constructed is often called 'componential analysis'. For a discussion *vide* Lyons [1969], pp. 470–81. (Obviously the implications of this section go considerably beyond the case of propositional languages.)

universal metalanguage, a universal dictionary of all languages becomes a real one. Note that, unlike the universal meaning algebra, a universal metalanguage need not be unique. Possibly a very rich natural language like English would be adequate, and if so then probably most other natural languages could be made to serve also.

The information which the dictionary gives is based on the assumption that the reader knows the metalanguage in which it is written but that he knows nothing else. This means that a dictionary entry will be of some such form as:

(1) 'chien' means dog

in which "'chien'" in the (French) object language is being mentioned in the sentence while 'dog' in the (English) metalanguage is being used.[73] It will not be of the form

(2) 'chien' means 'dog'.

In (1) there is only one object language and one metalanguage while in (2) there are two object languages and a metalanguage. This fact is obscured because one of the object languages happens to be the same as the metalanguage. If we take

(3) 'chien' means 'κύων'

then it is quite clear that understanding the metalanguage is not sufficient to give the meaning of 'chien'. All that an understanding of the metalanguage will do is enable us to extract the information that a certain French word means the same as a certain Greek word.[74] Likewise (2) gives us the information that a certain French word means the same as a certain English word. Because the language in which (2) is expressed is also English then if we understand (2) we know what 'chien' means; but the proposition which (2) expresses does not tell us this and if (2) is translated it will not tell us the meaning of 'chien'. The proposition expressed by (1), however, does tell us the meaning of (1) and this information would survive translation.

This last point has probably been elaborated more than it is worth but it needs to be made if only to clear up some misunderstandings of a theory of meaning developed by Jerrold Katz.[75] Katz' theory of meaning, which appears to have been influential in some linguistic circles, is rather obscurely presented and Katz does not himself seem terribly clear about the nature of the entities required in it. Most of

[73] Cf. Appendix I, pp. 245–7.

[74] "'chien' means *κύων*" is of course not a sentence at all, of English or any other natural language. On the general theory of quotation *vide* pp. 104–8 *infra*.

[75] More correctly, it was developed by Katz and Fodor [1963], Katz and Postal [1964] and Katz [1966].

those, and they include many philosophers, who have objected to it have done so on the assumption that a Katz dictionary is simply a recipe for translating sentences into 'semantic markerese'.[76] Katz denies this and says that the items in the lexical entry are 'to be regarded as constructs of a linguistic theory, just as terms such as "force" are regarded as labels for constructs in natural science'.[77]

Now perhaps Katz' semantical theory is not the kind of 'algebra of meanings' which we have elaborated but it could come close to it. It is the failure to distinguish between sentences like (1) and (2) on p. 57 which makes it look as though Katz is not doing genuine semantics (though Katz himself is not absolutely clear about this distinction), but if there is a universal system of concepts then there is no reason in principle why there could not be a language which had words for them all.[78] That there is a pretty strong empirical assumption about the actual world we are in but if something like it were true then a Katz-type dictionary would be at least a theoretical possibility.

Katz' dictionary also contains what he calls 'selection restrictions'; these are rules which prevent the combination of words which would make 'absurd' sentences. We have already seen that if principles 4.1 and 4.2 (p. 52) are abandoned then we can sometimes have sentences with absurd meanings. This means that the algebra will generate restrictions on what will go with what and given the meanings of the symbols we can say, in our universal metalanguage, whether they will go with one another. What needs stressing here is that the 'selectional restrictions' are consequent upon the semantic interpretation; they are not rules which prohibit certain semantic evaluations. As such it seems less misleading to have them as we have done as properties directly of the algebra of meanings and only derivatively properties of the sentences.

Indeterminacy

Since we are temporarily considering matters of language-use, as opposed to semantics in the strict sense, we shall briefly discuss an important feature of natural languages and indicate how it can be accommodated. This is the vagueness or indeterminacy of natural language. Suppose that somebody says

[76] This phrase is due to Lewis [1970], p. 18. It seems to me that Katz' semantics is in fact far closer to Lewis' own than Lewis' remarks would appear to suggest.

[77] Katz [1966], p. 156. Cf. also Katz and Postal [1964].

[78] At least if they were only countably many. The Arabic-numeral example of p. 30 shews that we could have infinitely many words; but a non-denumerable infinity would pose problems.

(1) Egypt has a hot climate.[79]

Probably most people would agree that it is true. But what *precisely* is the proposition expressed by (1)? Suppose we go back to the idea of a proposition as a set of possible worlds and try our Chapter One trick of shewing people each world in turn. What we shall probably find is that for some worlds they give a clear 'yes' or 'no' to the question whether (1) is true in that world but in others some will say 'yes', some 'no' and others will not know what to say. What can we do here? For each of these unclear worlds the two possible answers represent the two possible ways of making the proposition expressed by (1) more precise, and one might say that to (1) there correspond, with respect to this world, two propositions which agree in the worlds where the answer was clear but disagree in this one. More generally we can consider the class of sets of worlds which represent all possible ways of making (1) completely precise. Since the worlds in which the truth value of (1) is not clear are all rather remote from the real one, there is no practical loss in not being able to say that one of these precise propositions is the meaning of (1).

If we take this line throughout the whole of the language we shall think of the meanings of the words as being given, not by a single value assignment but by a class of value assignments which represent all the possible ways in which the vague sentences of ordinary language can be made precise. We shall call such a class a 'communication class'. The idea is that it does not matter, for the practical purposes of communication, which precise proposition we have in mind.[80] Which is another way of saying that we have no precise proposition in mind.

Suppose that **K** is a class of models for a propositional language $\mathscr{L}$. With respect to any sentence α of $\mathscr{L}$ there are three possibilities:

(i) α is true in all members of **K**.
(ii) α is true in some but not all members of **K**.
(iii) α is true in no members of **K**.

In case (i) we can say that α is **K**-true, in case (ii) that it is **K**-indeterminate and in case (iii) that it is **K**-false. Thus we may speak of a sentence

[79] As elsewhere in this chapter, the fact that we are here going beyond the sentences of a propositional language does not affect the point we are making. We could in any case imagine that (1) is represented by a simple sentence symbol. Cf. Austin's comments in [1962], p. 142 about 'France is hexagonal'.

[80] Alternative approaches to vagueness are found in Lewis [1970], p. 64 f, and Goguen [1969]. Probably the truth is that a number of different factors are involved.

lacking a truth-value. But note here that unlike the situation on p. 52f there is no reason to prevent α from having a value in all members of **K**.

This approach to indeterminacy also provides an alternative explanation for nonsensical sentences. Consider:

(2) This toothpaste smells red.

Now there is nothing about our use of the word 'smells' either to require or to prevent it from having the meaning:

4.9 'x smells ϕ' where ϕ is a colour word means that x has the smell normally associated with things of colour ϕ.

This means that the communication class of English will contain some meaning assignments in which 'smells' is given this meaning and others in which it is not, and thus for some members of the communication class (2) may be true while for others it is false. The reason of course is simple. In the real world smells are not as a rule associated with colours and so there would not arise any situations where it would make any practical difference in which way we were using the word 'smells'. We have to imagine a world rather remote from the real world before the decision becomes a sensible one. The air of absurdity about 'This toothpaste smells red' arises because with respect to the communication class of English, it is neither true nor false.

Another area in which the notion of a communication class might play a practicable part is in explaining what Quine has called the indeterminacy of translation.[81] Quine's contention is roughly that in translating from one language to another we can never be sure that what we end up with means exactly the same as what we began with. We can note two things which might explain some of the features of translation to which Quine draws attention. Firstly, the range of things which count as possible meanings for an expression is so great that the chances of two languages having words with exactly the same meanings is probably very small. Secondly, some assignments in the communication class of one language may correspond with some assignments in the communication class of another language but others may not. This explains how there may be no instances of exact translation but many instances which are enough in that the translated word corresponds to something in the communication class of each language. Thus translation, though never perhaps exact, is nevertheless possible.

[81] Quine [1960]; especially pp. 73–9.

A similar situation applies with respect to synonymy. Two sentences α and β are synonymous with respect to a meaning assignment V iff $V^+(\alpha) = V^+(\beta)$. However, it might happen that some models in a communication class make α and β synonymous while others do not. As before, although we, unlike Quine,[82] have a perfectly well defined notion of synonymy yet we, this time like Quine, agree that cases of pure synonymy in a natural language may be virtually non-existent and that the best we can hope for is synonymy for practical purposes. I.e., α is synonymous with β for *some* assignments in the communication class of the language in question.

A similar line can be taken over the notion of analyticity. By our account a sentence α is analytic in a meaning assignment V iff $V^+(\alpha)$ is true in all worlds, i.e. iff $V^+(\alpha)$ is logically or necessarily true.[83] Here too a sentence may be analytic in one member of a communication class but not in another member of the class. Thus it might appear that the search for analyticity in natural language is a vain one. Hopefully we have said enough to shew why this might appear so and why it is not worrying.

[82] Quine [1953], pp. 20–37.

[83] Our own analysis of analyticity or conceptual necessity does not depend on the notion of synonymy (*vide* p. 44) so we are unworried by objections to analyticity which depend on that notion.

PART TWO

Categorial Languages

CHAPTER FIVE

Pure Categorial Languages

Zero-order languages

Before we generalize the definition of language to include symbols and expressions of all syntactic categories it proves convenient to introduce a kind of language which is syntactically very little more complex than propositional languages but which enables us to raise some rather important semantical questions. We shall call these languages *zero-order languages*.[84]

A zero-order language is formed by adding to a propositional language a new basic category and some new functor categories. The new basic category is what we shall for the present refer to as the category of *names* (we say 'for the present' because in Part III we shall suggest a rather different analysis for names, at least as they occur in natural languages); the new functor categories are all predicates. By Φ_0 we shall understand a finite set of names and for each natural number *n*, Φ_n is a finite set of *n*-place predicates. The definition is as follows:

A zero-order language $\mathscr{L}$ is an ordered triple $\langle \Phi, \Delta, \mathrm{S} \rangle$, where $\Phi = \langle \Phi_0, \ldots, \Phi_m \rangle$ and $\Delta = \langle \Delta_0, \ldots, \Delta_k \rangle$ are finite sequences of pairwise disjoint (possibly empty) finite sets. Δ^+ is, as in Part I, the set of propositional functors and $\Phi^+ \cup \Delta^+$ is the set of symbols of $\mathscr{L}$. S is the (unique) smallest set such that:

5.1 $\Delta_0 \subseteq \mathrm{S}$

5.2 If $x_1, \ldots, x_n \in \Phi_0$ and $\varphi \in \Phi_n$ then $\langle \varphi, x_1, \ldots, x_n \rangle \in \mathrm{S}$

5.3 If $\alpha_1, \ldots, \alpha_n \in \mathrm{S}$ and $\delta \in \Delta_n$ then $\langle \delta, \alpha_1, \ldots, \alpha_n \rangle \in \mathrm{S}$

[84] Cf. Cresswell [1972b].

The name category, Φ_0, is, as we have said, a basic category, while the derived predicate categories form sentences out of names. Those familiar with predicate logic will see that zero-order languages are generalizations of the language of the predicate calculus without quantifiers (whence the name) in exactly the same sense as propositional languages are generalizations of the language of the propositional calculus.

In terms of our 'categorial' way of describing languages (p. 15), if names are of category 1 then k-place predicates are of category

$$\langle 0, \overbrace{1, \ldots, 1}^{k\text{-times}} \rangle$$

or alternatively (using s and n);

$$s/(\overbrace{n, \ldots, n}^{k\text{-times}})$$

and a zero-order language set out as a phrase-structure grammar would contain as well as 1.3–1.5 (p. 16)

5.4 $$s \to \langle \overbrace{s/n, \ldots, n}^{k\text{-times}}, \overbrace{n, \ldots, n}^{k\text{-times}} \rangle$$

as well as lexical rules assigning each member of Φ_k to its appropriate category. Notice that the category of sentence is still the only category which contains complex expressions.

The interest of zero-order languages is principally because of the new category of names. The category of names is important because the values of things in this category have no restrictions placed on them. This is unlike the category of sentences whose values are propositions. There is no reason why propositions should not be named, or anything else for that matter. However to begin with we shall simply assume that we have a class or domain, which we shall call **D**, of values for the names. Members of **D** have sometimes been called 'individuals' and the members of Φ_0, 'individual symbols' (often divided into individual constants and individual variables) but this does not seem a good name unless we want to include among the individuals sets, properties, propositions, worlds and the like. We shall just speak of it as **D** for the present as we shall later (Chapter Seven) have something to say about what its members are.

Another question which arises in the semantical analysis of intensional logics is whether **D** should comprise things which might exist but do not as well as those which actually do. Luckily this need not concern us at the moment since even if each world has its own domain associated with it we can always form the union of all these domains and let that union be **D**. Names will still be assigned members of **D**.

In our exposition of zero-order languages we shall, for convenience, take propositions simply as sets of worlds, as in Chapter One, though of course the reasons for complicating this story are still as valid as they were in Chapter Three. Later in the chapter we shall take care that our general development does not presuppose any particular analysis of propositions.

An indexical model structure for a zero-order language is a triple $\langle \mathbf{W}, \mathbf{D}, w_1 \rangle$ where **W** is a set (of possible worlds) and **D** a domain of 'things' and $w_1 \in \mathbf{W}$. An assignment V is now a somewhat extended thing satisfying, in addition to 1.9 and 1.10, the requirement:

5.5 If $x \in \Phi_0$ then $\mathrm{V}(x) \in \mathbf{D}$.

Since predicates are a certain kind of functor the sorts of values they have are fixed by the principle of p. 18. Predicates make sentences out of names so their values should be functions which make propositions out of members of **D**. I.e., where $\varphi \in \Phi_n$, $\mathrm{V}(\varphi)$, which we can write ω_φ, is an n-place operation such that where $a_1, \ldots, a_n \in \mathbf{D}$, $\omega_\varphi(a_1, \ldots, a_n) \subseteq \mathbf{W}$.

Where $\varphi \in \Phi_1$, i.e. where φ is a one-place predicate, ω_φ is called a *property*. Note that this is the wide logician's use of 'property' in which, say, standing three hundred yards from the biggest wooden building in the world is a property; viz., the operation ω such that for any $a \in \mathbf{D}$, $\omega(a)$ is the proposition that a is standing three hundred yards from the biggest wooden building in the world. (And remember that this proposition is the set of those and only those worlds in which a is standing three hundred yards from the biggest wooden building in the world.) Many philosophers would be unhappy with this as a property since the construction of another wooden building taller than the one a is standing three hundred yards from seems an odd way to effect a change in a's properties. I have no wish to defend either the wide or the narrow use of the word 'property' but simply state how it is being used in this book. Where ω is an n-place operation from $\mathbf{D}^n$ to $\mathscr{P}\mathbf{W}$ we shall sometimes speak of it, by extension, as an *n-place property*, though the word 'relation' would probably be more correct in such cases.

Given a value assignment V of this kind to the symbols of a zero-order language we can extend it to a value assignment V^+ to all the sentences of the language as follows:

5.6 If $\alpha \in \Delta_0$ then $V^+(\alpha) = V(\alpha)$

5.7 If $x_1, \ldots, x_n \in \Phi_0$ and $\varphi \in \Phi_n$ then $V^+\langle \varphi, x_1, \ldots, x_n \rangle = \omega_\varphi(V(x_1), \ldots, V(x_n))$

5.8 If $\alpha_1, \ldots, \alpha_n \in S$ and $\delta \in \Delta_n$ then $V^+(\langle \delta, \alpha_1, \ldots, \alpha_n \rangle) = \omega_\delta(V^+(\alpha_1), \ldots, V^+(\alpha_n))$

Intensional objects

We have proceeded in such a way that each member of Φ_0 is given an absolute assignment from **D**. Often in intensional logic it is thought that the assignment to an individual symbol should be world-relative.[85] Though such a procedure is possible it makes for considerable technical complications, particularly when we come to define more general kinds of languages. It is therefore desirable to shew that all the advantages of world-relative assignments can be obtained using absolute assignments and do not necessitate any change in our definition of models.

The plausibility of world-relative assignments is no doubt strongest when we are dealing with complex names derived from predicates to form definite descriptions. Such complex names as

the Prime Minister of New Zealand

do not occur in zero-order languages but they can certainly occur in languages we shall consider later in this chapter; and in any case there is no reason why we should not introduce a name which is supposed to do, in a zero-order language, what

the Prime Minister of New Zealand

does in English. Similarly

will always be a British subject

is a complex predicate expression in English but there is no reason why there should not be a one-place predicate in a zero-order language which does the same job. So consider the sentence:

(1) ***the Prime Minister of New Zealand will always be a British subject***

This sentence is ambiguous; suppose that the present Prime Minister at some time in the future, after he has ceased to be Prime Minister, also ceases to be a British subject but that the then Prime Minister is,

[85] *Vide* Hughes and Cresswell [1968], p. 199 f (footnote 151). The bracketing suggestion made there really amounts to the requirement that a descriptive phrase have scope. This point is amplified in Chapter Nine (pp. 147–50).

of course, a British subject. On one reading (1) is true, for at no time is there a Prime Minister who is not a British subject; but at some time the present Prime Minister ceases to be a British subject and so in another sense (1) is false.

To simplify the discussion let us suppose there are only two people u_1 and u_2 (we could dream up some rather fanciful names like 'Kirk' or 'Muldoon' but we shall stick to the prosaic ones) and two times (or worlds) w_1 and w_2. Suppose that w_2 is later than w_1 and that u_1 is Prime Minister at w_1 and u_2 at w_2. Suppose further that u_1 is a British subject at w_1 but not at w_2 while u_2 is a British subject at both times.

To put (1) into a sentence of a zero-order language let $\varphi \in \Phi_1$ represent the predicate ***will always be a British subject*** and $x \in \Phi_0$ be the name which behaves like ***the Prime Minister of New Zealand***. (1) then becomes

(2) $\langle \varphi, x \rangle$

Suppose that V and V′ are two value assignments which bring out the ambiguity of (2). We shew how this can be done without departing from the procedure set out on p. 67 of giving an absolute assignment to the members of Φ_0.

What we must do is to think of φ as something which might be true not only of ordinary people but of what have been variously called *intensional objects* or *individual concepts*,[86] 'objects' like, for instance, the thing which is u_1 in w_1 and u_2 in w_2. This 'object' is a genuine set-theoretical entity. It is the function ρ (whose domain is $\{w_1, w_2\}$) such that $\rho(w_1) = u_1$ and $\rho(w_2) = u_2$. If we allow our domain **D** to contain (instead of, or perhaps as well as, the 'ordinary' things, u_1 and u_2) functions from worlds (or times) into things then we can simply say in a case like this that $V(x) = \rho$. The ambiguity in (1) can then be resolved by giving different assignments to x in (2). Let $V'(x)$ be the constant function C^{u_1}. This is the function such that $C^{u_1}(w_1) = u_1$ and $C^{u_1}(w_2) = u_1$.

Assuming that we know which of the 'ordinary' objects u_1 and u_2 is a British subject in which world, we can state in formal terms a semantic rule for φ. $V(\varphi)$ remember is a one-place operation ω_φ whose domain is **D** and whose range comprises sets of worlds. Its semantic rule is, for $w \in \mathbf{W}$ and $a \in \mathbf{D}$:

5.9 $w \in \omega_\varphi(a)$ iff for all w' later than w, $a(w')$ is a British subject in w'.

[86] *Vide* Hughes and Cresswell [1968], pp. 196–8. Scott [1970], p. 152 calls them individual concepts.

We suppose that $V'(\varphi) = V(\varphi)$. It is easy to see that with $V(x)$ and $V'(x)$ as the functions defined above, $V^+(2)$ is true while $V'^+(2)$ is false, and that these two assignments bring out the ambiguity of (1).

$V(\varphi)$ is a function from worlds to sets of individual concepts (intensional objects). It is if you like a property which is true or false of individual concepts. In the case of ω when it is the meaning of ***will always be a British subject*** it had to be such if we were to be able to treat ***the Prime Minister of New Zealand*** as a name which could be given an absolute assignment from **D**.

There are, however, some properties for which it does not matter whether they are thought of as holding between individuals or individual concepts. Suppose that $\psi \in \Phi_1$ is intended to mean the same as

is a British subject

Consider the evaluation of $\langle \psi, x \rangle$ in a world w, and suppose that x is assigned a function from worlds to things. To know whether $\langle \psi, x \rangle$ is true in w it is sufficient to know whether the value at w of the function $V(x)$ is a British subject at w. For if $(V(x))(w) = (V(y))(w)$ then $w \in V^+(\langle \psi, x \rangle)$ iff $w \in V^+(\langle \psi, y \rangle)$.

A property of this kind is said to be an *extensional property*. Note that the fact that all properties can be construed as denoting functions from worlds to *n*-tuples of functions rather than *n*-tuples of things (i.e. they are conceived as relating intensional objects) does not prevent some of them from being extensional.[87]

An *n*-place property ω (*vide* p. 67) is *extensional* iff the following holds for any $a_1, \ldots, a_n, b_1, \ldots, b_n \in \mathbf{D}$ and $w \in \mathbf{W}$:

5.10 If $a_1(w) = b_1(w), \ldots, a_n(w) = b_n(w)$ then $w \in \omega(a_1, \ldots, a_n)$ iff $w \in \omega(b_1, \ldots, b_n)$.

(If we allow **D** to contain other things than functions whose domains are sets of worlds we can allow ω to be trivially extensional if some of the *a* and *b* are not such functions.)

By extension we may say that a predicate is extensional with respect to a value assignment iff it is assigned an extensional property.

Categorial languages

We want now to give a quite general definition of a *pure categorial language*.[88] Languages of this kind have been given several names.

[87] Scott [1970], p. 155 f.

[88] A *pure* categorial language to distinguish it from the extended kind of categorial language we shall introduce in the next chapter.

Richard Montague calls them 'disambiguated languages', David Lewis 'categorial grammars'.[89] Strictly each of these authors has defined them in slightly different ways, Montague algebraically and Lewis in terms of phrase-structure grammars, and our definition will be a little different too. They all, however, come to the same thing. The languages we have met so far have had two basic categories, names and sentences, and numbers of functor categories, either sentence-makers out of sentences or sentence-makers out of names. There have been symbols in all categories but so far complex expressions in only one category, that of sentence. Further, the functor categories have applied to things all in the same category; they have made sentences either out of other sentences or out of names, never out of a combination of names and sentences, and never out of other functors or predicates.[90] All this will now be remedied.

Where *Nat* is the set of natural numbers 0, 1, 2 ... etc. then the set *Syn* of *syntactic categories* is the smallest set satisfying:

5.11 $\text{Nat} \subseteq \text{Syn}$

5.12 If $\tau, \sigma_1, \ldots, \sigma_n \in \text{Syn}$ then $\langle \tau, \sigma_1, \ldots, \sigma_n \rangle \in \text{Syn}$

The idea here is that the members of Nat are the basic syntactic categories and that $\langle \tau, \sigma_1, \ldots, \sigma_n \rangle$ is the derived or functor category of things which make a thing of category τ out of things of category $\sigma_1, \ldots, \sigma_n$.[91] One may wonder why it is that we call the natural numbers 'syntactic categories'. The answer is that the role of the syntactic categories is solely to index certain sets. Perhaps we should follow Montague[92] and call them *category indices* since all they do is act as labels. We let 0 and 1, the first two members of Nat, be the indices for sentences and names respectively and shall, from now on, use them in place of *s* and *n*.[93]

We can now define a pure categorial language $\mathscr{L}$ as follows. $\mathscr{L}$ is an ordered pair $\langle F, E \rangle$ where F is a function from Syn whose range is a set of pairwise disjoint finite sets of which all but finitely many are

[89] Montague [1970a], Bar Hillel [1964] and Lewis [1970].

[90] Prior used to be fond of entities of this sort; *vide* his [1971]. G. E. Hughes tells me that he sometimes used the name 'connecticate', a sort of portmanteau word from 'connective' and 'predicate'.

[91] Thus Φ_0 will be F_1, Φ_1 will be $F_{\langle 0, 1 \rangle}$ and so on. (Cf. p. 15 f *supra*.)

[92] Montague [1970a], p. 377.

[93] 0 and 1 are the only basic categories we take seriously. On p. 215 *infra* we introduce 2 for the category of common noun. Chapter Fourteen explains why we do not consider imperatives and questions as basic categories though one could give reasons for doing so.

empty and the members of which are the *symbols* of $\mathscr{L}$. I.e., where $\sigma \in \text{Syn}$, F_σ is the finite set of symbols of category σ. It is important that each F_σ should be finite and also that there should be symbols of only finitely many categories since otherwise $\mathscr{L}$ might contain infinitely many symbols and we have already remarked (p. 19) why this should not be so.

E is that function from Syn whose range is the system of smallest sets which satisfy the following conditions:

For any $\sigma, \tau, \sigma_1, \ldots, \sigma_n, \in \text{Syn}$

5.13 $F_\sigma \subseteq E_\sigma$

5.14 If $\alpha_1, \ldots, \alpha_n \in E_{\sigma_1}, \ldots, E_{\sigma_n}$ respectively and $\delta \in E_{\langle\tau,\sigma_1,\ldots,\sigma_n\rangle}$ then $\langle\delta,\alpha_1,\ldots,\alpha_n\rangle \in E_\tau$.

E_σ is called the set of *expressions* (or sometimes *well-formed* expressions) of category σ. If we denote by E^+ the set of expressions of $\mathscr{L}$ of all syntactic categories then it can be shewn[94] that there is a unique E whose E^+ is the smallest set (i.e. is contained in all the other sets) satisfying 5.13 and 5.14. Thus, while F may be arbitrary, once it is given E is fixed and will contain *only* expressions made up from the symbols of $\mathscr{L}$ by the formation rules 5.13 and 5.14.

We also must assume that $\mathscr{L}$ is grounded (cf. p. 14) in the sense that where $\delta \in E_{\langle\tau,\sigma_1,\ldots,\sigma_n\rangle}$ and $\alpha_1 \in E_{\sigma_1},\ldots,\alpha_n \in E_{\sigma_n}$ then $\langle\delta,\alpha_1,\ldots, \alpha_n\rangle \notin F^+$. This will ensure that no symbol is of more than one category. (Cf. p. 249.)

Those who find these rules rather puzzling should go back to the discussion of propositional languages on pp. 13–17 and write 0 in place of *s* and E_0 in place of S. Thus 1.1 and 1.2 become

(i) $F_0 \subseteq E_0$

(ii) If $\delta \in F_{\overbrace{\langle 0,\ldots,0\rangle}^{n+1 \text{ times}}}$ and $\alpha_1, \ldots, \alpha_n \in E_0$, then $\langle\delta,\alpha_1,\ldots,\alpha_n\rangle \in E_0$;

which are instances of 5.13 and 5.14. Using 1 as the index for names and with $F_{\langle 0,\overbrace{1,\ldots,1}^{n \text{ times}}\rangle}$ replacing Φ_n we can also exhibit the formation rules of zero-order languages as instances of 5.13 and 5.14.

We shall now define a notion of interpretation which is a generalization of that of p. 18f for propositional languages. To avoid making a decision about whether a proposition is to be a set of worlds as in Chapter One, or an entity of the more sophisticated kind described in

[94] *Vide* Appendix II, p. 248f. This is the most complex theorem of its kind we have to prove.

Chapter Three, or any other notion of proposition which may come to hand, we shall simply assume that we have a set of propositions, and for the notion of truth a subset of true propositions. We shall also assume that we have suitable domains for the other basic categories. Once the domains of the basic categories are given, the kinds of values which expressions in the functor categories have is fixed. The simplest way of doing this is to make the system of domains a function from syntactic categories to sets of the required type.

A model structure for a pure categorial language $\mathscr{L}$ is an ordered pair $\langle \mathbf{D}, \mathbf{T} \rangle$ in which $\mathbf{D}$ is a function from Syn whose values are sets providing that

5.15 If $\sigma = \langle \tau, \sigma_1, \ldots, \sigma_n \rangle$ then $\mathbf{D}_\sigma$ is a set of total or partial functions from $\mathbf{D}_{\sigma_1} \times \ldots \times \mathbf{D}_{\sigma_n}$ into $\mathbf{D}_\tau$.

(I.e., if $\omega \in \mathbf{D}_\sigma$ then, if it is to have a value, its first argument must be in $\mathbf{D}_{\sigma_1}$, the second in $\mathbf{D}_{\sigma_2}$ and so on and its value will be in $\mathbf{D}_\tau$.)

$\mathbf{D}_0$ is therefore the set of propositions, and is what we have been referring to as $\mathbf{P}$. $\mathbf{D}_1$ will be the domain of 'things' and is what we have called $\mathbf{D}$. $\mathbf{T} \subseteq \mathbf{D}_0$. $\mathbf{D}^+$ is the union of all the domains.

Notice that we are allowing partial functions in our domains; there is of course no reason why a particular $\langle \mathbf{D}, \mathbf{T} \rangle$ should not contain only total functions but the extra freedom enables us to take care of the problem mentioned on p. 53 of expressions without a value. Indeed our system of domains plays some of the role of a meaning algebra as in Chapter Four (p. 52f).

We get a model $\langle \mathbf{D}, \mathbf{T}, \mathrm{V} \rangle$ by adding an assignment function V from symbols of $\mathscr{L}$ into the domains of $\mathbf{D}$ such that

5.16 For any $\sigma \in$ Syn, where $\delta \in \mathrm{F}_\sigma$ then $\mathrm{V}(\delta) \in \mathbf{D}_\sigma$.

Where δ is in a functor category and there is no confusion over different V's we usually write ω_δ.

We now want to extend V to an induced assignment V^+ to expressions in all the categories. We shall use the notation ω_δ to refer to $\mathrm{V}^+(\delta)$ where δ is any expression in a functor category and not just a symbol as before. V^+ is defined by induction on the construction of α:

5.17 If δ is a symbol (i.e. if $\delta \in \mathrm{F}^+$) then $\mathrm{V}^+(\delta) = \mathrm{V}(\delta)$.

5.18 If α is $\langle \delta, \alpha_1, \ldots, \alpha_n \rangle$ for some n then

$$\mathrm{V}^+(\langle \delta, \alpha_1, \ldots, \alpha_n \rangle) = \omega_\delta(\mathrm{V}^+(\alpha_1), \ldots, \mathrm{V}^+(\alpha_n)).$$

(Obviously $\delta, \alpha_1, \ldots, \alpha_n$ are shorter than $\langle\delta,\alpha_1,\ldots,\alpha_n\rangle$ and so we may use the induction hypothesis.) The uniqueness of V^+ for grounded categorial languages follows exactly as it did for propositional languages (*vide* p. 19n) though since the domains of **D** may contain partial functions there may be expressions which are undefined.

We now want to prove an analogue of theorem 1.14 (p. 20) and shew that for any suitably large **D** and **T** there is a model $\langle \mathbf{D},\mathbf{T},\mathrm{V}\rangle$ which makes true precisely the members of some arbitrarily given set of sentences.

We shall say that a system **D** of domains is *stratified* iff:

(i) $\{\mathbf{D}_\sigma : \sigma \in \mathrm{Nat}\}$ is a set of pairwise disjoint infinite sets of individuals.

(ii) for $\sigma = \langle\tau,\sigma_1,\ldots,\sigma_n\rangle$, $\mathbf{D}_\sigma$ contains all the total and partial functions from $\mathbf{D}_{\sigma_1} \times \ldots \times \mathbf{D}_{\sigma_n}$ into $\mathbf{D}_\tau$.[95]

THEOREM **5.19** *If* **D** *is a stratified system of domains and* **T** *and* $\mathbf{D}_0 - \mathbf{T}$ *are infinite then for any subset* A *of* E_σ *there is an assignment* V *such that* α *is true in* $\langle\mathbf{D}, \mathbf{T}, \mathrm{V}\rangle$ *iff* $\alpha \in \mathrm{A}$.

PROOF: Let π be a 1–1 mapping of E_0 into $\mathbf{D}_0$ such that $\pi(\alpha) \in \mathbf{T}$ iff $\alpha \in \mathrm{A}$, and of expressions of every other basic category σ into $\mathbf{D}_\sigma$.[96] We shew how to induce a 1–1 mapping π^+ of categories in other expressions in such a way that if $\alpha \in \mathrm{E}_\sigma$ then $\pi^+(\alpha) \in \mathbf{D}_\sigma$. The induction is on the 'order' of syntactic categories. I.e., supposing π^+ to have been defined for categories $\tau, \sigma_1, \ldots, \sigma_n$ we shew how to define it for category $\langle\tau,\sigma_1,\ldots,\sigma_n\rangle$.

5.20 If $\sigma \in \mathrm{Nat}$ and $\alpha \in \mathrm{E}_\sigma$ then $\pi^+(\alpha) = \pi(\alpha)$.

5.21 If $\sigma = \langle\tau,\sigma_1,\ldots,\sigma_n\rangle$ then since $\tau, \sigma_1, \ldots, \sigma_n$ are of lower order than $\langle\tau,\sigma_1,\ldots,\sigma_n\rangle$ we may assume that π^+ has been defined for them. The members of $\mathbf{D}_{\langle\tau,\sigma_1,\ldots,\sigma_n\rangle}$ can be partial functions so let $\pi^+(\delta)$ be that function which is defined only for those $a_1, \ldots, a_n \in \mathbf{D}_{\sigma_1}, \ldots, \mathbf{D}_{\sigma_n}$ such that for some $\alpha_1, \ldots, \alpha_n : a_1, \ldots, a_n = \pi^+(\alpha_1), \ldots, \pi^+(\alpha_n)$. For such $a_1, \ldots, a_n$ let $(\pi^+(\delta))(a_1,\ldots,a_n) = \pi^+(\langle\delta,\alpha_1,\ldots,\alpha_n\rangle)$. (Since $\langle\delta,\alpha_1,\ldots,\alpha_n\rangle$ is of category τ then $\pi^+(\langle\delta,\alpha_1,\ldots,\alpha_n\rangle)$ is already defined and since **D** is stratified, $\pi^+(\alpha) \in \mathbf{D}_{\sigma_n}$.)

[95] This condition is probably more restrictive than it need be but it makes the proof easier. An intended system of domains (*vide* p. 99) will not in fact be stratified.

[96] The stratification condition ensures that for any distinct categories σ and τ, $\mathbf{D}_\sigma$ and $\mathbf{D}_\tau$ will be disjoint. This means that there can be a 1–1 π of the required kind, and that the π^+ induced by π will also be 1–1.

We are now in a position to define V.

5.22 If $\alpha \in F_\sigma$ (for any $\sigma \in$ Syn) $V(\alpha) = \pi^+(\alpha)$.

Obviously V is an assignment of the required kind (since $\pi^+(\alpha) \in \mathbf{D}_\sigma$). Thus $\langle \mathbf{D}, \mathbf{T}, V\rangle$ is a model.

LEMMA **5.23** *If* $\alpha \in E_\sigma$ *then* $V^+(\alpha) = \pi^+(\alpha)$.

The proof is by induction on the construction of α.

If α is a symbol of $\mathscr{L}$ then the lemma holds by definition of V and 5.22. Suppose α is $\langle \delta, \alpha_1, \ldots, \alpha_n\rangle$ where $\delta \in E_{\langle \tau, \sigma_1, \ldots, \sigma_n\rangle}$ and $\alpha_1, \ldots, \alpha_n \in E_{\sigma_1}, \ldots, E_{\sigma_n}$; then $V^+(\alpha) = \omega_\delta(V^+(\alpha_1), \ldots, V^+(\alpha_n))$. But by induction hypothesis $\omega_\delta = \pi^+(\delta)$ and $V^+(\alpha_1) = \pi^+(\alpha_1), \ldots, V^+(\alpha_n) = \pi^+(\alpha_n)$. So

$$\begin{aligned} V^+(\alpha) &= (\pi^+(\delta))(\pi^+(\alpha_1), \ldots, \pi^+(\alpha_n)) \\ &= \pi^+(\langle \delta, \alpha_1, \ldots, \alpha_n\rangle) \qquad \text{(by 5.21)} \\ &= \pi^+(\alpha) \end{aligned}$$

Now if $\alpha \in E_0$ then $w_1 \in \pi(\alpha)$ iff $\alpha \in A$

$\therefore w_1 \in V^+(\alpha)$ iff $\alpha \in A$

i.e. α is true in $\langle \mathbf{D}, \mathbf{T}, V\rangle$ iff $\alpha \in A$; and the theorem is proved. **Q.E.D.**

Frege's Principle

Categorial languages satisfy a very important principle about meanings. The meaning of an expression in a categorial language is of course its value under some particular assignment. All interpretations satisfy the principle that the meaning of any complex expression is determined by the meanings of its parts. Or to be more precise the meaning of the whole expression is a function of the meanings of its parts. For historical reasons we call this *Frege's Principle*. This name must not be taken to imply that the principle is explicitly stated in Frege.[97]

We can formulate a weaker and a stronger version of the principle. The weaker version states simply:

5.24 In any model $\langle \mathbf{D}, \mathbf{T}, V\rangle$ there is a unique assignment V^+ to every complex expression.

[97] Cf. Scott [1970], p. 164. The ascription to Frege is more a tribute to the general tenor of his views on the analysis of language. As far as an explicit statement of the principle is concerned, the version which he does state seems to be the erroneous one that the reference (extension?) of a sentence is a function of the references of its parts (Frege [1892], p. 35, translated [1952], p. 64; *vide* also Church [1956], pp. 8 f). A great deal of the ingenuity of Frege's theories of sense and reference seems due to his need to avoid the disastrous consequences of this mistake.

This is a version of Frege's principle for reasons stated on p. 19. That V^+ depends uniquely on V was shewn there (for propositional languages) and on p. 74 (for categorial languages quite generally). What this principle says is simply that the assignment to the symbols determines the assignment to the complex expression.[98]

To state the stronger version of Frege's principle we introduce some new notation. We shall use

$\alpha \overset{\gamma/\delta}{\approx} \beta$

to mean that α differs from β only in having γ as a well-formed part in 0 or more places where β has δ. $\overset{\prime}{\approx}$ is strictly a four-place relation. We let it be the least[99] relation such that:

5.25 If α is β then $\alpha \overset{\gamma/\delta}{\approx} \beta$

5.26 If α is γ and β is δ then $\alpha \overset{\gamma/\delta}{\approx} \beta$

5.27 If α is $\langle\alpha_1,\ldots,\alpha_n\rangle$ and β is $\langle\beta_1,\ldots,\beta_n\rangle$ and $\alpha_1 \overset{\gamma/\delta}{\approx} \beta_1, \ldots, \alpha_n \overset{\gamma/\delta}{\approx} \beta_n$ then $\alpha \overset{\gamma/\delta}{\approx} \beta$.

We can now state the stronger version of Frege's principle for categorial languages.

5.28 If $\alpha \overset{\gamma/\delta}{\approx} \beta$ then in any model $\langle \mathbf{D},\mathbf{T},\mathrm{V}\rangle$ if $V^+(\gamma) = V^+(\delta)$ then $V^+(\alpha) = V^+(\beta)$.

The proof is an easy and obvious induction on the construction of α and β using 5.18.

Frege's principle does not hold for ordinary language. Indeed it might be plausible to maintain that this is the most crucial difference between the artificial languages we have been describing and the language we use in everyday communication. Counter-examples to Frege's principle in ordinary language can be given by producing cases of syntactic ambiguity.

One kind of ambiguity can arise when the same symbol belongs to two different syntactic categories and gives a different meaning to the whole sentence according as it is treated in one category rather than another. Prime examples are newspaper headlines:

[98] An example of a semantics in intensional logic which does not satisfy Frege's principle is that given for S0.5 in Cresswell [1966a], for there it would be possible to have a world in which say *Lp* is false while *Lq* is true though *p* and *q* might be true in exactly the same worlds. One can however rewrite this semantics so that it does satisfy Frege's principle, as shewn in Cresswell [1970], p. 357.

[99] Remember that a relation is a set of ordered *n*-tuples (p. 242 n). $\overset{\prime}{\approx}$ is therefore a set of quadruples. We can therefore speak about the smallest relation. For the structure of a proof that it is unique, cf. p. 248 f.

(1) ***women lay observers at Vatican Council***

(2) ***eighth Army push bottles up Germans***[100]

According as ***lay*** is a verb or an adjective we get a different meaning for (1) and according as ***push*** in (2) is a verb and ***bottles*** a noun or ***push*** a noun and ***bottles*** a verb we get a different meaning for (2). (1) and (2) perhaps are not so much counter-examples to Frege's principle as examples of the fact that the same sequence of symbols can be given two distinct grammatical analyses. This cannot happen in the case of categorial languages as we have defined them, for two reasons. First, the classes of symbols in different syntactic categories are disjoint; i.e., no symbol has more than one grammatical analysis[101] (unlike ***lay***, ***push*** and ***bottles*** in (1) and (2)). Second, the scope of each functor is fixed so that we cannot have an ambiguity about which expressions a functor is operating on.

It is cases of this latter kind which provide counter-examples to Frege's principle:

(3) ***this room needs painting badly***

The ambiguity is resolved here by shewing whether the adverb ***badly*** modifies the verb ***needs*** or the participle ***painting***. One could resolve the ambiguity by giving the appropriate grammatical analysis and could regard the sentence as not just the sequence of symbols but the sequence together with its grammatical analysis.[102] If we adopt this view the grammatically analysed sentence may not constitute a counter-example but the ambiguity will still be present in that the sequence, which is after all all that is present on the surface (unless we assume some subtle features of intonation or something of the kind), will be ambiguous among different grammatically analysed sentences. It is of course true that when (3) crops up in practice one of the interpretations is so obviously more sensible that the alternatives are not even considered. In general, ordinary language has so developed that the distinctions it enshrines are those we need in ordinary communication.

[100] Spiegl [1965].

[101] If a symbol has two different meanings we have a case of what is sometimes called 'lexical ambiguity'. Our semantics does not yet allow for this (but *vide* p. 213 *infra*), and so this is another respect in which our languages differ from ordinary language. But lexical ambiguity does not provide a counter-example to Frege's principle.

[102] Or by what linguists call a 'phrase marker' (*vide* Chomsky [1957], p. 87 n). An example of a phrase marker for propositional languages is found on p. 17 *supra*.

Ambiguities of scope cannot arise in categorial languages, and indeed the definition even allows a limited amount of playing about with the order of the symbols. Each complex expression of $\mathscr{L}$ will have the form $\langle\delta, \alpha_1, \ldots, \alpha_n\rangle$ for some n. In evaluating this expression we have of course to know which is the functor since the evaluation depends on applying the value of the functor to the values of the remaining symbols. As we have set out categorial languages the functor is always the first member of the n-tuple. But there is no need for this to be so. Given that $\alpha_1, \ldots, \alpha_n$ are of category $\sigma_1, \ldots, \sigma_n$ respectively and the whole expression is of category τ, then the category of δ will be $\langle\tau, \sigma_1, \ldots, \sigma_n\rangle$ which is of higher order (in the sense of p. 74) than $\tau, \sigma_1, \ldots, \sigma_n$. The functor is that member of the expression which is of higher category than any other member of the expression; so that provided we keep the same order among the other members of the expression we may put the functor wherever we please. Thus it does not matter whether we have $\langle\delta, \alpha, \beta\rangle$ or $\langle\alpha, \beta, \delta\rangle$ or $\langle\alpha, \delta, \beta\rangle$ provided that α precedes β.

This liberalization of the formation rules for expressions does of course require that we keep a tight hold on our bracketing. Consider

(1) $\langle\delta, \alpha, \langle\delta, \beta, \gamma\rangle\rangle$

With the functor written at the front this is just as unambiguous when treated as a single sequence with no internal brackets,[103] viz.

(2) $\langle\delta, \alpha, \delta, \beta, \gamma\rangle$

but if we allow the functors to go wherever they like in the expression we can re-write (1) as

(3) $\langle\alpha, \delta, \langle\beta, \delta, \gamma\rangle\rangle$

When this is treated as a single sentence we get

(4) $\langle\alpha, \delta, \beta, \delta, \gamma\rangle$

and this sequence is also what we get by deleting the brackets in the equally well-formed:

(5) $\langle\langle\alpha, \delta, \beta\rangle\, \delta, \gamma\rangle$

For a live case of the ambiguity of (4) we can use the propositional calculus formula $p \supset q \supset r$, which has a different meaning depending on whether it is read as $((p \supset q) \supset r)$ or $(p \supset (q \supset r))$.

[103] This discovery seems due to Łukasiewicz [1929] whose bracket-free notation was for a time quite popular and is still used by some logicians. Note however that the brackets '⟨' and '⟩' are not symbols of a categorial language but merely metalinguistic signs to indicate how the ordered sets are made up. Thus $\langle\alpha, \langle\beta, \gamma\rangle\rangle$ indicates a pair whose first member is α and whose second is $\langle\beta, \gamma\rangle$ while $\langle\langle\alpha, \beta\rangle, \gamma\rangle$ indicates a pair whose first member is $\langle\alpha, \beta\rangle$ and whose second is γ (cf. Appendix I, p. 242).

In later chapters we shall in fact shew that many ambiguities in ordinary language can be resolved by putting brackets in in different ways. These ambiguous sentences can be thought of as obtained from sentences of a categorial language (probably with the liberalization we have just mentioned about the position of the functor) by the deletion of brackets; the point being that the sentences of ordinary language generally have no more than a linear ordering (spatial in the case of writing and temporal in the case of speaking) to indicate scope. Generally the ambiguity is resolved by extra-linguistic information such as which interpretation would produce the more sensible thing to say in the circumstances.

The idea that there is underlying the 'surface' language we actually use a 'deep' or 'base' level which satisfies Frege's principle is one which is playing an important, albeit at times controversial, part in current linguistic theory.[104] It would be nice to think that this level could be represented by a categorial language or by a language of the slightly augmented kind to be considered in the next chapter. We shall in later chapters have something to say about this and also on the difficult and obscure question of just how the surface language is related to the base language.

[104] The most explicit statement of Frege's principle in current linguistic theory seems to be in Katz [1966], p. 152, and Katz and Fodor [1963]. Katz does not ascribe the principle to Frege, and in Katz [1967] gives the impression that it is his own. The 'projection rules' of Katz and Postal [1964] are attempts to shew how the base language satisfies Frege's principle.

CHAPTER SIX

Abstraction and λ-categorial Languages

In this chapter we consider a way of extending the already rich class of pure categorial languages, which seems to be required in order to account for certain important linguistic phenomena.

Quantifiers

In ordinary English words like 'everyone', 'no one', 'nothing' and so on have the grammatical status of noun-phrases and look as though they can be treated as names. E.g., just as one can say 'Bill loves Arabella' so one can say 'Everyone loves someone'. But unless we are very careful, and moreover unless we do some rather complicated semantical manoeuvring, treating them in this way causes problems. One problem concerns negation. If it is false that Bill loves Arabella then we can describe this by saying, 'Bill does not love Arabella'; but if it is false that everyone loves Arabella and we say, 'Everyone does not love Arabella', what we get might also mean that no one loves Arabella. It by no means follows that simply because it is false that everyone loves Arabella that it is true that everyone does not love Arabella, for some may and others may not.

If we are dealing with a one-place predicate there is a way out which can easily be fitted in to a categorial language. Suppose that ***sleeps*** $\in F_{\langle 0,1\rangle}$ in some categorial language. If ***Bill*** $\in F_1$[105] then we have $\langle$***sleeps***, ***Bill***$\rangle$ as a sentence. We do not want to have ***everyone*** $\in F_1$ for the reasons we have just described, for even if possible it is not natural

[105] We are now using the notation introduced on p. 71 f, whereby, instead of speaking about Φ_0 and Φ_1, we speak of F_1 and $F_{\langle 0,1\rangle}$.

to evaluate ⟨***everyone*, *sleeps***⟩ in a possible world by seeing whether the thing denoted by ***everyone*** does in fact satisfy the property denoted by ***sleeps*** in the possible world in question. What we want rather is to treat ***sleeps*** as the argument of ***everyone*** and say that ⟨***everyone*, *sleeps***⟩ is true iff the property denoted by ***sleeps*** does in fact satisfy the higher-order property denoted by ***everyone*** in the possible world in question. The higher-order property denoted by ***everyone*** is simply the property which holds of those and only those properties which are universally instantiated by things of the appropriate kind; in this case people. Thus ***everyone*** is of category $\langle 0, \langle 0, 1\rangle\rangle$.

This works well for one-place predicates but runs into difficulties when we have two-place predicates. Take 'Everyone loves someone'. ***loves*** is a two-place predicate, i.e., ***loves*** $\in F_{\langle 0,1,1\rangle}$. Since ***everyone*** and ***someone*** are of the same syntactic category then if ***everyone*** $\in F_{\langle 0,\langle 0,1\rangle\rangle}$ so is ***someone***. It follows that there is no way of making ⟨***loves*, *someone***⟩ a well-formed sequence of any syntactic category, and *a fortiori* not of the predicate category $\langle 0, 1\rangle$ so that ***everyone*** can apply to it. It is possible to treat transitive verbs as of category $\langle\langle 0,1\rangle,\langle 0,\langle 0,1\rangle\rangle\rangle$ as Richard Montague does;[106] but this is not natural, and in any case does not allow for the ambiguity in 'Everyone loves someone', which depends on whether there is claimed to be a universal beloved (say Jones) or not.

The way out of this problem taken by symbolic logic is to make use of the notion of a variable. Let us assume a denumerably infinite set X of dummy names which we shall call 'variables' and refer to as x, y, z etc. We can then form 'open' sentences like ⟨***sleeps***, x⟩ which means that x (at present an unspecified something) sleeps or, ⟨***loves***, x, y⟩ which means that an unspecified x loves the same or a different unspecified y. The claim that everyone sleeps is now made by saying that the open sentence ⟨***sleeps***, x⟩ is true for every appropriate value for x and the whole sentence may be written

(1) ⟨***everyone***, x, ⟨***sleeps***, x⟩⟩

The claim that someone sleeps is written as

(2) ⟨***someone***, x, ⟨***sleeps***, x⟩⟩

and means that ⟨***sleeps***, x⟩ is true for at least one appropriate value of x.

Armed with this notation we may tackle sentences involving two-place predicates and can even resolve the ambiguity of[107]

[106] Montague [1973], p. 223.

[107] Chomsky [1957], p. 100 f, has the example 'everyone in the room knows at least two languages', though he does not seem to think it is ambiguous.

everyone loves someone

by distinguishing between

(3) ⟨***everyone***, x, ⟨***someone***, y, ⟨***loves***, x, y⟩⟩⟩

and

(4) ⟨***someone***, y, ⟨***everyone***, x, ⟨***loves***, x, y⟩⟩⟩

To get the meaning of (3) we first get the meaning of

⟨***someone***, y, ⟨***loves***, x, y⟩⟩

This open sentence means that an unspecified x loves someone for it says that the sentence ⟨***loves***, x, y⟩ is true for some value of y. So (3) must mean that it is true of every x that x loves someone. There is nothing to require that it be the same person who is loved by all the x's. In (4) the embedded sentence

⟨***everyone***, x, ⟨***loves***, x, y⟩⟩

means that everyone loves the unspecified y. And if as (4) says this is true of some y, then there must be a single y (there may be more of course but there is at least one) such that everyone loves that y.

By changing the order of the variables we get both readings of the analogously ambiguous

someone loves everyone

Thus:

(5) ⟨***everyone***, x, ⟨***someone***, y, ⟨***loves***, y, x⟩⟩⟩

and

(6) ⟨***someone***, x, ⟨***everyone***, y ⟨***loves***, y, x⟩⟩⟩

Since the variables in X are regarded as symbols of category 1 (for they stand in place of names) examples (3)–(6) suggest that the quantifiers are simply functors of category ⟨0, 1, 0⟩. However to think of them thus would be to misconceive their role; they are in fact of category ⟨0, ⟨0, 1⟩⟩. To see what is wrong with regarding a quantifier as a two-place functor whose first argument is a variable and whose second argument a sentence we shall look at the way they would then have to be evaluated.

Let us imagine a model in which $V(x) = V(y) = a$ and in which the property V(***sleeps***) is true (in the real world of the model) of a but not true of all individuals. If ***everyone*** is a functor of category ⟨0, 1, 0⟩ then by applying Frege's principle (p. 76) it is easy to see that since $V(x) = V(y)$

(7) V^+(⟨***everyone***, x, ⟨***sleeps***, y⟩⟩) = V^+(⟨***everyone***, x, ⟨***sleeps***, x⟩⟩)

Now in

(8) ⟨***everyone***, x, ⟨***sleeps***, y⟩⟩

the quantifier is vacuous, for (8) means that for every value of x, *y* sleeps, which says just the same thing as that *y* sleeps, which, in the model we are considering, is true. However

(9) ⟨***everyone***, *x*, ⟨***sleeps***, *x*⟩⟩

says that everyone sleeps and this, in the same model, is intended to be false. Thus (7) does not satisfy the intended interpretation. Yet (7) follows by the valuation rules of p. 73 on the assumption that ***everyone*** is a functor of category ⟨0,1,0⟩. So ***everyone*** cannot be a functor of this category.[108]

In fact to understand how quantifiers work we must go back to our original idea that a quantifier is a functor of category ⟨0,⟨0,1⟩⟩, i.e., it forms a sentence by operating on an argument of category ⟨0,1⟩. Our difficulty arose when we came to complex predicates. Suppose that we want to say that everyone loves Arabella. What we need is a way of forming a predicate out of,

⟨***loves***, ***Arabella***⟩

Since our formation rules do not allow us to do this directly we introduce a 'logical' symbol λ and variables to form what is known as an *abstract* as follows:[109]

(10) ⟨λ, *x*, ⟨***loves***, *x*, ***Arabella***⟩⟩

is to indicate the property of being an *x* such that *x* loves Arabella. This abstract is to count as being of category ⟨0,1⟩ and so we can form the sentence

⟨***everyone***, ⟨λ, *x*, ⟨***loves***, *x*, ***Arabella***⟩⟩⟩

which means that the property of loving Arabella is one which is universal among people. We can of course also have

⟨***everyone***, ⟨λ, *x*, ⟨***sleeps***, *x*⟩⟩⟩

but here ⟨λ,*x*,⟨***sleeps***,*x*⟩⟩ is just a redundant way of expressing the same thing as ***sleeps***.

A property like the one expressed by (10) can be thought of in the following way. For every appropriate value of *x* (i.e. every member of $\mathbf{D}_1$ since $x \in X$) the values assigned to ***loves*** and ***Arabella*** will give a value in $\mathbf{D}_0$ to the open sentence ⟨***loves***,*x*,***Arabella***⟩. If the value of *x* is *a* then the value of ⟨***loves***,*x*,***Arabella***⟩ will be the proposition that *a* loves Arabella. Suppose that V is a value assignment. Where $a \in \mathbf{D}_1$ we shall let $V_{a/x}$ be the assignment just like V except that $V_{a/x}(x) = a$. Just as V induces an assignment V^+ to complex expressions so $V_{a/x}$

[108] Unless we follow the procedure adopted by Montague and Lewis referred to in footnote 143 on p. 111.

[109] This is due to Church [1940]. The idea of treating quantifiers as ordinary functors applying to abstracts is also discussed in Feys [1946] and Prior [1971], pp. 43–7; *vide* also Tichý [1971], pp. 283–5.

induces an assignment $V^+_{a/x}$ The property expressed, under V, by (10) can therefore be defined as that function ω from $\mathbf{D}_1$ into $\mathbf{D}_0$ such that for any $a \in \mathbf{D}_1$

$$\omega(a) = V^+_{a/x}(\langle \textbf{\textit{loves}}, x, \textbf{\textit{Arabella}}\rangle)$$

The idea of course is that $V^+_{a/x}(\langle \textbf{\textit{loves}}, x, \textbf{\textit{Arabella}}\rangle)$ is the proposition that *a* loves Arabella and that the property of loving Arabella is the function such that for any $a \in \mathbf{D}_1$, $\omega(a)$ is the proposition that *a* loves Arabella.

To see that this does indeed mean what we want it to mean let us look at

$$\langle \lambda, x, \langle \textbf{\textit{sleeps}}, x\rangle\rangle$$

Since $\textbf{\textit{sleeps}} \in F_{\langle 0,1\rangle}$ then, by the principles of p. 73, V(***sleeps***) is a function from $\mathbf{D}_1$ into $\mathbf{D}_0$. I.e., given an individual it forms a proposition, in particular the proposition that that individual sleeps. Let us call this function ω_{sleeps}. By the rules just outlined above $V^+(\langle \lambda, x, \langle \textbf{\textit{sleeps}}, x\rangle\rangle)$ is that function ω such that for any $a \in \mathbf{D}_1$, $\omega(a) = V^+_{a/x}(\langle \textbf{\textit{sleeps}}, x\rangle) = (V^+_{a/x}(\textbf{\textit{sleeps}}))(V^+_{a/x}(x))$. Now $V^+_{a/x}(x) = a$ and $V^+_{a/x}(\textbf{\textit{sleeps}}) = \omega_{sleeps}$, since $V^+_{a/x}(\textbf{\textit{sleeps}}) = V_{a/x}(\textbf{\textit{sleeps}})$ and $V_{a/x}$ differs from V only in the value for *x*. So for any $a \in \mathbf{D}_1$, $\omega(a) = \omega_{sleeps}(a)$; i.e., $\omega = \omega_{sleeps}$ as required.

Using abstraction to make complex predicates of category $\langle 0,1\rangle$ out of variables of category 1 and sentences (of category 0) we can then treat the quantifiers as straightforward functors of category $\langle 0,\langle 0,1\rangle\rangle$. In fact it will turn out that there are many other useful expressions of this type and that abstraction proves to be a very deep and powerful tool in linguistic analysis. Although most cases of abstraction that we shall use in Part III will involve abstracts only of category $\langle 0,1\rangle$ we shall in this chapter present the theory in a completely general way with variables of each syntactic category.

λ-categorial languages

We now shew how to describe in general form the addition of variables and λ's to any categorial language. Unlike any of the symbols we have met so far, λ is a logical constant with a fixed interpretation. Given any (pure) categorial language $\mathscr{L}$, we shew how to extend it to a language $\mathscr{L}^\lambda$ which will be called the *λ-categorial extension* of $\mathscr{L}$. We shall shew that in a certain sense $\mathscr{L}^\lambda$ is unique. $\mathscr{L}^\lambda$ will be called a *λ-categorial* language.

λ is to be some entity not in Syn or in $\mathscr{L}$. X is a function from Syn such that for any $\sigma \in$ Syn, X_σ is a denumerably infinite set disjoint from any X_τ (for $\sigma \neq \tau$) and from any set made up out of the symbols of $\mathscr{L}$. X_σ is the set of variables of type σ and X^+ is to denote the set of all variables.

The system E^λ of sets of expressions of $\mathscr{L}^\lambda$ can now be defined. It is the (unique) function from Syn whose values are the smallest sets satisfying the following; where $\sigma, \tau, \sigma_1, \ldots, \sigma_n \in$ Syn

6.1 $X_\sigma \subseteq E^\lambda_\sigma$

6.2 $F_\sigma \subseteq E^\lambda_\sigma$

6.3 If $\delta \in E^\lambda_{\langle\tau,\sigma_1,\ldots,\sigma_n\rangle}$ and $\alpha_1, \ldots, \alpha_n \in E^\lambda_{\sigma_1}, \ldots, E^\lambda_{\sigma_n}$ then $\langle\delta,\alpha_1,\ldots, \alpha_n\rangle \in E^\lambda_\tau$

6.4 If $\beta \in X_\sigma$ and $\alpha \in E^\lambda_\tau$ then $\langle\lambda,\beta,\alpha\rangle \in E^\lambda_{\langle\tau,\sigma\rangle}$

Since λ is not a functor there is no need to have as Montague does[110] a λ for each syntactic category (sometimes we use x, y etc. as meta-variables for members of the X_σ's). These formation rules allow us to have abstracts of other syntactic categories than $\langle 0,1\rangle$. In fact they allow abstracts of category $\langle\tau,\sigma\rangle$ where τ and σ are any categories whatever.

Given a model as defined on p. 73 for a categorial language $\mathscr{L}$ we shew how it induces a unique value assignment to all the expressions of $\mathscr{L}^\lambda$. The uniqueness of this induced assignment defines the sense in which $\mathscr{L}^\lambda$ is unique for it is independent of the particular things chosen as the variables. We assume therefore that we have a system of domains and a value assignment to the symbols of $\mathscr{L}$.

6.5 Let ν be a function with domain X^+ (i.e. the set of all variables) such that if $x \in X_\sigma$ then $\nu(x) \in \mathbf{D}_\sigma$.

(ν is a bit like an assignment function to variables but it proves more perspicuous to distinguish it from an ordinary assignment function.)

6.6 For any $x \in X_\sigma$ and $a \in \mathbf{D}_\sigma$ let $(\nu, a/x)$ be the function such that for $y \in X^+$ distinct from x, $(\nu,a/x)(y) = \nu(y)$ while $(\nu,a/x)(x) = a$.

We let $\mathbf{D}^+$ be the class of everything in the domain of any category and N be the class of all functions of the kind described in 6.5. Where $\nu \in N$, by V_ν we mean the value assignment such that

[110] Montague [1970a], p. 384. Montague treats λ as an ordinary functor. (*Vide* footnote p. 111 *infra*.)

6.7 If δ is a symbol of $\mathscr{L}$ (an $\mathscr{L}$-constant) then $V_v(\delta) = V(\delta)$.
6.8 If $x \in X^+$ then $V_v(x) = v(x)$.

(Remember that the symbols of $\mathscr{L}^\lambda$ are precisely the symbols of $\mathscr{L}$ and the variables in X^+.)

Let V_N be $\{V_v : v \in N\}$. Obviously given V, V_N is uniquely determined. We now shew how given V_N we can increase it to a class V_N^+ of assignments to all expressions in a uniquely determined fashion. For the ordinary functors things work as they did in categorial languages (cf. 5.18, p. 73) and for λ as we have indicated on p. 84. The full definition is as follows:

6.9 If α is a symbol of $\mathscr{L}^\lambda$ (i.e. either a symbol of $\mathscr{L}$ or a member of X^+) then for any $v \in N$, $V_v^+(\alpha) = V_v(\alpha)$.

6.10 If α is $\langle \delta, \alpha_1, \ldots, \alpha_n \rangle$ where $\delta \in E_{\langle \tau, \sigma_1, \ldots, \sigma_n \rangle}$ and $\alpha_1, \ldots, \alpha_n \in E_{\sigma_1}, \ldots, E_{\sigma_n}$, then for any $v \in N$, $V_v^+(\alpha) = \omega_\delta(V_v^+(\alpha_1), \ldots, V_v^+(\alpha_n))$ (where ω_δ is of course $V_v^+(\delta)$).

6.11 If α is $\langle \lambda, x, \beta \rangle$ where $x \in X_\sigma$ and $\beta \in E_\tau$, then $V_v^+(\alpha) = \omega$ where ω is that function from $\mathbf{D}_\sigma$ into $\mathbf{D}_\tau$ such that if $a \in \mathbf{D}_\sigma$ then $\omega(a) = V^+_{(v, a/x)}(\beta)$.

(By the induction hypothesis $V_v^+(\beta)$ is already defined for any $v \in N$ and in particular for $(v, a/x)$.)

We remarked in our discussion in Chapter Five that the members of $\mathbf{D}_\sigma$ might be partial functions. This means that $V_v^+(\beta)$ could be undefined for some $v \in N$. If $\omega(a)$ does not have a value then obviously a cannot be in its domain and so ω is a partial function too. Also it may happen that the function defined by 6.11 for an abstract in E_σ is not a member of $\mathbf{D}_\sigma$. In this case also the abstract will be undefined. In Chapter Seven we shall have a look at the domains of the intended interpretation and shall say a little more on the question of undefined expressions. If we have a system of domains which satisfies the restrictions of the classical type hierarchy then we can have models in which the values of all expressions in the functor categories are total, but the interpretation we shall favour will not have this nice property.

Where $\langle \lambda, x, \alpha \rangle$ is an abstract α is called the *scope* of the abstract and any occurrence of x in α is said to be *bound* in $\langle \lambda, x, \alpha \rangle$. An occurrence of a variable which is not bound is called *free*. Obviously the same variable may be both bound and free in the same expression. In languages in which variable-binding occurs a distinction is sometimes drawn between *closed* and *open* expressions. A closed expression is an expression in which no variable occurs free. An open expression is one which does contain free variables. An open sentence is sometimes called a *formula*, the term 'sentence' being restricted to closed sentences.

THEOREM **6.12** *If* α *is a closed expression then if* $\nu,\mu \in N$, $V_\nu^+(\alpha) = V_\mu^+(\alpha)$.

We first prove

LEMMA **6.13** *For any expression* α, *if* μ *and* ν *coincide on the variables free in* α *then* $V_\nu^+(\alpha) = V_\mu^+(\alpha)$.

Proof by induction on the construction of α.

Case 1: α is a variable.
Then α is free in α and so by the hypothesis of the lemma and 6.8, $V_\nu^+(\alpha) = V_\mu^+(\alpha)$.

Case 2: $\alpha \in F^+$.
Then $V_\nu^+(\alpha) = V(\alpha)$ and $V_\mu^+(\alpha) = V(\alpha)$ (by 6.7).

Case 3: α is $\langle \delta, \alpha_1, \ldots, \alpha_n \rangle$ $(\delta \neq \lambda)$.
Then $V_\nu^+(\langle \delta, \alpha_1, \ldots, \alpha_n) = (V_\nu^+(\delta))(V_\nu^+(\alpha_1), \ldots, V_\nu^+(\alpha_n))$.
But obviously if μ and ν coincide on the variables free in α then they coincide on the variables free in δ, α_1, ..., α_n and so by induction hypothesis:

$$\begin{aligned}(V_\nu^+(\delta))(V_\nu^+(\alpha_1), \ldots, V_\nu^+(\alpha_n)) &= ((V_\mu^+(\delta))(V_\mu^+(\alpha_1, \ldots, V_\mu^+(\alpha_n)) \\ &= V_\mu^+(\langle \delta, \alpha_1, \ldots, \alpha_n \rangle).\end{aligned}$$

Case 4: α is $\langle \lambda, x, \beta \rangle$.
Then if $x \in X_\sigma$ and $\beta \in E_\tau$ then for any $a \in \mathbf{D}_\sigma$ $(V_\nu^+(\langle \lambda, x, \beta))(a) = V_{(\nu,a/x)}(\beta)$ and $(V_\mu^+(\langle \lambda, x, \beta \rangle))(a) = V_{(\mu,a/x)}^+(\beta)$. Now if μ and ν coincide on all variables free in α then they coincide on all variables free in β except possibly x. But $(\nu, a/x)$ and $(\mu, a/x)$ coincide on x so $(\nu, a/x)$ and $(\mu, a/x)$ coincide on all variables free in β (since x is the only variable which could be free in β but not in α). Whence by induction hypothesis:

$$V_{(\nu,a/x)}^+(\beta) = V_{(\mu,a/x)}^+(\beta)$$

for all $a \in \mathbf{D}_\sigma$.

Thus $V_\nu^+(\langle \lambda, x, \beta \rangle)$ and $V_\mu^+(\langle \lambda, x, \beta \rangle)$ coincide for all arguments and thus are equal. **Q.E.D.**

Now clearly if α has no free variables then any ν and $\mu \in N$ coincide on the free variables in α and so by lemma 6.13, $V_\mu^+(\alpha) = V_\nu^+(\alpha)$ which proves theorem 6.12.

We can therefore simply speak of $V^+(\alpha)$ when α is closed, and the meaning of closed expressions is thus completely determined by the assignment to the symbols of $\mathscr{L}$.[111]

λ-conversion

For pure categorial languages, as for propositional languages, it was relatively easy to prove a theorem (5.19, p. 74) which shewed how we could always give a model which verified those and only those members of an arbitrarily given set of sentences. The case with λ-categorial languages is not so easy. Take e.g. the case of some $\alpha \in F_{\langle \tau, \sigma \rangle}$ and consider $x, y \in X_\sigma$. Then both $\langle \lambda, x, \langle \alpha, x \rangle \rangle$ and $\langle \lambda, y, \langle \alpha, y \rangle \rangle \in E_{\langle \sigma, \tau \rangle}$ and, further, the rules for semantic evaluation convince us of the following three facts: in any model

6.14 $V^+(\langle \lambda, x, \langle \alpha, x \rangle \rangle) = V^+(\langle \lambda, y, \langle \alpha, y \rangle \rangle)$

6.15 $V^+(\langle \lambda, x, \langle \alpha, x \rangle \rangle) = V^+(\alpha)$

and where $\beta \in F_n$.

6.16 $V^+(\langle \langle \lambda, x, \langle \alpha, x \rangle \rangle, \beta \rangle) = V^+(\langle \alpha, \beta \rangle)$.

This shews that unlike pure categorial languages the semantical framework of λ-categorial languages does treat some expressions as equivalent for every interpretation. This is quite reasonable when we remember that λ is in effect a logical constant and these rules reflect its meaning. It is perhaps not the usual sort of logical constant like the PC truth functors and may well be a constant which acts at a rather deeper level than they do. The principles underlying 6.14–6.16 are sometimes called principles of *λ-conversion* and they are due to Alonzo Church.[112]

In order to state these principles in their general form for λ-categorial languages we require a couple of definitions. We first define the notion of *bound alphabetic variant*.

6.17 If α and β differ only in that α has free x where β has free y then $\langle \lambda, x, \alpha \rangle$ is a bound alphabetic variant of $\langle \lambda, y, \beta \rangle$.

6.18 If γ is a bound alphabetic variant of δ, and α and β differ only in that α has γ where and only where β has δ then α is a bound alphabetic variant of β.

[111] Since a particular formula will contain only finitely many free variables, lemma 6.13 enables us to omit reference to a member of N, provided we give values for all the variables free in the formula. Thus, if α contains only $x_1, \ldots, x_n$ as free variables, we may write simply: $V^+_{a_1/x_1, \ldots, a_n/x_n}(\alpha)$; since for any ν, $\mu \in N$: $V^+_{(\nu, a_1/x_1, \ldots, a_n/x_n)}(\alpha) = V^+_{(\mu, a_1/x_1, \ldots, a_n/x_n)}(\alpha)$.

[112] Church [1941].

(Bound alphabetic variance is the smallest equivalence relation to satisfy 6.17 and 6.18).

We now define the result of substituting an expression for a variable.

6.19 Where $\alpha \in E_\tau$ and $\beta \in E_\sigma$ and $x \in X_\sigma$ then if α' is a bound alphabetic variant of α in which no variable free in β occurs, $\alpha[\beta/x]$ is α' with β replacing x wherever the latter occurs free in α.

(Note that the arbitrariness of α' determines $\alpha[\beta/x]$ only to within bound alphabetic variance. This does not matter since bound alphabetic variants always have the same value, but if the arbitrariness is thought undesirable we can always order the bound alphabetic variants of a formula and take the first which satisfies the required condition.)

We shall say that α can be converted into β by the principles of λ-conversion iff α conv β, where conv is the least equivalence relation satisfying the following:

6.20 Where α and β are bound alphabetic variants of one another then α conv β.

6.21 If $\alpha \in E_\tau$ and $x \in E_\sigma$ and $\beta \in E_\sigma$ then $\langle\langle\lambda, x, \alpha\rangle, \beta\rangle$ conv $\alpha[\beta/x]$.

6.22 If $\alpha \in E_{\langle\tau,\sigma\rangle}$ and $x \in X_\sigma$ and x does not occur free in α then $\langle\lambda, x, \langle\alpha, x\rangle\rangle$ conv α.

We now want to say what it is for a pair of expressions to be intersubstitutable with respect to a set of sentences. Roughly speaking where A is a set of sentences we want to say that α and β are A-intersubstitutable (A-indistinguishable) if any formula containing α is in A iff the same formula, but perhaps containing β somewhere in place of α, is also in A.

The proper definition of this relation would follow the lines of 5.25–5.27 of p. 76 but would of course need to be a little more complex because of the presence of variable-binding. We can then say that a set A of expressions is λ-closed iff wherever α conv β then α and β are A-intersubstitutable.

A theorem of semantic generality for a language $\mathscr{L}^\lambda$ would then say that for any suitable model structure $\langle \mathbf{D}, \mathbf{T}\rangle$ and any λ-closed set A of sentences of $\mathscr{L}^\lambda$ there is a model $\langle \mathbf{D}, \mathbf{T}, V\rangle$ which is characteristic for A. The conditions for a suitable model structure are discussed in Chapter Seven (pp. 98–100). Such a theorem is almost certainly possible but the details of the proof would be incredibly tortuous and the task will not be attempted here.[113]

λ-categorial languages and ordinary language

We began our chapter with a consideration of quantifiers and saw how to resolve the ambiguity between the various senses of

(1) ***everyone loves someone***

and

(2) ***someone loves everyone***

Let us now look a little more closely at the relation between these English sentences and their formalized counterparts. Taking (1) we get

(3) $\langle \textbf{\textit{everyone}}, \langle \lambda, x, \langle \textbf{\textit{someone}}, \langle \lambda, y, \langle \textbf{\textit{loves}}, x, y\rangle\rangle\rangle\rangle\rangle$

and

(4) $\langle \textbf{\textit{someone}}, \langle \lambda, y, \langle \textbf{\textit{everyone}}, \langle \lambda, x, \langle \textbf{\textit{loves}}, x, y\rangle\rangle\rangle\rangle\rangle$.

(3) and (4) require several operations to transform them into (1). But recall the remarks at the end of Chapter Five (p. 78 f) where we saw that so long as the order of the arguments is preserved the functor can be placed wherever we please. Applied to (3) and (4) this liberalization allows us to have,

(5) $\langle \textbf{\textit{everyone}}, \langle \lambda, x, \langle\langle \lambda, y, \langle \textbf{\textit{loves}}, x, y\rangle\rangle, \textbf{\textit{someone}}\rangle\rangle\rangle$

and

(6) $\langle\langle \lambda, y, \langle \textbf{\textit{everyone}}, \langle \lambda, x, \langle \textbf{\textit{loves}}, x, y\rangle\rangle\rangle\rangle, \textbf{\textit{someone}}\rangle$

It is in fact only in the position of ***someone*** relative to its argument that (5) differs from (3) and (6) from (4). (5) is synonymous with (3) and when evaluated by the semantic rule for ***someone*** suggested on p. 81 f gives the interpretation which does not require a universal beloved while (6) is synonymous with (4) and does require one.

The interesting thing about (5) and (6) is that when we delete the λ's and the variables, i.e., when we regard the sentences as sequences of symbols of the original language $\mathscr{L}$, we get the sequence

(7) $\langle \textbf{\textit{everyone}}, \textbf{\textit{loves}}, \textbf{\textit{someone}}\rangle$

In Part III we shall argue that a great deal of natural language is obtainable by this process of deletion of elements in an expression in a λ-categorial language. Notice that the underlying syntax of (7) can only be got by 'deriving' ***loves*** from $\langle \textbf{\textit{loves}}, x, y\rangle$ and so on.

On p. 79 f we alluded to the distinction between surface structure and deep structure. The sentences of a λ-categorial language are what

[113] Some idea of the complexity can be seen from the completeness proof for second-order logic in Cresswell [1972c], pp. 315–18.

we shall propose in Part III as the deep structure of English. The result of deleting the λ's and the variables gives us something which is very much nearer to the surface structure. It will not, however, quite do as it stands so we shall refer to it as the *shallow structure* of the λ-categorial language.[114]

If we regard (7) as the shallow structure of (5) and (6) then the grammatical analysis necessary for the interpretation of (7) cannot be obtained by analysis of the shallow structure. It was in fact the impossibility of shallow structure analysis which forced us on p. 81 to go beyond pure categorial languages.

(7), we have said, is ambiguous between (5) and (6) because it can be obtained from them by deletion of the purely logical elements. It can also be so obtained from the following two sentences:

(8) $\langle \boldsymbol{everyone}, \langle \lambda, x, \langle\langle \lambda, y, \langle \boldsymbol{loves}, y, x \rangle\rangle\, \boldsymbol{someone} \rangle\rangle\rangle$

(9) $\langle\langle \lambda, y, \langle \boldsymbol{everyone}, \langle \lambda, x, \langle \boldsymbol{loves}, y, x \rangle\rangle\rangle\rangle\, \boldsymbol{someone} \rangle$.

(8) and (9) differ from (5) and (6) only in having $\langle \boldsymbol{loves}, y, x \rangle$ in place of $\langle \boldsymbol{loves}, x, y \rangle$. (8) means what we would ordinarily express by (2) (someone loves everyone) when the someone need not be unique and (9) means what (2) does when the someone is unique. What our analysis seems to require is that (1) and (2) can be so understood as to be synonymous. If we were claiming that (1) and (2) under normal circumstances mean the same then we would of course be wrong. However if we claim that (2) *could* be understood to mean the same as (1) it is not so obviously silly.

I would say that under normal circumstances (1) means the same as (5), under somewhat special circumstances the same as (6), and under very special circumstances the same as (8) or (9). Let me give examples of these special circumstances. For (6) imagine the following contribution to a conversation:

(10) In that country all the people love their president. Isn't it frightening to be in a place where everyone loves someone.

Here (1) occurs as an embedded sentence with the meaning of (6). For (8) and (9) we seem to need to go beyond normal conversational English but there is nothing ungrammatical about a hymn which contains the lines

114 Some reasons why it will not do will appear in Chapter Twelve, and a formal analysis of the relation between surface and shallow structure will be given in Chapter Thirteen.

For you weeps someone bitterly
For you and all humanity
And everyone loves someone kind
'Tis God who does, for all he's pined.

There is, as far as I know, no such hymn, and perhaps it would be unworthy of the logician hymn-writer Isaac Watts, but it at least provides a case in which the sentence 'Everyone loves someone' must be understood as (9). To get (8) we would need something like:

For everyone loves someone dear
Loves you your mother, never fear.

If these examples are valid then we have some reason for suggesting that possible meanings of sentences of natural languages can be given by λ-categorial sentences from which the natural language sentences are obtained by deletion of the logical symbols. On this view an important task for the linguist will be to give an explanation of why some of these are less natural than others. E.g., given (1) he must shew why it is that although (5), (6), (8) and (9) are all *possible* readings yet (5) is the only really natural one and (8) and (9) are very unlikely indeed. There are of course formal differences among (5), (6), (8) and (9). E.g., a rule which says that the symbol with widest scope is normally put first[115] will select (5) in preference to (6). (Such a rule would be supported by the fact that 'Someone is loved by everyone' would be a natural way of expressing (6).) And a rule which says that the order of the variables after the λ's ought to correspond with their order as arguments of the predicate might rule out (8) and (9). These rules would need careful formulation but they do not seem impossible to state. It must be stressed that they would be rules about what an ordinary language sentence *probably* means or does not mean and therefore will presumably be part of empirical linguistics.

It might be found that some rules are specific to certain languages (inflected languages for instance will allow much freer variation of word order) while others are universal among all human languages. Some rules, like the ones we have just suggested, may depend only on the form of the deep structure sentences while others may depend on their meaning. We must, however, defer any further consideration of topics of this kind until we have shewn how to represent a much larger class of English sentences by the use of λ-categorial languages. That task we take up in Part III.

[115] Cf. G. Lakoff [1971a], pp. 238–41.

CHAPTER SEVEN

The Metaphysics of Categorial Languages

In the last two chapters our semantics have been based on a system **D** of domains. One of these, $\mathbf{D}_0$, is the domain of propositions and in Chapter Three we had a certain amount to say about it. Our task in this chapter will be to look at what sorts of things the other domains will contain. In fact the only important question concerns the domains of the basic categories, for the kinds of things which have to be in the function domains are then fixed (though there is still the question of whether to include them all).

Although we have allowed infinitely many basic categories we have, in our examples, used only two; the category 0 of sentences and the category 1 of what we have been calling 'names'. Since in Chapter Nine we shall suggest that names in ordinary language should be treated as of category $\langle 0, \langle 0, 1 \rangle \rangle$ our use of this word for symbols of category 1 is perhaps inapposite (it would be tempting and perhaps not overly misleading to call them 'logically proper names' if it were not that this phrase has acquired all sorts of unpleasant associations; when we want absolute strictness we shall speak simply of symbols of category 1). $\mathbf{D}_1$ under its intended interpretation is the domain of 'things'. We have already explained (p. 66) why we do not like the alternative 'individuals' (for we want to say that sets, functions, propositions and the like are all things) but we have not really said what things are.

Our set of propositions in Chapter Three was based on a set **B** of basic particular situations. Now this set **B** was intended to be rich enough to provide the ingredients of every possible world. It is desirable therefore to shew how talk about things can be analysed by set-theoretical construction out of **B**.

Basic individuals

In order to give some plausibility to our more general thesis we need first to shew how the everyday things of the physical world might be analysed in terms of **B**. We shall define a class of *basic individuals* which is intended to comprise things like physical objects, events, states, processes, and the like. A basic individual ρ is a function from a world to a part of that world. Remember that a world w is a subset of **B** and therefore a part of w is a subset of w. Strictly, since a subset of a world can itself be a world a basic individual ρ is a function from possible worlds into possible worlds provided that for any world w, $\rho(w)$ is a subset of w. $\rho(w)$, i.e. the value of the function ρ in the world w, is called the *manifestation* of ρ in w. An alternative would be to call it the *extension* of ρ in w.

In terms of the illustrative model of p. 38 f the manifestation of an individual ρ in a world w would be a space-time portion of w. Say ρ is some particular blackboard. Then, where w is the real world, $\rho(w)$ is that subset of space-time which makes up the blackboard throughout its history. It would be implausible to identify the blackboard with its manifestation, for we can ask 'Would the blackboard have been better placed nearer the window?' and one cannot ask this of a space-time slice.

It should be clear that the same basic individual can exist in more than one world, though its manifestation may be different in different worlds. Where the manifestation of a basic individual ρ in a world w is null then we can say that ρ does not exist in w. These two facts mean that talk about properties which an individual might have but does not have will be in order[116] and so will talk about individuals which do not

[116] The problem of how to decide when the thing someone is talking about can exist in other worlds, and what sort of properties it must have if it exists in these other worlds, i.e. the problem of deciding what properties are 'essential' to it (cf. Quine [1953], pp. 154–6), is in our view simply the problem of telling how to know what it is that someone is talking about; and it is therefore a problem for a theory of language use and not for semantics proper. Thus we have almost no contribution to make in the traditional debate about essentialism. Cf. Hintikka [1969], p. 138. Some philosophers, e.g. Lewis [1968], would claim that a thing can exist only in one world. Whether this is so or not can only be answered by attempts, like the one of the present chapter, to say what an individual is. The advice of Scott [1970], p. 144, to take an individual as primitive is good perhaps for logicians, but not I think for philosophers, nor for anyone interested in the relation between language and the world.

exist. The need to be able to suppose that a thing might be other than it is, which means being able to suppose a possible world in which that thing exists but with different properties, ought to be an obvious one. The need to be able to talk about what does not exist arises because in speaking of other worlds than the real one, say in telling stories, we may want to attribute properties (like, say, 'is wiser than any actually existing person') to individuals which indeed exist in that world but not in ours.[117]

Our blackboard example involves a physical object but it should be clear that an event, such as the battle of Waterloo, can also be seen in this way. Notice that our approach indicates a method of solution to the problem of saying just what is wrong and what is right about the statement

(1) The battle of Waterloo is nothing more than a certain movement of elementary physical particles.

A movement of elementary particles can be described as a certain subset of **B** by saying which points of space are occupied at which moments of time. (1) is true in the sense that the value of the battle of Waterloo function in the real world, and indeed in any world, is a movement of elementary physical particles. However (1) taken in another way is false. This is because we can also understand the particular movement of elementary particles in a particular world as an event. If we can accept an absolute space-time framework then we can form the function whose value for *any* world is the set of space-time points which is the value in the actual world of the battle of Waterloo function. It is functions of this kind which might be said to represent *absolutely physical* individuals, and if (1) is meant to assert the identity of the battle of Waterloo and the absolutely physical individual which coincides with it in the real world then (1) is false, since although the battle of Waterloo has a manifestation (possibly null) in each world it need not be the same manifestation in each; and this is why seeing it as a battle is different from seeing its manifestation as an absolutely physical event.

The situation here is analogous to, but must be distinguished from, the case of individual concepts as described on pp. 68–70. An indi-

[117] Cf. Scott [1970], p. 145, and Cocchiarella [1969], p. 35 f, also Lambert and van Fraassen [1970], pp. 8–11. Scott, like myself, appears to have been rather reluctantly converted by such examples as the one given in the text, to seeing the necessity for trans-world quantification. Many philosophers of course have doubts about trans-world comparisons, e.g. Hintikka [1969], pp. 144–6, and [1970], p. 140 f.

vidual concept is certainly a function from worlds but its values are individuals. The introduction of individual concepts can only be achieved after we have got clear on the notion of an individual. The reason we chose the word 'manifestation' rather than Carnap's word 'extension' for the value of an individual in a world was because 'extension' suggests that it is the value of the function which is the individual and not the function itself.[118]

Note that our range of basic individuals is far wider than any ordinary notion of things. E.g. we have said nothing to require that the manifestation of a basic individual in a given world has to be in any way spatio-temporally continuous.[119] Since we have been prepared to count events and processes as basic individuals perhaps restrictions of this kind would have been too severe. But more drastically we also allow functions which might bear no correspondence to anything anyone would recognize as a physical thing; functions whose manifestations in different worlds seem to form no describable pattern.

We must distinguish here between questions of ontology and questions of demarcation.[120] We have said that physical things have the status of functions of a certain kind. There is now the quite different problem of marking off those which human beings can recognize as things. About this problem we refuse to pronounce and shall say that just as we considered postulating a set of humanly graspable propositions, so there might be also a set of humanly graspable things.

Another feature of natural language which we considered in Chapter Four also applies to our analysis of things. That is the indeterminacy we discussed on pp. 58–61. E.g., given the analysis

[118] Scott [1970], p. 171 f, quotes Kaplan as defending the extensional way of taking properties, by stressing the ontological primacy of individuals over individual concepts. Our own metaphysics is not open to Kaplan's objection, since we have defined *individuals*. What we would claim to have shewn though, is that even ordinary individuals are not purely extensional entities.

[119] Obviously our class of basic individuals is far bigger than the class of 'basic particulars' in Strawson [1959], p. 39. Strawson is using 'basic' in a slightly different sense; in our terms he may be said to be attempting to mark out those individuals which are basic to the human understanding (cf. footnote 50, *supra*); and so there is no need for us to get involved in a pseudo-controversy about whether material objects are basic, or are set-theoretical constructions.

[120] Alternatively one could simply distinguish between saying what kind of a thing something is and giving a definition of that thing, cf. Montague [1969], p. 162. Montague discusses all sorts of philosophical entities in something of the same spirit as we do.

of a blackboard as a function from worlds to sub-worlds (worlds and sub-worlds being sets of space-time points), it is easy to imagine two functions differing from each other only in that in one world the manifestation of one of them occupies a very small number of extra space-time points so close to the points common to both that no one can detect them. Might we not get a situation in which one person is talking about one and another talking about the other? But how could you ever tell? The first point is that there are two blackboards since there will be properties the one has which the other lacks. But the second, and most important point, is that no observable property[121] can distinguish between them and that for practical purposes they can be considered to be the same. It is here that the notion of a communication class comes to our rescue. For the semantics of a natural language will be determined by a class which only makes as fine distinctions as are required. And a case where a difference between two things is undetectable to the language-users is simply an extreme case of something making no practical difference. A similar situation arises where the values of the functions coincide in all worlds except some which are so remote from the real one that we would not know how the thing we are talking about would be manifested in them.

On p. 46 f we alluded to the objection to set-theoretical analysis in metaphysics. Perhaps this objection has its strongest appeal when we are analysing an everyday physical object like a blackboard. Surely a function from worlds to worlds is a very rarified and abstract object? Do not nominalists fight shy of admitting sets and functions into their ontology and only do so reluctantly when forced? Yet they certainly believe in blackboards. The view that a function from worlds to worlds is an abstract entity is a question-begging one if being an abstract entity rules out being also a physical object. For on the analysis I am proposing some functions from worlds to worlds *are* physical objects and so the right conclusion is that not all such functions are abstract entities.[122] The objection must say more. The

[121] At least, no property observable to the language-user. We are of course not trying to say that two things are to be regarded as the same if there is no way of perceiving the difference between them; only that it makes no practical difference to regard them as the same. In some cases the indeterminacy seems tied to the very notion of the thing. E.g. in the case of clouds, hills and colour surfaces there are no precise identity criteria. (These examples are given in Routley [1971], p. 625, though Routley does not draw quite the conclusions we do.)

[122] One could, if one liked, define an abstract entity as any theoretical construction which is not a function whose domain is **W** and whose range contains the null set, i.e. any entity whose existence is not contingent.

objection must hold that the nature of ordinary physical objects and events is well enough known to shew that they behave in certain ways in which set-theoretical entities do not behave; and I would maintain that this cannot be shewn.

I recognize of course and have frequently been stressing that the analysis I am proposing is subject to philosophical scrutiny. But it must not be facile scrutiny. As an example of facile scrutiny consider the following, equally question-begging, instance of the general argument outlined above: the objection is that physical objects cannot be sets, because we can perceive physical objects through the senses. But whoever saw a set coming down the road? The question here is begged because whatever the analysis of 'seeing' is in terms of the metaphysics I have been sketching, it will at least be a two-place property and there is no reason why the proposition $\omega_{sees}(a, b)$ should not be true in a world w when a and b are sets. If b is the blackboard function and a the Mr Jones function, then the test of the analysis will be whether the worlds in which

$$\omega_{sees}(a, b)$$

is true are the worlds in which we would be happy to say that Mr Jones sees the blackboard. As far as the set coming down the road is concerned, one might well be prepared to say that one sees a set of three men coming down the road because one sees each of the men. I.e. for some sets, although the set is distinct from its members yet to see the set is just to see the members. But in any case the question is not whether anyone would be happy to say that a thing is a set or a function; the question is whether it *is* a set or a function.

Things

Basic individuals of course are only one kind of thing. The peculiarity of the name category is that its domain should contain everything that there is. Since we are limiting ourselves to set-theoretical constructions out of **B** an upper limit to the domain $\mathbf{D}_1$ would be the universe class of our chosen set theory with the members of **B** as 'individuals' in the technical sense which that word bears in set theory.[123] I.e., the domain of the variables in the first-order set-theoretical metalanguage would comprise the members of **B** together with all sets whose existence was entailed by the axioms. The axioms would be ones of some

[123] Cf. Lemmon [1969], p. 9 f. The incorporation of individuals into axiomatic set theory is discussed in Suppes [1960], p. 20 f (though Suppes is working in a version of set theory which does not have the distinction between sets and classes).

standard system of set theory, say those of NBG (p. 241), together with an axiom to ensure that **B** is a set.

On the assumption that NBG is consistent the universe U_B of all the individuals and sets in its domain will not be so big as to lead us into contradictions such as Russell's but ought to be big enough for all we want to do.

We cannot quite identify $\mathbf{D}_1$ with U_B since $\mathbf{D}_1$ in a model is the value of the function **D** for the syntactic category 1, and therefore must be a set, while U_B is of course a proper class. We can insist that $\mathbf{D}_1 \subseteq U_B$, and more generally for any $\sigma \in$ Syn we can have $\mathbf{D}_\sigma \subseteq U_B$. We also want $\mathbf{D}_1$ to include everything that is in any domain since we want everything to be nameable.

We shall say that **D** is an *intended system of domains* based on a set **B** of basic particular situations iff:

7.1 where **P** is constructed out of **B** as on p. 42, $\mathbf{D}_0 = \mathbf{P}$
7.2 for any category σ, $\mathbf{D}_\sigma \subseteq \mathbf{D}_1 \subseteq U_B$
7.3 If $\sigma = \langle \tau, \sigma_1, \ldots, \sigma_n \rangle$ then $\mathbf{D}_\sigma$ is a set of total or partial functions from $\mathbf{D}_{\sigma_1} \times \ldots \times \mathbf{D}_{\sigma_n}$ into $\mathbf{D}_\tau$.

Given that $\mathbf{D}_\tau, \mathbf{D}_{\sigma_1}, \ldots, \mathbf{D}_{\sigma_n}$ are sets, a standard set-theoretical proof ensures that $\mathbf{D}_\sigma$ will be too. Since $\mathbf{D}_1$ contains each $\mathbf{D}_\sigma$ it does not matter whether we speak of the union of all the $\mathbf{D}_\sigma$ as $\mathbf{D}^+$, as has been our practice, or as $\mathbf{D}_1$. $\mathbf{D}^+$ better emphasizes its universality, while $\mathbf{D}_1$ better emphasizes that it limits the range of V for symbols of category 1.

7.2 makes the use of partial functions as values of expressions in the functor categories (cf. pp. 53, 73 f and 86) not merely desirable but necessary. For consider a function in $\mathbf{D}_{\langle 0, 1 \rangle}$. This will be a function whose arguments are all in $\mathbf{D}_1$ yet which (by 7.2) is itself in $\mathbf{D}_1$, and it is a plausible set-theoretical principle that no function can apply to itself.[124] Thus, if all functions in $\mathbf{D}_{\langle 0, 1 \rangle}$ were required to be total, $\mathbf{D}_{\langle 0, 1 \rangle}$ would have to be empty, for there are no total functions of the required kind.

Considerations of this kind will rule out assignments which might lead to paradoxical entities. For instance, we cannot define a property true of those and only those properties not true of themselves. If we wanted our domains to contain only total functions then we should have to order them in a hierarchy with $\mathbf{D}_1$ consisting of individuals,

[124] This is guaranteed by what is sometimes known as the *Axiom of Regularity* or the *Axiom of Foundation* (cf. Lemmon [1969], p. 105, axiom A10). It also rules out such 'cycles' as $x \in y$, and $y \in x$, or $x \in y$, $y \in z$ and $z \in x$, and so on.

$\mathbf{D}_{\langle 0,1\rangle}$ of properties of individuals and so on. This would be undesirable for it would mean that one could only name individuals whereas we want to allow anything to be named. By allowing partial functions in the domains, and therefore by admitting the possibility of expressions which do not have a value, we ensure that intended models for λ-categorial languages are possible. The assumed consistency of the set-theoretical metalanguage (for although our metalanguage is English the formal definition of our semantics can be carried out in a formalization of NBG in first-order logic) guarantees that no intended model is contradictory but does not guarantee that a model exists and, as we have seen, if the members of a functor domain are required to be total then there will be no intended models.

Self-reference

If we are to take our metaphysics seriously then we must assume that the language itself is part of the world. For the present we are still not interested in the kinds of things symbols are (we take that question up in Chapter Eight) but we must certainly recognize *that* they are and that both they and complex expressions and all the rest are in $\mathbf{D}_1$. Further, an interpretation of a language is a set-theoretically describable pattern of interrelations between symbols and things in the world. So talk of the relation between language and the world is talk of relations among members of $\mathbf{D}_1$.

The fact that language and the relations between language and the world are all parts of the domain of values for the language, and so can be talked about in the language, raises the interesting question of the status of self-referential statements.[125] What we shall prove is that Tarski's result, that a truth predicate for a language cannot be defined within the language itself, holds for categorial languages given an intended system of domains.

Let us look at the simplest case of paradoxical self-reference. Suppose that we have a sentence κ of a language $\mathscr{L}$, whose meaning is supposed to be 'κ is false'. I.e., assuming for the moment that propositions are simply sets of worlds,[126] the meaning rule for κ is:

7.4 For any $w \in \mathbf{W}$, $w \in \mathrm{V}(\kappa)$ iff $w \notin \mathrm{V}(\kappa)$.

It ought to be obvious that there is no such set as $\mathrm{V}(\kappa)$. If there were then every member w would be such that $w \in \mathrm{V}(\kappa)$ iff $w \notin \mathrm{V}(\kappa)$.

[125] Semantical study of languages in which self-reference is possible occurs in van Fraassen [1970].

[126] Treating propositions simply as sets of worlds will not affect any of the points we make in this section.

But this condition holds for no w, so $V(\kappa) = \varnothing$. But then $w \in \varnothing$ iff $w \notin \varnothing$, and this is contradictory. So although V appears to be a value assignment which assigns a set of worlds to a simple sentence symbol it is not in fact one.

Such a case may seem artificial. To put up a simple sentence symbol with such a contradictory rule for assignment hardly tells us much about paradoxes of self-reference. We can get something which looks much more like a traditional version of one of these paradoxes if we suppose $E_{\langle 0, 1\rangle}$ to contain the predicate ***is false***. (We have for the moment to assume that this is a one-place predicate. Nothing here turns on the fact that in English it is actually a copula + adjective.) The semantic rule for ***is false*** is the following:[127]

7.5 V(***is false***) is that function $\omega \in E_{\langle 0, 1\rangle}$ such that for any $w \in \mathbf{W}$ and $a \in \mathbf{D}_1$, $w \in \omega(a)$ iff $a \in E_0$ and $w \notin V(a)$.

Our present hypothesis, remember, is that language is part of the world, more specifically that the expressions of a language are all in $\mathbf{D}_1$, and in particular that there is nothing to prevent an a in $\mathbf{D}_1$ being in E_0. Because $a \in E_0$ we can speak of $V(a)$. We shall shew that 7.5 is just as contradictory a meaning rule as 7.4.

Suppose that there is some symbol $\alpha \in F_1$ such that:

7.6 $V(\alpha) = \langle$***is false***$, \alpha\rangle$

Since language is part of the world then $\langle$***is false***$, \alpha\rangle \in \mathbf{D}_1$. Further, since α is a symbol of $\mathscr{L}$ there is no restriction on what we may assign to it and in particular no obstacle to a V which assigns it $\langle$***is false***$, \alpha\rangle$. Where V(***is false***) $= \omega$ then $w \in V(\langle$***is false***$, \alpha\rangle)$ iff $w \in \omega(V(\alpha))$; and by 7.5, given that $\langle$***is false***$, \alpha\rangle \in E_0$, $w \in \omega(V(\alpha))$ iff $w \notin V(V(\alpha))$. But by 7.6 $V(\alpha) = (\langle$***is false***$, \alpha\rangle)$ and so $w \in V(\langle$***is false***$, \alpha\rangle)$ iff $w \notin V(\langle$***is false***$, \alpha\rangle)$.

Since the nature of α is quite irrelevant to the preceding argument we need only require that F_1 is non-empty and that ***is false*** $\in E_{\langle 0, 1\rangle}$ to ensure that there can be an assignment satisfying 7.6. This means that for any $\mathscr{L}$ whose E_1 is non-empty there can be no assignment which satisfies 7.5.

[127] Note that this rule must not be confused with [V~] on p. 32 which does not yield any sort of paradox. Likewise 7.7 *infra* (p. 102) must not be confused with a rule for a one-place operator ϕ meaning 'it is the case that' and having the rule: $\omega_\phi(a) = a$.

The impossibility of a V satisfying 7.5 shews that a categorial language cannot contain a truth predicate in the sense of Tarski.[128] Where $\phi \in F_{\langle 0,1\rangle}$ we shall say that ϕ is a truth predicate for $\mathscr{L}$ with respect to an assignment V iff:

7.7 Where $w \in \mathbf{W}$ and $a \in \mathbf{D}_1$, $w \in \omega_\phi(a)$ iff $w \in V(a)$.
(I.e. $\langle \phi, a \rangle$ is true in w under V iff a is a sentence of $\mathscr{L}$ which is true in w under V.)

Suppose that $\mathscr{L}$ contains a truth predicate. I.e. suppose that there is an assignment V for which 7.7. holds. We shew that in that case there is an assignment for which 7.5 holds. We define an ω satisfying 7.5 as follows:

7.5′ For any $w \in \mathbf{W}$ and $a \in \mathbf{D}_1$, $\omega(a) = \mathbf{W} - \omega_\phi(a)$.

It is easy to see that an ω which satisfies 7.5′ also satisfies 7.5 since $w \in \omega(a)$ iff $w \notin \omega_\phi(a)$; i.e. (by 7.7) iff $w \notin V(a)$. Since there is no assignment satisfying 7.5 then there is no assignment satisfying 7.7. I.e., a truth predicate for $\mathscr{L}$ is impossible.

What is the moral of this? Tarski thought it was to avoid ordinary language and stick to formalized languages. But categorial languages are formalized. The fact is that to avoid the paradoxes, according to Tarski's advice, one should cease being interested in languages rich enough for them to arise in. If it were simply that the paradoxes arise in ordinary languages and not formalized ones then one might indeed say: so much the worse for ordinary (or formalized) languages; but when they arise in languages having a certain kind of richness, whether formalized or not, then we must look at what happens.

When we try to define a truth predicate for $\mathscr{L}$ we find that we cannot do it because it entails assignments which are in fact contradictory. Yet we appear, in Chapters Five and Six, to have defined quite generally a truth predicate for all categorial languages. Our immediate retort is of course that these definitions were given in the English metalanguage in which this book is written and so do not count as defining a truth predicate.

This defence would put an end to the matter were it not for the fact that part of our aim has been to explore languages which, though artificial, are getting closer and closer to a natural language – for

[128] Tarski [1935]. The passage referred to is in the English translation (Tarski [1956]) on p. 164 f.

convenience, English. If our aim is to be realized then the very metalanguage we are using must be capable of translation into a λ-categorial language. Our metalinguistic truth predicate then becomes a truth predicate for a λ-categorial language in that λ-categorial language, and there is no such predicate. So our metalanguage cannot be translated into a λ-categorial language.

The standard solution to this dilemma goes something like this. When we talk about the relations between a language and the world there is nothing to prevent a definition in the metalanguage of a truth predicate for the object language. If we want a truth predicate for that metalanguage, we express it in a language one level higher, and so on. We might then say that we have a general truth definition for a hierarchy of languages in that we have a schema which defines truth in $\mathscr{L}_i$ in the hierarchy in terms of $\mathscr{L}_{i+1}$. 'True' then becomes systematically ambiguous but, used with caution, it can still be regarded as a truth predicate for a 'language' which is in reality a hierarchy of languages.

The members of this hierarchy do not need to be very different from one another. In the first place they can be syntactically identical, i.e., can contain exactly the same symbols and formation rules. In the second place they can coincide semantically everywhere but in a very small area; to be precise, everywhere but when they are talking about the relation between language and the world or between one language and another. And even then, as we have just noted, the expressions which in $\mathscr{L}_{i+1}$ refer to expressions in $\mathscr{L}_i$ will mean the same things about $\mathscr{L}_i$ as do the same expressions of $\mathscr{L}_{i+2}$ about $\mathscr{L}_{i+1}$. We have already seen (p. 59 f) that there are reasons for regarding the semantics of natural languages as somewhat vague classes of meaning assignments rather than as single assignments.[129] Since the hierarchy of metalanguages need not differ syntactically we can regard its members as all in the communication class of the natural language and can treat the hierarchy as a hierarchy of meaning assignments for the same language rather than as a hierarchy of different languages. Thus we can explain why natural language appears to enable the definition of a truth predicate for itself despite the fact that such a predicate is inconsistent.

[129] If a situation should emerge in which the communication class of English allows assignments which give different results in a real situation, we get an example of what might be what is referred to by saying that ordinary language is 'inconsistent'.

Quotation

In talking about expressions of a language it is often useful to have a device which makes, out of an expression, a name-like symbol which refers to the expression. This process is called quotation. There is no theoretical reason why quotation should be restricted to expressions, and a general theory of quotation will describe the process of adding to a language anything at all in such a way that the added thing produces a symbol which is its name. In general any member of $\mathbf{D}^+$ is eligible for the quotation operation but the symbol so formed is always a member of F_1.

Suppose that $\mathscr{L}$ is a λ-categorial language and that $\langle \mathbf{D}, \mathbf{T}, \mathrm{V} \rangle$ is a model for $\mathscr{L}$. An entity *qu* is said to be a *quotation symbol for* $\mathscr{L}$ *under* $\langle \mathbf{D}, \mathbf{T}, \mathrm{V} \rangle$ iff for any $a \in \mathbf{D}^+$:

7.8 if $\langle qu, a \rangle \in F_1$ then $V(\langle qu, a \rangle) = a$

What this means is that in a λ-categorial language a quotation symbol is any entity which, when occurring as the first member of an ordered pair, makes a symbol whose value is the second member of that ordered pair. We shall call a pair of the form $\langle qu, a \rangle$ a *quotation* and we shall call *a* the *quoted entity*.[130]

We have called *qu* a quotation symbol though it is not strictly a symbol of $\mathscr{L}$. 7.8 requires that the whole quotation be a symbol of $\mathscr{L}$ but unless *qu* and *a* are already symbols 7.8 does not make them so. In most usual cases, however, the quoted entity will be, if not a symbol, at least an expression of $\mathscr{L}$, or of some other language. (For all that our general theory does, as it should, allow it, the idea of putting quotation marks around Big Ben has an odd ring to it.) It is undoubtedly the fact that α is already an expression of a language which makes it plausible to have $\langle qu, \alpha \rangle$ as also an expression of a language, for the extra symbol being introduced will not produce expressions which are radically different from the ones one already has.

[130] In Chapter Eight (pp. 122–4) we consider the difference between quoting an expression and quoting an utterance or token of that expression. At present we are still working with a definition of language so general that its symbols need not be sets of utterances. Note that '*qu*' is a symbol of the (enriched English) metalanguage of the present book. There is no reason to suppose that '*qu*' is a quotation symbol in English, and therefore no reason to suppose that when I write '$\langle qu, a \rangle$' I am referring to the first letter of the Roman alphabet. This point is no doubt obvious but worth mentioning because Tarski's objection to one definition of truth in colloquial languages ((6) on p. 159 of [1956]) appears to depend on taking quotation marks in the object language to be also quotation marks in the metalanguage. Also, perhaps, Quine's quasi quotes (*vide* Quine [1940], pp. 33–7) should best be regarded as the names of quotation symbols.

When a quoted entity is an expression it can have all sorts of properties.[131] It can have certain physical properties, depending on the kind of entity it is; it can have certain syntactical and structural properties depending on its role in $\mathscr{L}$: and it can have certain semantical properties, for our introduction of quotations in 7.8 made essential reference to a model. Quotational contexts can take account of all the properties of an expression and not merely its semantical properties. They are thus said to be *opaque*;[132] for consider two expressions α and β and an assignment V such that

(1) $V(\alpha) = V(\beta)$

Obviously it will not in general follow that

(2) $V(\langle qu, \alpha\rangle) = V(\langle qu, \beta\rangle)$

since the fact that α and β have the same meaning does not require that they are the same expression, and by 7.8, (2) will only be true if α and β are the same expression. Frege's principle then does not apply unrestrictedly through quotational contexts.[133] We shall be particularly interested, however, in looking at properties which do hold of an expression in virtue of its meaning.

To take an example of how the semantic properties of a word can survive quotation, let us have a look at how to express the view of philosophers who claim that entailment is a relation, albeit of a semantic kind, between sentences rather than propositions.[134] We suppose then that ***entails*** $\in F_{\langle 0, 1, 1\rangle}$. Thus if α and β are two sentences

(3) $\langle$***entails***$, \langle qu, \alpha\rangle, \langle qu, \beta\rangle\rangle$

will be a sentence. As the semantic rule for ***entails*** we propose:

7.9 For any $w \in \mathbf{W}$, $w \in \omega_{\boldsymbol{entails}}(a,b)$ iff a and b are sentences and $V(a) \subseteq V(b)$.

Entailment will then indeed be a relation between sentences; it will be that relation which holds iff the set of worlds which is the meaning of a is included in the set of worlds which is the meaning of b.

We have the following:

[131] This is stressed in Quine [1940], p. 23 f. It is also discussed by Goddard and Routley [1966], though they seem to want to use a different symbol depending on the sort of property attributed to the quoted entity.

[132] Opaque in Quine's sense; *vide* [1953], p. 142.

[133] Technically the principle is saved by regarding $\langle qu, \alpha\rangle$ as a symbol of $\mathscr{L}$; though, as we go on to shew, the fact that it is a symbol need not mean that we cannot attribute an internal structure to it.

[134] E.g. Quine [1940], p. 28. (Quine uses the term 'logical implication'.)

7.10 $w \in V(\langle \textit{\textbf{entails}}, \langle qu, \alpha\rangle, \langle qu, \beta\rangle\rangle)$
$\quad$ iff $w \in \omega_{\textit{\textbf{entails}}}(V(\langle qu, \alpha\rangle), V(\langle qu, \beta\rangle))$
$\quad$ iff $w \in \omega_{\textit{\textbf{entails}}}(\alpha, \beta)$
$\quad$ iff $V(\alpha) \subseteq V(\beta)$.

In Chapter Two (p. 33) we discussed an alternative way of looking at entailment. There ***entails*** (or rather ⥽) was a two-place propositional functor in $F_{\langle 0,0,0\rangle}$ with the semantic rule

7.11 For any $w \in \mathbf{W}$ and $a, b, \in \mathbf{D}_0$, $w \in \omega_{⥽}(a,b)$ iff $a \subseteq b$.

From this we easily obtain

7.12 $w \in \langle ⥽, \alpha, \beta\rangle$ iff $V(\alpha) \subseteq V(\beta)$.

7.11 is obviously a simpler rule than 7.9 and seems to have the same effect. But 7.11's advantages are not merely simplicity. It is easy to shew that a rule of the kind 7.9 is just as paradoxical as 7.5 and 7.7 were shewn to be on pp. 101 and 102. All we need to assume is that $\mathscr{L}$ has symbols α and β in F_1 such that

7.13 $V(\alpha) = \langle \textit{\textbf{entails}}, \alpha, \langle qu, \beta\rangle\rangle$

and

7.14 $V(\beta) = \varnothing$.

(I.e. β's value is the empty set of worlds; if $\mathscr{L}$ under V does not have such symbols as α and β then it is easy to consider a language and an assignment obtained from $\mathscr{L}$ by these additions.)

By 7.9, 7.13 and 7.14 we have for any $w \in \mathbf{W}$:

7.15 $w \in V(\langle \textit{\textbf{entails}}, \alpha, \langle qu, \beta\rangle\rangle)$
$\quad$ iff $w \in \omega_{\textit{\textbf{entails}}}(V(\alpha), V(\langle qu, \beta\rangle))$
$\quad$ iff $w \in \omega_{\textit{\textbf{entails}}}(\langle \textit{\textbf{entails}}, \alpha, \langle qu, \beta\rangle\rangle, \beta)$
$\quad$ iff $V(\langle \textit{\textbf{entails}}, \alpha, \langle qu, \beta\rangle\rangle) \subseteq V(\beta)$
$\quad$ iff $V(\langle \textit{\textbf{entails}}, \alpha, \langle qu, \beta\rangle\rangle) \subseteq \varnothing$
$\quad$ iff for all $w \in \mathbf{W}$, $w \notin V(\langle \textit{\textbf{entails}}, \alpha, \langle qu, \beta\rangle\rangle)$

This argument is not an argument against the introduction of the quotation symbol nor even an argument against taking semantic properties of sentences into account, but it may serve as a warning of the care needed in formulating such apparently innocuous principles as 7.9.[135]

[135] In fact 7.9 only gets us into trouble when we have a name which is to be the name of the sentence in which it occurs. Set-theoretical constraints will rule out the formation of this name by a quotation symbol, since $\langle qu, \alpha\rangle$ would then have to be one of the symbols in α. There is no doubt that, with suitable restrictions, 7.9 could be made a consistent definition.

Rules like 7.9 not only cause paradoxes of self-reference, but also cause problems when it comes to the question of whether to translate quoted expressions.

We shall not develop a full-scale theory of translation[136] except to formulate a rather rough and ready criterion for translations. We shall frequently be speaking of a language under a particular meaning assignment and so shall use the expression $\mathscr{L}/V$ to mean 'language $\mathscr{L}$ under meaning assignment V'. We are ignoring the system of domains since for the present we regard them as an extra-linguistic constant feature of the situation.

7.16 An expression α of a language $\mathscr{L}/V$ is a translation of an expression β of a language $\mathscr{L}'/V'$ iff $V(\alpha) = V'(\beta)$.

If *qu* is a quotation symbol in both $\mathscr{L}/V$ and $\mathscr{L}'/V'$ then we have for any $a \in \mathbf{D}^+$

7.17 $V(\langle qu, a\rangle) = a = V'(\langle qu, a\rangle)$.

Hence quoted expressions survive without translation.[137]

This means that if ***entails*** is to have the same meaning in $\mathscr{L}/V$ and $\mathscr{L}'/V'$ then where α and β are sentences:

7.18 $V(\langle \textbf{\textit{entails}}, \langle qu, \alpha\rangle, \langle qu, \beta\rangle\rangle) = V'(\langle \textbf{\textit{entails}}, \langle qu, \alpha\rangle, \langle qu, \beta\rangle\rangle)$
(or, what comes to the same thing, if there are two words which we might label $\textbf{\textit{entails}}_{\mathscr{L}/V}$ and $\textbf{\textit{entails}}_{\mathscr{L}'/V'}$, the two sentences will be translations).

But suppose that $\mathscr{L}/V$ and $\mathscr{L}'/V'$ are exactly the same in syntax and the same in semantics except that for some sentences α and β

7.19 $V(\alpha) = \varnothing$ and $V(\beta) = \mathbf{W}$

and

7.20 $V'(\alpha) = \mathbf{W}$ and $V'(\beta) = \varnothing$.

If we apply 7.9 we get the following (by the reasons of p. 106):

(a) $w \in V(\langle \textbf{\textit{entails}}, \langle qu, \alpha\rangle, \langle qu, \beta\rangle\rangle)$ iff $V(\alpha) \subseteq V(\beta)$

and

(b) $w \in V'(\langle \textbf{\textit{entails}}, \langle qu, \alpha\rangle, \langle qu, \beta\rangle\rangle)$ iff $V'(\alpha) \subseteq V'(\beta)$,

but by the definition of V and V′

[136] Such a theory is developed in Montague [1970a], p. 383 f.

[137] Notice that the same argument will still apply even if we have two quotation symbols, so that *qu* is a quotation symbol of $\mathscr{L}/V$ and *qu′* of $\mathscr{L}'/V'$.

$$V(\alpha) \subseteq V(\beta) \text{ but } V'(\alpha) \nsubseteq V'(\beta)$$

so 7.18 is false.

What are we to make of this? 7.16 and 7.17 guarantee that $\langle qu, \alpha \rangle$ and $\langle qu, \beta \rangle$ in $\mathscr{L}/V$ are translations of themselves in $\mathscr{L}'/V'$ and ***entails*** seems to have the same meaning (defined by 7.9) in both languages yet the two sides of 7.18 are not translations. The paradox arises from the assumption that because ***entails*** in each language obeys 7.9 it has the same meaning. But if we write ω for V(***entails***) and ω' for V′(***entails***) it is easy to see that $\omega \neq \omega'$, for by 7.9:

$$w \in \omega(\alpha, \beta) \text{ iff } V(\alpha) \subseteq V(\beta)$$

and

$$w \in \omega'(\alpha, \beta) \text{ iff } V'(\alpha) \subseteq V'(\beta)$$

and as we have said, one of the right hand sides of these is true but the other false. Thus for at least one pair of arguments from $\mathbf{D}_1$ (and remember sentences of languages are members of $\mathbf{D}_1$), ω and ω' do not coincide.

The point that needs stressing here is that the paradoxes and troubles we have been discussing do not arise because of the use of the quotation symbol. They arise from the peculiar nature of semantical rules like 7.9. There is, I maintain, only one sort of quotation, and philosophers who have thought there were more have done so because they have attributed differences in the kinds of properties expressions may have to different ways of talking about them. Of course the study of rules like 7.9 (and 7.5) is crucial in discussing the semantics for natural language and it is probably one of the most difficult and obscure areas in the philosophy of language. I would be the last to claim that what I have done in the last two sections has done much more than skim the surface but I would like to think that what I have said is enough to shew that problems of self-reference and quotation do not invalidate the application of formal semantics to languages approaching natural languages in the complexity of their structure.

CHAPTER EIGHT

Pragmatics

Our theory of meaning has been based on the assumption that the entities which are the values, in a given model, of expressions in functor categories are determined by the entities which are values of expressions in the basic categories. The values of sentences have been propositions and the values of names have been things. Now the domain $\mathbf{D}_1$ of things has to be wide enough to include everything there is and so in a sense no reconsideration of what its members ought to be will make it any larger than it is already. The domain $\mathbf{D}_0$ of propositions however is, in an intended system of domains (*vide* p. 99), constructed in a fairly specific way out of the set **B** of basic particular situations (*vide* pp. 42–4). What we are now going to consider are reasons for modifying the assumption that the meaning of a sentence is a proposition. We shall mainly give ordinary-language examples but the formal development will deal with λ-categorial languages.

Contexts of use

Sentences whose values seem not to be propositions include those which have been called context-dependent. The sort of context meant is often called a *context of use*.[138] As an example, consider the following two lines of an anonymous poem:[139]

(1) I am Master of this College,
What I don't know isn't knowledge.

[138] Montague [1970a], p. 379.
[139] Quoted in the *Faber Book of Comic Verse*, p. 270.

Now in any world the truth of (1) will depend on who the 'I' refers to and the time the sentence speaks of, for it may well be true of some people at some times but not of other people or at other times. This means that (1) as normally understood in English does not have as its value a proposition as we have defined it.

If we were to apply our present theory of meaning to sentences like (1) directly we should be forced to say that they are ambiguous; and worse, potentially infinitely ambiguous, for the meaning of (1) can change depending upon who is saying it, when he is saying it and possibly other features as well so that, e.g., it may not mean today what it meant yesterday. In some circumstances it has, on this view, no meaning at all, for we may not be supplied with an utterer or an utterance time. Yet this is absurd for we all know what (1) means. And the reason is clear. We know the meaning because we know, given an utterer and utterance time, what proposition a token of (1) asserts. I.e., the meaning of (1) can be thought of as a function from a complex bundle of all the relevant 'contextual information' to a proposition. That is why Richard Montague has called the formal analysis of context dependence 'pragmatics',[140] though it is equally arguable that since we are analysing the *meaning* of (1) it should still be regarded as semantics.

It is possible to regard a possible world itself as part of the context and the meaning of a sentence as a function from a context and (or including) a possible world[141] to a truth value. Indeed our formal development has not required that the things we have called possible worlds be possible worlds at all. They could be this whole 'contextual package' of a time, place, utterer etc. *and* a possible world. Let us follow Dana Scott for the moment and call such packages 'indices'[142] (it is a short word and when neutrality is desirable a good word). A sentence then can be assigned a set of indices (or, if you prefer, for it comes to the same thing, a function from indices into truth values). This means that the value of the sentence (1) will be the set of complete contexts in which it is true. If the context is one which supplies a for the speaker, t for the time and a world w, then $\langle a, t, w \rangle$ will be a member of the meaning of (1) iff in world w, a is the master of the college at t and what a does not know at t is not knowledge at t. Thus

[140] Montague [1970b], p. 68.

[141] Or a heaven, if we want to incorporate the analysis of Chapter Three into an approach of this kind.

[142] Scott [1970], p. 149 f. *Vide* also Montague [1970a], p. 379, and Lewis [1970], especially pp. 22–5, 62–5.

$\langle a,t,w\rangle$ may be a member of $V^+((1))$ while $\langle b,t,w\rangle$ may not be since b may be someone who does not satisfy the condition at t in w, or $\langle a,s,w\rangle$ may not be since a may not satisfy the condition at s in w. If we regard a proposition as a set of possible worlds then it is certainly true that (1) will assert different propositions for different speakers and times since the set $\{w \in \mathbf{W}: \langle a,t,w\rangle \in V^+((1))\}$ may well be different from $\{w \in \mathbf{W}: \langle b,t,w\rangle \in V^+((1))\}$ or from $\{w \in \mathbf{W}: \langle a,s,w\rangle \in V^+((1))\}$. But this does not make the meaning of (1) a variable thing.

If we look closely at (1) we see that time and speaker coordinates are not sufficient: to get the full meaning we must know what 'Master of this College' means, and to know that we must know which college is being talked about. It is not clear what sort of contextual feature supplies this information. The postulation of a 'college coordinate' would certainly do it but this would mean that we should have to have such a coordinate in all value assignments and, if so, why not a country, climate, religion, or 'previous drinks' coordinate?[143]

The trouble with the 'coordinate' approach to contextual dependence is that it seems to require that we give in advance a finite list of contextual features to be taken into account when evaluating a sentence. It is my opinion that there is no such list and that the contextual features to be taken into account depend on the meaning of the sentence. I will therefore set out a rather different manner of dealing with the problem of context-dependence; one which will, I hope, go a little more deeply into the nature of language than does the coordinate or indexical approach.

Utterances

In evaluating (1) we claimed that what was needed was to know at least who said it and when. But (1) might have been said by many different people on many different occasions. It is these occasions of use, or utterances as we shall call them, of (1) which can be said to

[143] A country coordinate would be needed for 'they're playing the National Anthem', climate for 'what a cold winter we had', religion for 'the gods are angry' and 'previous drinks' (as in Cresswell [1972b], p. 8) for 'just fetch your Jim another quart'. Lewis [1970], p. 24 resolves some of these by an 'indicated object' coordinate but one cannot be sure that more generality is not desirable. Both Montague and Lewis have an *assignment coordinate* (Montague [1970a], p. 386 and Lewis, loc. cit.), which enables them to regard the values of the free variables of a formula as supplied by the context. This enables them to reduce λ-categorial languages to pure categorial languages. Both the analysis of context-dependence adopted here, and our attitude to the relation between formal and natural languages as described on pp. 90–2 and taken up again in Part III, do not mix easily with this approach, and any theoretical advantages it might have would be quickly dissipated.

express propositions, and what we shall claim is that a context of use is a property of utterances.

To know what proposition is expressed by (1) we must ask what properties it has. The answer obviously, from what we have said, is: its being uttered by a certain person at a certain time indicating a certain institution (college). Any two utterances of (1) which coincide in these respects will express the same proposition. We shall say that a property ω specifies an utterer, utterance time and indicated institution iff there is a person a, a time t and an institution i such that for any thing b and world w, $\omega(b)$ is true in w iff in world w, b is uttered at time t by a, indicating institution i. Any property of utterances which specifies a speaker, time and indicated institution will be a suitable context for (1) and all utterances of (1) having that property will express the same proposition.

All this suggests that the meaning of (1) should be a function from properties into propositions. It should be a partial function since, as we have seen, not all properties will make an utterance express a proposition. The meaning of (1) will be something like the following:[144]

8.1 V((1)) is that function θ from properties into propositions such that if ω is a property which specifies an utterer a, utterance time t and indicated institution i then $\theta(\omega)$ is the proposition that a is Master of College i at time t and that what a does not know at t is not knowledge at t. If ω is not a property which specifies an utterer, utterance time and indicated institution then ω is not in the domain of θ (so that $\theta(\omega)$ is then undefined).

We are proposing to call certain functions (total or partial) from properties into propositions *open propositions*. This is by analogy with an open sentence. An open sentence, remember (p. 86f), is a sentence with a variable in it and it is called 'open' because its meaning does not become determinate until the variable is given a value. Likewise an open proposition does not have a propositional value until its argument place is filled by a property in its domain. In our terminology an open proposition is not a proposition: it is a function from proper-

[144] The circularity of this definition is apparent only. We are using an English metalanguage to describe the meaning of an English sentence. If we were putting V(1) forward as a way of teaching someone the meaning of (1) then it would, of course, be self-defeating. We are presupposing our discussion in Part I of the nature of propositions. The proposition in the present example is a humanly graspable one, which can be expressed in the English metalanguage (cf. p. 50f).

ties into propositions. When we speak of propositions without qualification we are to be understood as excluding open propositions. Another way of marking the distinction is to speak of the open proposition as the *meaning* of a sentence and the proposition which is its value for a given property as the *sense* of the sentence (with respect to that property). This terminology is used by Montague and may be helpful. Note also that properties are functions from things into propositions, not from things into open propositions.

We shall try now to make this all a bit more precise. We have called the use of a sentence on a particular occasion an utterance and will not be more specific than that. Whether the use of a sentence consists in the writing (or reading) of a mark or set of marks on a surface or of the production of certain sounds is not our concern though we do not mean to deny that it is of genuine philosophical interest. It seems better to take an utterance as an event rather than as an object since a single object, such as a road sign saying 'stop now', may be thought of as asserting different propositions at different times. (In this case we can think of a new utterance occurring as each motorist approaches and reads the sign.) All the same our definition will not require this and will put no restrictions on the kind of things utterances are.[145]

We shall say that a pure categorial language $\mathscr{L}$ is an *utterance language* iff its symbols are sets. By an *utterance*[146] of a symbol α of $\mathscr{L}$ we mean simply a member of α. Where $\mathscr{L}^\lambda$ is the λ-categorial extension of $\mathscr{L}$ then by the proper symbols of $\mathscr{L}^\lambda$ we mean, as before, the symbols of $\mathscr{L}$. We do not require that the variables of $\mathscr{L}^\lambda$ be sets. We define a *token* of an expression α in the following way. A token $\mathfrak{a}$ of α is a sequence whose first member is a member of the first proper symbol of α, whose second is a member of the second proper symbol of α and so on.

E.g., suppose α is

$$\langle \delta_1, \langle \lambda, x_1, \langle \delta_2, x_1, \alpha_1 \rangle \rangle, \langle \delta_2, \alpha_2, \langle \lambda, x_2, \langle \delta_1, \alpha_2, x_2 \rangle \rangle \rangle \rangle$$

145 Montague in Staal [1969], p. 274, cites approvingly the analysis in Bar Hillel [1963] of an utterance token as a pair consisting of a context and an expression. This of course makes the notion of a token clear if we have the notion of a context. I happen to believe that the notion of an utterance, difficult as it may be, is probably clearer than that of a context. Kasher [1971], p. 84 f, splits an utterance up into an *inscription* and a *linguistic setting*.

146 This definition will be modified *infra* pp. 209–15 to take care of cases in which two or more symbols combine to make one word. For absolute strictness we should use the phrase, 'symbol utterance', since we refer to tokens of expressions also as 'utterances'.

then where $\mathfrak{d}_1$, $\mathfrak{d}_2$, $\mathfrak{a}_1$, $\mathfrak{a}_2$ are members of δ_1, δ_2, α_1 and α_2 respectively

$$\langle \mathfrak{d}_1, \mathfrak{d}_2, \mathfrak{a}_1, \mathfrak{d}_2, \mathfrak{a}_2, \mathfrak{d}_1, \mathfrak{a}_2 \rangle$$

will be a token of α.

We no not include in a token anything to represent the λ's and the variables so that a token has all the possibilities of ambiguity described on pp. 90–2. This is a desirable state of affairs because it means that the λ's variables and so on are not part of the token utterances and accords well with the view that they belong in the deep structure and not on the surface.

We pause for a moment to observe that we have been rather more liberal in our definition of 'token of an expression' than its standard use would warrant. E.g., consider an utterance of the word 'the' (as just now written by me say), an utterance of the word 'cow' by a New Zealand dairy farmer some time last year, the word 'jumped' as written in the sand at Waikanae beach, the word 'over' as printed in Monday's *Evening Post*, the word 'the' (as written by me two lines ago) and the word 'moon' as said by an astronaut as he takes a giant step for mankind. This sequence would count, according to the above definition, as a token (given a suitable language) of the sentence 'the cow jumped over the moon'. Of course this is implausible but we can excuse ourselves, first, by saying that there seems no effective way of ruling this sort of case out and, second, by the fact that since our aim is to prove something true of all tokens of sentences then if we can prove it true of all tokens in this wide sense the result will still be true of all those tokens which would be classed as genuine utterances according to our normal intuitions. In any case properties which a token of a sentence must have in order for it to express a proposition will in general include the property of being a genuine utterance; whatever that property is.[147] There is therefore no need for us to make any formal distinction between 'genuine' tokens and others.

A property ω whose domain is restricted to utterances of $\mathscr{L}$ we shall call a *context property* (for $\mathscr{L}$) and we shall use as variables for context properties the letters '$\mathfrak{p}$', '$\mathfrak{q}$', '$\mathfrak{r}$' etc. It is to be understood that just as expressions have already been said to be part of the domain $\mathbf{D}_1$ of

[147] Thus when John Gielgud says to Laurence Olivier 'I am thy father's ghost', his utterance does not express the proposition that Gielgud is Olivier's father's ghost. A play is attempting to portray a possible world, in this case it is a world in which a tenth-century Dane, speaking sixteenth-century English, utters a genuine token of 'I am thy father's ghost'. This token does express a proposition, the proposition that the speaker is the ghost of Hamlet's father. Of course we include possible utterances as well as actual ones in our domain of utterances.

'things' in any interpretation so also tokens of expression are in $\mathbf{D}_1$. Thus context properties will still be functions from $\mathbf{D}_1$ into propositions. And the properties too, of course, are themselves members of $\mathbf{D}_1$ (*vide* p. 99).

Context-dependent interpretations

We have said that a context is a property but this is not quite good enough, for the families of properties which form suitable contexts for a sentence must be ordered in a certain way. For instance a property will be a suitable context for (1) if it specifies a speaker, time and indicated institution. Obviously it will still be a context if it gives other information as well, and further the proposition expressed by (1) will still be the same proposition. Another thing we must ensure is that an utterance can never have two independent properties which might make it express two different propositions. (Of course someone who doesn't know the relevant properties of the utterance may be in doubt about which proposition is expressed, but that is a different matter.)

Given a domain $\mathbf{D}_1$ of things and a set $\mathbf{P}$ of propositions, a property based on $\mathbf{D}_1/\mathbf{P}$ is a function from $\mathbf{D}_1$ into $\mathbf{P}$ (cf. p. 67). A proposition will either be a set of worlds as in Chapter One or a set of heavens as in Chapter Three. In either case we may speak of a proposition as being true or false in a world w (cf. pp. 24 and 43).

Given $\mathbf{D}_1$ and $\mathbf{P}$ we shall say that:

8.2 A family Ω of context properties based on $\mathbf{D}_1/\mathbf{P}$ is a *context family generated by* $\mathfrak{p}^*$ iff for any context property $\mathfrak{p}: \mathfrak{p} \in \Omega$ iff for any token $\mathfrak{a}$ and world w, if $\mathfrak{p}(\mathfrak{a})$ is true in w then $\mathfrak{p}^*(\mathfrak{a})$ is true in w. (Obviously every context property generates a context family.)

By an *open proposition based on* $\mathbf{D}_1/\mathbf{P}$ we mean a total or partial function θ from context properties based on $\mathbf{D}_1/\mathbf{P}$ such that:

8.3 If $\mathfrak{p}$ is in a context family generated by $\mathfrak{p}^*$, and $\mathfrak{p}^*$ is in the domain of θ, then $\theta(\mathfrak{p}) = \theta(\mathfrak{p}^*)$.

8.4 If $\mathfrak{p}$ and $\mathfrak{q}$ are in the domain of θ and $\theta(\mathfrak{p}) \neq \theta(\mathfrak{q})$ then, for any world w and any token $\mathfrak{a}$, at most one of $\mathfrak{p}(\mathfrak{a})$ and $\mathfrak{q}(\mathfrak{a})$ is true in w.

Any member $\mathfrak{p}$ of a context family Ω generated by $\mathfrak{p}^*$ will be a property which gives all the information that $\mathfrak{p}^*$ does, in that if $\mathfrak{a}$ is $\mathfrak{p}$ in w then $\mathfrak{a}$ is $\mathfrak{p}^*$ in w. $\mathfrak{p}$ may give more information as well. Thus if $\mathfrak{p}^*(\mathfrak{a})$ is true in any w iff $\mathfrak{a}$ is uttered by u, $\mathfrak{p}(\mathfrak{a})$ may be true iff $\mathfrak{a}$ is uttered by u at time t. In this case Ω will be the set of all context properties which entail the property of being uttered by u.

Suppose we are given a set **B** of basic particular situations and consequently a set **P** of propositions defined in terms of **B** as on pp. 42–4. By an *intended context-dependent system of domains based on* **B** we mean a function **D** from Syn such that for any σ, τ, $\sigma_1, \ldots, \sigma_n \in$ Syn:

8.5 $\mathbf{D}_0$ is a set of open propositions based on $\mathbf{D}_1/\mathbf{P}$.
8.6 $\mathbf{D}_\sigma \subseteq \mathbf{D}_1 \subseteq \mathbf{U}_\mathbf{B}$.
8.7 If $\sigma = \langle \tau, \sigma_1, \ldots, \sigma_n \rangle$ then $\mathbf{D}_\sigma$ is a set of total or partial functions from $\mathbf{D}_{\sigma_1} \times \ldots \times \mathbf{D}_{\sigma_n}$ into $\mathbf{D}_\tau$. (Note that this definition parallels that of p. 99 with the one exception in the definition of $\mathbf{D}_0$.)

A *context-dependent interpretation* for $\mathscr{L}^\lambda$ based on **D** is got by adding an assignment function V exactly as on p. 85f. We cannot define a model since the members of $\mathbf{D}_0$, being open propositions, cannot be true or false except with reference to a context property.

Given a context-dependent interpretation for a language $\mathscr{L}^\lambda$ we shall say that:

8.8 An utterance $\mathfrak{a}$ expresses a proposition a in a world w iff $\mathfrak{a}$ is a token of a sentence α and there is some context property $\mathfrak{p}$ such that $\mathfrak{p}(\mathfrak{a})$ is true in w and $V^+(\alpha)(\mathfrak{p}) = a$.

Since $\mathfrak{a}$ may be a token of other sentences besides α it may well express many different propositions. But *qua* token of α we want it to be unambiguous. I.e., we must rule out the possibility that $\mathfrak{a}$ may have two distinct properties $\mathfrak{p}$ and $\mathfrak{q}$ such that $V^+(\alpha)(\mathfrak{p}) \neq V^+(\alpha)(\mathfrak{q})$. Since $V^+(\alpha)$ is an open proposition then by 8.4 (p. 115) if $V^+(\alpha)(\mathfrak{p}) \neq V^+(\alpha)(\mathfrak{q})$ then at most one of $\mathfrak{p}$ and $\mathfrak{q}$ will be true of $\mathfrak{a}$ in w.

An utterance expresses a proposition with respect to a world. For it may happen that a token of, say, (1) has properties in one world different from the properties it has in another. (1) is in fact the last half of a poem which runs:

(2) First come I, my name is Jowett,
There's no knowledge but I know it.
I am Master of this College,
What I don't know isn't knowledge.

It refers to Benjamin Jowett who was Master of Balliol College, Oxford, from 1870 to 1893. It is highly unlikely that Jowett, in the real world, ever uttered a token of (2) and if so all utterances of (2), and probably of (1) as well, in the real world are not genuine ones. Yet of course there are possible worlds in which Jowett did utter (2) seriously and did express a proposition. Which proposition he expressed will be a contingent matter and in each world will depend on the properties the utterance has in that world.

We shall now feed back our formal definitions into a simple sentence of a categorial language. Take:

(3) ⟨***sleeps***, ***Jones***⟩

where ***Jones*** $\in F_1$ and ***sleeps*** $\in F_{\langle 0, 1 \rangle}$.
Let us say that Jones is a member of $\mathbf{D}_1$ and that V(***Jones***) = Jones. V(***sleeps***) will have to be a function from $\mathbf{D}_1$ into open propositions. As a first shot let us try the following:

8.9 V(***sleeps***) is that function ω from members of $\mathbf{D}_1$ to open propositions such that if $a \in \mathbf{D}_1$, $\omega(a)$ is the open proposition θ such that if $\mathfrak{p}$ is a context property which specifies a time t (cf. p. 112) then $\theta(\mathfrak{p})$ is the proposition that a is asleep at t. Otherwise $\mathfrak{p}$ is not in the domain of θ (so that θ is undefined for that argument).[148]

With this rule $V^+((3))$ will be the open proposition θ such that if $\mathfrak{p}$ is a context property which specifies a time t then $\theta(\mathfrak{p})$ is the proposition that Jones is asleep at t.

Unfortunately things are not quite as simple as that. First the argument of ***sleeps*** may also be a context-dependent expression as in[149]

(4) ⟨***sleeps***, ***I***⟩

We certainly do not want to say that the proposition expressed by (4) at a time t is that the functional entity denoted by ***I*** is asleep at t; for that entity is a function ζ such that if $\mathfrak{p}$ is a property which specifies an utterer u[150] then $\zeta(\mathfrak{p})$ is u, and it is $\zeta(\mathfrak{p})$, i.e. u, which would be claimed to be asleep, not ζ. The second point is that by our account on p. 112 to say that a property $\mathfrak{p}$ is a property which specifies a time t is to say that for any utterance $\mathfrak{a}$ and any world w $\mathfrak{p}(\mathfrak{a})$ is true in w iff $\mathfrak{a}$ is uttered in w at t; and as we said on p. 115 any property which specifies other things in addition will also be a context. So instead of saying simply that $\mathfrak{p}$ specifies a time t we should say rather that $\mathfrak{p}$ is in a

148 This shews we are taking ***sleeps*** in the sense of the continuous present (cf. *infra* p. 193 f).

149 We shall have something to say on p. 190 on the question of subject-predicate agreement. For the present we simply take (4) as a rather artificial rendering of 'I sleep'.

150 To say that $\mathfrak{p}$ specifies an utterer u, is to say that for any utterance a of $\mathscr{L}$, $\mathfrak{p}(\mathfrak{a})$ is true in a world w iff $\mathfrak{a}$ is uttered in w by u. We have no analysis to offer of what it is for u to utter $\mathfrak{a}$.

context family generated (in the sense of p. 145) by a property $\mathfrak{p}^*$ which specifies a time *t*.

We shall define an *open individual* as a function ζ whose domain is a set of context properties such that:

8.10 If $\mathfrak{p}$ and $\mathfrak{q}$ are in the same context family (*vide* p. 115) then $\zeta(\mathfrak{p}) = \zeta(\mathfrak{q})$.

8.11 If $\mathfrak{p}$ and $\mathfrak{q}$ are in the domain of ζ and are in different context families then for any utterance $\mathfrak{a}$ at most one of $\mathfrak{p}(\mathfrak{a})$ and $\mathfrak{q}(\mathfrak{a})$ is true in any world *w*.

This definition was not introduced along with the definition of an open proposition because open individuals will be in $\mathbf{D}_1$ in any case and so they do not necessitate any change in our general definition.

8.12 V(***I***) is the open individual ζ such that where $\mathfrak{p}$ is a property in a context family generated by a property $\mathfrak{p}$ which specifies an utterer *u* then $\zeta(\mathfrak{p}) = u$. Otherwise $\mathfrak{p}$ is not in the domain of ζ.

The revised definition of V(***sleeps***) is:

8.13 V(***sleeps***) is that function ω from open individuals to open propositions such that if ζ is an open individual then $\omega(\zeta)$ is the open proposition θ such that if $\mathfrak{p}$ is a property in the context family generated by a property $\mathfrak{p}^*$ which specifies a time *t* then $\theta(\mathfrak{p})$ is the proposition that $\zeta(\mathfrak{p})$ is asleep at *t*.

This procedure assumes that the argument of ***sleeps*** is always assigned an open individual. In the case of ***Jones*** it would have to be the constant function whose value for every context property is Jones. But let us see how 8.13 combines with 8.12 to give the intended value of (4):

$$\begin{aligned} V(\langle \boldsymbol{sleeps}, \boldsymbol{I} \rangle) &= \omega_{\boldsymbol{sleeps}}(V(\boldsymbol{I})) \\ &= \omega_{\boldsymbol{sleeps}}(\zeta) \end{aligned}$$

where ζ satisfies 8.12.

Now (4) will only express a proposition with respect to a property in a context family generated by a $\mathfrak{p}^*$ which specifies both a time *t* of utterance and an utterer *u* since by 8.13 any open proposition formed by $\omega_{\boldsymbol{sleeps}}$ is a function whose domain consists of context properties which

(a) are in a family generated by a property which specifies a time *t* and

(b) are in the domain of V(***I***) – which means that they must be in a family generated by a property which specifies an utterer *u*.

It is easy to see that the intersection of two families of this kind will be a family generated by a property which specifies a time *t* and an utterer *u*. If $\mathfrak{p}$ is in a context family generated by a property which specifies a time *t* and an utterer *u* then where $V(\langle \textbf{\textit{sleeps}}, \textbf{\textit{I}} \rangle) = \theta$, by 8.13 $\theta(\mathfrak{p})$ is the proposition that $\zeta(\mathfrak{p})$ is asleep at *t*; so that $\theta(\mathfrak{p})$ is the proposition that the utterer specified by $\mathfrak{p}$ is asleep at the time specified by $\mathfrak{p}$. Which means (by 8.8, p. 116) that any utterance of (4) by *u* at *t* expresses the proposition that *u* is asleep at *t*.[151]

If we want to evaluate a complex sentence in a given context we sometimes need to know only the values of the parts of the sentence in that context,[152] but sometimes we need to know more. Consider the symbol ***past*** $\in F_{\langle 0, 0 \rangle}$. Applying it to (3) we get[153]

(5) $\langle \textbf{\textit{past}}, \langle \textbf{\textit{sleeps}}, \textbf{\textit{Jones}} \rangle\rangle$

To know the value of (5) with respect to a property which specifies a time *t* we need to have more than the proposition that Jones is asleep at *t* because the truth of (5) at time *t* in a given world will not depend on any feature of the proposition that Jones is asleep at *t*. (5) will be true at *t* in *w* iff Jones is asleep at some *t′* earlier than *t*. So ***past*** operates on the whole meaning of $\langle \textbf{\textit{sleeps}}, \textbf{\textit{Jones}} \rangle$. In rough terms we can say that a sentence $\langle \textbf{\textit{past}}, \alpha \rangle$ is true in *w* with respect to a property $\mathfrak{q}$ in a context family which specifies *t* iff the meaning of α is a function θ such that for some property $\mathfrak{p}$, like $\mathfrak{q}$ except in specifying a time *t′* earlier than *t*, the value of θ at $\mathfrak{p}$ is a proposition which is true in *w* (*vide* 12.4, p. 195). This justifies us in regarding V(***past***) as a function from open propositions to open propositions as indeed it should be by the principles of p. 115.

Presuppositions

There are many undoubtedly meaningful sentences which appear not to express a proposition unless certain conditions are fulfilled. We think of Russell's

[151] Assuming that no genuine utterance can occur when the utterer is asleep (perhaps a dubious assumption), it should be easy to see how our meaning rules ensure that every genuine token of (4) must express a false proposition. It would be equally easy to shew that every genuine token of $\langle \textbf{\textit{exists}}, \textbf{\textit{I}} \rangle$ and $\langle \textbf{\textit{thinks}}, \textbf{\textit{I}} \rangle$ must express a true proposition. This does not of course shew that the propositions they express are anything but contingent and publicly falsifiable.

[152] Contexts of this kind are called 'distributive contexts' on p. 9 of Cresswell [1972b]. The erroneous impression is given in that article that all contexts are distributive. Our present approach involves no loss since we can always define the effect of a distributive context. (In the way in which, on p. 70 *supra*, extensional properties of individuals were shewn to be expressible in terms of properties of individual concepts.)

[153] The modifications suggested *infra*, p. 210, will give us **slept** for ***past, sleeps.***

(1) The present king of France is bald.

(1) is sometimes said to *presuppose* that there is exactly one present king of France. Russell thought that (1) asserted, among other things, that there is exactly one present king of France, and that therefore (1) is currently false. To say that it presupposes that there is exactly one king of France is, on the other hand, to say that a current utterance of it does not express a proposition at all and that (1) is therefore neither true nor false.

The first thing we are to note about this solution is that it must be *utterances* of (1) which express or fail to express a proposition. Utterances of (1) made in, say, 1750 certainly might have expressed propositions. This suggests that sentences like (1) can be dealt with by the theory of context dependence which we have been developing in this chapter. For we have been regarding the meanings of sentences as open propositions, viz. as partial functions from properties into propositions. Since they are partial functions a given token $\mathfrak{a}$ of a sentence α might not have any of the properties in the domain of the open proposition assigned to α. In such a case $\mathfrak{a}$ will fail to express a proposition, by the definition on p. 116.

We can now look at the meaning of (1). It is not part of the purpose of this book to put forward particular semantical analyses of words in English or any other language and whenever we do so it is for illustration only. In the present instance we are not suggesting that the semantical rule we shall give reflects the normal English treatment of definite descriptions but it seems to formalize at least one intuitively reasonable proposal.[154] Nor are we concerned at the moment to shew how to analyse complex descriptive phrases like 'the present king of France' or complex predicates like 'is bald'. We shall suppose that the first is a name of category 1 and the second a predicate of category $\langle 0, 1\rangle$. Let us refer to the first as α and the second as δ. Thus (1) can be thought of as having the form:

(2) $\langle \delta, \alpha\rangle$

We propose for δ the rule:

8.14 V(δ) is that function ω from individuals to open propositions such that for any individual a, $\omega(a)$ is the open proposition θ such that if $\mathfrak{p}$ is a context property which specifies a time t (cf. p. 112) then $\theta(\mathfrak{p})$ is true in a world w iff a is bald at t in w.

[154] The view of presupposition that I am trying to formalize is that of Strawson [1950], though some of the details differ.

(This definition has been given in the style of 8.9 (p. 117). It should of course be complicated along the lines of 8.13 but the extra complication is more likely to obscure the point being made than to assist it.) And for α:

8.15 $V(\alpha)$ is the open individual ζ (cf. p. 118) such that for any context property $\mathfrak{p}$, $\zeta(\mathfrak{p}) = k$ if $\mathfrak{p}$ is a property such that, in any world w and for any utterance $\mathfrak{a}$, $\mathfrak{p}(\mathfrak{a})$ is true in w iff k is the one and only king of France in w at the time at which $\mathfrak{a}$ occurs. Otherwise $\mathfrak{p}$ is not in the domain of ζ (so that $\zeta(\mathfrak{p})$ is then undefined).

Now by 8.8 (p. 116) an utterance token of (1) will express a proposition only if it has a property which is in the domain of the open proposition which is the meaning of (1). By 8.15 this will only be so if the utterance occurs when there is exactly one king of France. Since $\theta(\mathfrak{p})$ lacks a value when there is no king of France, no utterance of (1) in the real world at present will express a proposition (by 8.8). To call the existence of a king of France a presupposition of (1) is simply to say that if it is false then no token of (1) will express a proposition.[155] Note that there is no suggestion here that it expresses a truth-valueless proposition, or a proposition with some third value.[156] It expresses no proposition at all. Yet (1) is meaningful: its meaning is an open proposition, that is, a function from properties into propositions.

Some philosophers would object to 8.15 on the ground that the kind of property needed for an utterance token of (1) to express a proposition according to that rule is one which requires knowledge of facts beyond those of which knowledge is in any case required for communication.[157] Thus it might be held that for successful

[155] Obviously we could give a rule for ***if*** along the same lines. $\langle \textit{\textbf{if}}, \alpha, \beta \rangle$ would express the proposition expressed by β if α is true, and no proposition if it is not.

[156] Woodruff [1970] proposes a three-valued logic which is supposed to represent Strawson's view of presupposition. Whether or not it represents Strawson, it will not quite do for us. Our propositions are always either true or false in any possible world. The advantage of an analysis in terms of a third truth value is that a sentence which lacks a presupposition can still be meaningful. Our analysis shares this advantage.

[157] Perhaps this requirement is unworrying. It seems a plausible principle to hold that someone may be presumed to know the *meaning* of what he says (if his utterance is a genuine one); but perhaps not the proposition his utterance expresses. E.g., John goes to sleep on Tuesday and wakes up after an hour mistakenly thinking he has slept for 25 hours. He utters a token of the sentence: 'The day before yesterday I went on a protest march'. The proposition his utterance expresses is that he marched on Sunday but the proposition he *thinks* it expresses is that he marched on Monday.

communication those in a communication situation require, or at least can reasonably be expected to know, who is uttering the sentence, when it is being uttered and so on, but they should not be expected to know whether or not there is a king of France. What is really presupposed, they will say, is not that there *is* a king of France, but merely that the speaker and hearer should believe of someone that he is the present king of France; and the utterance of (1) will then express the proposition that that person is bald. As we have said there is nothing sacred about 8.15 and it could easily be modified in the direction indicated by our last remarks.

A more extreme line is to say that (1) might be true even though the speaker and hearer know that there is no present king of France but both intend to say of a particular person that he is bald and use the expression 'the present king of France' to refer to him.[158] This does seem to be a situation which cannot be covered by a meaning rule for the description and it seems best accounted for by saying that the phrase is not being used with its accustomed meaning but is being used as if it were a name made up for the purpose. We shall later (pp. 238–40) discuss situations in which a sentence cannot have its usual meaning. In these situations the context affects what is said in a more radical way than the way considered in this chapter. Our present theory of context shews how the meaning of the sentence combines with the context to give a proposition. The more radical kind of contextual situation is one in which the context forces a different meaning or no meaning at all on the sentence. This latter situation is one whose study belongs to a theory of language-use rather than semantics proper and is perhaps what would more normally be described as real pragmatics than would what we have so far been doing.

Contexts and quotation

Our theory of quotation was general enough to allow anything at all to be quoted. In particular we can quote not only expressions but tokens of expressions; not only $\langle qu, \alpha \rangle$ but also $\langle qu, \mathrm{a} \rangle$ may be symbols of F_1. Now α and a are unquestionably different things and so $V(\langle qu, \alpha \rangle) \neq V(\langle qu, \mathrm{a} \rangle)$ in any assignment in which qu is a quotation symbol. Thus a sentence in which $\langle qu, \alpha \rangle$ occurs, and the same sentence but with $\langle qu, \mathrm{a} \rangle$ in its place, may well differ in truth value in some world.

[158] E.g. Donellan [1966] and [1970].

The question which now arises is that of the status of tokens of these sentences. Technically $\langle qu, \alpha \rangle$ and $\langle qu, \mathfrak{a} \rangle$ are symbols. But this causes a difficulty, for even if $\mathscr{L}$ is an utterance language, $\langle qu, \alpha \rangle$ and $\langle qu, \mathfrak{a} \rangle$ are ordered pairs and not sets of utterances, so that we cannot say here as we did of other symbols that an utterance of a quotation is just a member of the quotation. This means that we must extend our definitions of 'utterance' and 'token'.

On p. 104 we alluded to the question of whether to treat *qu* as a logical symbol which would be deleted in obtaining the surface language or as a proper symbol.[159] If we treat it as the latter and it occurs in an utterance language it will have to be a set whose members are utterances. One way of obtaining a token of $\langle qu, \alpha \rangle$, and perhaps the way followed in natural language, is to let it be the sequence whose first member is a member of *qu* (if *qu* is a proper symbol), whose second member (or whose first if *qu* is a logical symbol) is a member of the first symbol of α, and so on. Defining a token of $\langle qu, \mathfrak{a} \rangle$ is not so easy for $\mathfrak{a}$ is already a token. One way is simply to tolerate the resultant ambiguity and let $\mathfrak{a}$ itself, possibly preceded by a token of *qu*, be a token of itself. This means that there will be no way of distinguishing between a token of $\langle qu, \alpha \rangle$ and $\langle qu, \mathfrak{a} \rangle$.

We are already allowing tokens to be ambiguous between different sentences and the extra ambiguity involved here is reflected in natural language. In fact it is very seldom that utterances are quoted. Normally when we want to talk about an utterance we do so by a description like:

(1) The first utterance of the word 'the' by Jones on Christmas Day of 1965.

One might just conceivably have occasion to say something like

(2) 'BLUE' is written in large letters for emphasis

but this would normally be in a situation in which the ambiguity admitted of only one sensible resolution. In any case one can avoid quoting tokens by paraphrasing (2) as

(3) This token of 'BLUE' is written in large letters

where what is being quoted is actually the word 'blue' and not a token of it, but the property being ascribed to that word is one of having a certain demonstratively indicated token written in large letters.

One could of course construct a language in which quotation of

[159] *qu* might be a logical (and therefore deleted) symbol in spoken languages but a proper symbol in written languages.

tokens was explicitly marked by some device.[160] The important thing to remember about what we have said is that there is no ambiguity in the original sentences but only in tokens of them.

We have distinguished between $\langle qu, \alpha \rangle$ and $\langle qu, \mathfrak{a} \rangle$ where α is a sentence (of a λ-categorial language) and $\mathfrak{a}$ is a token of α, but of course one may well wish to quote the shallow structure of α, as indeed our ordinary language examples have done. Let $s(\alpha)$ be the sequence formed by taking the proper symbols of α in the order in which they occur in α. This is not the same as a token of α, for the members of $s(\alpha)$ are the actual symbols and not their members. We may frequently wish to have the quotation $\langle qu, s(\alpha) \rangle$, particularly where there are two non-synonymous sentences α and β such that $s(\alpha) = s(\beta)$ and we want to form a sentence like

(4) What he actually said was $\langle qu, s(\alpha) \rangle$ but I don't know what he meant by it

(the doubt being about whether to take it as a surface instance of α or of β). Here too we have a slight problem in obtaining a token since (4) may well be true while the following is false:

(5) What he actually said was $\langle qu, \alpha \rangle$ but I don't know what he meant by it.

If we obtain the token of both (4) and (5) by taking the sequence of instances of the proper symbols in order we shall find that any token of the one is also a token of the other (and their surface sentences are identical). We have here a similar situation to the one above. We can either say that the ambiguity in the surface structure of (4) and (5) does no more than reflect the ambiguity of $s(\alpha)$ and $s(\beta)$ and so need not be resolved at the surface or the token level, or we can incorporate devices such as extra proper symbols to deal with it. Probably the former course is closest to natural language and the latter, if ever needed, would be required only for certain specialized fields of discourse, probably in philosophy.

The important thing however is to be alive to the differences in the deep structure and, as we have shewn, our theory of quotation involves no difficulties or ambiguities at that level.

[160] As we have used different kinds of letters for token variables and expression variables. Various possible conventions of this kind are described in Goddard and Routley [1966].

PART THREE

English as a Categorial Language

CHAPTER NINE

Some Parts of Speech

Our discussion of natural languages will be restricted to the formal treatment of English. A compelling reason for this is to avoid the question of how far the formal features of English are peculiar to it and how far they occur more widely. This question is one of immense philosophical and linguistic importance but it would seem better to have taken substantial steps toward the formalization of one language before asking how universally applicable the methods used are. The other reason is that it is likely that many, if not most, of the problems we come across in trying to formalize English may well occur, even if in a superficially different form, in the treatment of other languages.[161]

A λ-categorial base for English

This part of the book will assume that the sentences of English are to be obtained from the sentences of a λ-categorial language $\mathscr{L}^\lambda$ by deletion of the logical symbols (viz. the λ's and the variables) in the way set out on pp. 90–2.

We propose to call the sentences of $\mathscr{L}^\lambda$ the *λ-deep structures* of English. Mostly we shall simply talk about the deep structures but always it will be in this technical sense. The phrase 'deep structure' has been chosen (rather advisedly) as the one which gets closest to what we are after. It has however acquired a very specialized sense in transformational theory, a sense from which we must dissociate ourselves. This specialized sense is one which can only be defined in

[161] Of course the real reason is that as a native English speaker I can act as my own informant.

theories which are based on Chomsky's *Aspects*[162] model of language description and is at the heart of the debate on the question of the autonomy of syntax. As we do not wish to take sides on this issue, we stress that our use of the phrase 'deep structure', though analogous, is not the same as the precise sense it has in Chomsky's writings. A similar warning applies to the terms 'surface structure' (*vide* p. 210) and 'shallow structure'. We define the *shallow structure*[163] of a sentence α of a λ-categorial language $\mathscr{L}^{\lambda}$ as the sequence $s(\alpha)$ which consists of the proper symbols of α (*vide* p. 90) in the order in which they occur in α.

In the next few chapters we shall attempt to shew how a wide class of English sentences can be thought of as obtained in this way; a class extensive enough to suggest that, with the refinements described in Chapter Thirteen (pp. 209–15), all of English might be so obtained. We will not, however, be providing even a partial grammar for English by doing this since there will be many shallow structures which will not be acceptable English sentences. We explore in Chapter Thirteen the question of how to formulate principles which restrict the deep structures to those which give acceptable surface sentences. If we were engaged in empirical linguistics it would be a legitimate criticism of this part of the book that we do not shew how to generate only those deep structures which are acceptable in English; but since our aim is the rather different one of trying to shew how the semantical theory we have been developing in Parts I and II can be applied to a natural language it is enough to shew that a significant range of sentences which *are* acceptable can be regarded as having λ-deep structures which reflect their intuitive meanings.

In this chapter we shall consider the question of the syntactic category into which we should put some of the major parts of speech recognized by traditional grammar, as they occur in deep structure. Although we use the traditional names we do not define them. It would be possible in principle, though tedious and unnecessary in practice, to say what, e.g., a noun is by giving a finite list of all the symbols which are to count as nouns in English. Since we are only

[162] Chomsky [1965]. A good introduction to the theory of semantic syntax or generative semantics is found in Lakoff [1971a]. We discuss it briefly on p. 146 f.

[163] The reason we do not call it 'surface structure' will appear as we proceed since we shall meet a number of structures which will clearly need further transformation to give us surface sentences. An account of the derivation of surface structure will be given early in Chapter Thirteen (pp. 209–15).

interested in the syntactic category they belong to in the deep structure there is no need for us to formulate principles for recognizing them in the surface structure. Actually at this stage not all the traditional grammatical distinctions will be preserved; e.g., we shall make no distinction between common nouns and intransitive verbs. It will be the task of later chapters to refine the rather rough and ready account we are about to present and, hopefully, in a series of ever diminishing circles, approach, so to speak, closer and closer to the natural language which is our ultimate, albeit at times elusive, goal.

The λ-categorial language $\mathscr{L}^{\lambda}$ on which English is to be based will have associated with it a meaning assignment V, based on some intended system of domains as described on pp. 98–100 or on a context-dependent system of domains as described on pp. 115–17. Actually, as we saw in Chapter Four (pp. 58–60), it should probably be characterized by a communication class of meaning assignments. In this part of the book we shall from time to time illustrate the semantics of $\mathscr{L}^{\lambda}$ for a given symbol by giving a rule which we think reflects the meaning of that word in English. It needs to be stressed that every time we do this we are merely illustrating what that meaning might be. In a number of cases it is pretty clear that the rule we present must be something of an over-simplification. We do not regard it as part of our task to say what the meaning of any word in English actually is but only to say enough to make plausible the idea of a λ-categorial deep structure.

When we give a semantic rule for illustration we shall usually do so as if the intended meaning assignment were based on a domain of propositions which (as in Chapter One, p. 24) are sets of possible worlds instead of (as in Chapter Three, p. 42) sets of heavens. This is because we are only offering rough and ready illustrations. To take an example, suppose we give the semantic rule for ***not*** by quoting [V~] on p. 32, viz.:

V(***not***) is that function $\omega \in \mathbf{D}_{\langle 0, 0 \rangle}$ such that for any $a \in \mathbf{D}_0$ and $w \in \mathbf{W}$, $w \in \omega(a)$ iff $w \notin a$.

What we really mean is that in any model in the communication class of the λ-categorial base of English ***not*** must be assigned a functor which makes out of a proposition (set of heavens) another proposition which is true in a world (i.e., contains that world-heaven) iff the original proposition is false in that world. But it is obviously much easier to speak as though it was only sets of worlds we had to deal with.[164]

Another point to notice is that we shall sometimes omit to mention the possibility of a function which is undefined for some arguments. Thus we may write, where, say, $\omega \in \mathbf{D}_{\langle 0, 1\rangle}$, that for any $w \in \mathbf{W}$ and $a \in \mathbf{D}_1$, $w \in \omega(a)$ iff .... It may happen that no total function satisfying this definition is in $\mathbf{D}_{\langle 0, 1\rangle}$ and what our rule is then to be interpreted as saying is that ω is to be some big partial function in $\mathbf{D}_{\langle 0, 1\rangle}$ whose domain includes all the things we intuitively want and which is such that for any a in the domain of ω, $w \in \omega(a)$ iff ....

All of these simplifications would be unwarranted if our purpose were to do any more than indicate reasons for supposing that every English sentence corresponds to a set of deep structures in a λ-categorial base.

Nominals

In the sentences

(1) ***John ran away***

(2) ***everyone loves someone***

(3) ***Arabella loves the Prime Minister of New Zealand***

John, ***everyone***, ***someone***, ***Arabella*** and ***the Prime Minister of New Zealand*** are all what we may call *nominals*.[165] If we assume that (1)–(3) are shallow sentences of a λ-categorial language then we are faced with the problem of giving a categorial analysis of the words in them. We have been treating ***John*** and ***Arabella*** as of category 1 and what we said on p. 68 would suggest that ***the Prime Minister of New Zealand*** should also be (a complex expression) of the same category. On the other hand ***everyone*** and ***someone*** were, in Chapter Six, quite clearly asserted to be of category $\langle 0, \langle 0, 1\rangle\rangle$.

If we want to have a λ-categorial language in which some of the nominals are of category 1 and others are of category $\langle 0, \langle 0, 1\rangle\rangle$ we shall have to say that the treatment of them all as of grammatically

[164] Also, of course, the meaning assignment for English must be a context-dependent one, but it proves somewhat easier to illustrate many of our semantic rules ignoring this for a while. Context-dependence in English is taken up in Chapter Eleven.

[165] Many linguists use the term 'noun phrase' but this might be confusing since nominals and complex noun expressions, on the view developed in this chapter, are quite different. Strictly if (1) is a shallow structure of a λ-categorial language sentence it should be represented as $\langle$***John, ran, away***$\rangle$, but since a shallow structure is simply a sequence we omit the angle brackets and commas, and represent it as we would an ordinary English sentence.

the same class in the shallow structure does not correspond with their status in deep structure; or to put the point in another way, that their 'grammatical form' does not correspond with their 'logical form'. This view indeed appears to be one which has been held by many logicians and philosophers.[166]

Now there are, as we shewed on pp. 80–3, very good reasons for not treating ***everyone*** and ***someone*** as of category 1 and so there are good reasons for not treating all nominals as of that category. But there are no good reasons for not treating all nominals as of category $\langle 0, \langle 0, 1\rangle\rangle$. We shall shew immediately that nothing is lost by letting ***John*** and ***Arabella*** be of category $\langle 0, \langle 0, 1\rangle\rangle$, and in a later section (pp. 147–50) that a great deal is to be gained by letting definite descriptions be of category $\langle 0, \langle 0, 1\rangle\rangle$.[167]

Given any categorial language $\mathscr{L}$ and an assignment V (in some intended system of domains as described on p. 99) to its symbols we can, as shewn on p. 87 f, speak of the induced assignment V^+ to all the closed expressions of the λ-categorial extension of $\mathscr{L}$. Consider then a closed expression β in E_1 such that for some $a \in \mathbf{D}_1$, $V^+(\beta) = a$. (E.g. if ***John*** $\in E_1$ and John $\in \mathbf{D}_1$ then we might have $V^+($***John***$) =$ John.) We want to define the conditions under which the assignment makes an expression α in $E_{\langle 0, \langle 0, 1\rangle\rangle}$ do the same work as β in the sense of picking out the same individual a of $\mathbf{D}_1$.

We shall say that α *corresponds referentially with* β *in* $\mathscr{L}$ *under* V iff $\beta \in E_1$ and $\alpha \in E_{\langle 0, \langle 0, 1\rangle\rangle}$[168] and

9.1 $V^+(\alpha)$ is that function ζ from $\mathbf{D}_{\langle 0, 1\rangle}$ into $\mathbf{D}_0$ such that for any $\omega \in \mathbf{D}_{\langle 0, 1\rangle}$, $\zeta(\omega) = \omega(V^+(\beta))$. (Obviously if $\omega(V^+(\beta))$ is undefined so is $\zeta(\omega)$.)

As a consequence of 9.1 we may prove the following:

9.2 If α corresponds referentially with β in $\mathscr{L}$ under V, γ is any expression in any category σ and $x \in X_1$, then $V^+(\langle \alpha, \langle \lambda, x, \gamma\rangle\rangle) = V^+(\gamma[\beta/x])$ where $\gamma[\beta/x]$ is as defined on p. 89.

9.2 is proved by the principles of λ-conversion.
Principle 6.21 of p. 89 guarantees that

$$V^+(\gamma[\beta/x]) = V^+(\langle\langle \lambda, x, \gamma\rangle, \beta\rangle)$$

[166] It is perhaps best known in the form of Russell's theory of descriptions; *vide* Whitehead and Russell [1910], especially p. 30 f.

[167] Cf. Harman [1970], p. 287 f.

[168] This definition could be generalized to certain other pairs of categories, but we only need it for the ones given.

and 6.10 of p. 86 shews that this is equal to

$$V^+(\langle\lambda, x, \gamma\rangle)(V^+(\beta))$$

which by 9.1 is

$$V^+(\alpha)(V^+(\langle\lambda, x, \gamma\rangle))$$

which is

$$V^+(\langle\alpha, \langle\lambda, x, \gamma\rangle\rangle)$$

thus satisfying 9.2.

9.2 can be illustrated by seeing how ***John*** functions when of category $\langle 0, \langle 0, 1\rangle\rangle$. Take a predicate like ***runs*** $\in F_{\langle 0, 1\rangle}$. Then $\langle$***John***, ***runs***$\rangle$ will be true iff V(***runs***) has the (higher-order) property of being instantiated by John, just as $\langle$***someone***, ***runs***$\rangle$ is true iff V(***runs***) has the property of being instantiated by someone. Given that F_1 contains, say, ***John****, designating John, 9.2 says that $\langle$***John***, ***runs***$\rangle$ is to be true (i.e., ***runs*** is among the predicates true of John) iff $\langle$***runs***, ***John****$\rangle$ is true (i.e., iff John satisfies the predicate ***runs***).

What all this shews is that if we have expressions of $\mathscr{L}^\lambda$ in E_1 then we can always have expressions in $E_{\langle 0, \langle 0, 1\rangle\rangle}$ which do the same work. Therefore a language which contains no proper symbols of category 1 is not inherently any poorer than one which does contain such symbols.

If $\alpha \in E_{\langle 0, \langle 0, 1\rangle\rangle}$ we shall call α a *logically proper name* in $\mathscr{L}$ under V iff:

9.3 $V^+(\alpha)$ is a function ζ for which there is some $a \in \mathbf{D}_1$ such that for every $\omega \in \mathbf{D}_{\langle 0, 1\rangle}$, $\zeta(\omega) = \omega(a)$.

The sense of 9.3 is that if α is a logically proper name under an assignment V then there is some $a \in \mathbf{D}_1$ such that where β is any one-place predicate, $\langle\alpha, \beta\rangle$ will, under V, be true in world w iff β is true of a. In such a case we can say that α picks out a. Notice that the definiens makes no reference to the word 'name'. Nor do we give any analysis of the process of using an expression to name something. On our approach this would be a confusion between meaning and use (*vide* p. 2 f). Given an adequate theory of language use we can say that a person is using α to name a (logically properly) iff the language $\mathscr{L}/V$ which he is using is one in which α is a logically proper name (in the sense of 9.3) which picks out a. Treating names as of category $\langle 0, \langle 0, 1\rangle\rangle$ enables us to remain neutral on the question of whether the proper names of ordinary language are logically proper or not. We do not have to pronounce on whether ***Socrates*** is really a logically proper name or a concealed description which means, say, 'the teacher of

Plato'; or on the equally difficult question of whether a person now using the word ***Plato*** can really be referring to Plato.

Our avoidance of issues such as those mentioned in the last paragraph may sound a little underhand. For, after all, although we may have no proper symbols of category 1 yet we have variables of category 1.[169] And surely, it might be said, the notion of a formula $\langle\delta, x\rangle$ being true where $\delta \in E_{\langle 0,1\rangle}$ and $x \in X_1$ depends on first knowing what it is like for $\langle\delta, \alpha\rangle$ to be true when α is a proper symbol of category 1. But even if this assumption is needed to teach someone how a variable of category 1 functions there is no reason why the pupil should not throw away the ladder after he has climbed up. Actually the role of the variables is explained in our English/set-theoretical metalanguage and it is enough that we can use this language precisely. That we can use it precisely in the definition of a λ-categorial language as set out on pp. 84–6 seems to me at least as certain as that we can use it anywhere else in logic and mathematics.

Nouns and verbs

Before we can discuss profitably the structure of nominals we need to say something about the symbols out of which they are made. In this section we shall look at nouns and verbs. Common count nouns are semantically one-place predicates.[170] The meaning of ***man*** is to be understood in terms of what it is to be a man or, if you like, in terms of the property of being a man. If we know what being a man is then we know what it is to say that every man runs or is mortal or that Arabella loves a handsome man. In the same way, the meaning of an intransitive verb like ***runs*** is to be understood as the property of running; i.e. intransitive verbs are also one-place predicates.

In Chapter Thirteen (pp. 215–17) we shall take up the question of how to incorporate the noun/verb distinction into our analysis of English. The situation is quite a complex one and for the present we shall find it easier to treat both nouns and intransitive verbs as of the same syntactic category in the deep structure though all the examples we put up will be chosen so as not to violate the distinction.

[169] Lewis [1970], p. 51 f, suggests a simplification which consists in taking verb phrases and common nouns as basic categories. But our view of the relation between deep and shallow structure fits better with leaving a class of variables of category 1.

[170] This of course means a predicate in the logical rather than the grammatical sense, viz. a member of $E_{\langle 0,1\rangle}$. Note that this view of common nouns automatically takes care of nearly all the points made in Bach [1968].

Given, therefore, a categorial language $\mathscr{L}$ as the deep structure of English we shall, for the moment, say that words which are nouns in the shallow structure are members of $F_{\langle 0,1\rangle}$ of $\mathscr{L}$ in the deep structure. Intransitive verbs are also in $F_{\langle 0,1\rangle}$ and transitive verbs are in $F_{\langle 0,1,1\rangle}$.[171]

At this point we should say something about rules of agreement. One feature of the shallow structure will be that while sequences of the form

(1) ⟨***I, run***⟩

and

(2) ⟨***John, runs***⟩

are both acceptable in English,

(3) ⟨***I, runs***⟩

and

(4) ⟨***John, run***⟩

are not. We allow both ***run*** and ***runs*** to be in $F_{\langle 0,1\rangle}$. Further, we insist that V(***run***) = V(***runs***). But we recall that the language is going to need what we call 'acceptability principles' which allow only certain λ-categorial sentences to yield acceptable shallow structures. These principles would rule out the deep structures of (3) and (4) (in this particular case the deep and shallow structures of (3) and (4) are identical).

In the rest of this part, where we are not concerned with acceptability principles, we shall usually cite our examples in a form which does not violate the agreement restrictions; while recognizing of course that in every case there will be equivalent deep structures which do violate them. A similar situation arises with words like ***I*** and ***me***, where in English at any rate the distinction seems to make little semantical contribution to the evaluation of expressions.[172] Many cases of plural-

[171] Possibly some verbs will be predicates of higher degree; e.g., ***gives*** might be in $E_{\langle 0,1,1,1\rangle}$.

[172] The only exception I can think of is in cases of structural ambiguity in which the shallow structure may be derived from two deep structures, only one of which satisfies the agreement restrictions. Thus

(a) ⟨***me, loves, he***⟩

can be derived either from

(b) ⟨***me***,⟨λ, *x*,⟨⟨λ, *y*,⟨***loves***, *x*, *y*⟩⟩, ***he***⟩⟩⟩

or

(c) ⟨***me***,⟨λ, *x*,⟨⟨λ, *y*,⟨***loves***, *y*, *x*,⟩⟩, ***he***⟩⟩⟩.

Only (c) satisfies the agreement principle. (Though even here, since only (b) makes the subject come before the verb, another important principle of English shallow

ization are also of this form and ***man*** and ***men*** will both occur in the deep structure with the same meaning. Pluralization, discussed on pp. 190–2, does sometimes however have semantic effect and because its effect is rather complicated we shall avoid it as far as possible in the examples we discuss in the next few chapters.

Determiners

In order to make nominals out of common nouns we need what linguists call *determiners*.[173] These ought to be words of category $\langle\langle 0,\langle 0,1\rangle\rangle,\langle 0,1\rangle\rangle$; for the nominals they make are of category $\langle 0,\langle 0,1\rangle\rangle$ and the common nouns they make them out of are of category $\langle 0,1\rangle$. Actually it turns out that we can make use of the principles of λ-conversion to get a simpler characterization. Words which make nominals out of common nouns include words like ***every***, ***a***, ***the***, ***most*** and some others. We shall approach the problem of constructing nominals out of common nouns by putting forward, for illustrative purposes only, tentative meaning rules for these four words in English and shewing how their meanings combine with the meanings of nouns and verbs to give us the meanings of sentences like

$\langle$***every***, ***man***, ***runs***$\rangle$

We repeat our warnings on pp. 120 and 129 about not taking any semantical rule as the final statement on English. We are restricting ourselves to assignments in which context is not taken into account. This will be remedied later (cf. pp. 179–82).

We suppose that ***every***, ***a***, ***the*** and ***most*** are all two-place functors whose arguments are both of category $\langle 0,1\rangle$; i.e. these four functors are members of $F_{\langle 0,\langle 0,1\rangle,\langle 0,1\rangle\rangle}$. (Actually we shall want the first argument to be a common noun and the second an intransitive verb but, until Chapter Thirteen (pp. 215–17), we have no way of marking this difference.) The values of expressions of category $\langle 0,1\rangle$ are one-place properties ω, ω' etc. We propose the following semantic rules:

structure, many speakers might prefer to tolerate the ungrammaticality.) Note that (b) is equivalent to the perfectly acceptable

(d) $\langle$***I***,$\langle\lambda, x,\langle\langle\lambda, y,\langle$***love***, $x, y\rangle\rangle$, ***him***$\rangle\rangle\rangle$

and (c) to

(e) $\langle$***he***,$\langle\lambda, x,\langle\langle\lambda, y,\langle$***loves***, $x, y\rangle\rangle$, ***me***$\rangle\rangle\rangle$.

[173] Bloomfield [1933], p. 203 f. There are many more determiners than the ones we discuss; e.g. all the numerals (though *vide* Jackendoff [1968]). Borkowski [1958] calls the numerals 'numerical quantifiers' and develops an arithmetic on this basis. (Though it may be better to use a symbol like ***coll***—p. 162 *infra*—to convert the numerals into proper names of numbers.)

9.4 V(***every***) is that function ζ in $\mathbf{D}_{\langle 0, \langle 0, 1\rangle, \langle 0, 1\rangle\rangle}$ such that for any $\omega, \omega' \in \mathbf{D}_{\langle 0, 1\rangle}$ and any $w \in \mathbf{W}$, $w \in \zeta(\omega, \omega')$ iff for every a in the domain of ω, if $w \in \omega(a)$ then $w \in \omega'(a)$.

9.5 V(***a***) is that function ζ in $\mathbf{D}_{\langle 0, \langle 0, 1\rangle, \langle 0, 1\rangle\rangle}$ such that for any $\omega, \omega' \in \mathbf{D}_{\langle 0, 1\rangle}$ and any $w \in \mathbf{W}$, $w \in \zeta(\omega, \omega')$ iff there is at least one $a \in \mathbf{D}_1$ such that $w \in \omega(a)$ and $w \in \omega'(a)$.

9.6 V(***the***) is that function ζ in $\mathbf{D}_{\langle 0, \langle 0, 1\rangle, \langle 0, 1\rangle\rangle}$ such that for any $\omega, \omega' \in \mathbf{D}_{\langle 0, 1\rangle}$ and any $w \in \mathbf{W}$, $w \in \zeta(\omega, \omega')$ iff there is exactly one a such that $w \in \omega(a)$; and for that a, $w \in \omega'(a)$.[174]

9.7 V(***most***) is that function ζ in $\mathbf{D}_{\langle 0, \langle 0, 1\rangle, \langle 0, 1\rangle\rangle}$ such that for any $\omega, \omega' \in \mathbf{D}_{\langle 0, 1\rangle}$ and any $w \in \mathbf{W}$, $w \in \zeta(\omega, \omega')$ iff of the a's such that $w \in \omega(a)$ there are more such that $w \in \omega'(a)$ than such that $w \notin \omega'(a)$.

From 9.4–9.7 we may easily obtain the following 'truth rules' for sentences:

9.8 $w \in \mathrm{V}^+(\langle$***every, man, runs***$\rangle)$ iff for every a such that $w \in$ V(***man***)(a), $w \in$ V(***runs***)(a). (I.e., ⟨***every, man, runs***⟩ is true in a world w iff every a of which ***man*** is true in w is a thing of which ***runs*** is true in w.)

9.9 $w \in \mathrm{V}^+(\langle$***a, man, runs***$\rangle)$ iff there is some a such that $w \in$ V(***man***)(a) and $w \in$ V(***runs***)(a) (i.e., iff there is something of which both ***man*** and ***runs*** is true in w).

9.10 $w \in \mathrm{V}^+(\langle$***the, man, runs***$\rangle)$ iff there is exactly one a such that $w \in$ V(***man***)(a) (i.e., iff there is exactly one man in w) and for this a, $w \in$ V(***runs***)(a).

9.11 $w \in \mathrm{V}^+(\langle$***most, men, run***$\rangle)$ iff of the a's such that $w \in$ V(***men***)(a) (i.e., of the things which are men in w) there are more a's such that $w \in$ V(***run***)(a) than $w \notin$ V(***run***)(a) (i.e., more of them run in w than don't).[175]

In quantificational logic ***every*** and ***a*** are usually one-place functors which operate on truth functional combinations. Thus, instead of

(1) ⟨***every, man, runs***⟩

[174] It is in 9.6 that we see the need for a context-dependent assignment. Obviously it is very implausible to suppose that a sentence containing a phrase like ***the man*** is to entail that there is one and only one man.

[175] We regard ***men*** in ⟨***most, men, run***⟩ as being semantically equivalent to ***man*** but required after ***most*** (as is ***run*** instead of ***runs***), in an acceptable deep structure. *Vide* p. 134 f.

we would have something like

(2) $\langle \boldsymbol{every}, \langle \lambda, x, \langle \supset, \langle \boldsymbol{man}, x\rangle, \langle \boldsymbol{runs}, x\rangle\rangle\rangle\rangle$

It is certainly true that with the appropriate rule for $\supset$ ([V$\supset$], p. 32) the rule for ***every*** can be rewritten as:

9.12 V(***every***) is that function ζ from properties into propositions such that for any $\omega \in \mathbf{D}_{\langle 0, 1\rangle}$ and $w \in \mathbf{W}$, $w \in \zeta(w)$ iff for every a in the domain of ω, $w \in \omega(a)$.

We have chosen not to do it this way since although 9.12 and [V$\supset$] capture precisely our 9.3 they do so at the expense of introducing a material implication functor into English. If we translate $\supset$ as ***if***, we are involved in the controversy about whether ***if*** in English is to be interpreted as material implication, and if we introduce $\supset$ as a technical symbol, then we are no further forward in the analysis of ***every*** in English. Although 9.4 may not reflect the ordinary English use of ***every*** the chances of its being accepted as an approximation are enormous compared with the chances of [V$\supset$]'s being accepted as reflecting the English use of ***if***. Moreover even if such manoeuvres will do in the case of 9.4 and 9.5 (and possibly 9.6) there seems no way of adapting them to 9.7. 'Most A's are B's' cannot be translated as: 'It is true of most things that either they are not A's or they are B's'.[176]

Given these functors of category $\langle 0, \langle 0, 1\rangle, \langle 0, 1\rangle\rangle$ we can now shew how they operate on nouns to give nominals. The deep-structure representation of the nominal ***every man*** is:

(3) $\langle \lambda, x_{\langle 0, 1\rangle}, \langle \boldsymbol{every}, \boldsymbol{man}, x_{\langle 0, 1\rangle}\rangle\rangle$

(The subscript on the variable indicates that it is a member of $X_{\langle 0, 1\rangle}$, i.e. a one-place predicate variable; up to now our illustrations have used only variables of category 1 and we have left them without subscripts.)

From the formation rules for λ-categorial languages (p. 85) we see that (3) is an abstract of type $\langle 0, \langle 0, 1\rangle\rangle$ since it makes a sentence $\langle \boldsymbol{every}, \boldsymbol{man}, x_{\langle 0, 1\rangle}\rangle$ out of a variable of type $\langle 0, 1\rangle$. Furthermore,

[176] Suppose there were ten things altogether and five were not A's, three were A's but not B's, and two were A's and B's; then obviously 'most A's are B's' is false, since only two of the five A's are B's, but it is true of most things (viz. seven out of the ten) that either they are not A's or they are B's. And any other alternative will have similar awkward consequences. As a two-place functor, however, ***most*** gives us no problems. Cf. Lewis [1970], p. 43, and Parsons [1970b], p. 372n (Parsons attributes this point to John Wallace).

principle 6.21, p. 89, assures us that the following two sentences are synonymous:

(4) $\langle\langle\lambda, x_{\langle 0,1\rangle}, \langle \textbf{\textit{every}}, \textbf{\textit{man}}, x_{\langle 0,1\rangle}\rangle\rangle, \textbf{\textit{runs}}\rangle$[177]

and

(5) $\langle \textbf{\textit{every}}, \textbf{\textit{man}}, \textbf{\textit{runs}}\rangle$

In a similar way we may generate the nominals:

(6) $\langle\lambda, x_{\langle 0,1\rangle}, \langle \textbf{\textit{a}}, \textbf{\textit{man}}, x_{\langle 0,1\rangle}\rangle\rangle$

(7) $\langle\lambda, x_{\langle 0,1\rangle}, \langle \textbf{\textit{the}}, \textbf{\textit{man}}, x_{\langle 0,1\rangle}\rangle\rangle$

(8) $\langle\lambda, x_{\langle 0,1\rangle}, \langle \textbf{\textit{most}}, \textbf{\textit{men}}, x_{\langle 0,1\rangle}\rangle\rangle$[178]

These nominals combine equally happily with transitive verbs. Suppose ***loves*** $\in F_{\langle 0,1,1\rangle}$. We can have:

(9) $\langle \textbf{\textit{every}}, \textbf{\textit{man}}, \langle\lambda, x_1, \langle\langle\lambda, y_1, \langle \textbf{\textit{loves}}, x_1, y_1\rangle\rangle, \textbf{\textit{Arabella}}\rangle\rangle\rangle$

and with ***woman*** $\in F_{\langle 0,1\rangle}$ we can have

(10) $\langle \textbf{\textit{every}}, \textbf{\textit{man}}, \langle\lambda, x_1, \langle\langle\lambda, y_1, \langle \textbf{\textit{loves}}, x_1, y_1\rangle\rangle, \langle\lambda, x_{\langle 0,1\rangle}, \langle \textbf{\textit{a}}, \textbf{\textit{woman}}, x_{\langle 0,1\rangle}\rangle\rangle\rangle\rangle\rangle$

(10) can be converted into:

(11) $\langle \textbf{\textit{every}}, \textbf{\textit{man}}, \langle\lambda, x_1, \langle \textbf{\textit{a}}, \textbf{\textit{woman}}, \langle\lambda, y_1, \langle \textbf{\textit{loves}}, x_1, y_1\rangle\rangle\rangle\rangle\rangle$

by principles of λ-conversion.[179]

Let us see just how it goes.

Using

(12) $\langle\langle\lambda, x_{\langle 0,1\rangle}, \langle\delta, \alpha, x_{\langle 0,1\rangle}\rangle\rangle, \beta\rangle$ conv. $\langle\delta, \alpha, \beta\rangle$

we may convert

(13) $\langle\lambda, x_{\langle 0,1\rangle}, \langle \textbf{\textit{a}}, \textbf{\textit{woman}}, x_{\langle 0,1\rangle}\rangle\rangle, \langle\lambda, y_1, \langle \textbf{\textit{loves}}, x_1, y_1\rangle\rangle$

into

(14) $\langle \textbf{\textit{a}}, \textbf{\textit{woman}}, \langle\lambda, y_1, \langle \textbf{\textit{loves}}, x_1, y_1\rangle\rangle\rangle$

and this represents precisely the difference between (10) and (11) when the functor is put behind its argument.

Using the truth rules 9.8 and 9.9 (but with $\langle\lambda, y_1, \langle \textbf{\textit{loves}}, x_1, y_1\rangle\rangle$ in place of ***runs***) we can see that (14) means that for at least one woman, x_1 loves that woman. Thus

(15) $\langle\lambda, x_1, \langle \textbf{\textit{a}}, \textbf{\textit{woman}}, \langle\lambda, y_1, \langle \textbf{\textit{loves}}, x_1, y_1\rangle\rangle\rangle\rangle$

is the property of loving a woman, and so (11) – and therefore (10) –

[177] A good way of reading $\langle\lambda, x, \alpha\rangle$ is 'is an x such that α' (Lewis [1970], p. 43 f). Thus (4) can be read (roughly) as 'runs is an $x_{\langle 0,1\rangle}$ such that every man $x_{\langle 0,1\rangle}$'s or 'runs is a one-place property x such that every man satisfies x'. Readings like this ought to help overcome any initial intuitive difficulty.

[178] Of course we can also form $\langle\langle\lambda, x_{\langle 0,1\rangle}, \langle \textbf{\textit{every}}, \textbf{\textit{runs}}\rangle\rangle\rangle$, which we do not want, but we shall see how expressions of this kind can be eliminated in Chapter Thirteen.

[179] One use of the principles of λ-conversion is, as here, to enable us to rearrange the order of the proper symbols. They also allow a single occurrence of a symbol to do the work of more occurrences.

says that this property is true of every man, i.e. that every man loves a woman.

If we want to claim that it is one woman that all men love we use:

(16) $\langle\langle\lambda, y_1, \langle$***every, man***$, \langle\lambda, x_1, \langle$***loves***$, x_1, y_1\rangle\rangle\rangle\rangle,$
$\langle\lambda, x_{\langle 0,1\rangle}, \langle$***a, woman***$, x_{\langle 0,1\rangle}\rangle\rangle\rangle$

Abstract nouns and mass nouns

Our discussion of nouns has been concerned exclusively with common count nouns like ***man*** or ***chair*** or ***flower***. Some nouns like ***virtue*** or ***Christmas*** seem to function rather differently. At times they function as logically proper names; to be sure, names of 'abstract' entities but entities of the sort our ontology is quite capable of dealing with. If ***virtue*** $\in \mathbf{D}_{\langle 0,\langle 0,1\rangle\rangle}$ and we know what virtue is and that it is in $\mathbf{D}_1$ we can say:

9.13 V(***virtue***) is that function $\zeta \in \mathbf{D}_{\langle 0,\langle 0,1\rangle\rangle}$ such that for any $\omega \in \mathbf{D}_{\langle 0,1\rangle}$, $\zeta(\omega) = \omega$(virtue).

Unfortunately, as with most abstract nouns, we can also treat virtue as a common count noun and say

(17) ***John possesses every virtue***

There is certainly a semantic link between ***virtue*** as the name of an abstract quality and ***virtue*** as the name of an instance of that quality and maybe a fully adequate linguistic and philosophical analysis should explain what it is. We shall opt out and merely say that the deep structure contains two words, ***virtue***$_1$ (in $F_{\langle 0,\langle 0,1\rangle\rangle}$) and ***virtue***$_2$ (in $F_{\langle 0,1\rangle}$), which are semantically closely related and identically realized in the surface structure (cf. *infra* p. 213).

A somewhat similar situation obtains with mass nouns. Our approach here will be pretty much that of Quine.[180] The idea is that ***water*** refers sometimes to the totality of all the water in the world (as a sort of 'thing' which extends over many discontinuous regions of space) and sometimes to a part of that water. We leave the notion of a 'part of all the water in the world' for others to explain.[181] On this view ***water*** would be in $F_{\langle 0,\langle 0,1\rangle\rangle}$ and would have the semantic rule:

9.14 V(***water***) is that function $\zeta \in \mathbf{D}_{\langle 0,\langle 0,1\rangle\rangle}$ such that for any $\omega \in \mathbf{D}_{\langle 0,1\rangle}$ and $w \in \mathbf{W}$, $w \in \zeta(\omega)$ iff there is some part $a \in \mathbf{D}_1$ of water such that $w \in \omega(a)$.

[180] Quine [1960], pp. 97–100; also Parsons [1970b].
[181] E.g. the 'calculus of individuals' of Goodman [1951], pp. 42–51, or the mereology of Leśniewski (*vide* Sobociński [1955]).

This means that the deep structure of

(18) ***John drinks water***

will be

(19) $\langle$***John***, $\langle\lambda, x_1, \langle\lambda, y_1, \langle$***drinks***, $x_1, y_1\rangle\rangle$, ***water***$\rangle\rangle$

and will be true in a world *w* iff John drinks in *w* something which is a part of the totality of water.

Mass nouns can also occur with some determiners.[182] We can have

(20) ***John drinks the water in the cup***

or

(21) ***John wants some water***

though not, in the same sense, ***a water*** or ***some waters***. If we deal with these cases as we did with abstract nouns we can say that ***water*** in (20) and (21) is, in deep structure, a distinct, though related, word. I.e., ***water***$_1$ is in $F_{\langle 0, \langle 0, 1\rangle\rangle}$ and obeys 9.14 while ***water***$_2$ is in $F_{\langle 0, 1\rangle}$ and is in many, but not all, respects like a common count noun and has the semantics:

9.15 V(***water***$_2$) is that function $\omega \in \mathbf{D}_{\langle 0, 1\rangle}$ such that for any $a \in \mathbf{D}_{\langle 0, 1\rangle}$ and $w \in \mathbf{W}$, $w \in \omega(a)$ iff *a* is part of the totality of water.

Adverbs and adjectives

Of these two parts of speech it is adverbs which seem to perform more functions than adjectives. Indeed with our present view of deep structure, adjectives turn out to be just a restricted kind of adverb. Adverbs can be thought of as modifying either transitive or intransitive verbs. Since we are using a λ-categorial language as deep structure it is easily shewn that all these jobs can be performed by expressions of the category $\langle 0,0\rangle$.[183]

[182] Cf. Quine [1960], p. 99 f. ***water*** in this sense can also be qualified by an adjective. Cf. 'blue styrofoam' in Parsons [1970b], p. 364. It would also be possible to introduce a 'logical' operator, rather like ***coll*** on pp. 162–5, to connect ***water***$_1$ and ***water***$_2$ so that we would need only one semantic rule.

[183] Though some adverbs may have to be analysed as predicate modifiers of category $\langle\langle 0,1\rangle,\langle 0,1\rangle\rangle$; e.g. ***willingly*** in:

(a) ***willingly John precedes Arabella***

(b) ***willingly Arabella follows John***

Assuming that ***John*** and ***Arabella*** are logically proper names and that ***John precedes Arabella*** means the same as ***Arabella follows John***, then if ***willingly*** $\in F_{\langle 0, 0\rangle}$, (a) and (b) would have to be synonymous; yet in (a) it is John who is willing and in (b) it is Arabella. The view of adverbs and adjectives as predicate modifiers is found in Reichenbach [1947], pp. 301–10 (cf. also Rennie [1971]). It is discussed in Parsons [1970a], who, at p. 325 f, opts for treating adverbs as sentence modifiers. (*Vide* also Lakoff [1970a], p. 220 f.) Work of this kind has also been done by Montague and J. A. W. Kamp (*vide* Montague [1970a], p. 394).

As an example suppose ***quickly*** $\in F_{\langle 0,0\rangle}$. Then we have

(1) $\langle\langle$***the, man, runs***$\rangle$, ***quickly***$\rangle$

as a sentence of $\mathscr{L}^{\lambda}$. But also we have

(2) $\langle\lambda, x_1, \langle\langle$***runs***$, x_1\rangle$, ***quickly***$\rangle\rangle$

as a complex expression of category $\langle 0, 1\rangle$. For ***quickly*** operates (backwards) on the sentence $\langle$***runs***$, x_1\rangle$ to form $\langle\langle$***runs***$, x_1\rangle$, ***quickly***$\rangle$ from which we can abstract the complex intransitive verb phrase (2) whose shallow structure is ***runs quickly***.

One rather significant feature of this treatment of adverbs is that when combined with our treatment of nominals it raises interesting possibilities of differences of scope. E.g., using (2) we may form the sentence

(3) $\langle$***the, man,*** $\langle\lambda, x_1, \langle\langle$***runs***$, x_1,\rangle$ ***quickly***$\rangle\rangle\rangle$

What we notice is that in (3) ***quickly*** is within the scope of ***the*** while in (1) ***the*** and everything else in the sentence is in the scope of ***quickly***. Any interpretation which reflected normal English would probably make (1) and (3) synonymous but the structure of (1) and (3) does not force them to be so. And it is easy to get sentences in which scope differences of this kind cause clear differences in meaning. Suppose ***no one*** (which for the moment we shall treat as one word) is in $F_{\langle 0,\langle 0,1\rangle\rangle}$ and ***tenderly*** is in $F_{\langle 0,0\rangle}$. We propose for ***no one*** the semantic rule:

9.16 V(***no one***) is that function ζ such that for any $\omega \in \mathbf{D}_{\langle 0,1\rangle}$ and any world w, $w \in \zeta(\omega)$ iff for every person $a \in \mathbf{D}_1$, $w \notin \omega(a)$.

Consider then the sentence

(4) ***Arabella loves no one tenderly***

Provided an unnatural reading is accepted this sentence is ambiguous in that it could mean that Arabella loves no one and she does it (viz. her non-loving) tenderly. I.e.,

(5) $\langle$***Arabella,*** $\langle\lambda, x_1, \langle\langle\langle\lambda, y_1, \langle$***loves***$, x_1, y_1\rangle\rangle$, ***no one***$\rangle$, ***tenderly***$\rangle\rangle\rangle$

However what it probably means is

(6) $\langle$***Arabella,*** $\langle\lambda, x_1, \langle\langle\lambda, x_{\langle 0,0\rangle}, \langle\langle\lambda, y_1, \langle\langle$***loves***$, x_1, y_1\rangle, x_{\langle 0,0\rangle}\rangle\rangle$, ***no one***$\rangle\rangle$, ***tenderly***$\rangle\rangle\rangle$

By the λ-conversion principle 6.21 of p. 89, (6) becomes

(7) $\langle$***Arabella,*** $\langle\lambda, x_1, \langle\langle\lambda, y_1, \langle\langle$***loves***$, x_1, y_1\rangle$, ***tenderly***$\rangle\rangle$, ***no one***$\rangle\rangle\rangle$

Here the property of being an x such that of no y is it true that x loves y tenderly is asserted as belonging to Arabella. I.e., Arabella loves no one tenderly. (6) is a case where λ-conversion is essential, for the interpretation of the sentence demands that although the adverb occurs at the end of the sentence its scope extends only as far as and does not include the penultimate word ***no one*** which is adjacent to it in the shallow structure and separates it from its argument.

Obviously one can iterate adverbs to form complex adverbial expressions. Thus we can have

(8) $\langle\langle\langle$***John, runs***$\rangle$, ***necessarily***$\rangle$, ***quickly***$\rangle$

which can also be expressed as

(9) $\langle\langle$***John, runs***$\rangle$, $\langle\lambda, x_0, \langle\langle x_0,$ ***necessarily***$\rangle$, ***quickly***$\rangle\rangle\rangle$

in which the abstract

(10) $\langle\lambda, x_0, \langle\langle x_0,$ ***necessarily***$\rangle$, ***quickly***$\rangle\rangle$

is of category $\langle 0,0\rangle$; and (8) is equivalent to (9) by λ-conversion. And quite generally any expression of category $\langle 0,0\rangle$, however formed, will count as an adverb in the deep structure though acceptability principles (like those mentioned on p. 134) may well prevent many of them from reaching the surface.

Our treatment of adjectives differs from that of those linguists who derive the attributive use of adjectives from their predicative use. Chomsky[184] derives

(8) ***a wise man is honest***

from

(9) ***a man is wise***

and

(10) ***a man is honest***

In (8) ***wise*** occurs attributively and qualifies ***man***. In (9) and (10) it is simply predicated of ***man***. Semantic reasons would suggest that the attributive use is prior. John Lyons gives the example[185]

(11) ***a small elephant is a large animal***

(11) shews that the meanings of ***large*** and ***small*** are bound up with the meanings of the things they qualify. If we think of common nouns as one-place predicates then adjectives are of category $\langle\langle 0,1\rangle,\langle 0,1\rangle\rangle$. Adjectives are not as general as adverbs, which can also be (as we have shewn) of other categories than the category $\langle\langle 0,1\rangle,\langle 0,1\rangle\rangle$ (e.g. $\langle\langle 0,1,1\rangle,\langle 0,1,1\rangle\rangle$ and so on). Adjectives of course only qualify

[184] Chomsky [1968], p. 25. A particularly illuminating discussion of the role of adjectives, which takes the word *good* as an example, is to be found in Chapter Six of Ziff [1960], pp. 200–47 and Chapter Seven of Vendler [1967], pp. 172–95.

[185] Lyons [1969], p. 466; though Lyons does not take this example to support the primacy of the attributive use of adjectives. The view is also discussed in Bach [1968], p. 102 f. Bach, however, seems to think that adjectives are either predicative (and so derive from verbs) or attributive, like ***alleged*** (and so derive from adverbs). He does not consider a case like ***large*** which can be used predicatively but whose semantics requires an attributive analysis.

common nouns (or complex common noun expressions[186]) and we shall bring out this additional difference in Chapter Thirteen.

To shew how the semantics for ***large*** works we shall give a tentative semantical rule:

9.17 V(***large***) is that function ζ from $\mathbf{D}_{\langle 0,1\rangle}$ into $\mathbf{D}_{\langle 0,1\rangle}$ such that if ω is a property whose domain consists of physical things then ω is in the domain of ζ and for any world w and any $a \in \mathbf{D}_1$, $w \in (\zeta(\omega)(a)$ iff a is larger than most of the b's such that $w \in \omega(b)$.

(I.e., given a property ω we find out whether a is a large ω (in w) by finding out whether it is larger than most of the things which are ω in w.[187] Note that we explain the meaning of ***large*** in terms of an absolute metalinguistic concept of relative largeness.)

Given 9.17 it is easy to see how a thing could be a large animal without being a large elephant. For if ω is the property of being an animal and ω' the property of being an elephant then a may well be larger than most animals and so $\zeta(\omega)(a)$ may be true without a's being larger than most elephants so that $\zeta(\omega')(a)$ may be false (all in some world w). It is not at all easy to see how an analysis of attributive adjectives in terms of predicative adjectives after the manner of (8), (9) and (10) could explain this in any natural way.

Even cases which can be handled as (8) was handled can be equally well handled in the way we have just described, much as extensional properties (p. 70) could be expressed in terms of intensional ones.[188]

Suppose that the phrase ***wise man*** means something which is wise as well as being a man. Then

9.18 V(***wise***) is the function ζ such that $w \in \zeta(\omega)(a)$ iff $w \in \omega(a)$ and a is wise in w.

In Chapter Eleven (p. 184 f) we discuss the question of how to incorporate the predicative use of adjectives into our deep structure.

[186] Complex common noun expressions will be those expressions of category $\langle 0,1\rangle$ which will be realized in the surface structure as complex nouns. In linguistics they have sometimes been spoken of as noun phrases, but in our deep structure they must be carefully distinguished from nominals. Common noun expressions are of category $\langle 0,1\rangle$, while nominals are of category $\langle 0,\langle 0,1\rangle\rangle$.

[187] This is rough because it is not so much the number of things of the appropriate kind but also their relative size. No matter how many fleas there were, or how few elephants, a large flea would still be a small animal.

[188] So much so that Lewis [1970], p. 27, speaks of extensional adjectives in a case like this.

Prepositions

Prepositions use nominals to make adverbial expressions.[189] In deep structure we shall treat them as of category $\langle\langle 0,0\rangle,1\rangle$. Usually the preposition in the shallow structure occurs immediately before the nominal it governs. Suppose that ***for*** $\in F_{\langle\langle 0,0\rangle,1\rangle}$. Then we have as a deep structure

(1) $\langle\lambda, x_0, \langle\langle\lambda, x_1, \langle\langle \textbf{\textit{for}}, x_1\rangle, x_0\rangle\rangle, \textbf{\textit{Arabella}}\rangle\rangle$

Superficially it might seem easier to have prepositions of category $\langle\langle 0,0\rangle,\langle 0,\langle 0,1\rangle\rangle\rangle$ so that they operate directly on nominals. In this case

(2) $\langle \textbf{\textit{for}}, \textbf{\textit{Arabella}}\rangle$

would, as it stands, be a well formed expression in the deep structure. The reason we have not done this is that there can arise cases in which the scope of the nominal relative to the preposition can cause differences in meaning. Suppose that ***pines*** $\in F_{\langle 0,1\rangle}$. Then the shallow structure

(3) ***everyone pines for someone***

is ambiguous. It may mean

(4) $\langle \textbf{\textit{everyone}}, \langle\lambda, x_1, \langle\langle\lambda, y_1, \langle\langle \textbf{\textit{pines}}, x_1\rangle, \langle \textbf{\textit{for}}, y_1\rangle\rangle\rangle, \textbf{\textit{someone}}\rangle\rangle\rangle$

or

(5) $\langle\langle\lambda, y_1, \langle \textbf{\textit{everyone}}, \langle\lambda, x_1, \langle\langle \textbf{\textit{pines}}, x_1\rangle, \langle \textbf{\textit{for}}, y_1\rangle\rangle\rangle\rangle\rangle, \textbf{\textit{someone}}\rangle$

(4) allows each person to pine for someone different while (5) requires that there be a single person whom everyone pines for.

Actually the situation is a little more complex than (4) and (5) would indicate since there is another sense of (3) in which a piner need have no particular person in mind. Cases of this kind can arise without the use of prepositions, as in

(6) ***Lacey hunts a mouse***

where it simply means that Lacey is mouse-hunting without there being any particular mouse she is hunting. Cases like (6) are notoriously difficult and will be discussed on pp. 170 f and 212 f. All we shall say here is that their solution in the prepositional cases is of a piece with their solution in the purely verbal cases.

The name 'preposition' arises because of the occurrence of a preposition before its nominal and prepositions occurring after the nominal have sometimes been called 'post-positions'. In our deep structure, of course, prepositions can occur either before or after the nominal they govern and there seems little objection to the view that

[189] Parsons [1970a], p. 323; also Geach [1970], pp. 10–13.

it is up to the acceptability principles to say that deep structures in which the preposition occurs after the nominal it governs do not in normal circumstances give rise to acceptable surface structures in English. In poetic contexts, however, the preposition can sometimes occur after its noun, as in

(7) ***they toiled the whole night through***

Prepositional phrases are not only adverbial but also, on occasions, adjectival. Thus not only can we say

(8) ***the man serves in the shop***

but we can also say

(9) ***the man in the shop runs***

At present of course this does not embarrass us since adjectives are just a restricted class of adverbs but we shall later (p. 216 f) have to take account of the fact that there is no difference between adverbial and adjectival prepositional expressions. The deep structure of (9) is

(10) $\langle \textbf{\textit{the}}, \langle \lambda, y_1, \langle\langle \lambda, x_1, \langle\langle \textbf{\textit{man}}, x_1\rangle, \langle \textbf{\textit{in}}, y_1\rangle\rangle\rangle, \langle \lambda, x_{\langle 0,1\rangle}, \langle \textbf{\textit{the}}, \textbf{\textit{shop}}, x_{\langle 0,1\rangle}\rangle\rangle\rangle\rangle, \textbf{\textit{runs}}\rangle$

Notice that (10) is one of the few examples we have produced in which we have a common noun expression with an argument of category 1.

The preposition ***of*** raises all sorts of problems, not the least of which is the number of distinct prepositions which deep structure should recognize for it (cf. *infra* p. 146). Here we shall merely shew how treating it as a preposition enables us to explain certain phenomena involving determiners which might otherwise look perplexing. As we have been using the words ***every*** and ***most*** they (like ***the*** and ***a***) have been of category $\langle 0, \langle 0, 1\rangle, \langle 0, 1\rangle\rangle$. But as well as sentences like

(11) ***some men run***

and

(12) ***most mayors sleep***

we have

(13) ***some of the men run***

and

(14) ***most of the mayors sleep***

These examples seem to involve essential use of the definite article followed by a plural noun, a phenomenon we shall discuss on p. 191. We shall not therefore attempt a semantical rule. The deep structure of (13) is

(14) $\langle \textbf{\textit{some}}, \langle \lambda, x_1, \langle\langle \lambda, x_{\langle 0,1\rangle}, \langle\langle \lambda, y_1, \langle\langle x_{\langle 0,1\rangle}, x_1\rangle, \langle \textbf{\textit{of}}, y_1\rangle\rangle\rangle, \langle \lambda, y_{\langle 0,1\rangle}, \langle \textbf{\textit{the}}, x_{\langle 0,1\rangle}, y_{\langle 0,1\rangle}\rangle\rangle\rangle\rangle, \textbf{\textit{men}}\rangle\rangle, \textbf{\textit{run}}\rangle$

By principles of λ-conversion (14) becomes[190]

(15) $\langle \textbf{\textit{some}}, \langle \lambda, x_1, \langle\langle \lambda, y_1, \langle\langle \textbf{\textit{men}}, x_1\rangle, \langle \textbf{\textit{of}}, y_1\rangle\rangle\rangle,$
$\langle \lambda, x_{\langle 0,1\rangle}, \langle \textbf{\textit{the}}, \textbf{\textit{men}}, x_{\langle 0,1\rangle}\rangle\rangle\rangle\rangle, \textbf{\textit{run}}\rangle$

Some determiners such as ***every***, ***a*** and ***the*** cannot take a preposition in this way while others such as ***some***, ***each***, ***all*** and ***most*** can.

Our treatment of prepositions perhaps needs a little defence since it is in conflict with the view that prepositions do not really occur in the deep structure at all. E.g. the phrase

(16) ***the love of God***

as it occurs in a sentence might be held to signal that in the deep structure there is an embedded sentence

(17) – ***loves God***

or

(18) ***God loves*** –

(17) and (18) therefore represent alternative ways of resolving a structural ambiguity in (16). Our approach, on the other hand, will say that the ambiguity is of a lexical kind depending on two meanings of ***of***.

This is not so implausible as it might appear. If, as Charles Fillmore has argued,[191] the meanings of verbs have built in to them a number of argument places which might represent, in the case of an activity, the agent, object, goal etc. of the activity, then there is no reason why V($\textbf{\textit{of}}_1$), say, might not be a function whose value for an individual x is the function which makes out of an activity of ϕ-ing the more specific activity of ϕ-ing by x as agent, while V($\textbf{\textit{of}}_2$) makes the activity of ϕ-ing with x as object. Our approach would have the effect of putting the analysis of (16) into the semantics rather than the syntax and it is perhaps no accident that Fillmore is one of those linguists who regard the semantic structure as having an important part to play in linguistic analysis. In Chapter Four we had a little to say about what a structured system of meanings might be like and in such a meaning algebra there

[190] Occasionally sentences of this kind may even reach the surface, though when they do so it is often with a changed word order. Thus, adapting an example of Lee [1971], p. 7, we might have: ***of the boys who left school early some boys arrived home late***. An analysis of this kind was criticized in Jackendoff [1968], p. 430 f. Jackendoff's own analysis, as I understand it, would make a determiner, like ***three*** say, behave like the nominal ***a trio***, for he makes ***three of the men*** have a structure similar to ***a group of the men*** (op. cit., p. 426 f). Probably the 'collective' symbol ***coll*** (p. 162) is involved in analyses of sentences like (15).

[191] Fillmore [1968], especially pp. 24–31. A discussion of the semantical role of ***with*** is found in Lakoff [1968]. A similar idea of course occurs in Aristotle's *Categories* (1b25–2a4).

would be no difficulty in shewing how the two senses of ***of*** are related to the meanings of (17) and (18) respectively.[192]

Nominals and scope

We have already seen in our discussion of adverbs how changes in the scope of an adverb relative to the scope of a nominal can sometimes effect changes in the meaning of the whole sentence. For further illustration we shall use the case of ***not*** with which we opened the discussion which led us in Chapter Six (pp. 80–3) to postulate quantifiers of category $\langle 0, \langle 0, 1\rangle\rangle$. ***not*** $\in F_{\langle 0,0\rangle}$ though in English it usually works by modifying an auxiliary verb like ***do*** or ***have***. We shall allow ourselves the rather archaic

(1) ***everyone loves not Arabella***

This sentence can be ambiguous between[193]

(2) $\langle\langle\lambda, y_1, \langle \textbf{\textit{everyone}}, \langle\lambda, x_1, \langle\langle \textbf{\textit{loves}}, x_1, y_1\rangle, \textbf{\textit{not}}\rangle\rangle\rangle\rangle, \textbf{\textit{Arabella}}\rangle$

and

(3) $\langle\langle\lambda, y_1, \langle\langle \textbf{\textit{everyone}}, \langle\lambda, x_1, \langle \textbf{\textit{loves}}, x_1, y_1\rangle\rangle\rangle, \textbf{\textit{not}}\rangle\rangle, \textbf{\textit{Arabella}}\rangle$

The difference is, as in the examples of p. 80, in the relative scope of ***everyone*** and ***not***. In (2) ***not*** is within the scope of ***everyone*** and in (3) ***everyone*** is within the scope of ***not***. In the case of quantifiers this difference of scope causes a difference of meaning, as illustrated by (2) and (3) where in (2) universal non-loving is predicated of Arabella while in (3) all we get is a denial of universal loving.

Many philosophical problems have arisen from failure to see that definite descriptions have scope and therefore require to be treated as of category $\langle 0, \langle 0, 1\rangle\rangle$. One of the first philosophers to discuss the formal analysis of descriptions was Russell[194] who, in this regard, was

[192] It perhaps needs saying that nothing in our present approach has ruled out the possibility of formulating the acceptability principles so that they depend on semantic structure; e.g., there is nothing to prevent a semantic analysis of the instrumental ***with*** which links it (in the manner of Lakoff [1968]) with the verb ***use***; and there is nothing to prevent this analysis being used to formulate acceptability principles. This is the reason why nothing in the present book need be incompatible with the hypothesis of generative semantics (at least as I understand this hypothesis); though I personally find the aims of generative semantics rather Utopian (cf. G. Lakoff [1970a], p. 195).

[193] Perhaps the ambiguity appears better in the more colloquial ***everyone does not love Arabella*** (though, as with the examples on p. 91, in ordinary conversation it is probably not ambiguous and means (3)).

[194] Although Russell (Whitehead and Russell [1910], pp. 173–5) recognized that definite descriptions have scope and Smullyan [1948] applied it to modal functors, neither of them seems to have quite realized that the introduction of scope made a difference in the syntactic category of the expression. Similar comments apply to Thomason and Stalnaker [1968]. It is a failure to see that it is

clearer about their scope than most of his successors. What Russell did was to shew that in the case of some words like ***not***, ***and***, and ***if*** (the 'truth functors' in fact, cf. p. 31 f) the scope of a definite description does not matter provided there is exactly one thing satisfying it. As Arthur Smullyan pointed out, in the case of modal words like ***necessarily*** the scope does matter, even when the uniqueness condition is satisfied.

For suppose that ***mayor*** and ***presides*** are both in $F_{\langle 0,1\rangle}$ (one a common noun of course and one an intransitive verb). We can illustrate the effect of the scope of ***not*** by

(4) ⟨⟨***the, mayor, presides***⟩, ***not***⟩

and

(5) ⟨***the, mayor***, ⟨λ, x_1, ⟨⟨***presides***, x_1⟩, ***not***⟩⟩⟩

In (4) ***the*** and ***mayor*** are both within the scope of ***not*** while in (5) ***not*** is within the scope of ***the***.[195] However no ambiguity will arise, on the assumption that there is (in each world) one and only one mayor, for in that case if it is true of the mayor that he does not preside then it must be false that the mayor presides.

Suppose now though that ***necessarily*** $\in F_{\langle 0,0\rangle}$ and that ⟨***necessarily***, α⟩ is true in w iff α is true in all worlds, and suppose that the mayor is defined to be the one who presides (at the appropriate meetings). Then we have (allowing backwards scope):

(6) ⟨⟨***the, mayor, presides***⟩, ***necessarily***⟩

as true but

(7) ⟨***the, mayor***, ⟨λ, x_1, ⟨⟨***presides***, x_1⟩, ***necessarily***⟩⟩⟩

as false since there are some worlds in which the person who is the mayor in the real world is not the mayor and so does not preside.

Notice that the difference in scope between (6) and (7) brings out precisely the difference we discussed on pp. 68–70 between the two senses of

(8) ***the Prime Minister of New Zealand will always be a British subject***

Our solution there was to resolve the ambiguity by making two different assignments of two different intensional objects (i.e. functions from worlds to individuals). In the present case we would have to

really the *scope indicator* which is the operator, and that the description itself plays the role of a bound variable, which has caused the notion of the scope of the description to remain opaque to so many philosophers. For a discussion *vide* Føllesdal [1966], pp. 104–10.

[195] If we took ⟨λ, $x_{\langle 0,1\rangle}$, ⟨***the, mayor***, $x_{\langle 0,1\rangle}$⟩⟩ as the subject of ⟨λ, x_1, ⟨⟨***presides***, x_1⟩, ***not***⟩⟩ we could more simply say that ***the mayor*** is within the scope of ***not***.

treat ***the mayor*** as of category 1 and either assign it the constant function whose value in any world is the thing which is the mayor in this world or the function whose value in any world is the thing which is the mayor in that world.

Our present semantics avoids any equivocation of this sort. The phrase ***the mayor*** is in deep structure

(9) $\langle \lambda, x_{\langle 0,1\rangle}, \langle \textbf{\textit{the}}, \textbf{\textit{mayor}}, x_{\langle 0,1\rangle}\rangle\rangle$

which is an expression of category $\langle 0,\langle 0,1\rangle\rangle$. Suppose that we have a value for ***mayor*** such that in any w there is exactly one a such that $w \in \omega_{\textbf{\textit{mayor}}}(a)$. Then the suggested semantics 9.6 (p. 136) for ***the***, will give the following (using the evaluation rules of p. 86):

9.19 $V^{+}(\langle \lambda, x_{\langle 0,1\rangle}, \langle \textbf{\textit{the}}, \textbf{\textit{mayor}}, x_{\langle 0,1\rangle}\rangle\rangle)$ is that function ζ from properties into propositions such that for any $\omega \in \mathbf{D}_{\langle 0,1\rangle}$:

$$\zeta(\omega) = V_{\langle \omega/x_{\langle 0,1\rangle}\rangle}(\langle \textbf{\textit{the}}, \textbf{\textit{mayor}}, x_{\langle 0,1\rangle}\rangle)$$
$$= V(\textbf{\textit{the}})(\omega_{\textbf{\textit{mayor}}}, \omega)$$

and $w \in V(\textbf{\textit{the}})(\omega_{\textbf{\textit{mayor}}}, \omega)$ iff there is exactly one a such that a is the mayor in w, and it is true of a that a satisfies ω in w.

Thus ***the mayor*** denotes the higher-order property which holds in a world w of a property ω iff ω holds in w of the thing which is the mayor in w. (6) and (7) distinguish between the case in which in each world the mayor in that world presides in that world and the case in which the thing which is the mayor in this world presides in every world.

On this analysis the predicate ***presides*** can stand for an ordinary property which is true in w of an individual a iff a presides in w. Properties of intensional objects are not necessary to resolve difficulties of the kind generated by ambiguities such as that of (1) on p. 68 or the example we have just been discussing. Nor is the introduction of intensional objects sufficient to resolve these apparent paradoxes. To see this we shall introduce the adverb ***allowably***. The sentence we shall look at is rather unnatural and we are going to iterate these clumsy adverbs in ways English would frown on.[196] However they do make the point. Our sentence is:

(10) ***the mayor allowably presides necessarily***

We assume the following rule for ***allowably***:

9.20 V(***allowably***) is that function ω in $\mathbf{D}_{\langle 0,0\rangle}$ such that for any

[196] A live case here would require a context-dependent assignment.

$w \in \mathbf{W}$ and $a \in \mathbf{D}_0$, $w \in \omega(a)$ iff there is some legally acceptable alternative world w' such that $w' \in a$.[197]

Consider the value of (10) in a world w. If, by analogy with Chapter Five, p. 69, we treat ***the mayor*** as a complex member of E_1 and try to bring out the ambiguity of (10) by assigning either the constant function whose value in any world is the thing which is the mayor in this world, or whose value in any world is the thing which is the mayor in that world, then we can express some of the meanings of (10) but we cannot express

(11) $\langle\langle$***the***, ***mayor***, $\langle\lambda, x_1, \langle$***allowably***, $\langle$***presides***, $x_1\rangle\rangle\rangle\rangle$, ***necessarily***$\rangle$.

Here ***the mayor*** is within the scope of ***necessarily*** but not within the scope of ***allowably***. (11) will be true in a world w iff for every world w' there is some world w'' which is a legal alternative to w' such that *the thing which is mayor in* w' presides in w''. The point is that the thing which presides in w'' need be neither the thing which is the mayor in the original world w (so the phrase could not be assigned a constant function) nor need it be the thing which is the mayor in w'' (so the phrase could not be assigned the function whose value in each world is the thing which is the mayor in that world). Indeed it is not at all clear that there is any intensional object which could be assigned to ***the mayor*** in order to give the meaning which (11) gives to (10).

Treating nominals as expressions of category $\langle 0, \langle 0, 1\rangle\rangle$, which may therefore have scope, avoids all these problems without any need for intensional objects. $\mathbf{D}_1$ will of course contain intensional objects because it contains everything (*vide* pp. 98–100) and we may from time to time wish to speak about such things, but paradoxes of the kind discussed above (and their relative, the 'morning star' paradox (p. 183 n)) neither need intensional objects nor can be resolved by their introduction.

[197] This rule means that ***allowably presides*** is interpreted to mean 'is permitted by law to preside'. More natural examples, like the one on pp. 68–70 in Chapter Five, can be given when we discuss context-dependent assignments in the deep structure of English.

CHAPTER TEN

More Parts of Speech

Among the parts of speech recognized by traditional grammar are what we might call 'logical' parts of speech. These are words whose function was thought of as the combining of the major parts together to form phrases, clauses or sentences. In a deep structure of the kind we are proposing they can be given a categorial analysis just like any other word, though it may happen that there are only a few in a particular class.

There are some important words we shall not be discussing in this chapter. These are words like the personal pronouns whose semantics demands that we be thinking of context-dependent assignments of the kind described in Chapter Eight. Of course it is context-dependent assignments which must eventually form the communication class of English but the function of a great many words can be more simply defined in the first instance in terms of an assignment which makes no reference to contexts of use.

The auxiliary *do*

It is not natural in English, though it is possible, to say

(1) ***Arabella sings not***

The natural way of expressing (1) is

(2) ***Arabella does not sing***

A verb like ***does*** in (2) is called an *auxiliary*. Other auxiliaries like ***will***, ***shall*** and ***have*** we shall leave until Chapter Twelve because they have essentially to do with tense and must therefore wait until we discuss a context-dependent assignment. Also there is the verb ***be*** which is going to get a special section on its own. (The reader will notice that we have been rather scrupulous in avoiding instances of this verb.)

Now ***do*** is also an ordinary transitive verb as in

(3) ***John does the work***

but in deep structure these uses can be distinguished. This is seen by the fact that the negation of (3) is not

(4) ***John does not the work***

(though this is as possible as (1) and as unnatural as (1)) but

(5) ***John does not do the work***

The auxiliary ***do*** (or ***does***)[198] makes a verb phrase out of a verb phrase and it can be seen as of category $\langle\langle 0,1\rangle,\langle 0,1\rangle\rangle$. (When it operates on a transitive verb it can always be seen as operating on the intransitive verb phrase which consists of the transitive verb plus its object.) Its position in acceptable English sentences will have to be severely restricted. It almost always occurs either just before the verb or separated by ***not***. Further we seldom have

(6) ***Arabella does sing***

The semantics of ***do*** is very simple: basically it preserves the meanng of its verb.

10.1 V(*do*) is that function $\zeta \in \mathbf{D}_{\langle\langle 0,1\rangle,\langle 0,1\rangle\rangle}$ such that for any $\omega \in \mathbf{D}_{\langle 0,1\rangle}$, $\zeta(\omega) = \omega$.

We can now formulate the deep structure of (2) as

(7) $\langle \textit{\textbf{Arabella}}, \langle \textit{\textbf{does}}, \langle \lambda, x_1, \langle \textit{\textbf{not}}, \langle \textit{\textbf{sing}}, x_1\rangle\rangle\rangle\rangle\rangle$

Now by 10.1

$\mathrm{V}(\textit{\textbf{does}})(\mathrm{V}^+(\langle \lambda, x_1, \langle \textit{\textbf{not}}, \langle \textit{\textbf{sing}}, x_1\rangle\rangle\rangle)) = \mathrm{V}^+(\langle \lambda, x_1, \langle \textit{\textbf{not}}, \langle \textit{\textbf{sing}}, x_1\rangle\rangle\rangle)$

By the rules for evaluating abstracts (pp. 83–6) we have for any $\nu \in N$ (where N is the set of all assignments to the variables of $\mathscr{L}^\lambda$) and for any $a \in \mathbf{D}_1$

$$w \in \mathrm{V}_\nu^+(\langle \lambda, x_1, \langle \textit{\textbf{not}}, \langle \textit{\textbf{sing}}, x_1\rangle\rangle\rangle)(a)$$

iff

$$w \in \mathrm{V}_{(\nu, a/x)}^+(\langle \textit{\textbf{not}}, \langle \textit{\textbf{sing}}, x_1\rangle\rangle)$$

and provided ***not*** obeys [V~] of p. 32 this last will be true iff

$$w \notin \mathrm{V}_{(\nu, a/x)}^+(\langle \textit{\textbf{sings}}, x_1\rangle)$$

i.e. iff $w \notin \mathrm{V}(\textit{\textbf{sings}})(a)$

For ***Arabella*** we assume of course that $w \in \mathrm{V}^+(\langle \textit{\textbf{Arabella}}, \alpha\rangle)$ iff

[198] Remember that (as noted on p. 134) we shall have ***do*** and ***does*** as symbols of the same category, with the same meaning.

$w \in (V^+(\alpha))$(Arabella), so that $w \in V^+(7)$ iff $w \notin V^+($***sings***$)$(Arabella), i.e. iff Arabella does not sing in w.

Conjunctions

Conjunctions in traditional grammar link, among other things, sentences. We shall initially discuss ***and*** and shall assume it to be in $F_{\langle 0,0,0\rangle}$ and to have the truth-functional meaning it has in logic (cf. p. 32) viz.:

10.2 V(***and***) is that function $\omega \in \mathbf{D}_{\langle 0,0,0\rangle}$ such that if $a, b \in \mathbf{D}_0$ then for any $w \notin W$, $w \in \omega(a,b)$ iff $w \in a$ and $w \in b$.

We do not want to insist that this is precisely its meaning but only that it seems a reasonable approximation and that seeing it in this way gives us a criterion for assessing the reasonableness of the analyses of sentences containing ***and*** which we are about to present.

The deep structure of some sentences is easy, e.g.

(1) ⟨⟨***John, sleeps***⟩, ***and***, ⟨***Arabella, sleeps***⟩⟩

Since ***and*** is a two-place functor we may, by the rules of p. 78, put it between its arguments as well as before or after them. The trouble with ***and*** in English arises because it very seldom links sentences in the shallow structure but usually appears between two parts of a compound nominal. Thus a more natural rendering of (1) in the shallow structure would be

(2) ***John and Arabella sleep***

At this point a transformational linguist might postulate rules which enable the derivation of (2) from (1).[199] We achieve the same result by obtaining (2) from a λ-categorial deep structure sentence which is equivalent by λ-conversion to (1), viz.:

(3) $\langle\langle\lambda, x_{\langle 0,1\rangle}, \langle\langle$***John***$, x_{\langle 0,1\rangle}\rangle,$ ***and***$, \langle$***Arabella***$, x_{\langle 0,1\rangle}\rangle\rangle\rangle,$ ***sleep***$\rangle$

((3) converts to (1) by principle 6.21 on p. 89.)

In accordance with the rule suggested in footnote 177 (p. 138) we can (very loosely) paraphrase (3) as: ***sleep*** is an $x_{\langle 0,1\rangle}$ such that John $x_{\langle 0,1\rangle}$'s and Arabella $x_{\langle 0,1\rangle}$'s.

We can also deal with cases which many linguists assume are only obtainable by proper deletion of lexical items, e.g.,

[199] Though some realization of the inadequacy of this procedure is shewn by Chomsky [1965], p. 145 f, where an index to indicate sameness of referent is attached to a noun. This idea is taken up in Bach [1968], pp. 105–12, and McCawley [1968a], pp. 136 *et seq.* and [1971] where a view much closer to ours is described. Indeed it may be that our own procedure represents one framework within which a fully formalized version of the proposals of these authors might be realized.

(4) ***John sleeps but Arabella does not***

The deep structure of (4) is[200]

(5) $\langle \textit{\textbf{John}}, \langle\langle \lambda, x_1, \langle \textit{\textbf{sleeps}}, \langle \lambda, x_{\langle 0,1\rangle}, \langle\langle x_{\langle 0,1\rangle}, x_1\rangle, \textit{\textbf{but}}, \langle \textit{\textbf{Arabella}}, \langle \textit{\textbf{does}}, \langle \lambda, y_1, \langle \textit{\textbf{not}}, \langle x_{\langle 0,1\rangle}, y_1\rangle\rangle\rangle\rangle\rangle\rangle\rangle\rangle\rangle\rangle\rangle$

By λ-conversion (5) becomes

(6) $\langle\langle \textit{\textbf{John}}, \textit{\textbf{sleeps}}\rangle, \textit{\textbf{but}}, \langle \textit{\textbf{Arabella}}, \langle \textit{\textbf{does}}, \langle \lambda, y_1, \langle \textit{\textbf{not}}, \langle \textit{\textbf{sleeps}}, y_1\rangle\rangle\rangle\rangle\rangle\rangle$

The shallow structure of (6) is

(7) ***John sleeps but Arabella does not sleeps***

(7) of course would have to be rejected by an agreement principle (because of the last ***sleeps***) so that it could not be an acceptable shallow sentence but it is very tempting to think of (2) as obtained from (7) by the deletion of the second ***sleeps***. Since ***sleeps*** is a proper symbol of $\mathscr{L}$ we may speak of this kind of deletion as *proper* deletion. It will be remembered that we are calling the deletion of the λ's and the variables *logical* deletion.

The question at issue is not just whether (2) should be derived from (7) but what principles govern proper deletion in general. Obviously we cannot derive (2) from

(8) ***John sleeps but Arabella does not run(s)***

But even when the two verb phrases are identical this may not be sufficient to permit the deletion. Consider

(9) ***John and Arabella have a child***

Either (9) means that they have the same child or it is ambiguous. In either case the meaning which says that they have a common child cannot be explained if (9) is derived from

(10) ***John have a child and Arabella have a child***

The ambiguity is resolved in our own theory by the alternative deep structures:

(11) $\langle\langle \lambda, x_{\langle 0,1\rangle}, \langle\langle \textit{\textbf{John}}, x_{\langle 0,1\rangle}\rangle, \textit{\textbf{and}}, \langle \textit{\textbf{Arabella}}, x_{\langle 0,1\rangle}\rangle\rangle\rangle, \langle \lambda, x_1, \langle\langle \lambda, y_1, \langle \textit{\textbf{have}}, x_1, y_1\rangle\rangle, \langle \lambda, x_{\langle 0,1\rangle}, \langle \textit{\textbf{a}}, \textit{\textbf{child}}, x_{\langle 0,1\rangle}\rangle\rangle\rangle\rangle\rangle$

and

(12) $\langle\langle \lambda, y_1, \langle\langle \lambda, x_{\langle 0,1\rangle}, \langle\langle \textit{\textbf{John}}, x_{\langle 0,1\rangle}\rangle, \textit{\textbf{and}}, \langle \textit{\textbf{Arabella}}, x_{\langle 0,1\rangle}\rangle\rangle\rangle, \langle \lambda, x_1, \langle \textit{\textbf{have}}, x_1, y_1\rangle\rangle\rangle\rangle, \langle \lambda, x_{\langle 0,1\rangle}, \langle \textit{\textbf{a}}, \textit{\textbf{child}}, x_{\langle 0,1\rangle}\rangle\rangle\rangle$

Since

(13) $\langle \lambda, x_1, \langle\langle \lambda, y_1, \langle \textit{\textbf{have}}, x_1, y_1\rangle\rangle, \langle \lambda, x_{\langle 0,1\rangle}, \langle \textit{\textbf{a}}, \textit{\textbf{child}}, x_{\langle 0,1\rangle}\rangle\rangle\rangle\rangle$

converts to

(14) $\langle \lambda, x_1, \langle \textit{\textbf{a}}, \textit{\textbf{child}}, \langle \lambda, y_1, \langle \textit{\textbf{have}}, x_1, y_1\rangle\rangle\rangle\rangle$

[200] ***but*** for present purposes can be treated as ***and*** though of course there are differences.

(which is in $E_{\langle 0, 1\rangle}$) then (11) converts to

(15) $\langle\langle \textbf{\textit{John}}, \langle \lambda, x_1, \langle \textbf{\textit{a}}, \textbf{\textit{child}}, \langle \lambda, y_1, \langle \textbf{\textit{have}}, x_1, y_1\rangle\rangle\rangle\rangle\rangle, \textbf{\textit{and}}, \langle \textbf{\textit{Arabella}}, \langle \lambda, x_1, \langle \textbf{\textit{a}}, \textbf{\textit{child}}, \langle \lambda, y_1, \langle \textbf{\textit{have}}, x_1, y_1\rangle\rangle\rangle\rangle\rangle\rangle$

which is the interpretation of (13) which does not require it to be the same child. (12) becomes

(16) $\langle \textbf{\textit{a}}, \textbf{\textit{child}}, \langle \lambda, y_1, \langle\langle \textbf{\textit{John}}, \langle \lambda, x_1, \langle \textbf{\textit{have}}, x_1, y_1\rangle\rangle\rangle, \textbf{\textit{and}}, \langle \textbf{\textit{Arabella}}, \langle \lambda, x_1, \langle \textbf{\textit{have}}, x_1, y_1\rangle\rangle\rangle\rangle\rangle\rangle$

(16) of course says that it is true of a child that both John has it and Arabella has it, and so insists that it is the same child.

This example shews that an apparently simple rule like one which gets the shallow structure of (4) from (7) by deletion of the second ***sleeps*** turns out, when fully formulated, to be rather complex and indeed appears to depend for its correct application on such semantic features as that if ***a child*** in (10) is meant to refer to one and the same child the rule does not apply. Our way of obtaining it makes both alternative deep structures of (10) mean precisely what is required. Of course we have thrown a very heavy burden on the principles which tell us which deep structures are acceptable in English.

or behaves in many ways like ***and***. We can give it a meaning rule which corresponds to [Vv] on p. 32 as 10.2, on p. 153, corresponds to [V&]. Most of our discussion of compound nominals carries over to ***or*** though there are some interesting cases when it is combined with ***not***.[201] Thus

(17) ***John loves not Arabella or Clarissa***

can have as deep structure either

(18) $\langle \textbf{\textit{John}}, \langle \lambda, x_1, \langle \textbf{\textit{loves}}, \langle \lambda, x_{\langle 0,1,1\rangle}, \langle \textbf{\textit{not}}, \langle\langle \textbf{\textit{Arabella}}, \langle \lambda, y_1, \langle x_{\langle 0,1,1\rangle}, x_1, y_1\rangle\rangle\rangle, \textbf{\textit{or}}, \langle\langle \textbf{\textit{Clarissa}}, \langle \lambda, y_1, \langle x_{\langle 0,1,1\rangle}, x_1, y_1\rangle\rangle\rangle\rangle\rangle\rangle\rangle\rangle\rangle$

or

(19) $\langle \textbf{\textit{John}}, \langle \lambda, x_1, \langle \textbf{\textit{loves}}, \langle \lambda, x_{\langle 0,1,1\rangle}, \langle \textbf{\textit{not}}, \langle \lambda, x_{\langle 0,0\rangle}, \langle\langle \textbf{\textit{Arabella}}, \langle \lambda, y_1, \langle x_{\langle 0,0\rangle}, \langle x_{\langle 0,1,1\rangle}, x_1, y_1\rangle\rangle\rangle\rangle, \textbf{\textit{or}}, \langle \textbf{\textit{Clarissa}}, \langle \lambda, y_1, \langle x_{\langle 0,0\rangle}, \langle x_{\langle 0,1,1\rangle}, x_1, y_1\rangle\rangle\rangle\rangle\rangle\rangle\rangle\rangle\rangle\rangle\rangle$

(18) must be interpreted as saying that he loves neither Arabella nor Clarissa while (19) says that either he doesn't love Arabella or that he doesn't love Clarissa. This can be seen by making the appropriate λ-conversions, which we leave to the reader.

The perceptive language-user will of course know that ***and*** and ***or*** often occur with ***both*** and ***either*** respectively and they can be negated

[201] Obviously (17) would be more natural if formulated using ***does*** but the extra complications would be irrelevant to the point made here.

in various ways with ***neither*** and ***nor***. These words can occur with semantic force as in:

(20) ⟨***both, men, run***⟩

and

(21) ⟨***either, man, runs***⟩

Here they are each of category ⟨0, ⟨0, 1⟩, ⟨0, 1⟩⟩ exactly as are ***every***, ***a***, ***the*** and ***most*** as discussed on pp. 135–7. Their semantics are akin to ***the*** except that whereas ***the*** in the present case makes a true sentence when there is exactly one man, and he runs, ***both*** makes a true sentence of (24) when there are exactly two men and they both run, while ***either*** makes a true sentence of (19) when there are exactly two men and one of them runs.

Now there is obviously a semantic link of some kind between (20) and the deep structure of

(22) ***both John and Arabella run***

and between (21) and

(23) ***either John or Arabella run***

but there seems no easy way of expressing this, particularly when we must also allow

(24) ***John both runs and sleeps***

and

(25) ***either John runs or Arabella sleeps***

We shall in fact find that the most convenient way of dealing with these cases is to regard the ***both*** and the ***either*** as shallow structure devices for indicating the scope of ***and*** and ***or*** in the deep structure.[202] We shall spend some time on pp. 217–24 in discussing the role of scope-indicating devices in the shallow structure and so shall not go any further into this particular application of them. The same remarks apply to such other 'compound' conjunctions as ***if – then*** –. (We shall not, even tentatively, propose [V⊃] as the meaning of this functor in view of the furore that would cause.)

Not all functors lend themselves in the way ***and*** and ***or*** do to the manufacture of compound nominals. E.g., although we can have

(26) ***John runs because Arabella sleeps***

with the deep structure

(27) ⟨⟨***John, runs***⟩, ***because***, ⟨***Arabella, sleeps***⟩⟩

we cannot have, as giving an acceptable shallow structure,

(28) ⟨⟨λ, $x_{\langle 0,1\rangle}$, ⟨⟨***John***, $x_{\langle 0,1\rangle}$⟩, ***because***, ⟨***Arabella***, $x_{\langle 0,1\rangle}$⟩⟩⟩, ***sleeps***⟩

[202] For a different account of ***either*** *vide* G. Lakoff [1971a], p. 256n.

I.e. there will have to an acceptability principle which blocks the derivation of

(29) ***John because Arabella sleeps***

On the other hand

(30) $\langle$***John***$, \langle\lambda, x_1, \langle$***sleeps***$, \langle\lambda, x_{\langle 0,1\rangle}, \langle\langle x_{\langle 0,1\rangle}, x_1\rangle,$
because$, \langle$***Arabella***$, \langle$***does***$, x_{\langle 0,1\rangle}\rangle\rangle\rangle\rangle\rangle\rangle\rangle$

yields the perfectly acceptable

(31) ***John sleeps because Arabella does***

In the case of ***and*** of course we have as acceptable both

(32) ***John sleeps and Arabella***

and

(33) ***John sleeps and Arabella does***

though in these latter cases the addition of ***too*** as the last word would make a more normal sentence.

One of the principal tasks in Chapter Thirteen will be to try to formulate what lies behind such facts as the acceptability of (30) and the non-acceptability of (28). All we shall say here is that an answer in the form of a rule for deletion of the second object when the verbs are linked by ***and*** but not when linked by ***because*** seems as much *ad hoc* and as little independently motivated as the observation that (30) is an acceptable deep structure but (28) is not. The important feature may well be that ***and*** and ***or*** obey the commutative and associative laws;[203] i.e. that $\langle\alpha, \textbf{\textit{and}}, \beta\rangle$ has the same value as $\langle\beta, \textbf{\textit{and}}, \alpha\rangle$ and that $\langle\alpha, \textbf{\textit{and}}, \langle\beta, \textbf{\textit{and}}, \gamma\rangle\rangle$ has the same value as $\langle\langle\alpha, \textbf{\textit{and}}, \beta\rangle, \textbf{\textit{and}}, \gamma\rangle$.

Before we leave a discussion of conjunctions we shall say a little about cases in which one of the arguments of the conjunction is inserted, almost parenthetically, into the middle of the other argument.[204] Thus

(34) ***John, because Arabella sleeps, runs.***

It would be possible to obtain this directly from a λ-categorial deep structure, viz.:

(35) $\langle\langle\lambda, x_{\langle 0,1\rangle}, \langle\langle$***John***$, x_{\langle 0,1\rangle}\rangle,$ ***because***$, \langle$***Arabella, sleeps***$\rangle\rangle\rangle,$ ***runs***$\rangle$

However, there seems no harm in saying that (34) is obtained from

(36) $\langle\langle$***John, runs***$\rangle,$ ***because***$, \langle$***Arabella, sleeps***$\rangle\rangle$

by the transposition of one of the arguments. The point is that written English by the use of commas, and spoken English by a subtle combination of pausing and intonation, seem to recognize that ***because***

[203] Though ***and*** in English is not always commutative, *vide infra*, p. 165.

[204] This is sometimes called *apposition*. The link between parenthetical insertion and apposition is seen in Bloomfield [1933], p. 186.

Arabella sleeps is an intruder in (34). A good, though intuitive, way of telling whether an expression is an intruder in this sense is to see whether enclosing it in parentheses in a written token of the whole sentence causes a difference of meaning. Although of course it has semantic effect in the sense that (34) clearly differs in meaning from the simple

(37) ***John runs***

(it says more) yet we can lift ***because Arabella sleeps*** bodily out of the place where it occurs and put it after ***John runs***.

We must, though, be very careful that a transformation of the kind needed to get (34) from (36) is only postulated when it can do no harm. We noted above (p. 154 f) that the temptation to postulate a rather similar sort of rule (involving deletion of repeated phrases) was one to be resisted if we were to avoid certain semantic anomalies.

Relative and reflexive pronouns

It is perhaps a little odd that we should discuss relative pronouns before personal pronouns. The answer is that personal pronouns are essentially context-dependent in a way relative pronouns are not and must therefore wait until the next chapter.

Relative pronouns make adjectives out of intransitive verb phrases (i.e. out of expressions of category $\langle 0,1\rangle$). Thus they are of category $\langle\langle\langle 0,1\rangle,\langle 0,1\rangle\rangle,\langle 0,1\rangle\rangle$; and we have the deep structure

(1) ⟨***the***, ⟨***man***, ⟨***who***, ***sleeps***⟩⟩, ***runs***⟩

In English there are two uses of relative pronouns. First, they can form what are known as restrictive relative clauses. This is the situation in (1) where ⟨***who***, ***sleeps***⟩ restricts ***man*** to form a one-place predicate (i.e. an expression of category $\langle 0,1\rangle$) which is true of only certain kinds of men, viz. those who sleep. The other kind, the so-called descriptive relative, occurs in a sentence like

(2) ***John, who drives a car, sings***

In this case we do not have several Johns from whom we want to pick out the one who drives a car in order to say that he sings. It is that in addition to the main sentence

(3) ***John sings***

we are being offered, parenthetically, the extra information that John drives a car. ***who drives a car*** is an intruder in the above sense.[205] If so then we should deal with it by deriving it from

(4) ***John sings who drives a car***

[205] Thus it is sometimes called an *appositive* relative clause.

This will not do as it stands. What will do is

(5) ***John sings and he drives a car***

The best way to see (2) is to imagine ***who*** as being derived from ***and he*** so that (2) comes first from

(6) ***John, and he drives a car, sings***

which comes from (5).

There is obviously some semantic reason for the use of the same word ***who*** for both restrictive and descriptive relative clauses but it is hard to say exactly what it is. It must have something to do with the fact that the meaning of (1) can be expressed as:

(7) ***the thing such that he is a man and he sleeps runs***

but (7) gives us no clue to a meaning rule for ***who***. The situation is like that of ***both*** and ***either*** on p. 156 where the words had two uses which were clearly related but not in an obvious way. In the absence of a better solution we shall treat the ***who*** in descriptive relatives as derived from ***and he*** at the beginning of a parenthetical clause[206] and the ***who*** in restrictive relative clauses as of category $\langle\langle\langle 0,1\rangle,\langle 0,1\rangle\rangle,\langle 0 1\rangle\rangle$ with the semantic rule:

10.3 V(***who***) is that function $\zeta \in \mathbf{D}_{\langle\langle\langle 0,1\rangle,\langle 0,1\rangle\rangle,\langle 0,1\rangle\rangle}$ such that for any $\omega, \omega' \in \mathbf{D}_{\langle 0,1\rangle}$, $(\zeta(\omega))(\omega')$ is that function in $\mathbf{D}_{\langle 0,1\rangle}$ such that for any human being $a \in \mathbf{D}_1$ and $w \in \mathbf{W}$, $w \in ((\zeta(\omega))(\omega')(a)$ iff $w \in \omega(a)$ and $w \in \omega'(a)$.

This rule is based on the assumption that ***who*** is only used when applied to a human being. A rule for ***which*** would be exactly the same except that it would exclude human beings. The rule for ***whom*** would be just as for ***who*** but principles of agreement would prevent the derivation of ***whom*** in (shallow) subject position. (The status of ***who*** in object position would seem to vary among English speech communities and perhaps even from person to person.)

Reflexive pronouns convert a two-place predicate like ***loves*** into a one-place predicate like ***loves himself***. But they do not do it in the same way that ***Arabella*** converts ***loves*** into ***loves Arabella***. ***himself*** is used to ensure that the single argument of ***loves himself*** occupies both

[206] I am not entirely happy about leaving descriptive relative clauses in the lurch like this since the phenomenon is quite a widespread one. Thus we can have ***the philosophical Greeks liked to talk*** (Bach [1968], p. 93) in which ***philosophical*** plays the part of a descriptive relative clause. The same phenomenon appears when one nominal complements another as in: ***the girl Miriam laughed.*** (Cf. Delorme and Dougherty [1972].)

argument places of ***loves***. Thus ***himself*** in the λ-base is of category $\langle\langle 0,1\rangle,\langle 0,1,1\rangle\rangle$ (which means that it can operate not only on a transitive verb but also on a complex expression made up, say, using a preposition like ***runs towards***).

The semantics for ***himself*** is simple:

10.4 V(***himself***) is that function $\zeta \in \mathbf{D}_{\langle\langle 0,1\rangle,\langle 0,1,1\rangle\rangle}$ such that for any $\omega \in \mathbf{D}_{\langle 0,1,1\rangle}$ and $a \in \mathbf{D}_1$, $(\zeta(\omega))(a) = \omega(a,a)$.

(***herself*** and ***itself*** have the same rule but will be affected by different restrictions in obtaining the shallow structure.)[207] Thus

(8) ***John loves himself***

has a a deep structure

(9) ⟨***John***, ⟨***loves***, ***himself***⟩⟩

Assuming that ***John*** is a logically proper name, which picks out John, 9.3 (p. 132) assures us that for any $\omega \in \mathbf{D}_{\langle 0,1\rangle}$, V(***John***)($\omega$) = ω(John).

Now V⁺(9) = V(***John***)(V⁺(⟨***loves***, ***himself***⟩))
= V⁺(⟨***loves***, ***himself***⟩)(John)
= V(***loves***)(John, John)

There are other shallow structures which can be derived from λ-bases which express reflexiveness; e.g. from

(10) ⟨***John***, ⟨λ, x_1, ⟨***loves***, x_1, x_1⟩⟩⟩

we may derive

(11) ***John loves***

The reason why (10) would be ruled out as unnatural is that (11) normally means that John loves someone and is an example of the intransitive use of transitive verbs which we discuss on p. 200 f. This is partly because the occasions on which we want to say that John loves himself are relatively fewer than those on which we want to say merely that he loves someone. Verbs which pick out actions which are frequently reflexive, like ***shaves***, do allow a derivation of the (10) to (11) kind; thus

(12) ⟨***John***, ⟨λ, x_1, ⟨***shaves***, x_1, x_1⟩⟩⟩

gives the acceptable shallow structure

(13) ***John shaves***

We can also of course obtain

(14) ***John shaves himself***

from a deep structure like (9).

[207] Or else V(***himself***) could be restricted to the case where *a* is male and (8) would be undefined if John is a woman.

The collective sense of nominals

Consider the sentence

(1) ***the men outnumber the women***

Suppose for the moment we treat ***the men*** and ***the women*** as unanalysed nominals.[208] Our procedure up to now would give the deep structure of (1) as

(2) $\langle$***the men***, $\langle\lambda, x_1, \langle\langle\lambda, y_1, \langle$***outnumber***, $x_1, y_1\rangle\rangle$, ***the women***$\rangle\rangle\rangle$

or

(3) $\langle\langle\lambda, y_1, \langle$***the men***, $\langle\lambda, x_1, \langle$***outnumber***, $x_1, y_1\rangle\rangle\rangle\rangle$, ***the women***$\rangle$

Let us further suppose, as seem plausible, the following rule for ***the men*** and ***the women***

10.5 V(***the men***) is that function $\zeta \in \mathbf{D}_{\langle 0, \langle 0, 1\rangle\rangle}$ such that if $\omega \in \mathbf{D}_{\langle 0, 1\rangle}$ and $w \in \mathbf{W}$ then $w \in \zeta(\omega)$ iff for every a in the intended set of men[209] $w \in \omega(a)$.

V(***the women***) is the same but with 'women' in place of 'men'. However, such an interpretation will not fit (1), for (1) does not mean that each man outnumbers each woman but rather that the intended set of men is larger than the intended set of women. Thus (2) and (3) are not deep structures for the natural sense of (1). In the case of (1), both (2) and (3) are clearly ruled out as deep structures and there is no question of ambiguity. Other cases do admit of ambiguity: e.g.,

(4) ***men who sweep chimneys diminish daily***

can, for those with robust imaginations, evoke the picture of next year's chimney sweeps being only a foot high, though it almost certainly means that there will be fewer sweeps about. Example (4) does not seem to involve equivocation in ***diminish*** but rather in what it is which is claimed to be diminishing and suggests that what we have here are two distinct uses of a nominal. Let us take (1) and see what is involved.

The predicate ***outnumber*** could be said to relate two sets when the second has fewer members than the first. We have to be a bit more careful than that since we may want to speak of a set determined by a condition (say the set of the men in a certain room) outnumbering a set determined by another condition (say the set of the women in a certain room). Suppose we want to have the proposition that the men in the room outnumber the women in the room. This will be the proposition which is true in a world w iff the set of men in the room in w is larger than the set of women in the room in w. It would thus seem

[208] This is to avoid complications over plurals, cf. *infra* p. 191.

[209] A rule like 10.5 really only makes sense in a context-dependent assignment, *vide infra*, pp. 174, 180 and 191.

better to let ***outnumber*** relate the two *properties* of being a man in the room and being a woman in the room since then the value of the proposition in w can be calculated by finding the value of the properties in w.

Actually it proves better still to give a definition of ***outnumber*** which applies to functions in $\mathbf{D}_{\langle 0, \langle 0, 1 \rangle\rangle}$ and says when one of them is to be understood as outnumbering another of them. What we want is to indicate that ***outnumber*** is to apply not to each man separately but to ***the men*** taken as a whole. The best way to deal with this is to say that V(***outnumber***) is a property which has as its argument the complicated functions which are V(***the men***) and V(***the women***), which (by the principles of p. 98 f) are of course in $\mathbf{D}_1$.

To make this work we want something which converts ***the men*** into a logically proper name (in the sense of 9.3, p. 132) of V(***the men***). This operator will be in $F_{\langle\langle 0, \langle 0, 1 \rangle\rangle, \langle 0, \langle 0, 1 \rangle\rangle}$ and will be referred to as ***coll***[210] (for ***the men*** is in $\langle 0, \langle 0, 1 \rangle\rangle$ and so, for us, are all names). We give the following semantics for ***coll***:

10.6 V(***coll***) is that function $\zeta \in \mathbf{D}_{\langle\langle 0, \langle 0, 1 \rangle\rangle, \langle 0, \langle 0, 1 \rangle\rangle\rangle}$ such that if $a \in \mathbf{D}_{\langle 0, \langle 0, 1 \rangle\rangle}$, $\zeta(a)$ is that function in $\mathbf{D}_{\langle 0, \langle 0, 1 \rangle\rangle}$ such that for any $\omega \in \mathbf{D}_{\langle 0, 1 \rangle}$, $(\zeta(a))(\omega) = \omega(a)$.[211]

This will make the deep structure of (1):

(5) $\langle\langle$***coll, the men***$\rangle, \langle \lambda, x_1, \langle\langle \lambda, y_1, \langle$***outnumber***$, x_1, y_1\rangle\rangle,$
$\langle$***coll, the women***$\rangle\rangle\rangle\rangle$

Since $\langle$***coll, the men***$\rangle$ and $\langle$***coll, the women***$\rangle$ are logically proper names then there is no difference in meaning caused by a difference in scope.[212] To see how (5) works we shall give a rule for ***outnumber***.

10.7 V(***outnumber***) is that function $\omega \in \mathbf{D}_{\langle 0, 1, 1 \rangle}$ such that for any $w \in \mathbf{W}$ and a, $b \in \mathbf{D}_1$, $w \in \omega(a,b)$ iff $a \in \mathbf{D}_{\langle 0, \langle 0, 1 \rangle\rangle}$ and $b \in \mathbf{D}_{\langle 0, \langle 0, 1 \rangle\rangle}$ and $\{x \in \mathbf{D}_1 : (\forall \omega \in \mathbf{D}_{\langle 0, 1 \rangle})(w \in a(\omega) \supset w \in \omega(x))\}$ contains more members than $\{x \in \mathbf{D}_1 : (\forall \omega \in \mathbf{D}_{\langle 0, 1 \rangle})(w \in b(\omega) \supset w \in \omega(x))\}$. (Remember that $\mathbf{D}_{\langle 0, \langle 0, 1 \rangle\rangle} \subseteq \mathbf{D}_1$.)

210 Although ***coll*** will appear in the shallow structure, it will not reach the surface (*vide infra*, p. 213 n). It would be what linguists call a 'zero morpheme'. Gleason [1961], p. 76, points out the dangers of having zero morphemes, and we shall be as sparing as possible in our use of them.

211 There may be no total function in $\mathbf{D}_{\langle\langle 0, \langle 0, 1 \rangle\rangle, \langle 0, \langle 0, 1 \rangle\rangle\rangle}$ satisfying 10.6. As we remarked *supra* p. 130 we must therefore take some big partial function whose domain takes in all the cases we want to consider.

212 G. Lakoff [1970a], p. 161. A common surface indicator of a 'collective' interpretation is the use of the word ***all*** as opposed to ***every***; *vide* Vendler [1967], pp. 72–6. Another is the use of the plural since words like ***every***, which do not allow the collective interpretation, seem to require the singular. (Of course a non-collective interpretation can occur with ***all*** and the plural as in ***all men run***.)

To see what this comes to we shall use it in the evaluation of (5). Given V(***the men***) and V(***the women***) as defined in 10.5 (p. 161) we have

$$\mathrm{V}^{+}(\langle \textbf{\textit{coll, the men}}\rangle) = \mathrm{V}(\textbf{\textit{coll}})(\mathrm{V}(\textbf{\textit{the men}}))$$

and by 10.6 this is that function $\zeta \in \mathbf{D}_{\langle 0, \langle 0, 1\rangle\rangle}$ such that for any $\omega \in \mathbf{D}_{\langle 0, 1\rangle}$

$$\zeta(\omega) = \omega(\mathrm{V}(\textbf{\textit{the men}}))$$

and similarly

$$\mathrm{V}^{+}(\langle \textbf{\textit{coll, the women}}\rangle)(\omega) = \omega(\mathrm{V}(\textbf{\textit{the women}})).$$

Since ⟨***coll, the men***⟩ and ⟨***coll, the women***⟩ are logically proper names we know, by the usual principles for evaluating abstracts (*vide* pp. 83–6), that $\mathrm{V}^{+}((5)) =$

(6) V(***outnumber***)(V(***the men***), V(***the women***))

By 10.7, $w \in (6)$ iff

(7) $\{x \in \mathbf{D}_1 : (\forall \omega \in \mathbf{D}_{\langle 0, 1\rangle})(w \in \mathrm{V}(\textbf{\textit{the men}})(\omega) \supset w \in \omega(x))\}$

contains more members than

(8) $\{x \in \mathbf{D}_1 : (\forall \omega \in \mathbf{D}_{\langle 0, 1\rangle})(w \in \mathrm{V}(\textbf{\textit{the women}})(\omega) \supset w \in \omega(x))\}$

Now by 10.5 (p. 161) we know that $w \in \mathrm{V}(\textbf{\textit{the men}})(\omega)$ iff for every y in the intended set of men (in w), $w \in \omega(y)$ and $w \in \mathrm{V}(\textbf{\textit{the women}})(\omega)$ iff for every y in the intended set of women (in w), $w \in \omega(y)$. Thus $x \in (7)$ iff x has (in w) all the properties which the members of the intended set of men have in w. And this means that $x \in (7)$ iff x is in the intended set of men; and that (7) is therefore the intended set of men. Similarly $x \in (8)$ iff x is in the intended set of women. Thus (6) is true in w iff the intended set of men in w contains more members than the intended set of women in w. The reasoning here is certainly involved but no more so, I think, than an adequate analysis of (1) demands.

A solution of roughly this kind would seem to be indicated for some problem cases raised by James McCawley.[213] We shall not attempt to discuss McCawley's proposals in detail except to say that operators like ***coll*** should be able to take care of such examples as

(9) ***those men went to Cleveland*** (together)

(10) ***the policemen broke up the demonstration***

and so on. Slightly more difficult are the collective uses of phrases made up with ***and***. Take, e.g.,

(11) ***John and Arabella fight***

One way of dealing with this is to take ***fight*** in the deep structure to be in $\mathrm{F}_{\langle 0, 1, 1\rangle}$. We assume (11) to mean that John and Arabella are fighting one another. If so, the deep structure for (11) could be

[213] McCawley [1968a], pp. 140–55, 161–9. *Vide* also Dougherty [1970].

(12) $\langle\langle\lambda, x_{\langle 0,1,1\rangle}, \langle\langle\lambda, x_1, \langle\langle\lambda, x_{\langle 0,0,0\rangle}, \langle\langle\lambda, y_1, \langle\langle x_{\langle 0,1,1\rangle}, x_1, y_1\rangle, x_{\langle 0,0,0\rangle}, \langle x_{\langle 0,1,1\rangle}, y, x_1\rangle\rangle\rangle, \textbf{\textit{John}}\rangle\rangle, \textbf{\textit{and}}\rangle\rangle, \textbf{\textit{Arabella}}\rangle\rangle, \textbf{\textit{fight}}\rangle$

By λ-conversion we get

(13) $\langle\langle\lambda, x_1, \langle\langle\lambda, y_1, \langle\langle \textbf{\textit{fight}}, x_1, y_1\rangle, \textbf{\textit{and}}, \langle \textbf{\textit{fight}}, y_1, x_1\rangle\rangle\rangle, \textbf{\textit{John}}\rangle\rangle, \textbf{\textit{Arabella}}\rangle$

which is equivalent to

(14) $\langle\langle \textbf{\textit{John}}, \langle\lambda, x_1, \langle\langle\lambda, y_1, \langle \textbf{\textit{fight}}, x_1, y_1\rangle\rangle, \textbf{\textit{Arabella}}\rangle\rangle\rangle, \textbf{\textit{and}}, \langle \textbf{\textit{Arabella}}, \langle\lambda, y_1, \langle\langle\lambda, x_1, \langle \textbf{\textit{fight}}, y_1, x_1\rangle\rangle, \textbf{\textit{John}}\rangle\rangle\rangle\rangle$

I am not sure that I altogether like this way of dealing with it and perhaps one should regard V(***fight***) as a one-place property of the collective 'John and Arabella' function. Then the deep structure of (11) would be

(15) $\langle\langle \textbf{\textit{coll}}, \langle\lambda, x_{\langle 0,1\rangle}, \langle\langle \textbf{\textit{John}}, x_{\langle 0,1\rangle}\rangle, \textbf{\textit{and}}, \langle \textbf{\textit{Arabella}}, x_{\langle 0,1\rangle}\rangle\rangle\rangle\rangle, \textbf{\textit{fight}}\rangle$

10.6 (p. 162) will ensure that

$V^{+}(\langle \textbf{\textit{coll}}, \langle\lambda, x_{\langle 0,1\rangle}, \langle\langle \textbf{\textit{John}}, x_{\langle 0,1\rangle}\rangle, \textbf{\textit{and}}, \langle \textbf{\textit{Arabella}}, x_{\langle 0,1\rangle}\rangle\rangle\rangle\rangle)$

will denote the property of properties which, in any world, are true of John and Arabella and the semantic rule for ***fight*** would be modelled on V(***outnumber***) and would among other things entail something to the effect that in a world *w*, V(***fight***)(*a*) is true if *a* determines a class in *w* (in the way ***the men*** determined a class in our earlier example) such that when the class is two-membered each member, in *w*, fights the other member.

A harder case is one which involves what is known as the *respectively* transformation.[214] Consider

(16) ***John and Arabella run and jump***

where this means that John runs and Arabella jumps. (This interpretation of (12) could be clinched by putting ***respectively*** at the end of the sentence; hence the name of the phenomenon.) This *can* be given the following deep structure:

(17) $\langle\langle\lambda, y_{\langle 0,1\rangle}, \langle\langle\lambda, x_{\langle 0,0,0\rangle}, \langle\langle\lambda, x_{\langle 0,1\rangle}, \langle\langle\lambda, y_{\langle 0,\langle 0,1\rangle\rangle}, \langle \textbf{\textit{John}}, \langle\lambda, x_{\langle 0,\langle 0,1\rangle\rangle}, \langle\langle\langle x_{\langle 0,\langle 0,1\rangle\rangle}, x_{\langle 0,1\rangle}\rangle, x_{\langle 0,0,0\rangle}, \langle y_{\langle 0,\langle 0,1\rangle\rangle}, y_{\langle 0,1\rangle}\rangle\rangle\rangle\rangle, \textbf{\textit{and}}, \langle\langle x_{\langle 0,\langle 0,1\rangle\rangle}, x_{\langle 0,1\rangle}\rangle, x_{\langle 0,0,0\rangle}, \langle y_{\langle 0,\langle 0,1\rangle\rangle}, y_{\langle 0,1\rangle}\rangle\rangle\rangle\rangle, \textbf{\textit{Arabella}}\rangle\rangle, \textbf{\textit{run}}\rangle\rangle\ \textbf{\textit{and}}\rangle\rangle, \textbf{\textit{jump}}\rangle$

By λ-conversion (17) becomes

(18) $\langle\langle\langle \textbf{\textit{John}}, \textbf{\textit{run}}\rangle, \textbf{\textit{and}}, \langle \textbf{\textit{Arabella}}, \textbf{\textit{jump}}\rangle\rangle, \textbf{\textit{and}}, \langle\langle \textbf{\textit{John}}, \textbf{\textit{run}}\rangle, \textbf{\textit{and}}, \langle \textbf{\textit{Arabella}}, \textbf{\textit{jump}}\rangle\rangle\rangle$

(17) is a monster and would need to be extraordinarily well motivated to be the deep structure of anything.

[214] McCawley, loc. cit.

The ***coll*** operator does not apply here quite so easily as it has done before. There are two reasons for this. The first is that, as we have been interpreting ***and***, $\langle\alpha, \boldsymbol{and}, \beta\rangle$ is synonymous with $\langle\beta, \boldsymbol{and}, \alpha\rangle$. Yet (16) is certainly not synonymous with

(19) ***Arabella and John run and jump***

under the *respectively* interpretation. The second difficulty is that although we can make a property out of ***run and jump***, viz.:

(20) $\langle\lambda, x_1, \langle\langle \boldsymbol{run}, x_1\rangle, \boldsymbol{and}, \langle \boldsymbol{jump}, x_1\rangle\rangle\rangle$

this property (given the standard rule for ***and***) will be true of something iff that thing both runs and jumps.

The first objection can be dealt with if we assume that ***and*** is not (as the logic books have it) commutative. Much is frequently made of the difference between

(21) ***she got married and had a baby***

and

(22) ***she had a baby and got married***

where ***and*** seems to mean something like ***and then***. If we interpret the ***then*** in a non-temporal way as merely indicating a later member of a sequence then we might have

(23) $\langle \boldsymbol{coll}, \langle\lambda, x_{\langle 0,1\rangle}, \langle\langle \boldsymbol{Arabella}, x_{\langle 0,1\rangle}\rangle, \boldsymbol{and}, \langle \boldsymbol{John}, x_{\langle 0,1\rangle}\rangle\rangle\rangle\rangle$

as referring to the property whose value in any world is the ordered pair consisting of Arabella and John. We might then use an operator which when applied to

(24) $\langle\lambda, x_1, \langle\lambda, y_1, \langle\langle \boldsymbol{run}, x_1\rangle, \boldsymbol{and}, \langle \boldsymbol{jump}, y_1\rangle\rangle\rangle\rangle$

could form a one-place predicate which is true of something iff it is an ordered pair the first member of which runs and the second jumps; ***respectively*** would then be a surface marker to indicate that a deep structure involving this operator is the intended one. A solution of this kind would appear to me to formalize some of what McCawley says[215] though the situation here seems very complex and only partially understood. I hope however to have said enough to shew that there is no reason to suppose that a λ-categorial base language will not be up to the task.

that clauses

The most straightforward way in which one sentence can be embedded in another in English is by means of the word ***that***:

(1) ***John says that Arabella sleeps***

[215] McCawley [1968a], p. 155 f.

We shall claim that ***that*** in (1) functions as a purely syntactic device which converts a sentence into a nominal but does not essentially change its value.[216] I.e., in the deep structure ***that*** $\in F_{\langle\langle 0, \langle 0, 1\rangle\rangle, 0\rangle}$ and has the semantic rule:

10.8 V(***that***) is the function ζ in $\mathbf{D}_{\langle\langle 0, \langle 0, 1\rangle\rangle, 0\rangle}$ such that $a \in \mathbf{D}_1$ is in the domain of ζ iff a is a proposition (remember that everything, including propositions, is in $\mathbf{D}_1$), and for any such a and any $\omega \in \mathbf{D}_{\langle 0, 1\rangle}$, $(\zeta(a))(\omega) = \omega(a)$.

If we allowed nominals to be of type 1 we could let ***that*** be in $F_{\langle 1, 0\rangle}$ and have the rule that V(***that***)$(a) = a$ for any proposition a. But we shall see that construing it as in $F_{\langle 0, \langle 0,1\rangle\rangle}$ has the advantages we have already seen with other nominals. We therefore get as deep structure for (1)

(2) $\langle$***John***, $\langle\lambda, x_1, \langle\langle\lambda, y_1, \langle$***says***, $x_1, y_1\rangle\rangle$,
$\langle$***that***, $\langle$***Arabella, sleeps***$\rangle\rangle\rangle\rangle\rangle$

We should perhaps say a word of justification for regarding expressions whose main operator is ***that*** ('*that* clauses' as they are sometimes called) as nominals, i.e. as expressions of category $\langle 0, \langle 0, 1\rangle\rangle$. The basic argument is that they can replace what are unquestionably nominals. E.g., as well as (1) we can have

(3) ***John says something***

and in place of

(4) ***John tells Arabella that Bill sleeps***[217]

we can have

(5) ***John tells Arabella the answer***

Cases in which we appear to get anomalies, like

(6) ***John says the answer***

or worse

(7) ***John says Arabella***

seem best treated as semantic. I.e., ***say*** in this sense is a verb which only makes sense when its second term denotes a proposition.

While we are on this point it is worth noting that many complex

[216] Because a ***that*** clause frequently complements another nominal (*vide supra*, note 206, p. 159), as in ***the claim that John lies is absurd***, they are often called complements, and ***that*** is called a *complementizer* (*vide* Jacobs and Rosenbaum [1968], pp. 163–78).

[217] This makes ***tells*** of category $\langle 0,1,1,1\rangle$. The verb ***say*** is interesting because it can also take quotations as arguments. It might be best to have two deep structure words $\textbf{\textit{say}}_1$ and $\textbf{\textit{say}}_2$ whose meanings, though closely related, are distinct. (Similarly with the verb ***entails*** which we discuss below.)

expressions which in logic are treated as propositional functors are really made up from predicates which operate on ***that*** clauses; e.g., in the deep structure of

(8) ***that John runs quickly entails that John runs***

entails is in $F_{\langle 0,1,1\rangle}$ and the deep structure is

(9) $\langle\langle$***that***$, \langle\langle$***John, runs***$\rangle,$ ***quickly***$\rangle\rangle,$
$\langle\lambda, x_1, \langle\langle\lambda, y_1, \langle$***entails***$, x_1, y_1\rangle\rangle, \langle$***that***$, \langle$***John, runs***$\rangle\rangle\rangle\rangle$

The semantics for ***entails*** is exactly the same as the rule for $\prec\!\!3$ on p. 33 except that we must of course restrict its domain to those members of $\mathbf{D}_1$ which are propositions.[218] I.e.,

10.9 V(***entails***) is that function $\omega \in \mathbf{D}_{\langle 0,1,1\rangle}$ such that for any $w \in \mathbf{W}$ and $a, b \in \mathbf{D}_1$,

(i) a and b are in the domain of ω iff a and $b \in \mathbf{D}_0$,

and

(ii) $w \in \omega(a,b)$ iff $a \subseteq b$.

When we evaluate (9) we see that it is true in any world precisely when $V^+(\langle\langle$***John, runs***$\rangle,$ ***quickly***$\rangle) \subseteq V^+(\langle$***John, runs***$\rangle)$.

On p. 105 we discussed an ***entails*** predicate which was a predicate of sentences. Although we are now treating ***entails*** as a predicate and not a functor as on p. 33 it should be clear that its semantics follows that of p. 33 and not the complex paradox-generating semantics of p. 106.

10.8 is not the only rule we might have for ***that***. Consider the two sentences

(10) ***John knows that Arabella runs***

(11) ***John knows not that Arabella runs***[219]

Obviously (10) entails that Arabella runs. But also it would seem that there is a sense in which (11) does as well.[220] A verb like ***know*** which behaves in this way we might call a *factive* verb. Since the semantics of 10.8 will not give us a deep structure in which (11) entails that Arabella runs, we shall introduce what we might call a *factive* ***that*** which we shall refer to as ***that′*** and for which we shall give a semantics

[218] There are also predicates ***is true*** and ***is false*** which stand to this sense of ***entails*** as the predicates discussed on p. 102 and p. 101 stand to the predicate ***entails*** of p. 105. Kneale [1972], p. 239, puts it this way: 'considered as a linguistic operator, the predicate "is true" undoes the nominalizing work of "that".' These predicates (unlike the ones mentioned in Chapter Seven) are of course just as non-paradox-generating as is this ***entails***.

[219] As with other cases, the auxiliary ***does*** complicates the example but can easily be accommodated.

[220] G. Lakoff [1970a], p. 176, makes the same point about ***realize***.

which enables us to do justice to the facts as they appear to be. To do this we need to make use of the fact that ***that*** clauses are nominals and therefore have scope. The semantic rule for ***that′*** is:

10.10 V(***that′***) is a function $\zeta \in \mathbf{D}_{\langle\langle 0, \langle 0, 1\rangle\rangle, 0\rangle}$ such that where $a \in \mathbf{D}_0$ then a is in the domain of ζ and for any $\omega \in \mathbf{D}_{\langle 0, 1\rangle}$, if ω is in the domain of $\zeta(a)$ then if $w \in \mathbf{W}$, $w \in (\zeta(a))(\omega)$ iff $w \in a$ and $w \in \omega(a)$. (As before we note that if $a \in \mathbf{D}_0$ then $a \in \mathbf{D}_1$.)

The difference between 10.8 and 10.10 is simply that for $\zeta((a))(\omega)$ to be true in a world w, the proposition a must be true in w.

Consider now the following deep structures for (10) and (11):

(12) $\langle\langle\lambda, y, \langle$***John***$, \langle\lambda, x, \langle$***knows***$, x, y\rangle\rangle\rangle\rangle, \langle$***that′***$, \langle$***Arabella***$,$ ***runs***$\rangle\rangle\rangle$

(13) $\langle\langle\lambda, y, \langle$***John***$, \langle\lambda, x, \langle\langle$***knows***$, x, y\rangle,$ ***not***$\rangle\rangle\rangle\rangle,$
$\langle$***that′***$, \langle$***Arabella***$,$ ***runs***$\rangle\rangle\rangle$

(13) is not the contradictory of (12) since in (13) ***not*** is within the scope of the ***that′*** clause. (12) of course has a contradictory. If we make (12) the whole scope of an initial ***not*** we have a sentence which simply negates it.[221] By 10.10 it follows that (12) entails that Arabella runs and so its contradictory cannot also entail this. What we shall shew, however, is that (13), like (12), and therefore unlike the contradictory of (12), does entail that Arabella runs.

Let $V^+(\langle\lambda, y, \langle$***John***$, \langle\lambda, x, \langle\langle$***knows***$, x, y\rangle,$ ***not***$\rangle\rangle\rangle\rangle) = \omega$.

Given an appropriate rule for ***knows*** and the rules for evaluating abstracts we see that for any $a \in \mathbf{D}_1$ in the domain of ω, and any $w \in \mathbf{W}$, $w \in \omega(a)$ iff John does not know a.

Now $V^+((13)) = V^+(\langle$***that′***$, \langle$***Arabella***$,$ ***runs***$\rangle\rangle)$.

I.e., where V(***that′***) is ζ as defined in 10.10 and $a = V^+(\langle$***Arabella***$,$ ***runs***$\rangle)$ and is the proposition that Arabella runs, then

$$V^+((13)) = (\zeta(a))(\omega).$$

By 10.10 $w \in (\zeta(a))(\omega)$ iff $w \in a$ and $w \in \omega(a)$. I.e., $V^+(13)$ is true iff Arabella runs in w and John does not know this.

Not all verbs take a factive ***that***. Thus

(14) ***John believes that Arabella runs***

seems to entail neither that Arabella runs nor that she does not. Perhaps 10.8 and 10.10 are mutually exclusive in the sense that some verbs, like ***believe***, are only followed by ***that*** while others, like ***know***,

[221] And of course λ-conversion can be used to get a deep structure equivalent to the negation of (3) but in which ***not*** has the position it has in (11). The possibility of a genuine contradictory of (12) means that even if ***know*** is a factive verb it can still have a non-factive negation.

are only followed by ***that′***. If this is so, then we need only have one ***that*** and use a semantic rule which works like 10.10 when its argument is the meaning of a factive verb and like 10.8 when its argument is the meaning of a non-factive verb.

On the other hand there might be some verbs which take both a factive and a non-factive ***that***. If this is so then we will need two symbols in the deep structure for there will be ambiguous surface sentences depending on whether the ***that*** clause is understood factively or non-factively.[222]

Infinitives

Another common way of embedding one sentence in another is by using what is sometimes known as the *accusative and infinitive* construction. The surface grammar of

(10) ***John wants Arabella to sing***

treats ***Arabella*** as the object of ***wants***, but in deep structure it seems best to treat ***Arabella to sing*** as an embedded sentence. The role of ***to*** in the English infinitive seems simply a surface marker to indicate how ***sing*** is to be treated and we could have ***to sing*** as one symbol in the deep structure. However, it seems best to treat ***to*** as analogous to an auxiliary with no semantic effect in the deep structure except as an indicator for the acceptability principles. We do though need a logical operator, which we shall write as ***inf***, whose job is to convert the sentence

(11) ⟨***Arabella, sing***⟩

into a nominal.[223] V(***inf***) = V(***that***) but ***inf*** never reaches the surface. V(***to***) = V(***do***) (10.1, p. 152) and simply preserves the meaning of its

[222] ***that*** is only one kind of complementizer. Another is ***whether***, as in ***John knows whether Arabella sleeps***. Like ***whether***, but somewhat different, is ***what***, as in ***John knows what the answer is***. The proper analysis of these is very difficult and we do not pursue it. Some helpful studies, in the context of transformational grammar, are found in Bresnan [1970] and Kiparsky and Kiparsky [1971]; and a more philosophical discussion occurs in Chapter Five (pp. 127–46) of Vendler [1967]. The latter articles are especially interesting from a semantical point of view and shew how incomplete our own discussion of these questions has been.

[223] There are other uses of the infinitive. E.g., in the sentence: ***those who came to scoff stayed to pray***, ***to*** appears to make an adverb (of purpose) out of an intransitive verb phrase. ***to scoff*** is what Jacobs and Rosenbaum [1968] call a *verb phrase complement*. Their example (op. cit., p. 193) is ***Joan condescended to work at the museum***. The difference between these kinds of infinitives can be brought out by considering the difference between ***Jeremy wants a man to dig the garden*** and ***Jeremy wants a spade to dig the garden***. There would also seem to be an adverbial ***that*** in ***I was upset that he came***.

verb. Its presence however is required if a structure containing ***inf*** is to be acceptable. Thus the deep structure of (10) is

(12) $\langle$***John***, $\langle\lambda, x_1, \langle\langle\lambda, y_1, \langle$***wants***, $x_1, y_1\rangle$, $\langle$***inf***, $\langle$***Arabella***, $\langle$***to***, ***sing***$\rangle\rangle\rangle\rangle\rangle$

Notice that ***to*** also indicates that ***sing*** and not ***sings*** is to follow it.

We can also say

(13) ***John wants to sing***

This has the deep structure

(14) $\langle$***John***, $\langle\lambda, x_1, \langle\langle\lambda, y_1, \langle$***wants***, $x_1, y_1\rangle\rangle$, $\langle$***inf***, $\langle\langle$***to***, ***sing***$\rangle, x_1\rangle\rangle\rangle\rangle$

There are possibilities of scope ambiguity in infinitival phrases; e.g.

(15) ***John wants a man to sing***

may have as deep structure either

(16) $\langle$***John***, $\langle\lambda, x_1, \langle\langle\lambda, y_1, \langle$***wants***, $x_1, y_1\rangle\rangle$, $\langle$***inf***, $\langle$***a***, ***man***, $\langle$***to***, ***sing***$\rangle\rangle\rangle\rangle\rangle$

or

(17) $\langle$***John***, $\langle\lambda, x_{\langle 0, \langle 0, 1\rangle\rangle}$, $\langle$***wants***, $\langle\lambda, x_{\langle 0, 1, 1\rangle}$, $\langle$***a***, ***man***, $\langle\lambda, z_1, \langle x_{\langle 0, \langle 0, 1\rangle\rangle}, \langle\lambda, x_1, \langle\langle\lambda, y_1, \langle x_{\langle 0, 1, 1\rangle}, x_1, y_1\rangle\rangle$, $\langle$***inf***, $\langle\langle$***to***, ***sing***$\rangle, z_1\rangle\rangle\rangle\rangle\rangle\rangle\rangle\rangle\rangle\rangle\rangle$

John and ***wants*** have been taken by λ-conversion out of their 'true' places in deep structure in order to obtain the order required in the shallow structure. (17) converts to

(18) $\langle$***a***, ***man***, $\langle\lambda, z_1$, $\langle$***John***, $\langle\lambda, x_1, \langle\langle\lambda, y_1, \langle$***wants***, $x_1, y_1\rangle\rangle$, $\langle$***inf***, $\langle\langle$***to***, ***sing***$\rangle, y_1\rangle\rangle\rangle\rangle\rangle\rangle\rangle$

Comparing (16) and (18) we notice that in (16) ***a man*** is within the scope of ***wants*** while in (18) ***wants*** is within the scope of ***a man***. (18) assumes that there is some particular man whom John wants to sing while (16) simply says that what John wants is that there be such a man. There is a spurious sense in which in (17) ***a man*** is within the scope of ***wants*** but the sense in which it is spurious should be clear. (17) is a case of the kind alluded to on p. 138 n in which we are using λ-conversion simply to do the work, of re-ordering.

A more difficult case involving verbs like ***wants*** occurs when they are followed only by a direct object as in

(19) ***Arabella wants a man***

Here too we may distinguish between a discriminating Arabella who wants some particular man and an Arabella who does not really mind which man it is.

There are at least two kinds of solution to this problem. The first says that (19) is a surface sentence whose shallow structure is something like

(20) ***Arabella wants to find a man***

The resolution of the ambiguity in (20) can then proceed exactly as did that of (15). We shall have something to say about this solution on pp. 212–14 when we discuss the relation between shallow and surface structure. It is a solution of this kind which seems to be favoured by many linguists.[224]

The second kind of solution is a variant of one given by Richard Montague;[225] this is to think of the things which can be wanted as of a number of kinds. First, we may want ordinary things, as when Arabella wants some particular man; second, we may want states of affairs, as when Arabella wants John to play the piano; and third, we may want indefinite intensional objects. In this third sense we are to think of

(21) $V^{+}(\langle\lambda, x_{\langle 0,1\rangle}, \langle \boldsymbol{a}, \boldsymbol{man}, x_{\langle 0,1\rangle}\rangle\rangle)$

as the object of Arabella's desire. It is a bit like saying that what Arabella wants is a generic object of a certain kind.[226] This solution of course throws the difficulty onto someone who is proposing to write a semantic rule for ***wants*** in English but if that difficulty should not prove insurmountable Montague's solution will do.

The incorporation of Montague's solution into our framework demands the use of the collective interpretation operator ***coll*** (p. 162). The deep structure of (19) then becomes

(22) $\langle \boldsymbol{Arabella}, \langle\lambda, x_1, \langle\langle\lambda, y_1, \langle \boldsymbol{wants}, x_1, y_1\rangle\rangle,$
$\langle \boldsymbol{coll}, \langle\lambda, x_{\langle 0,1\rangle}, \langle \boldsymbol{a}, \boldsymbol{man}, x_{\langle 0,1\rangle}\rangle\rangle\rangle\rangle\rangle\rangle$

The evaluation of (22) would, with the appropriate rule for ***wants*** of the sort just indicated, proceed like the evaluation of (6) on p. 163 f.

If we are concerned with only one language the choice between these two ways of dealing with (19) will probably depend upon how much we want to keep semantics out of syntax. If it should turn out (a possibility we suggest, though by no means espouse, in Chapter Thirteen, pp. 211–15) that the deep structure should be regarded as

[224] E.g. Bach [1968], p. 119 f and, with some reservations, G. Lakoff [1970a], p. 220 f.

[225] Montague [1973]. Montague's solution appears to be simpler in his presentation because he treats intransitive verb phrases as of category ⟨⟨0,1⟩,⟨0,⟨0,1⟩⟩⟩. A consequence of this, however, is that he is unable to regard (19) as ambiguous. One of its meanings would have to be paraphrased as 'A man is such that Arabella wants him'.

[226] This is the way Lewis [1970], pp. 52–4, sees what Montague is doing. (It must of course be pointed out that what we have called 'Montague's solution' is really a family of solutions, only one of which coincides in every detail with what Montague says.)

a sort of universal system of concepts which underlies many or all natural languages, then it may well be that the first solution makes for more interesting generalizations than Montague's, but choices of this kind we leave to others.[227]

[227] A mine of examples will be found in Partee [1970]. Many of these are dealt with in Montague [1973]. Our own discussion ought to indicate how Montague's solution can be dealt with by us. The most difficult cases are those involving bound variables (*vide infra*, p. 178 f) such as ***Arabella wants a man so that she can marry him***. To shew how a Montague approach would tackle these cases would lead us too far astray.

CHAPTER ELEVEN

Context-dependence in English

Personal pronouns

Among the symbols which count as nominals are words like ***I***, ***you***, ***he***, ***she***, ***it*** etc.[228] We have already in Chapter Eight discussed how ***I*** is to be treated in a context-dependent interpretation of a λ-categorial language in which it is a member of F_1. Our first task in this chapter is to modify its semantic rule, along the lines suggested by 9.2 (p. 131), for a language in which it is of category $\langle 0, \langle 0, 1 \rangle \rangle$. We assume that $\mathbf{D}$ is an intended system of context-dependent domains. This means that $\mathbf{D}_0$ is a set of open propositions (in the sense of p. 115) and the other domains are appropriately built up as set out on p. 116. We give the following rule for ***I***:

11.1 V(***I***) is a function[229] $\zeta \in \mathbf{D}_{\langle 0, \langle 0, 1 \rangle \rangle}$ such that any $\omega \in \mathbf{D}_{\langle 0, 1 \rangle}$ which contains animate things in its domain is in the domain of ζ and for any such ω, $\zeta(\omega)$ is the following open proposition: For any context property $\mathfrak{p}$, $\mathfrak{p}$ is in the domain of $\zeta(\omega)$ iff $\mathfrak{p}$ is in a context family (*vide* p. 115) which specifies an utterer. Where $\mathfrak{p}$ specifies u as utterer then $(\zeta(\omega))(\mathfrak{p}) = (\omega(u))(\mathfrak{p})$.

With this rule for ***I*** we do not need either the open individuals of p. 118 or the complicated rule for predicates which we stated for ***sleep*** in 8.13 but can use a version like 8.9 (p. 117).[230]

[228] There are also the plural forms of these words; *vide infra*, pp. 190–2.
[229] We say *a* function rather than *the* function for the reasons mentioned in footnote 211 (p. 162).
[230] Note that V(***sleep***) = V(***sleeps***).

11.2 V(***sleep***) is a function ω in $\mathbf{D}_{\langle 0,\, 1\rangle}$ such that for any a in its domain $\omega(a)$ is the open proposition such that if $\mathfrak{p}$ is in a context family which specifies a time of utterance t then $(\omega(a))(\mathfrak{p})$ is true in any $w \in \mathbf{W}$ iff a is asleep at t in w.

We shew how this enables the proper evaluation of

(1) ⟨***I***, ***sleep***⟩

V^{+}(⟨***I***, ***sleep***⟩) is (V(***I***))(V(***sleep***)) and by 11.1 this will be the open proposition θ such that $\theta(\mathfrak{p})$ is true in w iff $\mathfrak{p}$ is in a context family which specifies an utterer u and (V(***sleep***)(u))($\mathfrak{p}$) is true in w. Now by 11.2 (V(***sleep***)(u))($\mathfrak{p}$) will be true in w iff $\mathfrak{p}$ is in a family which specifies a time t and u is asleep at t. Thus $\theta(\mathfrak{p})$ will be true iff $\mathfrak{p}$ is in a context family which specifies an utterer u and a time t and u is asleep at t. This means that a token of (1) uttered by u at t will express the proposition that u is asleep at t. The case with ***you*** is similar except that it depends on a context family which specifies a person who is being addressed.

More difficult cases are the third person pronouns ***he***, ***she*** and ***it***. This can be seen by comparing them with ***I*** and ***you***. If a person utters a token of

(2) ⟨***I***, ***sleep***⟩

or

(3) ⟨***I***, ⟨λ, x_1, ⟨⟨λ, y_1, ⟨***love***, x_1, y_1⟩⟩, ***you***⟩⟩⟩

there is only one utterer and, in favourable cases, one person being addressed. In the case of ***he***, however, we cannot determine the reference in such a straightforward way. The only kind of rule which seems to make any sense is the rule that ***he*** means the person the utterer is talking about, or intends to refer to. These terms are difficult in that the notions of what it is to talk about something or refer to something cause notorious philosophical problems. They are indeed among the hardest questions which a theory of language use must come to grips with. However this in itself need not worry us since whatever the proper philosophical ar**al**ysis of the problem may be, we do talk about and refer to things and we can know what we are talking about or referring to.

If an account of this kind is to be given for personal pronouns it would look something like:

11.3 V(***he***) is a function $\zeta \in \mathbf{D}_{\langle 0,\, \langle 0,\, 1\rangle\rangle}$ such that for any $\omega \in \mathbf{D}_{\langle 0,\, 1\rangle}$ in its domain $\zeta(\omega)$ is the open proposition such that for any context property $\mathfrak{p}$, $\mathfrak{p}$ is in the domain of $\zeta(\omega)$ iff $\mathfrak{p}$ is in a context family which specifies that a male person or animal u is the thing which is being talked about; for any such $\mathfrak{p}$, $(\zeta(\omega))(\mathfrak{p}) = (\omega(u))(\mathfrak{p})$.

The rule for ***she*** is exactly the same except that the word 'female' replaces 'male' and the rule for ***it*** is like the rule for ***he*** except that 'male person or animal u' is replaced by 'something u which is not a human being'. These last qualifications may not represent English exactly, since in stories, for instance, stones can speak and might be described as ***he***, we speak of ships as ***she*** and we may, in certain circumstances, use ***it*** to speak of human beings. But at least the rules might be considered to approximate to English usage and that is good enough for the points being made here. 11.3 will provide for

(4) $\langle \boldsymbol{he}, \boldsymbol{runs} \rangle$

the meaning θ, viz. the open proposition such that if $\mathfrak{p}$ specifies an intended referent u and a time t then for $w \in \mathbf{W}$, $w \in \theta(\mathfrak{p})$ iff u is running at t.

The trouble with 11.3 comes with cases of multiple reference. In a sentence like

(5) ***he says that he sleeps***

it is possible that the two ***he***'s are intended to refer to different people as when (5) is the answer to

(6) ***what does the mayor say about the town clerk?***

This is just an acute form of a more general difficulty.[231] Mostly a token of a sentence will be talking about many people, some of them the intended referents of the personal pronouns and others not. We suppose that the deep structure contains not one but a number of personal pronouns. We shall speak of $\boldsymbol{he}_1$, $\boldsymbol{he}_2$ etc.[232] These will all be realized in the surface structure as **he** (*vide* p. 213). There will also be versions of ***him***, ***she***, ***her***, ***it*** etc. Two pronouns with the same subscript have as value the same individual in accordance with 11.4 to be given below (p. 176). This means that (5) is ambiguous and its alternative deep structures would be of some such form as:

(7) $\langle\langle\lambda, x_1, \langle \boldsymbol{he}_1, \langle\lambda, y_1, \langle \boldsymbol{says}, x_1, y_1\rangle\rangle\rangle, \langle \boldsymbol{that}, \langle \boldsymbol{he}_1, \boldsymbol{sleeps}\rangle\rangle\rangle$

or

(8) $\langle\langle\lambda, x_1, \langle \boldsymbol{he}_1, \langle\lambda, y_1, \langle \boldsymbol{says}, x_1, y_1\rangle\rangle\rangle, \langle \boldsymbol{that}, \langle \boldsymbol{he}_2, \boldsymbol{sleeps}\rangle\rangle\rangle$

[231] Jourdain [1918], p. 26, cites a line from one of William Cowper's hymns: ***Satan trembles when he sees the weakest saint upon his knees*** (*Hymns Ancient and Modern*, No. 246) as an example of ambiguous pronominal reference.

[232] If the possibility of infinitely many symbols is worrying, we can easily characterize the series, using some arbitrary symbol ***sub***, as ***he***, $\langle \boldsymbol{sub}, \boldsymbol{he}\rangle$, $\langle \boldsymbol{sub}, \langle \boldsymbol{sub}, \boldsymbol{he}\rangle\rangle$ etc.

where $\boldsymbol{he}_1$ and $\boldsymbol{he}_2$ are two separate members of $F_{\langle 0, \langle 0, 1\rangle\rangle}$ and (7) is intended to be interpreted in such a way that it is the same ***he*** being referred to both times. The context tells us which deep structure to select.

We want to make sure that for a deep structure to be acceptable the indices of the pronouns increase from left to right, with of course the proviso that an index may be repeated to indicate identity of referent with that of an earlier pronoun. $\boldsymbol{he}_n$ in the deep structure will therefore be represented by the nth referentially distinct 𝔥𝔢 in the token. (Two 𝔥𝔢's are referentially distinct iff they are intended to refer to different people.) We shall give the rule for $\boldsymbol{he}_n$:

11.4 $V(\boldsymbol{he}_n)$ is a function $\zeta \in \mathbf{D}_{\langle 0, \langle 0, 1\rangle\rangle}$ such that for any $\omega \in \mathbf{D}_{\langle 0, 1\rangle}$ which is in the domain of ζ, $\zeta(\omega)$ is the following open proposition. Any context property $\mathfrak{p}$ is in the domain of $\zeta(\omega)$ iff $\mathfrak{p}$ is in a context family generated by a context property $\mathfrak{p}^*$ for which there is some male person or animal u such that for any $w \in \mathbf{W}$ and any utterance $\mathfrak{a}$, $\mathfrak{p}^*(\mathfrak{a})$ is true in w iff the utterer of $\mathfrak{a}$ in w intends in w to refer to u by the nth referentially distinct 𝔥𝔢 in $\mathfrak{a}$. For any $\mathfrak{p}$ in the domain of $\zeta(\omega)$, $(\zeta(\omega))(\mathfrak{p}) = (\omega(u))(\mathfrak{p})$.

Take first a simple case:

(9) $\langle \boldsymbol{he}_1, \boldsymbol{sleeps}\rangle$

Now V(***sleeps***) = V(***sleep***) and so, by combining 11.2 on p. 174 with 11.4, we get

$$V^+(\langle \boldsymbol{he}_1, \boldsymbol{sleeps}\rangle) = (V(\boldsymbol{he}_1))(V(\boldsymbol{sleeps}))$$

This will be the open proposition θ such that $\theta(\mathfrak{p})$ is true in w iff $\mathfrak{p}$ is in a family which specifies u as the intended referent of $\boldsymbol{he}_1$ in w and $(V(\boldsymbol{sleeps}))(u)(\mathfrak{p})$ is true in w. Now by 11.2, $(V(\boldsymbol{sleeps})(u))(\mathfrak{p})$ will be true in w iff $\mathfrak{p}$ is in a context family which specifies a time t and u is asleep at t. Thus $\theta(\mathfrak{p})$ will be true iff $\mathfrak{p}$ is a property which is in a context family which specifies a time t of utterance and which specifies u as the intended referent of $\boldsymbol{he}_1$ and u is asleep at t.

This means that any token of (9) which is uttered at t by someone who intends the 𝔥𝔢 to refer to u expresses the proposition that u is asleep at t.

Let us look at the more complicated (5) and assume its deep structure is (8). We suppose that in addition to the rule for ***sleeps*** we have the following rules for ***says*** and ***that*** (cf. p. 166):

11.5 V(***says***) is that function ω in $\mathbf{D}_{\langle 0, 1, 1\rangle}$ such that for any $a, b \in \mathbf{D}_1$, $\omega(a, b)$ is the open proposition such that if $\mathfrak{p}$ is in a context family which specifies a time of utterance t then $(\omega(a))(\mathfrak{p})$ is true in any $w \in \mathbf{W}$ iff b is a proposition, and a asserts b at t in w.

11.6 V(***that***) is that function ξ in $\mathbf{D}_{\langle\langle 0, \langle 0, 1\rangle\rangle, 0\rangle}$ such that for any open proposition $\theta \in \mathbf{D}_0$ (so that $\theta \in \mathbf{D}_1$ also), $\xi(\theta)$ is the functor ζ such that for any $\omega \in \mathbf{D}_{\langle 0, 1\rangle}$, and any context property $\mathfrak{p}$, $((\zeta(\omega))(\mathfrak{p}) = (\omega(\theta(\mathfrak{p})))(\mathfrak{p})$.

We now want to evaluate (8). We already know that

11.7 V(⟨***he***$_2$, ***sleeps***⟩) is the open proposition θ such that if $\mathfrak{p}$ specifies a time t and ***he***$_2$-reference u_2 then $\theta(\mathfrak{p})$ is the proposition that u_2 is asleep at t.

11.8 V$^+$(⟨***that***, ⟨***he***$_2$, ***sleeps***⟩⟩) is by 11.6 the function $\zeta \in \mathbf{D}_{\langle 0, \langle 0, 1\rangle\rangle}$ such that for any $\omega \in \mathbf{D}_{\langle 0, 1\rangle}$, and any context property $\mathfrak{p}$, $((\zeta(\omega))(\mathfrak{p}) = (\omega(\theta(\mathfrak{p})))(\mathfrak{p})$, where V$^+$(⟨***he***$_2$, ***sleeps***⟩) is θ. Where $\mathfrak{p}$ is in a context family which specifies an utterance time t and an intended ***he***$_2$-referent u_2 then by 11.7 $\theta(\mathfrak{p})$ is true in w iff u_2 is asleep in w at t.

By 11.5 and the rules for evaluating abstracts (pp. 83–6) we have:

11.9 V$^+$(⟨λ, x_1, ⟨***he***$_1$, ⟨λ, y_1, ⟨***says***, x_1, y_1⟩⟩⟩⟩) is the function ω in $\mathbf{D}_{\langle 0, 1\rangle}$ such that for any $a \in \mathbf{D}_1$, $\omega(a)$ is the open proposition such that if $\mathfrak{p}$ is a context property which specifies t as the time of utterance and u_1 as the intended referent of ***he***$_1$ then $(\omega(a))(\mathfrak{p})$ is true in any world w iff u_1 asserts a at time t.

Whence

11.10 V$^+$(⟨⟨λ, x_1, ⟨***he***$_1$, ⟨λ, y_1, ⟨***says***, x_1, y_1⟩⟩⟩⟩,
⟨***that*** ⟨***he***$_2$, ***sleeps***⟩⟩⟩)($\mathfrak{p}$)
will be true in w iff $(\omega(\theta(\mathfrak{p}))(\mathfrak{p})$ is true in w where ω is as in 11.9 and θ as in 11.8.

This means that if $\mathfrak{p}$ is a context property which specifies an utterance time t, an intended ***he***$_1$-referent u_1 and an intended ***he***$_2$-referent u_2, then V$^+$((8))($\mathfrak{p}$) is a proposition true in w iff in w, u_1 asserts at t the proposition that u_2 is asleep at t.

This approach to personal pronouns may also be the way to deal with proper names like ***Arabella*** which, in natural languages, do not refer to a unique person though each genuine occasion of use does so refer. We could thus have ***Arabella***$_1$, ***Arabella***$_2$ and so on, and a semantic rule to the effect that ***Arabella***$_n$ denotes the person the utterer intends it to denote. The 'meaning' of proper names would then be a function from contexts to functions which act as logically proper names.[233]

Pronouns as bound variables

There is another use of personal pronouns in English which makes them very like bound variables in logic.[234] Now in λ-categorial languages we have variables but we do not as a rule allow them to reach the shallow structure; what we want is some way of doing this. Since we are allowing as symbols of the deep structure $\boldsymbol{he}_1$, $\boldsymbol{he}_2$ etc. we shall also allow a symbol $\boldsymbol{he}^\dagger$ which is of category $\langle 1,1\rangle$. In general we want arguments to be variables so that when $x \in X_1$

$$\langle \boldsymbol{he}^\dagger, x\rangle$$

will be in E_1. Of course expressions like

$$\langle \boldsymbol{he}^\dagger, \langle \boldsymbol{he}^\dagger, x\rangle\rangle$$

will also be in E_1 but we shall insist that our acceptability principles rule out as unacceptable any expressions which contain iterated $\boldsymbol{he}^\dagger$'s. We also of course need $\boldsymbol{she}^\dagger$, $\boldsymbol{it}^\dagger$,$\boldsymbol{him}^\dagger$ and $\boldsymbol{her}^\dagger$.

The semantics for $\boldsymbol{he}^\dagger$ is simple.

11.11 $V(\boldsymbol{he}^\dagger)$ is that function $\omega \in \mathbf{D}_{\langle 1,1\rangle}$ such that for any $a \in \mathbf{D}_1$, $\omega(a) = a$.

The idea behind this semantics is that $\boldsymbol{he}^\dagger$ is really no more than a variable-indicating sign in the deep structure which is to be allowed to reach the surface. A typical sentence containing $\boldsymbol{her}^\dagger$ is:

(1) ***every man who sees her***† ***loves Arabella***

The deep structure of (1) is

(2) $\langle\langle\lambda, y_1, \langle \boldsymbol{every}, \langle \boldsymbol{man}, \langle \boldsymbol{who}, \langle\lambda, x_1, \langle \boldsymbol{sees}, x_1, \langle \boldsymbol{her}^\dagger, y_1\rangle\rangle\rangle\rangle\rangle, \langle\lambda, x_1, \langle \boldsymbol{loves}, x_1, y_1\rangle\rangle\rangle\rangle, \boldsymbol{Arabella}\rangle$

It would be possible to treat ***her*** in (1) as an ordinary personal pronoun is we say that the linguistic context of (1) makes it clear that it is Arabella who is being referred to but it seems much more pleasant to regard the context as specifying that ***her*** here functions as the signal for a bound variable.[235] We must of course allow the possibility that

[233] Another way of dealing with proper names is hinted at in Lewis [1970], p. 63 f.

[234] Chomsky [1968], p. 39. Of course the acceptability principles will need to tell us when pronouns of this kind (*anaphoric* pronouns as they are sometimes called) can occur naturally in English. *Vide* Ross [1967] for some discussion of this sort of problem. For some complexities in connection with the anaphoric ***it*** *vide* G. Lakoff [1970b].

[235] A solution along these lines should be possible for the 'migs and pilots' problem of Karttunen [1971]. What sentences I have been able to come up with

(1) might have a deep structure in which ***her*** is a more ordinary personal pronoun, as when it is said with an emphasis and a pointing gesture to someone other than Arabella.

Another use of bound variable pronouns helps in the analysis of certain 'impersonal' constructions. Suppose that ***appears*** $\in F_{\langle 0, 1\rangle}$. Then we have the equivalence of

(3) $\langle\langle\lambda, x_1, \langle\langle \textit{\textbf{it}}^\dagger, x_1\rangle, \textit{\textbf{appears}}\rangle\rangle, \langle \textit{\textbf{that}}, \langle \textit{\textbf{John}}, \textit{\textbf{runs}}\rangle\rangle\rangle$

and

(4) $\langle\langle \textit{\textbf{that}}, \langle \textit{\textbf{John}}, \textit{\textbf{runs}}\rangle\rangle, \textit{\textbf{appears}}\rangle$

(4) gives a slightly less natural shallow structure than (3) but given the rules for ***it***† and principles of λ-conversion, (3) and (4) are synonymous.

In this section we have presented two ways of dealing with the personal pronouns as if they were quite separate; but of course they are not. The bound variable pronoun occurs when some other element in the sentence is the means for indicating what is being talked about. If it were possible to develop 'paragraph semantics' one might be able to bind a variable in another sentence under certain conditions, and thus many pronouns which have now to be accommodated by a rule like 11.4 could be treated by one like 11.11. Indeed in many cases 11.4 can be regarded as a 'stand in' rule until such a time as the study of semantics progresses far enough for it to be replaced by one like 11.11. Presumably this could not be done in all cases, however, for there seem to be other ways of indicating what one is talking about than by language.

More about the definite article

Most definite descriptions in English are not in fact true of a unique individual. Nor are they intended to be. A phrase like ***the man*** as it occurs in

(1) ***the man sleeps***

does not presuppose[236] that there is exactly one man. What it does presuppose though is that there is only one man being spoken about. The situation is like the case with ***he*** except that we have the noun which follows ***the*** to restrict the possibilities of reference.

are exceedingly complex and only partially solve the puzzle (to be more specific, I can do, at enormous cost, ***the pilot who shot at it hit the mig that chased him*** but I have not yet been able to do ***the pilot who shot at it hit a mig that chased him***), cf. Harman [1970], p. 292 and McCawley [1971], p. 227.

[236] The sense of 'presuppose' is the one explained in Chapter Eight on pp. 119–22. In that chapter we only considered definite descriptions which were claimed (at any given time) to hold of exactly one thing.

11.12 For any context property $\mathfrak{p}$ we shall say that $\mathfrak{p}$ is an **e**-specifying property iff **e** is a subset of $\mathbf{D}_1$ and $\mathfrak{p}$ is in a context family generated by a property $\mathfrak{p}^*$ such that for any utterance $\mathfrak{a}$ and world w, $\mathfrak{p}^*(\mathfrak{a})$ is true in w iff the things the utterer of $\mathfrak{a}$ in w is intending to talk about are all in **e**.

(Of course, as with the pronouns, there are difficult questions posed by 11.12 for a theory of language use.)
The rule for ***the*** is now as follows[237]

11.13 V(***the***) is a function $\zeta \in \mathbf{D}_{\langle 0, \langle 0, 1\rangle, \langle 0, 1\rangle\rangle}$ such that for any ω, ω' in its domain, any context property $\mathfrak{p}$ is in the domain of $\zeta(\omega, \omega')$ iff there is some subset **e** of $\mathbf{D}_1$ such that $\mathfrak{p}$ is an **e**-specifying property and for any $w \in \mathbf{W}$ there is exactly one $a \in \mathbf{e}$ such that $w \in (\omega(a))(\mathfrak{p})$. For such a $\mathfrak{p}$, $w \in (\zeta(\omega, \omega'))(\mathfrak{p})$ iff $w \in (\omega'(a))(\mathfrak{p})$.

Let us now evaluate the deep structure of (1) viz.:

(2) ⟨***the***, ***man***, ***sleeps***⟩

We suppose that

11.14 V(***man***) is the open property ω such that for any context property $\mathfrak{p}$ which specifies a time of utterance t, $(\omega(a))(\mathfrak{p})$ is true in a world w iff a is a man at t in w.[238]

Now $V^+(2) = (V(\textit{\textbf{the}}))(V(\textit{\textbf{man}}), V(\textit{\textbf{sleeps}}))$ and so by 11.13 $(V^+(2))(\mathfrak{p})$ will be true in a world w iff for some $\mathbf{e} \subseteq \mathbf{D}_1$, $\mathfrak{p}$ is an **e**-specifying context family and there is exactly one $a \in \mathbf{e}$ such that $w \in (V(\textit{\textbf{man}})(a))(\mathfrak{p})$ and for this a, $w \in (V(\textit{\textbf{sleeps}})(a))(\mathfrak{p})$. This means that, of the things $\mathfrak{p}$ specifies as being talked about, a is the only one such that $w \in (V(\textit{\textbf{man}})(a))(\mathfrak{p})$.

By 11.14 $w \in (V(\textit{\textbf{man}})(a))(\mathfrak{p})$ iff $\mathfrak{p}$ specifies a time of utterance t and a is a man at t. Thus if $(V^+(2))(\mathfrak{p})$ is true in w, a must be the one and only thing being talked about which is a man at t. By 11.2 (p. 174) $w \in (V(\textit{\textbf{sleeps}})(a))(\mathfrak{p})$ iff a is asleep at t, so $(V(2))(\mathfrak{p})$ will be true in w iff the one and only thing being talked about which is a man at the time of utterance is asleep at the time of utterance.

Thus any token of (2) uttered at t when the only man its utterer has in mind is Jones, will express the proposition that Jones sleeps at t.

[237] It may be necessary in a sentence like ***the men chase the men*** (when said e.g. in answer to the question, 'What do the men with the spears do to the men with the shields?') to have $\textit{\textbf{the}}_1$, $\textit{\textbf{the}}_2$ etc. in the deep structure, but normally the common noun expression which follows ***the*** will be specific enough to disambiguate within the sentence.

[238] Notice that common nouns may sometimes be time-dependent. For nouns in which this is crucial like ***widow***, *vide infra*, p. 198 f.

In the case of (2) the only sense in which ***man*** is context-dependent is with respect to time. ***man*** is independent of the intentions of the utterer. In some descriptive phrases, however, the noun does seem to be dependent on the intentions of the utterer. Consider e.g.:

(3) ***every mayor likes the picture***

(3) has the deep structure:

(4) $\langle \textbf{\textit{every}}, \textbf{\textit{mayor}}, \langle \lambda, x_1, \langle\langle \lambda, y_1, \langle \textbf{\textit{likes}}, x_1, y_1 \rangle\rangle, \langle \lambda, x_{\langle 0,1 \rangle}, \langle \textbf{\textit{the}}, \textbf{\textit{picture}}, x_{\langle 0,1 \rangle} \rangle\rangle\rangle\rangle\rangle$

which may refer to all (past and present) mayors of a certain town. In this case the context property would have to specify a particular municipality $\mathfrak{m}$. But on other occasions we may wish to refer to the mayors of several different towns, as in

(5) $\langle$***every, mayor, objects***$\rangle$

In this latter case what we want is that ***mayor*** should require a context property which specifies a class $\mathfrak{M}$ of municipalities and makes ***mayor*** be the property of being the mayor of one of the municipalities in $\mathfrak{M}$.

That common nouns are frequently context-dependent is a point that has often been overlooked. I hope to have said enough to shew how wide-ranging can be the ways in which this dependence is manifested.

It is possible to have a ***the*** which acts as a bound variable. In the sentence

(6) ***a man came and a boy came but the man left***

it is almost certain that ***the man*** refers to the man who came with the boy. Of course we could say that in a natural token of (6) ***the man*** is intended so to refer and that 11.13 therefore covers the case. However just as 11.4 in the case of ***he*** might be seen as a way of opting out of the analysis rather than as the giving of one, so 11.13 might be held to be a way of avoiding the same work for ***the***. Where, as in (6), a definite article is intended to link with an expression elsewhere in the same sentence, there would seem to be good reason for having a ***the***† which is analogous to ***he***†.[239] The semantics of ***the***†, however, appears

[239] As remarked on p. 179 *supra* we are not engaging in any semantics which go beyond a single sentence. In certain cases, however, a conjoined sentence like (6) can give the same effect. (Robbins [1968], p. 130.) Thus (6) could be thought of as replaced by the two sentences: ***a man came and a boy came. the man left.*** (Cf. Vendler [1967], p. 63.) Vendler (op. cit., p. 52) claims that ***the*** signals a (possibly deleted) restrictive relative clause. This is not in conflict with 11.13 since the relative clause can be regarded as how the speaker would, if called upon, specify the class he has in mind. The fact that he has not done so in an actual sentence has, Vendler says, (op. cit., p. 66) 'no philosophical significance'.

to involve a number of difficulties and so we shall content ourselves with merely noting that our analysis of the definite article needs a little refinement if it is to do full justice to the anaphoric ***the***.

The verb *to be*

We have so far avoided using any illustrations involving the verb ***be***. This has made many of our examples sound a little forced when more natural ones seem to hand. The verb ***be*** deserves a section on its own and because some, though not all, of what we say about it concerns context-dependence we have deferred it until this chapter.

Philosophers have distinguished three main uses of the verb ***be*** in English: first, the existential use (now rare) of attributing existence to something;[240] second, the ***is*** of identity; and third, the ***is*** of predication. We shall say little about the first of these, even though a discussion could be illuminating. In looking at the other two uses we shall maintain that the ***is*** of identity and the ***is*** of predication are the same, though

(1) ***Bill is a man***

and

(2) ***the mayor is the winner***

have a simpler analysis than

(3) ***Bill is large***

The semantic rule for the ***is*** of identity is simple: ***is*** $\in F_{\langle 0,1,1\rangle}$ and

11.15 V(***is***) is that function $\omega \in \mathbf{D}_{\langle 0,1,1\rangle}$ such that if $\mathfrak{p}$ is a context property and $a, b \in \mathbf{D}_1$ then for any $w \in \mathbf{W}$, $w \in (\omega(a,b))(\mathfrak{p})$ iff $a = b$.

The first thing we notice is that although ***is*** is defined in a context-dependent assignment its meaning does not depend on that assignment. This fact may at first seem rather curious in view of the fact that ***is*** in English is tensed. Our discussion of tenses on pp. 193–9 will however shew that tensed verbs in the surface structure frequently signal tense operators in the underlying structure which operate on whole sentences and are not essentially connected with the verb until the surface sentence is obtained.

[240] The existential ***is*** may well be involved when locative or temporal adverbials occur as in ***a man is in the room*** (Chomsky [1970], p. 208) or ***the demonstration was on Thursday***. Such an ***is*** is in $F_{\langle 0,1\rangle}$ though the acceptability principles will have to rule out sentences in which it is unqualified like ***the demonstration was*** (Lyons [1969], p. 345). Lyons [1969], p. 322 f (*vide* also Lyons [1967]) argues that the copula should not occur at all in deep structure but this seems to make too little of the difference between ***Miriam is pretty*** and ***Miriam is here***.

The deep structure of (1) is

(4) $\langle \textit{\textbf{Bill}}, \langle \lambda, x_1, \langle\langle \lambda, y_1, \langle \textit{\textbf{is}}, x_1, y_1 \rangle\rangle, \langle \lambda, x_{\langle 0,1 \rangle}, \langle \textit{\textbf{a}}, \textit{\textbf{man}}, x_{\langle 0,1 \rangle} \rangle\rangle\rangle\rangle\rangle$

Assuming that ***Bill*** is a logically proper name (*vide* p. 132), there is no worry about the relative scopes of it and ***a man***. (4) means that the property of being identical with a man applies to Bill, i.e. that Bill is a man. Further, if we accept the time-dependent meaning of ***man*** reflected in 11.14 (p. 180), then being identical with a man means being identical with something which is a man at the time of utterance, and thus (4) asserts that Bill is now a man.

In (2) the relative scopes of ***the mayor*** and ***the winner*** can affect the logical status of the sentence. We can see this more clearly if we use the adverb ***necessarily*** (with the semantics as on p. 148) and form

(5) ***the mayor is necessarily the winner***

If (5) has the deep structure[241]

(6) $\langle \textit{\textbf{the}}, \textit{\textbf{mayor}}, \langle \lambda, x_1, \langle\langle \lambda, y_1, \langle\langle \textit{\textbf{is}}, x_1, y_1 \rangle, \textit{\textbf{necessarily}} \rangle\rangle, \langle \lambda, x_{\langle 0,1 \rangle}, \langle \textit{\textbf{the}}, \textit{\textbf{winner}}, x_{\langle 0,1 \rangle} \rangle\rangle\rangle\rangle\rangle$

then it is true if the mayor is the winner since, by 11.15, if $\omega(a,b)(\mathfrak{p})$ is true in any world then it is true in every world. However, its more natural deep structure is probably not (6) but

(7) $\langle\langle \lambda, x_{\langle 0,\langle 0,1 \rangle\rangle}, \langle\langle \textit{\textbf{the}}, \textit{\textbf{mayor}}, \langle \lambda, x_1, \langle\langle \lambda, y_1, \langle \textit{\textbf{is}}, x_1, y_1 \rangle\rangle, x_{\langle 0,\langle 0,1 \rangle\rangle} \rangle\rangle\rangle, \textit{\textbf{necessarily}} \rangle\rangle, \langle \lambda, x_{\langle 0,1 \rangle}, \langle \textit{\textbf{the}}, \textit{\textbf{winner}}, x_{\langle 0,1 \rangle} \rangle\rangle\rangle$

(7) is simply a version, re-ordered by λ-conversion, of

(8) $\langle\langle \textit{\textbf{the}}, \textit{\textbf{mayor}}, \langle \lambda, x_1, \langle\langle \lambda, y_1, \langle \textit{\textbf{is}}, x_1, y_1 \rangle\rangle, \langle \lambda, x_{\langle 0,1 \rangle}, \langle \textit{\textbf{the}}, \textit{\textbf{winner}}, x_{\langle 0,1 \rangle} \rangle\rangle\rangle\rangle\rangle, \textit{\textbf{necessarily}} \rangle$

In (8) all the nouns are within the scope of ***necessarily*** and (8) (and therefore (7)) is true iff in every world the thing which is the mayor in that world is also the thing which is the winner in that world. For a given context which specifies an intended municipality, an intended game and a time of utterance, (7) will be true or false depending on various logical properties of the particular mayor and game.

We now turn to (3). As we said on p. 142 the semantic role of adjectives is best understood when we see them as noun modifiers. This means that the meaning of ***large*** is revealed by the way it operates on a noun to form a more complex common noun expression. Thus we get

(9) $\langle \textit{\textbf{large}}, \textit{\textbf{flea}} \rangle$

or

[241] It should be obvious that (5) has exactly the same structure as ***the morning star is necessarily the evening star*** and therefore the form of our solution to this well-known paradox should be clear.

(10) ⟨***large, animal***⟩

Very roughly where α is of category $\langle 0, 1\rangle$

$$\langle \textbf{\textit{large}}, \alpha\rangle$$

means something larger than most things which are α.

What this means is that if we are told that something is large we are entitled to ask, 'large what?' Thus the meaning of (3) is not specified. The answer to the 'large what?' question is given by what we shall call a 'comparison property' which is usually supplied by the context.[242] In the case of (3) it is almost certainly the property of being a person, but it is not always so clear since

(11) ***Arabella is large***

may have a different meaning depending on whether Arabella is being asserted to be a large child, large woman or large person. Unless we are to regard (11) as ambiguous, we must have the context specify the property which the adjective is intended to modify. This applies particularly to predicates which admit of degrees but can apply in so widely diverse areas that it is better to let it apply quite generally. E.g., it has been argued that the colour of red hair would not be considered red if found in a coat.[243] Our analysis of predicative adjectives requires us to put in the deep structure a symbol whose meaning is context-determined and whose sole function is to indicate the intended comparison property.

11.16 We shall say that a context property $\mathfrak{p}$ specifies $\omega \in \mathbf{D}_{\langle 0, 1\rangle}$ as a *comparison property* iff $\mathfrak{p}$ is in a context family generated by a property $\mathfrak{p}^*$ such that for any utterance $\mathfrak{a}$ and world w, $\mathfrak{p}^*(\mathfrak{a})$ is true in w iff the utterer of $\mathfrak{a}$ in w intends the open property ω to be the standard of comparison for the adjective he is using predicatively in $\mathfrak{a}$.

We now assume that the deep structure contains a symbol $\boldsymbol{a}^*$ which is not allowed to reach the surface and whose semantics is like that of $\boldsymbol{a}$ in 9.5 on p. 136. Actually we shall have $\boldsymbol{a}^*$ of category $\langle\langle 0,\langle 0,1\rangle\rangle,\langle 0,1\rangle\rangle$ with the semantics.

11.17 $V(\boldsymbol{a}^*)$ is a function $\zeta \in \mathbf{D}_{\langle\langle 0, \langle 0, 1\rangle\rangle, \langle 0, 1\rangle\rangle}$ such that if ω is in the domain of ζ and ω' in the domain of $\zeta(\omega)$ and $\mathfrak{p}$ is any context

[242] The connection between attributive and predicative adjectives is actually a very subtle one and we are probably oversimplifying things here. Some indication of its complexity can be found in Bolinger [1967b].

[243] Bambrough [1971], p. 73: 'Ginger Rogers has red hair. If there were a coat of exactly the same shade of colour as Ginger Rogers' hair it would not be a red coat.'

property: for any $w \in \mathbf{W}$, $w \in \zeta((\omega, \omega'))(\mathfrak{p})$ iff there is some $\boldsymbol{a} \in \mathbf{D}_1$ such that $w \in (\omega(a))(\mathfrak{p})$ and $w \in (\omega'(a))(\mathfrak{p})$.

We now introduce a symbol ***comp*** in $F_{\langle 0, 1\rangle}$, also deleted in reaching the surface:

11.18 V(***comp***) is that function $\omega \in \mathbf{D}_{\langle 0, 1\rangle}$ such that where $\mathfrak{p}$ specifies ω' as a comparison property then for any a in the domain of ω', $(\omega(a))(\mathfrak{p}) = (\omega'(a))(\mathfrak{p})$.

The deep structure of (10) now becomes:

(12) $\langle \textbf{\textit{Arabella}}, \langle \lambda, x_1, \langle\langle \lambda, y_1, \langle \textbf{\textit{is}}, x_1, y_1\rangle\rangle, \langle \textbf{\textit{a*}}, \langle \textbf{\textit{large}}, \textbf{\textit{comp}}\rangle\rangle\rangle\rangle\rangle$

To evaluate this, let us suppose that $\mathfrak{p}$ specifies the property of being a woman as the standard of comparison. By 11.18 V(***comp***) in this context is the same as V(***women***) in this context. The property suggested for large will make ⟨***large***, ***comp***⟩ a property true of things which are larger than most comps, i.e. most women. Thus (12) reflects what we said above in our discussion of (11).

PART FOUR

English as a Natural Language

CHAPTER TWELVE

Words and Morphemes

Surface structure

In Part III we were concerned with the relation between what we have called the 'deep structure' and the 'shallow structure' of English. The idea behind this metaphor is that English sentences of the kind we actually use, form what we might call the 'surface structure' of the language, and these other levels represent stages which are progressively closer to the 'underlying' meanings of the surface sentences. Up to now we have said little to shew that the surface structure of a sentence cannot be identified with its shallow structure. The phenomena discussed in this chapter, however, shew that this identification cannot be carried through.

In Chapter Thirteen (pp. 209–15) we shall be presenting a formal account of the relation between shallow structure and surface structure. The present chapter deals with cases in which we shall want the deep structure to contain symbols which only reach the surface in combination with other symbols. E.g. we shall want our deep structure to have a symbol ***ed*** whose meaning will be a past operator. I.e.,

(1) ⟨⟨***Arabella, sleep***⟩, ***ed***⟩

will be true in a world with respect to a context property which specifies a time *t* iff

(2) ⟨***Arabella, sleep***⟩

is true with respect to a property which is like the first except in specifying some *t′* earlier than *t*. The shallow structure of (1) is

(3) ⟨***Arabella, sleep, ed***⟩

In Chapter Thirteen we shall be concerned about how to get from

sleep ed to the surface **slept**.[244] In this chapter we shall be concerned with the deep structure role of symbols like ***ed*** which are realized in the surface structure by the modifications they cause in other words. If we wanted to adopt linguists' terminology we could call the symbols of the λ-base *morphemes*, though we shall normally only speak about a *morpheme* when we have in mind a symbol which does not have a surface realization as a separate word.

Pluralization

When we look at the semantic effect of pluralization in English we see that it occurs in at least three main areas and that its manner of operation in the deep structure is different in each.

First a pronoun like ***he***, ***she*** or ***it*** can be pluralized as in

(1) ⟨***they***, ***run***⟩

though proper names cannot; second, common count nouns can be pluralized, and when they are they form nominals, as in

(2) **men run**

and third, we can form plural expressions like

(3) **the men run**

(4) **all men run**

(5) **some men run**

We shall treat the pronoun case first since it seems the simplest. Since the number of personal pronouns is small it seems better simply to add ***they***[245] as an extra symbol with its own semantic rule. The rule will be very like the rule for ***he*** in that we shall have in the deep structure ***they***$_1$, ***they***$_2$, ... etc., and will obtain a possible deep structure in the same way as on p. 176.

12.1 V(***they***$_n$) is a function $\zeta \in \mathbf{D}_{\langle 0, \langle 0, 1\rangle\rangle}$ such that for any $\omega \in \mathbf{D}_{\langle 0, 1\rangle}$, which is in the domain of ζ, $\zeta(\omega)$ is the following open proposition: for any context property $\mathfrak{p}$, $\mathfrak{p}$ is in the domain of $\zeta(\omega)$ iff $\mathfrak{p}$ is in a context family which specifies a group **e** of things as the intended referent of ***they***$_n$. For such a $\mathfrak{p}$ and any $w \in \mathbf{W}$, $w \in \zeta(\omega)(\mathfrak{p})$ iff for every member a of **e**, $w \in (\omega(a))(\mathfrak{p})$.

The other cases require slightly different treatment. In all of (2), (3), (4) and (5) the pluralization in the surface structure applies to the

[244] From here on we use sans serif bold typeface to indicate elements in the surface structure as opposed to the shallow structure. *Vide infra* pp. 209–11. (The difference is not always clear and occasionally it is a mere matter of taste whether we cite the shallow form or the surface form.)

[245] and ***them***. Sometimes ***they*** and ***them*** act as bound variable indicators. When they do their semantics is no different from that of ***he***†, p. 178.

noun ***man*** but the semantic effect it has is different. We can therefore have a functor ***pl*** which is, like ***every***, ***a*** and ***the***, in category $\langle 0, \langle 0,1\rangle, \langle 0,1\rangle\rangle$.[246] This would make the deep structure of (1)

(6) ⟨***pl***, ***man***, ***run***⟩

There is no trouble about getting **men** from ***pl***, ***man***; that is done by the method described on pp. 209–11. We need of course to ensure that in (6), or in the equally allowable

(7) ⟨***man***, ***pl***, ***run***⟩

pl applies to ***man*** in getting the surface structure.

The meaning of (2) in English is not quite as clear as we might like. It may mean that every man runs or that most men run, or perhaps merely that some men run. But at any rate (2) is neither worse nor better off in this regard than (6) would make it.

In the case of (3), although it is ***man*** which is pluralized in the surface structure, the semantic effect of the pluralization is to change the meaning of ***the***.[247] The function of the pluralizing of ***man*** in the surface structure is simply to indicate that it is the plural ***the*** which is to be selected in the deep structure.

The meaning rule for the plural ***the*** would probably go somewhat as follows:

12.2 V(***the***$_{pl}$) is a function $\zeta \in \mathbf{D}_{\langle 0, \langle 0, 1\rangle, \langle 0, 1\rangle\rangle}$ such that for any ω, ω' in its domain, any context property $\mathfrak{p}$ is in the domain of $\zeta(\omega, \omega')$ iff there is some subset **e** of $\mathbf{D}_1$ such that $\mathfrak{p}$ is an **e**-specifying property (cf. 11.12, p. 180) and for any $w \in \mathbf{W}$ and $a \in \mathbf{e}$, if $w \in (\omega(a))(\mathfrak{p})$ then $w \in (\omega'(a))(\mathfrak{p})$.

The idea is that 12.2 will make (3) true if, of the things which are being spoken about, all of them who are men are running.

all and ***some*** are a little different. (4) is the same in meaning as

(8) ***every man runs***

and the pluralization of ***man*** has no semantic effect and can therefore be covered by agreement restrictions (*vide* p. 134 f). (5) means that at least two men run. It is possible, though unnatural except in logician's English, to say

(9) ***some man runs***

and if we allow this then the function of the pluralization of ***man*** in

[246] Cf. Quine [1960], p. 90.

[247] In many languages a plural determiner has a different surface form. Some of the plural personal pronouns behave at times like determiners; *vide* Postal [1970].

the surface structure (5) is to indicate that it is the 'at least two' ***some*** rather than the 'at least one' ***some*** which is intended.

Other uses of plurals seem either to have no semantic effect or to be reducible to one of the cases considered here. Pluralization seems very much a surface device for indicating a variety of different though related semantic phenomena and it is little wonder that formal languages have avoided it as much as possible.[248]

Other morphemes

In the surface structure of English, adverbs are frequently made out of adjectives by adding **-ly**. In most cases the meaning of the adverb can be calculated from the meaning of the adjective. E.g., if we think of ***runs*** and ***runner*** as having the same meaning in deep structure then ***runs quickly*** is to have the same deep structure meaning as ***quick runner***.

However, as far as the deep structure is concerned, it is easier to take ***quickly*** as basic and define ***quick*** from it.

In general, given α as a symbol of category $\langle 0,0\rangle$ it is easy to define the corresponding adjective β simply as

$$\langle \lambda, x_{\langle 0,1\rangle}, \langle \lambda, x_1, \langle\langle x_{\langle 0,1\rangle}, x_1\rangle, \alpha\rangle\rangle\rangle$$

Not all adverbs have meanings which depend on their adjectives. Thus

(1) **John is a hard man**

is not synonymous with

(2) **John is hardly a man**

In fact it seems more profitable to treat each case on its own. This means doubling up the lexicon but since there are only finitely many English adjectives there is no theoretical objection.[249]

Other suffixes are those which make abstract nouns out of properties, e.g. ***redness*** and ***doghood*** are both of category $\langle 0,\langle 0,1\rangle\rangle$ and ***ness*** and ***hood*** have a semantic role akin to the ***coll*** on p. 162. They provide us with nominals which enable us to talk about things which are the values of expressions which are not nominals. Although some shortening of the lexicon (i.e., the number of distinct proper symbols) may be possible by giving a semantic rule for such endings it is not

[248] Gleason [1961], p. 226, says 'the category of plural in English gathers together a rather diverse assortment of concepts.' He cites Chinese (op. cit., pp. 7 and 223) as an example of a language which manages to do without number most of the time.

[249] This is another instance where those who want to bring as much semantics into syntax as they can will be able to carry the deep-structure analysis further than I have chosen to do.

obvious to me that we might not avoid confusion by regarding ***redness*** as a separate word whose only connection with ***red*** is the connection we choose to give it when specifying its semantic role. We have however raised the possibility of letting the meaning of ***redness*** be determined from the meaning of ***red*** by using the meaning of ***ness***.

A better case could be made out for having morphemes to express comparatives and superlatives. This is particularly so since we can form these in other ways than by word endings. If we regard **better** as merely the surface representation of ***more good***, then by treating ***more*** and ***most***[250] as adverbs and ***than*** as a preposition the deep structure analysis of comparatives is simply a question of giving meanings to these two words.

Time, tense and aspect

The verbs which have occurred in our illustrations so far have all been given in the grammatical simple present tense of English. Thus we have had sentences like

(1) ⟨***John, sleeps***⟩

or

(2) ⟨***Arabella, runs***⟩

In using these as examples however we have failed to make a distinction between what we might call grammatical tense and semantical tense, or surface-structure tense and deep-structure tense. Grammatically in English the simple present of the verb ***sleep*** is (in the third person) ***sleeps*** as in (1), that of ***run*** is ***runs*** and that of ***love*** is ***loves***. However **sleeps** in English does not as a rule denote the semantical simple present tense. The semantical simple present tense of the verb ***sleep*** is that property ω such that for any $a \in \mathbf{D}_1$ and any context property $\mathfrak{p}$ in a family which specifies a time t and any $w \in \mathbf{W}$,

$$w \in (\omega(a))(\mathfrak{p}) \text{ iff } a \text{ is asleep at } t$$

The case of the semantical simple present of ***run*** is similar. Wherever we have given semantical rules for verbs (as e.g. on pp. 117, 174) it has been the semantical simple present we have defined even though the verb forms we have used, like ***sleeps*** and ***runs***, do not in English designate this tense. For we normally say things like

(3) **Miriam runs to school every day**

or

(4) **Jeremy sleeps in the afternoon**

[250] This is a different (though related) ***most*** from the one of p. 136. We should use ***most***$_1$ and ***most***$_2$.

where we intend to pick out repeated action occurring on and off for a period containing the present and some of the (immediate) past and future as well. The true semantical simple present of verbs like ***run*** and ***sleep*** (which might be described as *activity* verbs) is found in what is sometimes called in English the present continuous (grammatical) tense,[251] viz.,

(5) **Miriam is running**

(6) **Jeremy is sleeping**

This section will be looking at the deep structure of the tense system and so we shall be primarily concerned with semantic tenses.[252] The first point to make is the primacy of the semantical simple present. Let us continue to use ***sleeps*** for this (despite what we have just now said).

The meaning of a sentence like (1) is time-dependent in that $V^{+}((1))(\mathfrak{p})$ will be true for a context property $\mathfrak{p}$ iff $\mathfrak{p}$ specifies a time t and John is asleep at t. If we regard ***runs*** in (1) as more properly represented by a stem and a present tense ending we should have to make the semantic rule for the stem not time-dependent and there is a difficulty about this. Suppose, for example, we let V(***sleep***) (where ***sleep*** is the verb-stem) be the property of being asleep at some time. Then V^{+}(***sleeps***) would have to be the open property of being asleep at the time of utterance supplied by the context. Even if this could be formulated for ***sleeps*** it is difficult to see how to write a general semantical rule for a ***pres*** morpheme which finds quite generally the property ω_{pres} which is the property of being ω at present. Indeed it is arguable that we can only make sense of the case for ***sleep*** because we have defined the stem property in terms of the present tense property: viz. to sleep (stemwise) is to be asleep (present-tense-wise) at some time.

Given the present tense it is easy to see how to get the past and future tenses. We suppose we have a symbol (morpheme) ***ed*** which is of category $\langle 0,0 \rangle$. The semantics for ***ed*** can be roughly stated, as on p. 119, by saying that $\langle$***ed***$,\alpha\rangle$ is true for a context property $\mathfrak{p}$ which specifies a time t iff α is true for a property which is just like $\mathfrak{p}$ except in specifying a time t' earlier than t. In order to make precise the notion

[251] Though even this can have other meanings, as in
John is running at the Olympics this year.

[252] The history of tense logic has been admirably chronicled by the founder of the subject, A. N. Prior (Prior [1967]). One is forced though to admit that formal systems of tense logic have very little to contribute to the analysis of the tense system of English. On the complexity of tense behaviour in English and other natural languages, *vide* R. Lakoff [1970].

of 'just like' involved in this rough statement, we shall introduce the following terminology:

12.3 For any time t, $\mathfrak{q}(t)$ is the context property such that, for any utterance $\mathfrak{a}$ and $w \in \mathbf{W}$, $w \in (\mathfrak{q}(t))(\mathfrak{a})$ iff $\mathfrak{a}$ is uttered at t in w. (i.e. $\mathfrak{q}(t)$ is the generating property of the context family which specifies t; cf. p. 115).

We are now in a position to state the rule for ***ed***.

12.4 V(***ed***) is that function $\omega \in \mathbf{D}_{\langle 0,0\rangle}$ such that for any $\theta \in \mathbf{D}_0$ and any context property $\mathfrak{p}$:

(a) $\mathfrak{p}$ is in the domain of $\omega(\theta)$ iff $\mathfrak{p}$ is in a context family which specifies an utterance time t.

(b) For any $w \in \mathbf{W}$, $w \in (\omega(\theta))(\mathfrak{p})$ iff there is some context property $\mathfrak{p}^*$ such that

(i) $\mathfrak{p}$ is in the context family generated by $\mathfrak{p}^* \cap \mathfrak{q}(t)$,

and

(ii) there is some t' earlier than t such that $w \in \theta(\mathfrak{p}^* \cap \mathfrak{q}(t'))$.

In the rest of the chapter, instead of giving each time an elaborate definition in terms of $\mathfrak{p}^* \cap \mathfrak{q}(t')$, we shall simply continue to speak of 'a context property $\mathfrak{q}$ exactly like $\mathfrak{p}$ except in specifying t''.

We must be careful about the relations between ***ed*** in the deep structure and the tense endings in the surface structure. We have little trouble with

(7) **John slept**

which is the surface realization of the shallow structure of

(8) $\langle\langle$***John, sleep***$\rangle$, ***ed***$\rangle$

With respect to a context property $\mathfrak{p}$ which specifies at time t, (8) will be true iff $\langle$***John, sleep***$\rangle$ is true for some $\mathfrak{q}$ which specifies a time t' earlier than t, i.e. iff John is asleep at some t' earlier than t. The difficulty comes with a sentence like

(9) **John slept yesterday**

The plausible rule for ***yesterday***, which is an adverb[253] in category $\langle 0,0\rangle$, is

12.5 V(***yesterday***) is that function $\omega \in \mathbf{D}_{\langle 0,0\rangle}$ such that where θ is any open proposition and $\mathfrak{p}$ any context property which specifies a time t of utterance, $(\theta(\omega))(\mathfrak{p})$ is true in any world w iff there is some context property $\mathfrak{q}$ exactly like $\mathfrak{p}$ except in specifying a time t' which is on the day before t and $\theta(\mathfrak{q})$ is true in w.

[253] It can also be an abstract noun.

With this rule the deep structure of (9) has to be

(10) ⟨⟨***John, sleep***⟩, ***yesterday***⟩

It can be neither

(11) ⟨⟨⟨***John, sleep***⟩, ***ed***⟩, ***yesterday***⟩

nor

(12) ⟨⟨⟨***John, sleep***⟩, ***yesterday***⟩, ***ed***⟩

(11) means that it was true at some time prior to yesterday that John is asleep; i.e., it is what we would normally express as

(13) **John had slept (by) yesterday**

(12) means that it was true some time in the past that John was asleep on the day before that.

The plain fact seems to be that English surface structure is not equipped to deal with embedded tense operators. ***yesterday*** always refers to the day preceding the utterance even if it occurs embedded in a tense operator. The use of the pluperfect as in (13) seems to be the surface signal for an ***ed*** inside the scope of another tense operator, and in (9) the past tense seems put in solely to agree with ***yesterday*** and has no semantic force.[254]

It should be clear that we could add a future tense operator which corresponds to ***will***. Its semantics will be exactly analogous with those for ***ed***. In English this operator occurs as an auxiliary verb and could perhaps be dealt with as we did with ***do*** on pp. 151–3.

As well as tense, English verbs recognize aspect. Thus although we have been using (1) to mean that John is asleep at the time of utterance its more usual use would be in what is sometimes called the *present progressive* tense. In the deep structure it proves most convenient to keep ***sleep*** and ***sleeps*** as the semantical simple present and, for the progressive tense, introduce a symbol ***prog*** which is, like ***ed***, in $F_{\langle 0, 0\rangle}$:

12.6 V(***prog***) is that function $\zeta \in \mathbf{D}_{\langle 0, 0\rangle}$ such that for any $\theta \in \mathbf{D}_0$ and any context property $\mathfrak{p}$ which is in a family which specifies a time t, and any $w \in \mathbf{W}: w \in (\zeta(\theta))(\mathfrak{p})$ iff

(i) there is a time t' before t and a time t'' after t such that there are moments which occur at intervals between t' and t''[255] and

(ii) where $\mathfrak{q}$ is a context property which is exactly like $\mathfrak{p}$ except in specifying one of these moments, then $w \in \theta(q)$.

[254] It may be that surface tenses have no semantic effect except to indicate the presence in the deep structure of a temporal operator which does not reach the surface.

[255] We may loosely describe these as moments in the *neighbourhood* of $\mathfrak{p}$ (or of t), cf. Scott [1970], p. 160, and Montague [1970b], p. 73.

Let us see what V(***prog***) (which is at best a somewhat tentative approximation to a meaning rule) comes to in a sentence like

(14) $\langle\langle$***John, sleeps***$\rangle$, ***prog***$\rangle$

Now $V^+((14)) = \zeta(V^+(\langle$***John, sleeps***$\rangle))$, and we know (cf. p. 117) that $w \in (V^+(\langle$***John, sleeps***$\rangle))(\mathfrak{q})$ iff $\mathfrak{q}$ is in a family which specifies a time t and John is asleep at t. By V(***prog***) (12.6) $w \in \zeta(V^+($***John, sleeps***$))(\mathfrak{p})$ iff there are moments in the neighbourhood of $\mathfrak{p}$, such that if $\mathfrak{q}$ specifies one of these moments then $w \in V^+(\langle$***John, sleeps***$\rangle)(\mathfrak{q})$. And what this means is that John is asleep at these moments. I.e., (14) is true in w at a time t iff John is asleep at intervals in the neighbourhood of t.

In the case of activity verbs the grammatical simple present in English is usually, as we have said, the present progressive. Verbs like ***love***, however, which are not strictly activity verbs (since whatever repeated activities ***John loves Arabella*** involves, we hardly want to say that it is true at a time t in virtue of John's loving Arabella at intervals in the neighbourhood of t), can be regarded as having a grammatical simple present whose meaning is their semantical simple present.[256]

The other kind of aspect is the *perfective* aspect. ***perf*** is also in $F_{\langle 0, 0\rangle}$ and has the rule

12.7 V(***perf***) is that function $\zeta \in \mathbf{D}_{\langle 0, 0\rangle}$ such that for any $\theta \in \mathbf{D}_0$, $w \in \mathbf{W}$ and context property $\mathfrak{p}$ which is in a family which specifies a time t, then $w \in ((\zeta(\theta))(\mathfrak{p})$ iff there is a time t' prior to t such that where $\mathfrak{q}$ is any property exactly like $\mathfrak{p}$ except in specifying a time t'' between t' and a time almost immediately prior to t, $\omega \in \theta(\mathfrak{q})$.

The perfective idea which 12.7 defines is a purely temporal one. To do full justice to the perfective aspect one ought perhaps to make some use of the notion of 'completed action'. We shall, however, let 12.7 stand since it can at least illustrate one part of the perfective aspect. A similar argument to the one used above for (14) should convince the reader that

(15) $\langle\langle$***John, sleeps***$\rangle$, ***perf***$\rangle$

will be true iff John was asleep from some moment prior to the present until a moment immediately prior to the present.

The tense and aspect operators can of course be iterated so that we can have, e.g.,

(16) $\langle\langle\langle$***John, sleep***$\rangle$, ***perf***$\rangle$, ***prog***$\rangle$

[256] Cf. Vendler [1967], Chapter Four, especially p. 99, for this and other distinctions between kinds of verbs.

or

(17) $\langle\langle\langle$***John, sleep***$\rangle$, ***prog***$\rangle$, ***perf***$\rangle$

The surface language does not always realize these unambiguously. Any of (15), (16), (17) and perhaps other combinations can on occasions be represented by either

(18) **John has slept**

or

(19) **John has been sleeping**

The pluperfect tense arises from a deep structure in which ***perf*** and ***ed*** are combined. Thus a possible deep structure for

(20) **John had slept**

is

(21) $\langle\langle\langle$***John, sleep***$\rangle$, ***perf***$\rangle$, ***ed***$\rangle$

The surface tense system of English and its relation to a deep structure of the kind we have been outlining is horribly complex. Much of it is done using auxiliaries and participles. We discuss participles later in this chapter (pp. 201–5) and will then have the machinery for obtaining deep structures which enable us to derive, by deletion of λ's and variables, shallow structures which can be realized in the familari way.

Before we leave the semantic discussion of aspect we shall look at certain paradoxes which arise if the scope of nominals in temporal contexts is ignored. We shall not pretend to a complete study of them but merely try to indicate what happens to them in our context-dependent assignments. Consider the following argument:[257]

(22) **Arabella is a widow**

(23) **Bill married Arabella**

(24) **Bill married a widow**

We suppose that Arabella is now a widow because Bill has died since he married her but that she was not a widow when he married her. The air of paradox arises because of an equivocation in (24). It could have either of the two deep structures

(25) $\langle \boldsymbol{Bill}, \langle \lambda, x_1, \langle\langle \lambda, y_1, \langle\langle \boldsymbol{marry}, x_1, y_1\rangle, \boldsymbol{ed}\rangle\rangle, \langle \lambda, x_{\langle 0,1\rangle}, \langle \boldsymbol{a}, \boldsymbol{widow}, x_{\langle 0,1\rangle}\rangle\rangle\rangle\rangle\rangle$

or

(26) $\langle \boldsymbol{Bill}, \langle \lambda, x_1, \langle\langle \lambda, x_{\langle 0,\langle 0,1\rangle\rangle}, \langle\langle\langle \lambda, y_1, \langle \boldsymbol{marry}, x_1, y_1\rangle\rangle, x_{\langle 0,\langle 0,1\rangle\rangle}\rangle, \boldsymbol{ed}\rangle\rangle, \langle \lambda, x_{\langle 0,1\rangle}, \langle \boldsymbol{a}, \boldsymbol{widow}, x_{\langle 0,1\rangle}\rangle\rangle\rangle\rangle\rangle$

(26), by λ-conversion, is equivalent to

(27) $\langle \boldsymbol{Bill}, \langle \lambda, x_1, \langle\langle \boldsymbol{a}, \boldsymbol{widow}, \langle \lambda, y_1, \langle \boldsymbol{marry}, x_1, x_2\rangle\rangle\rangle, \boldsymbol{ed}\rangle\rangle\rangle$

[257] Quine [1960], p. 170, and [1970], p. 397.

In (25) ***marry*** is within the scope of ***ed*** but ***widow*** is not, while in (27) both ***marry*** and ***widow*** are within the scope of ***ed***. This means that (25) says that Bill (in the past) married someone who is now a widow. (25) follows from (22) and (23) but does not represent the normal sense of (24). (27) represents the normal sense of (24) but does not follow from (22) and (23).

In the surface structure there are various words which indicate deep structure scope. If we say

(28) **the king won**

this would normally have a deep structure corresponding to (18), viz.,

(29) $\langle\langle$***the, king, win***$\rangle$, ***ed***$\rangle$

If we wanted to shew that ***the*** and ***king*** were outside the scope of ***ed*** we would probably indicate this in the surface structure by a word like **present** and say

(30) **the present king won**

which means that the person who is now king won, whether or not he was king when he won (in contrast to (28)). (30) would have as deep structure

(31) $\langle$***the***, $\langle$***present, king***$\rangle$, $\langle\lambda, x_1, \langle\langle$***win***$, x_1\rangle$, ***ed***$\rangle\rangle\rangle$

In deep structure ***present*** is redundant (we can give it a semantics which ensures that $V^+(\langle$***present, king***$\rangle) = V($***king***$))$ but it is necessary in the surface structure to indicate which deep structure should be selected. We shall indicate the mechanics of this sort of thing on pp. 217–20.

Verb modification

In this section, as in the last, we shall be more interested in the semantics of the constructions we discuss than their precise formulation in English.

We think of the passive as formed by an operator ***en***. This operates on transitive verbs, i.e., predicates of category $\langle 0,1,1\rangle$, to produce intransitive verb phrases. It is thus of category $\langle\langle 0,1\rangle,\langle 0,1,1\rangle\rangle$. The semantics for ***en*** is as follows:

12.8 V(***en***) is that function ζ in $\mathbf{D}_{\langle\langle 0,1\rangle,\langle 0,1,1\rangle\rangle}$ such that for any $\omega \in \mathbf{D}_{\langle 0,1,1\rangle}$, and any context property $\mathfrak{p}$ and any $a \in \mathbf{D}_1$ and $w \in \mathbf{W}$, $w \in ((\zeta(\omega))(a))(\mathfrak{p})$ iff there is some $b \in \mathbf{D}_1$ such that $w \in (\omega(b,a))(\mathfrak{p})$.

We shall go through an example to see what this rule comes to:

(1) $\langle$***Bill***, $\langle$***love, en***$\rangle\rangle$

(which is the present deep structure of **Bill is loved**). Since the passive construction does not essentially depend on context we shall work with the simpler version of 12.8 obtained by deleting all reference to $\mathfrak{p}$.

$$w \in \mathrm{V}^+(1) \text{ iff } w \in (\mathrm{V}(\textbf{\textit{Bill}}))((\mathrm{V}(\textbf{\textit{en}}))(\mathrm{V}(\textbf{\textit{love}}))$$
$$\text{i.e., iff } w \in ((\mathrm{V}(\textbf{\textit{en}}))(\mathrm{V}(\textbf{\textit{love}})))(\mathrm{Bill})$$
$$\text{i.e., iff } w \in (\mathrm{V}(\textbf{\textit{love}}))(b, \mathrm{Bill}) \text{ for some } b \in \mathbf{D}_1$$
$$\text{i.e., iff some one loves Bill in } w.$$

Note that $\langle \textbf{\textit{love}}, \textbf{\textit{en}} \rangle$ is an intransitive verb phrase. We can if we wish form out of (1) the sentence

(2) $\langle\langle \lambda, x_1, \langle\langle \textbf{\textit{Bill}}, \langle \textbf{\textit{love}}, \textbf{\textit{en}} \rangle\rangle, \langle \textbf{\textit{by}}, x_1 \rangle\rangle\rangle, \textbf{\textit{Arabella}} \rangle$

in which ***by***, a preposition, forms an adverbial expression out of ***Arabella*** and this modifies (1). The meaning of ***by*** will of course have to ensure that (2) is equivalent to

(3) $\langle \textbf{\textit{Arabella}}, \langle \lambda, x_1, \langle\langle \lambda, y_1, \langle \textbf{\textit{love}}, x_1, y_1 \rangle\rangle, \textbf{\textit{Bill}} \rangle\rangle\rangle$

As with tense, there is no way of indicating scope in the surface structure by the position of the ***en***.

There are many verbs in English which can be used either transitively or intransitively. E.g. we can use

(4) **Bill loves**

as a perfectly good way of saying that Bill loves someone. One could deal with (4) by saying that ***loves*** in the deep structure of (4) is a separate lexical item (in $F_{\langle 0, 1 \rangle}$) from ***loves*** in (3), but this hardly does justice to the community of meaning between the two cases. Alternatively one could supply a dummy object (call it ***intrans***, the intransitive-making object) so that (4) would have the deep structure

(5) $\langle \textbf{\textit{Bill}}, \langle \lambda, x_1, \langle\langle \lambda, y_1, \langle \textbf{\textit{loves}}, x_1, y_1 \rangle\rangle, \textbf{\textit{intrans}} \rangle\rangle\rangle$

This way would be necessary if the scope of ***intrans*** was ever important. ***intrans*** would have the same semantics as ***someone*** but the rules for obtaining its surface structure would ensure that ***loves intrans*** had the surface realization **loves**. However since ***intrans*** always seems to have minimal scope it is better to think of it simply as an operator of category $\langle\langle 0, 1 \rangle, \langle 0, 1, 1 \rangle\rangle$ like the passive operator but with a different semantics, viz.:

12.9 V(***intrans***) is that function $\zeta \in \mathbf{D}_{\langle\langle 0, 1 \rangle, \langle 0, 1, 1 \rangle\rangle}$ such that if $\omega \in \mathbf{D}_{\langle 0, 1, 1 \rangle}$ and $\mathfrak{p}$ is any context property and $a \in \mathbf{D}_1$ and $w \in \mathbf{W}$, then $w \in ((\zeta(\omega))(a))(\mathfrak{p})$ iff there is some $b \in \mathbf{D}_1$ such that $w \in (\omega(a, b))(\mathfrak{p})$.

Note that the only difference between 12.8 and 12.9 is the order of a and b in $\omega(a, b)$. It can be seen that if (4) has the deep structure

(6) $\langle \textbf{\textit{Bill}}, \langle \textbf{\textit{loves}}, \textbf{\textit{intrans}} \rangle\rangle$

then it will be true iff Bill loves someone (or perhaps something).

Not all verbs form an intransitive in this way and the acceptability principles will have to ensure that only surface structures are permitted for those which do.

A slightly more complicated situation is found in the so-called *ergative* verbs.[258] If we have an intransitive verb like ***flies*** we can often make a transitive verb out of it as in

(7) ***Bill flies a 'plane***

Here the ***flies*** in (7) means something like 'causes to fly'. Suppose we have an operator ***erg*** in category $\langle\langle 0,1,1\rangle,\langle 0,1\rangle\rangle$ with the semantics

12.10 V(***erg***) is that function $\zeta \in \mathbf{D}_{\langle\langle 0,1,1\rangle,\langle 0,1\rangle\rangle}$ such that where $\omega \in \mathbf{D}_{\langle 0,1\rangle}$, a, $b \in \mathbf{D}_1$, $w \in \mathbf{W}$ and $\mathfrak{p}$ is in a context family which specifies a time t of utterance, then $w \in ((\zeta(\omega))(a,b))(\mathfrak{p})$ iff a brings about at t in w the proposition $(\omega(b))(\mathfrak{p})$.

The deep structure of (7) is

(8) $\langle \textit{\textbf{Bill}}, \langle \lambda, x_1, \langle\langle \lambda, y_1, \langle\langle \textit{\textbf{erg}}, \textit{\textbf{flies}}\rangle, x_1, y_1\rangle\rangle,$
$\langle \lambda, x_{\langle 0,1\rangle}, \langle \textit{\textbf{a}}, \textit{\textbf{'plane}}, x_{\langle 0,1\rangle}\rangle\rangle\rangle\rangle\rangle$

which is true at t iff Bill is causing a 'plane to fly at t. ***erg flies*** of course is realized on the surface as **flies**.

Many linguists cite as examples of ergative verbs verbs in which the surface realization is quite different for the transitive and intransitive senses. Thus ***kill*** is often used for $\langle$***erg***, ***die***$\rangle$.[259] For our purposes, however, there seems little point in not regarding these as separate lexical items. The meaning of ***kill*** will have to be specified as 'cause to die' but there seems no reason to suppose that the two words have any more in common than that (though this raises important questions of linguistic principle to which we shall return on pp. 213–15). By contrast, some verbs which seem to have both transitive and intransitive senses do not seem quite to fit the pattern of 12.10. E.g. ***walk*** in

(9) ***Bill walks the dog***

seems to mean that Bill takes the dog for a walk rather than that Bill causes the dog to walk (which he might very well do without walking it).

Participles

We shall take as our starting point for this section the idea that participles are verbal adjectives. By this we mean that a participle is an expression of category $\langle\langle 0,1\rangle,\langle 0,1\rangle\rangle$ made up out of a verb and such other things as (possibly) a tense and passive operator. We shall also

[258] Lyons [1969], p. 360.

[259] Lyons [1969], pp. 351–60. Though, as Chomsky ([1971], p. 189 n) remarks, ***kill*** differs from ***cause to die*** in virtue of the directness of the connection.

consider how participles combine in English to express various distinctions of tense and aspect.

We shall claim that in deep structure there is a participle-making operator which we shall write as ***ing***.[260] We do not restrict ***ing*** to forming the present active participle, despite what its appearance might suggest. Our contention is that tense, voice and aspect, which surface structure participles all have, should be represented in the deep structure by the operators ***ed***, ***will***, ***perf***, ***prog*** and ***en***. We shall also claim that the surface distinction between the participle used as a verb and used as an adjective reflects a deep structure difference of scope and that the deep structure status of the participle is the same in both cases.

ing is of category $\langle\langle\langle 0,1\rangle,\langle 0,1\rangle\rangle,\langle 0,1\rangle\rangle$; i.e., it makes an adjective out of an intransitive verb phrase. Thus:

(1) $\langle \boldsymbol{run}, \boldsymbol{ing}\rangle$

is an adjective of category $\langle\langle 0,1\rangle,\langle 0,1\rangle\rangle$. Transitive verbs can also be dealt with directly as in

(2) $\langle \lambda, y_1, \langle\langle \lambda, x_1, \langle \boldsymbol{love}, x_1, y_1\rangle\rangle, \boldsymbol{ing}\rangle\rangle$

which is of category $\langle\langle\langle\langle 0,1\rangle,\langle 0,1\rangle\rangle,\langle 0,1\rangle\rangle,1\rangle$, though it is occasionally more convenient to supply an object first to convert the transitive verb into an intransitive verb phrase. In addition, those transitive verbs which can be used intransitively will have participles for their intransitive sense. E.g. the intransitive sense of ***love*** has the participle:

(3) $\langle\langle \boldsymbol{love}, \boldsymbol{intrans}\rangle, \boldsymbol{ing}\rangle$

The semantics for ***ing*** is fairly straightforward:

12.11 V(***ing***) is that function $\zeta \in \mathbf{D}_{\langle\langle\langle 0,1\rangle,\langle 0,1\rangle\rangle,\langle 0,1\rangle\rangle}$ such that if ω, ω' are in $\mathbf{D}_{\langle 0,1\rangle}$, $w \in \mathbf{W}$ and $\mathfrak{p}$ is any context property, then for any $w \in \mathbf{W}$, $w \in ((\zeta(\omega))(\omega')(\mathfrak{p})$ iff for any $a \in \mathbf{D}_1$ $w \in (\omega(a))(\mathfrak{p})$ and $w \in (\omega'(a))(\mathfrak{p})$.

Let us see what 12.11 gives for

(4) $\langle\langle \boldsymbol{run}, \boldsymbol{ing}\rangle, \boldsymbol{man}\rangle$

For any $a \in \mathbf{D}_1$, context property $\mathfrak{p}$ and $w \in \mathbf{W}$:

$$w \in \mathrm{V}^+((4))(\mathfrak{p}) \text{ iff } w \in ((\mathrm{V}(\boldsymbol{ing}))(\mathrm{V}(\boldsymbol{run})))(\mathrm{V}(\boldsymbol{man}))(a)(\mathfrak{p})$$
$$\text{iff } w \in \mathrm{V}(\boldsymbol{run})(a)(\mathfrak{p}) \text{ and } w \in (\mathrm{V}(\boldsymbol{man})(a))(\mathfrak{p}).$$

I.e. (4) will be true in w iff $\mathfrak{p}$ specifies an utterance time t and (in w) a

[260] There is another use of the present participle. ***sleeping car*** means a car for sleeping in, not a car which is asleep. In spoken English this is frequently marked by stress. Thus, we have ***sleéping car*** but ***sleeping dóg***. It seems best accounted for by a separate morpheme ***ing****. Phenomena of this kind are studied extensively in Lees [1960].

is a man at t and a runs at t. I.e., a running man (at a time t) is something which is both a man at t and is running at t.

We make the passive participle by attaching ***en*** to the verb before ***ing***. Thus we can get

(5) $\langle\langle$***love, en***$\rangle$, ***ing***$\rangle$

which in the surface structure would be **loved**. The participle **loved** in surface English seems to be both active, as in

(6) **Arabella has loved**

and passive as in

(7) **Arabella is loved**

Sometimes we want to combine tense and aspect in the participles. The deep structure of

(8) **a running man**

will be

(9) $\langle\lambda, x_{\langle 0,1\rangle}, \langle$***a***, $\langle\langle\langle$***run, prog***$\rangle$, ***ing***$\rangle$, ***man***$\rangle$, $x_{\langle 0,1\rangle}\rangle\rangle$

if it means a man who runs from time to time.

In English, as we have observed on p. 194, the surface realization of the semantical simple present tense of ***run*** would occur in sentences like

(10) **Arabella is running**

The deep structure of (10) is

(11) $\langle$***Arabella***, $\langle\lambda, x_1, \langle\langle\lambda, y_1, \langle$***is***, $x_1, y_1\rangle\rangle$, $\langle$***a****, $\langle\langle$***run, ing***$\rangle$, ***comp***$\rangle\rangle\rangle\rangle\rangle$

By 12.11, (11) will be true iff Arabella is running and is a member of the intended comparison class. Provided that class is chosen as one of which Arabella is a member then (11) can be regarded as saying simply that Arabella is running (at the time of utterance).

The grammatical simple present in English, as we have noted, usually signals the progressive aspect; i.e.

(12) **Arabella runs**

does not usually have the deep structure

(13) $\langle$***Arabella, runs***$\rangle$

which we have been attributing to it, but rather,

(14) $\langle$***Arabella***, $\langle$***runs, prog***$\rangle\rangle$

The simple past

(15) **Arabella ran**

seems best rendered as

(16) $\langle\langle$***Arabella, run***$\rangle$, ***ed***$\rangle$

although, as we saw on p. 195 f, ***ed*** cannot occur in the presence of a temporal adjective like ***yesterday***.

The perfective aspect is conveyed by the verb **have**. This can be thought of as marking the deep structure ***be perf*** and combining with the present or past active participle depending on the tense required. Thus we may get

(17) $\langle \boldsymbol{Arabella}, \langle \lambda, x_1, \langle\langle \lambda, y_1, \langle \boldsymbol{is}, x_1, y_1\rangle\rangle, \langle \boldsymbol{a}^*, \langle\langle \boldsymbol{perf}, \boldsymbol{run}\rangle, \boldsymbol{ing}\rangle, \boldsymbol{comp}\rangle\rangle\rangle\rangle$

where ***is a* perf*** is realized as **has**, and ***run***, ***ing*** (which is really the active participle) is realized as **run**.

Alternatively we may get

(18) $\langle\langle \boldsymbol{Arabella}, \langle \lambda, x_1, \langle\langle \lambda, y_1, \langle \boldsymbol{is}, x_1, y_1\rangle\rangle, \langle \boldsymbol{a}^*, \langle\langle \boldsymbol{perf}, \boldsymbol{run}\rangle, \boldsymbol{ing}\rangle, \boldsymbol{comp}\rangle\rangle\rangle\rangle, \boldsymbol{ed}\rangle$

which could be rearranged (by λ-conversion) so that the ***ed*** would occur with the ***is*** and the ***perf***, and ***is perf ed*** could be realized as **had**.

(Note that, just as in the case of ***do*** on p. 152, there is also a genuine verb ***have*** which has no more than an historical connection with the auxiliary.)

Future tenses are also dealt with by an auxiliary in English but ***shall*** and ***will***, like ***do***, apply directly to the verb and not to the participles. We shall not detail the semantic rules, but ***shall*** and ***will*** can also be combined with other tense and aspect indicators. The tense structure of English is a very complicated business and we have said only so much as is necessary to shew that the framework we have been developing seems to pose no insuperable objections to the accommodation of this phenomenon.

A distinction is sometimes drawn between the verbal and adjectival uses of a participle. This distinction can be conveniently brought out by the ambiguous sentence

(19) **they are visiting relatives**

Taking ***are*** as meaning the same as ***is***, we can resolve the ambiguity by the two deep structures

(20) $\langle\langle \lambda, z_1, \langle \boldsymbol{they}, \langle \lambda, x_1, \langle\langle \lambda, y_1, \langle \boldsymbol{are}, x_1, y_1\rangle\rangle, \langle \boldsymbol{a}^*, \langle\langle\langle \lambda, y_1, \langle \boldsymbol{visit}, y_1, z_1\rangle\rangle, \boldsymbol{ing}\rangle, \boldsymbol{comp}\rangle\rangle\rangle\rangle\rangle\rangle, \langle \lambda, x_{\langle 0,1\rangle}, \langle \boldsymbol{pl}, \boldsymbol{relative}, x_{\langle 0,1\rangle}\rangle\rangle\rangle$

and

(21) $\langle \boldsymbol{they}, \langle \lambda, x_1, \langle\langle \lambda, y_1, \langle \boldsymbol{are}, x_1, y_1\rangle\rangle, \langle\langle \boldsymbol{visit}, \boldsymbol{intrans}\rangle, \langle \lambda, x_{\langle 0,1\rangle}, \langle \boldsymbol{pl}, \boldsymbol{relative}, x_{\langle 0,1\rangle}\rangle\rangle\rangle\rangle\rangle\rangle$

(20) is obtained by forming the participle of the transitive verb ***visit*** in the way described on p. 202 and then treating ***relative*** as its object. In (21) we form the transitive verb to ***visit*** and then its participle which is an adjective used attributively to qualify ***relative***. There is no

easy way of bringing this out in the surface structure without seeming to have to claim that **visiting** has two uses, an adjectival and a verbal one.

Gerunds

We now turn to gerunds. It has been recognized[261] that there are in English at least two kinds of gerunds, viz. what have been called *nominal gerunds* and *verbal gerunds*. The difference can be illustrated by the following three sentences

(1) **I hate Bill leaving litter**

(2) **I hate Bill's leaving litter**

(3) **I hate Bill's leaving of litter**

(1) is a case of a verbal gerund. In it there is a subordinate sentence containing a verb of which ***Bill*** is the subject and ***litter***[262] the object. In (3), on the other hand, ***leaving*** is simply a noun in its own right and is a straightforward nominal gerund. (2) is a little more difficult, but seems open to analysis by regarding ***leaving litter*** as the gerund of the complex verb-phrase ***leave litter***. If so then the gerunds in (1), (2) and (3) represent the nominalization of a whole sentence, a one-place predicate and a two-place predicate respectively. We shall introduce three symbols, $\boldsymbol{nom}_1$, $\boldsymbol{nom}_2$ and $\boldsymbol{nom}_3$ to do the required jobs.

$\boldsymbol{nom}_1$ plays the role of the ***inf*** on p. 169. This means $\boldsymbol{nom}_1$ is in category $\langle\langle 0,\langle 0,1\rangle\rangle,0\rangle$ and $V(\boldsymbol{nom}_3) = V(\boldsymbol{inf}) = V(\boldsymbol{that})$.[263] Indeed it is easy to see that (1) has the same meaning as

(4) **I hate Bill to leave litter**

Since **leaving** is a single word there is no reason why we cannot have $\boldsymbol{leaving} \in F_{\langle 0,1,1\rangle}$ with the rule:

$$V(\boldsymbol{leaving}) = V(\boldsymbol{leave})$$

Of course the acceptability principles will require the presence of ***nom*** in the deep structure so that we do not get deep structures like

(5) $\langle \boldsymbol{Bill}, \langle\lambda, x_1, \langle\langle\lambda, y_1, \langle \boldsymbol{leaving}, x_1, y_1\rangle\rangle, \boldsymbol{litter}\rangle\rangle\rangle$

as acceptable complete sentences.

The deep structure of (1) is

(6) $\langle \boldsymbol{I}, \langle\lambda, x_1, \langle\langle\lambda, y_1, \langle \boldsymbol{hate}, x_1, y_1\rangle\rangle,$
$\langle \boldsymbol{nom}_1, \langle \boldsymbol{Bill}, \langle\lambda, x_1, \langle\langle\lambda, y_1, \langle \boldsymbol{leaving}, x_1, y_1\rangle\rangle, \boldsymbol{litter}\rangle\rangle\rangle\rangle\rangle\rangle$

[261] E.g. by Wasow and Roeper [1972]. Our analysis has much in common with theirs. Cf. also Chomsky [1970].

[262] Since ***litter*** is a mass noun it can, when unqualified, stand without a determiner (*vide* p. 139 f).

[263] Or perhaps V(***that'***) (cf. p. 167 f) since **I do not like Bill leaving litter** seems to entail that Bill leaves litter.

nom$_2$ is a more genuine kind of gerund-forming operator and makes a noun out of an intransitive verb phrase; i.e. it is of category $\langle\langle 0,1\rangle, \langle 0,1\rangle\rangle$. But in order to analyse (2) we have to do something about **Bill's**. This is a combination of the nominal ***Bill*** and what we shall call the *possessive morpheme*, ***s***.[264] ***s*** is of category $\langle\langle 0,\langle 0,1\rangle,\langle 0,1\rangle\rangle,1\rangle$ for it makes a determiner out of an expression in category 1. (We note that just as **the house** and **every house** are nominals, so is **Bill's house**. ***s*** cannot operate directly on a nominal, however, since otherwise we could not disambiguate **everyone loves someone's wife**.) The deep structure of (2) is

(7) $\langle\langle\lambda, y_1, \langle \boldsymbol{I}, \langle\lambda, x_1, \langle \boldsymbol{hate}, x_1, y_1\rangle\rangle\rangle\rangle, \langle\lambda, x_{\langle 0,1\rangle}, \langle \boldsymbol{Bill}, \langle\lambda, x_1, \langle\langle \boldsymbol{s}, x_1\rangle, \langle \boldsymbol{nom}_2, \langle\lambda, z_1, \langle\langle\lambda, y_1, \langle \boldsymbol{leaving}, z_1, y_1\rangle\rangle, \boldsymbol{litter}\rangle\rangle\rangle, x_{\langle 0,1\rangle}\rangle\rangle\rangle\rangle\rangle$

We first note that ***leaving*** is assigned the same value as ***leave*** (or ***leaves***). In order to work out the meaning of (7) we shall discuss the meaning of the new symbols ***s*** and ***nom***$_2$.

The semantic rule for ***s*** will be something like the following:

12.12 V(***s***) is a function $\zeta \in \mathbf{D}_{\langle\langle 0,\langle 0,1\rangle,\langle 0,1\rangle\rangle,1\rangle}$ such that if a is in its domain and $\langle\omega,\omega'\rangle$ is in the domain of $\zeta(a)$ then for any context property $\mathfrak{p}$ and $w \in \mathbf{W}$, $w \in (\zeta(a))(\omega,\omega')(\mathfrak{p})$ iff both:

(a) There is exactly one $b \in \mathbf{D}_1$ such that (i) $w \in (\omega(b))(\mathfrak{p})$, and (ii) either b is an object and belongs to a in w or b is an action and is performed by a in w; and also:

(b) for this b, $w \in (\omega'(b))(\mathfrak{p})$

Before trying to apply 12.12 to (7) we shall try it on a simpler sentence:

(8) **Bill's cat runs**

This has the deep structure

(9) $\langle \boldsymbol{Bill}, \langle\lambda, x_1, \langle\langle \boldsymbol{s}, x_1\rangle, \boldsymbol{cat}, \boldsymbol{runs}\rangle\rangle\rangle$

By the rules for evaluating abstracts we have for any $a \in \mathbf{D}_1$

(10) $\mathrm{V}^+(\langle\lambda, x_1, \langle\langle \boldsymbol{s}, x_1\rangle, \boldsymbol{cat}, \boldsymbol{runs}\rangle\rangle)(a)$

as true in a world w (for a context property $\mathfrak{p}$) iff

$(\mathrm{V}(\boldsymbol{s})(a))(\mathrm{V}(\boldsymbol{cat}), \mathrm{V}(\boldsymbol{runs}))$

is. By 12.12 this will be so iff *firstly*, there is exactly one b such that b

[264] Cf. p. 144. ***s*** is like a preposition and can often be replaced by ***of*** provided a suitable determiner (usually ***the***) is added. Thus, **Bill's house** can be replaced by **the house of Bill.** When ***s*** applies to a complex nominal it is realized in the surface by a modification of the last word of the nominal, as in: **the man in the queue's raincoat** (cf. Gleason [1961], p. 137 f); thus the ambiguity in **the son of Pharaoh's daughter** (Heb. 11: 24).

belongs to a and $w \in (\mathrm{V}(\boldsymbol{cat})(b))(\mathfrak{p})$, i.e. iff b is (in w) the only cat belonging to a (clearly no b such that $w \in (\mathrm{V}(\boldsymbol{cat})(b))(\mathfrak{p})$ is an action, for no cats are actions, so that the second part of the clause doesn't apply), and *secondly*, $w \in (\mathrm{V}(\boldsymbol{runs})(b))(\mathfrak{p})$, i.e. b runs. All of which means that (9) is true iff there is exactly one cat belonging to Bill and that cat runs.

(7), by similar though more complex processes, can be shewn to be true iff there is exactly one thing which is both an action of leaving litter and is performed by Bill, and that action is something I hate. To get this reading we need a semantic rule for ***nom***$_2$. The simplest rule is

12.13 $\mathrm{V}(\boldsymbol{nom}_2)$ is the function $\zeta \in \mathbf{D}_{\langle\langle 0,1\rangle,\langle 0,1\rangle\rangle}$ such that for any $\omega \in \mathbf{D}_{\langle 0,1\rangle}$, $\zeta(\omega) = \omega$.

On this view the only function performed by ***nom***$_2$ is the changing of a verb-phrase into a complex common noun expression.

Zeno Vendler[265] appears to want to go further and suggests that nominal gerunds (or as he calls them *perfect nominals*) have very different semantic properties from verbal gerunds. To take account of Vendler's points we would need to modify 12.13. Here we merely note that our framework does allow a semantical difference between (1) and (2) if we choose to put it into the meaning rules for ***nom***$_1$ and ***nom***$_2$.

Turning finally to (3) we have ***nom***$_3$ in category $\langle\langle 0,1\rangle,\langle 0,1,1\rangle\rangle$. ***nom***$_3$ makes a noun out of a transitive verb. This gives us the following deep structure for (3)

(11) $\langle\langle\lambda, y_1, \langle \boldsymbol{I}, \langle\lambda, x_1, \langle \boldsymbol{hate}, x_1, y_1\rangle\rangle\rangle\rangle, \langle\lambda, x_{\langle 0,1\rangle},$
$\langle \boldsymbol{Bill}, \langle\lambda, x_1, \langle\langle \boldsymbol{s}, x_1\rangle, \langle\lambda, y_1, \langle\langle\lambda, z_1, \langle\langle\langle \boldsymbol{nom}_3, \boldsymbol{leaving}\rangle, y_1\rangle,$
$\langle \boldsymbol{of}, z_1\rangle\rangle\rangle, \boldsymbol{litter}\rangle\rangle, x_{\langle 0,1\rangle}\rangle\rangle\rangle\rangle\rangle$

One important difference between the verbal gerund of (1) and the nominal gerunds of (2) and (3) concerns the situation when the verb lacks a subject. Consider the difference between

(12) **I hate leaving litter**

and

(13) **I hate the leaving of litter**

[265] Vendler [1967], pp. 122–46. It might even be possible to have a number of different rules for ***nom***$_2$. Thus ***nom***$_2$* might have the rule 12.13 (which is a rule which tends to make (1) and (2) synonymous) while ***nom***$_2$** might have a rather different rule. Such a procedure might be one way in which our framework could deal with the ambiguity in Chomsky's example ([1968], p. 27): **I disapprove of John's drinking.**

In (12) ***I*** has to be the subject of the embedded sentence but in (13) it does not. The deep structure of (12) is parallel to the infinitival case of the (14) on p. 170 and is

(14) $\langle \boldsymbol{I}, \langle \lambda, x_1, \langle\langle \lambda, y_1, \langle \boldsymbol{hate}, x_1, y_1\rangle\rangle,$
$\langle \boldsymbol{nom}_1, \langle\langle \lambda, y_1, \langle \boldsymbol{leaving}, x_1, y_1\rangle\rangle, \boldsymbol{litter}\rangle\rangle\rangle\rangle$

The point here is that ***nom***$_1$ operates on whole sentences and therefore leaves a dangling free variable which is picked up by the ***I***. With (13) the case is quite other:

(15) $\langle\langle \lambda, y_1, \langle \boldsymbol{I}, \langle \lambda, x_1, \langle \boldsymbol{hate}, x_1, y_1\rangle\rangle\rangle\rangle,$
$\langle \lambda, x_{\langle 0,1\rangle}, \langle \boldsymbol{the}, \langle \lambda, y_1, \langle\langle \lambda, z_1, \langle\langle\langle \boldsymbol{nom}_3, \boldsymbol{leaving}\rangle, y_1\rangle,$
$\langle \boldsymbol{of}, z_1\rangle\rangle\rangle, \boldsymbol{litter}\rangle\rangle, x_{\langle 0,1\rangle}\rangle\rangle\rangle$

Since ***nom***$_3$ (and ***nom***$_2$ also) operates on a verb phrase there is no dangling subject to be catered for.

Gerunds can be combined with tense and aspect operators though there appear to be certain restrictions on the acceptability of some combinations. To take up that question, however, would lead us further afield than we are prepared to go.

CHAPTER THIRTEEN

Obtaining Natural Languages

In the light of the observations in the last chapter it can be seen that there is a need for certain theoretical refinements in the formal definitions of Part II. We have postponed this until we are in a position to use the tentative account of the λ-deep structure of English to illustrate the need for our more complicated account. The essence of the refinement is to provide a method for getting from the shallow structure to the surface structure. It will also provide us with a definition of 'surface structure'.

A revised account of utterance languages

Our definition of utterance languages on p. 113, although adequate for the points we wished to make in Chapter Eight, will not quite do as it stands. The reason may be seen by a consideration of the phenomena discussed in Chapter Twelve. Consider for example the sentence

(1) ⟨⟨***John***, ***sleep***⟩, ***ed***⟩

As we saw on p. 194 ***ed*** is best regarded in the deep structure as a symbol of category ⟨0, 0⟩. Since ***ed*** and ***sleep*** are distinct symbols, then in an utterance language as defined in Chapter Eight they would have to be distinct classes of utterances and a token of (1) would have to be of the form

(2) $\langle \mathfrak{John}, \mathfrak{sleep}, \mathfrak{ed} \rangle$

where $\mathfrak{John} \in$ ***John***, $\mathfrak{sleep} \in$ ***sleep*** and $\mathfrak{ed} \in$ ***ed***. In fact a token of (1) has the form

(3) $\langle \mathfrak{John}, \mathfrak{slept} \rangle$

To get from (1) to (3) therefore we add what we shall call an *amalgamation function*.

13.1 An amalgamation function[266] $\mathfrak{A}$ for a categorial language $\mathscr{L}$ is a function whose domain is a finite subset of the set of all finite sequences of proper symbols of $\mathscr{L}$ and whose range is a set of sets.

In the case of (1) we would have

$$\mathfrak{A}(\langle \textit{sleep}, \textit{ed}\rangle) = \textbf{slept}$$

where **slept** is a class of tokens, in fact the class of all possible utterances of the English word 'slept'. $\mathfrak{A}$ does some of the work that linguists put into the 'phonological component' but such a description can be misleading. Phonology seems more properly to be thought of as the study of the ways we might independently classify the members of the sets in the range of $\mathfrak{A}$ according to certain principles of sound production. We are interested in classifying tokens of sentences in terms of their semantic properties. $\mathfrak{A}$ is a part of the semantical analysis of $\mathscr{L}$ and to call it a phonological rule would betray a lack of understanding of its proper role. As we shall see, there are some cases in which $\mathfrak{A}$ makes a not insignificant semantical contribution.

We can shew how $\mathfrak{A}$ works by an example. Given a deep structure sentence α we first obtain the shallow structure $s(\alpha)$ as on p. 124. $s(\alpha)$ is the sequence consisting of the proper symbols of $\mathscr{L}$ in the order in which they occur in α. Suppose e.g. that $s(\alpha)$ is

$$\langle \alpha_1, \alpha_2, \alpha_3, \alpha_4, \alpha_5\rangle$$

i.e., α_1 is the first proper symbol in α, α_2 (perhaps the same symbol as α_1 or perhaps not) is the second and so on. Now suppose that $\langle \alpha_1, \alpha_2\rangle$, α_3, $\langle \alpha_4, \alpha_5\rangle$ are all in the domain of $\mathfrak{A}$ and that

$$\mathfrak{A}(\langle \alpha_1, \alpha_2\rangle) = \mathbf{a}_1$$

$$\mathfrak{A}(\alpha_3) = \mathbf{a}_2$$

and

$$\mathfrak{A}(\langle \alpha_4, \alpha_5\rangle) = \mathbf{a}_3$$

where $\mathbf{a}_1$, $\mathbf{a}_2$ and $\mathbf{a}_3$ are all sets. Then a surface structure of α (there could be more than one) would be $\mathbf{a}$ where

$$\mathbf{a} = \langle \mathbf{a}_1, \mathbf{a}_2, \mathbf{a}_3\rangle$$

And where $\mathfrak{a}_1 \in \mathbf{a}_1$, $\mathfrak{a}_2 \in \mathbf{a}_2$ and $\mathfrak{a}_3 \in \mathbf{a}$; then

[266] Cf. Montague [1970a], p. 377. Montague has simply a relation. Our $\mathfrak{A}$ is a function because we want the shallow structure, in conjunction with $\mathfrak{A}$, to determine the surface structure completely. Any stylistic surface variants short of those which depend on features of the tokens (such as, e.g., intonation) are reflected in the deep and shallow structures.

$\langle \mathfrak{a}_1, \mathfrak{a}_2, \mathfrak{a}_3 \rangle$

would be a token of **a** and therefore of α.

This example should make it clear how the general case would go.

With this revised definition of 'token' comes a consequential redefinition of the notions we introduced in Chapter Eight, like 'context property' and such. All the points made in that chapter still hold good when this has been carried out.

An interesting question now arises about whether $\mathfrak{A}$ should be called a semantical or a syntactical function. As long as we restrict ourselves to a single language the question is no more than a terminological one, though even here we can, I think, produce reasons for saying that $\mathfrak{A}$ has semantic effect. The question is whether we should think of a rule which says

13.2 $\mathfrak{A}(\langle \textit{sleep}, \textit{ed} \rangle) =$ **slept**

as telling us something about the meaning of **slept** or not. Part of the answer to this question depends upon the nature of ***sleep*** and ***ed***. Until now, in so far as we have looked at this question at all, we have thought of ***sleep*** at least, if not ***ed***, as a class of utterances, but now it is **slept** which is the class of utterances. The role of ***sleeps*** and ***ed*** has become much more abstract. In fact we can now go back to the liberality of Chapter One and allow the proper symbols of $\mathscr{L}$ to be anything we like.[267]

If we were looking at several languages we might take this idea even further since we might even regard the 'symbols' of $\mathscr{L}$ as 'universal human concepts'. This means that we might have two languages $\mathscr{L}/\mathfrak{A}$ and $\mathscr{L}/\mathfrak{A}'$ which differ only in the surface realization of the underlying $\mathscr{L}$. Some such phenomenon as this might explain why a philosophical attempt to discover the meaning of words like **good**, **know**, **believe**, **reality**, etc. is not an examination of the English language.

We cannot of course simply identify an expression of $\mathscr{L}^\lambda$ with its meaning because, e.g., even if

(4) $\langle$***John***, ***sleeps***$\rangle$

is a sequence in which ***John*** and ***sleeps*** are not English words but universal concepts, the meaning of (4) is still obtained by the operation

[267] Deep structures now become like bound variables. Just as $\langle \lambda, x, \langle \alpha, x \rangle \rangle$ and $\langle \lambda, y, \langle \alpha, y \rangle \rangle$ are synonymous and the structural role of the x can be played equally well by y, so the role of the λ-deep structure does not require any account to be given of the nature of the symbols.

of the ***John*** function on the ***sleeps*** function.[268] Also, since the meanings of symbols of a natural language are probably given by means of a communication class of the kind outlined (for propositional languages) on pp. 58–61, a class of assignments might still be needed even if the symbols of $\mathscr{L}$ are universal concepts. For it may be that the same vague concept occurs in several different languages.

Be all this as it may, we must repeat that we have not imposed any restrictions on the nature of symbols of $\mathscr{L}$. Anything which plays the required role will do. One could indeed formulate the connection between the surface language and the meaning without reference at all to $\mathscr{L}$, just as in combinatory logic one can formulate quantification theory without bound variables, but such a formulation would be too complicated to be illuminating.

We have illustrated the use of $\mathfrak{A}$ in the case of tenses. Obviously we can deal similarly with any of the phenomena discussed in Chapter Twelve. Furthermore we can deal with the more troublesome

(5) ***Arabella wants a man***

of p. 170 f. Actually we are interested in the surface sentence:

(6) ⟨**Arabella, wants, a, man**⟩

and, just as **slept** represents ⟨***sleep, ed***⟩, we could say that **wants** is composed of ⟨***wants, to*, find****⟩. This means that the deep structure of (6) is

(7) $\langle \textit{\textbf{Arabella}}, \langle \lambda, x_1, \langle\langle \lambda, y_1, \langle \textit{\textbf{wants}}, x_1, y_1\rangle\rangle,$
$\langle \textit{\textbf{to}}^*, \langle\langle \lambda, z_1, \langle \textit{\textbf{find}}^*, x_1, z_1\rangle\rangle, \langle \lambda, x_{\langle 0,1\rangle}, \langle \textit{\textbf{a}}, \textit{\textbf{man}}, x_{\langle 0,1\rangle}\rangle\rangle\rangle\rangle\rangle\rangle\rangle$

The shallow structure then becomes

(8) ⟨***Arabella, wants, to*, find*, a, man***⟩

We suppose that $\mathfrak{A}$(***Arabella***) = **Arabella**, $\mathfrak{A}$(***a***) = **a**, $\mathfrak{A}$(***man***) = **man**, and $\mathfrak{A}$(⟨***wants, to*, find****⟩) = **wants**. This gives us (6) as (8)'s surface structure.

to* and ***find**** are symbols of $\mathscr{L}$ and so are ***to*** and ***find***. V(***to****) = V(***to***) and V(***find****) = V(***find***) but ***to**** and ***to*** and ***find**** and ***find*** are distinct symbols. The reason for this is that we want to have $\mathfrak{A}$(***wants***) = **wants**, $\mathfrak{A}$(***to***) = **to**, and $\mathfrak{A}$(***find***) = **find**.

We want this so that the deep structure which is like (7) except that ***to*** and ***find*** replace ***to**** and ***find**** will give us

(9) ⟨***Arabella, wants, to, find, a, man***⟩

[268] The theory of meaning in Lewis [1970], pp. 31–40, is in fact an attempt to combine a system of concepts of the present kind with an algebra of meanings of the kind described *supra* on pp. 53–6 since Lewis' 'meanings' also give the value of the function at each stage.

as a shallow structure from which we may derive

(10) ⟨**Arabella, wants, to, find, a, man**⟩

as a surface sentence. Since the sequence ⟨***wants***, ***to***, ***find***⟩ (unlike ⟨***wants***, ***to****, ***find****⟩) is not in the domain of 𝔄 we cannot obtain (6) from (9). And since ***to**** and ***find**** are neither of them in the domain of 𝔄 (although ***wants*** and ⟨***wants***, ***to****, ***find****⟩ are both) we cannot obtain (10) from (8). If we adopt this solution to the problem raised by (6) then we have a more compelling reason for saying that 𝔄 contributes to giving the meaning of the surface sentence and that (8) represents a stage at which it has got some of its meaning but not all of it.

In some cases 𝔄 can be used to block a surface realization of an unacceptable shallow structure. E.g., the shallow structure

(11) ⟨***Arabella***, ***wants***, ***inf***, ***to***, ***find****, ***a***, ***man***⟩

will not yield any surface sentence since ***find**** must occur with a ***to**** in order to produce a sequence in the domain of 𝔄.[269] However, there are many acceptability principles which 𝔄 cannot replace. E.g., the structures

(12) ⟨***me***, ***run***⟩

(13) ⟨***I***, ***runs***⟩

must be blocked even though ***me***, ***I***, ***run*** and ***runs*** are all in the domain of 𝔄. (Note here that the symbols of $\mathscr{L}$ cannot be entirely semantical entities, for although V(***run***) = V(***runs***), yet ***run*** and ***runs*** must be distinct symbols. If $\mathscr{L}$ is a concept language perhaps ***run*** would be a concept and ***runs*** would be, say, ⟨***run***, 3⟩, i.e., the pair made up of the concept and the number 3. 𝔄 would then realize the first as **run** and the second as **runs**.)

The function 𝔄 enables us to deal in an obvious and simple way with cases of lexical ambiguity. Lexical ambiguity arises where two distinct symbols have a common realization. E.g., where ***light***$_1$ means 'not heavy' and ***light***$_2$ means 'not dark' then

𝔄(***light***$_1$) = 𝔄(***light***$_2$) = **light**

Here both ***light***$_1$ and ***light***$_2$ are in $F_{\langle\langle 0,1\rangle,\langle 0,1\rangle\rangle}$; but of course **light** can also be a common noun and so we might have ***light***$_3$ $\in F_{\langle 0,1\rangle}$. Here too

𝔄(***light***$_3$) = **light**

The case of ***light***$_2$ and ***light***$_3$ is interesting for it is no accident that they

[269] 𝔄 can thus be used for the task we called *proper* deletion on p. 153 f. Viz. the preventing of certain deep structure symbols from reaching the surface. E.g. 𝔄(***coll***) (cf. p. 162) = ∅, 𝔄(***inf***) = ∅ (p. 169), 𝔄(***comp***) = ∅, 𝔄(***a****) = ∅ (p. 184 f), 𝔄(***nom***) = ∅ (p. 205) etc.

are both realized in the same way. As a language grows it is natural for a surface word to be extended to cover senses which although distinct (and therefore rightly represented by distinct symbols in the λ-base) are yet closely related.[270] Take, e.g., the verb ***water*** as in

(14) ***Arabella waters the garden***

In some cases the relations between identically realized words can be expressed by general patterns. One such pattern was discussed by means of the particle ***erg*** on p. 201. Using $\mathfrak{A}$ we can have

$$\mathfrak{A}(\langle \textit{erg}, \textit{fly}\rangle) = \textbf{fly}$$
$$\mathfrak{A}(\langle \textit{erg}, \textit{flies}\rangle) = \textbf{flies} \text{ etc.}$$

and even such cases as

$$\mathfrak{A}(\langle \textit{erg}, \textit{die}\rangle) = \textbf{kill}$$

Another case in which something of this sort may be going on is in a verb like **build**. We can say:

(15) **John and Arabella are building at Ngaio**

(15) **Fletcher Construction do not build houses**

(17) **Cecil builds every weekend**

In (15) John and Arabella are getting someone else to build them a house. Thus they might ask Fletcher Construction to build it for them. But even if Fletcher Construction did build it for them they would employ such a man as Cecil who does the work. The question here is whether to have three separate words in the λ-categorial language. There is no objection of principle to this. Since we are granting that $\mathfrak{A}$ should be regarded as contributing to the semantic analysis we do not have to assume that the realization of ***build***$_1$, ***build***$_2$ and ***build***$_3$ as **build** is an accident. Alternatively one might try to say that there is an underlying ***build*** concept and that the various senses of **build** are got by operating on this.[271] The basic sense might be as found in (17). We might then have a logical particle ***emp*** so that

$$\langle \textit{emp}, \textit{build}\rangle$$

means (roughly) 'employs people who build' and $\mathfrak{A}(\langle \textit{emp}, \textit{build}\rangle) =$ **build**. The sense of **build** involved in (15) might then be represented as

$$\langle \textit{erg}, \langle \textit{emp}, \textit{build}\rangle\rangle$$

with $\mathfrak{A}$ taking this also into **build**. We shall remain neutral on the question of whether this should be done this way or simply by having ***build***$_1$, ***build***$_2$, ***build***$_3$. There is certainly an important topic here in the

[270] The idea that two things have the same name because, although distinct, they are closely related was noted by Aristotle in *Metaphysics* Γ2 (1003a34–b5) where he discusses the meanings of ***health*** and of ***medical***.

[271] For a sustained attempt to carry out this sort of analysis *vide* Fillmore [1968]. Cf. also Staal [1967].

philosophical analysis of the idea of an action but whether this interest is enough to take the analysis into the λ-base is to me very unclear.

The noun-verb distinction

In our account of English deep structure in Part III we made no distinction between common nouns and intransitive verb phrases. Both were of category $\langle 0,1\rangle$. The time has now come to remedy this situation. Our solution will be a simple one, so simple that if it could have been applied in an absolutely regular way we would have introduced it at the beginning of Part III. The basic idea is that common nouns, although semantically of the same category as intransitive verb phrases, are syntactically of a different category.[272] What we do is introduce the additional basic category 2 of common noun expressions.

We take care of the semantical situation by the simple requirement that

13.3 $\mathbf{D}_2 = \mathbf{D}_{\langle 0,1\rangle}$

Certain consequential changes now have to be made. First, the class of determiners (pp. 135–9) must now be of category $\langle 0,2,\langle 0,1\rangle\rangle$. This means that

(1) $\langle$***the, runs, man***$\rangle$

will now be ruled out as an ill-formed expression since ***runs*** is not of category 2 and ***man*** is no longer of category $\langle 0,1\rangle$. Second, adjectives will now become of category $\langle 2,2\rangle$. Note that this immediately allows us to generate complex common noun expressions. For if ***happy*** $\in F_{\langle 2,2\rangle}$ then $\langle$***happy, man***$\rangle \in E_2$ and so we can have:

(2) $\langle$***the***, $\langle$***happy, man***$\rangle$, ***runs***$\rangle$

The relative pronoun ***who*** (p. 158 f) becomes of category $\langle\langle 2,2\rangle, \langle 0,1\rangle\rangle$ for it makes an adjectival expression out of an intransitive verb phrase; and certain other changes of this nature will have to be made.

The awkward cases which cause this approach to be not entirely regular arise with adverbs and prepositions. Adverbs not only modify verbs (or whole sentences) as in

(3) ***the man sleeps quietly***

but they also modify adjectives as in

(4) ***the quietly confident man sleeps***

[272] Montague [1972]. Lewis [1970], p. 20, has a category C of common noun. Intensions of common nouns are functions from indices to sets.

(3) requires ***quietly*** to be of category $\langle 0,0\rangle$ while (4) requires it to be of category $\langle 2,2\rangle$.

Our solution to this problem will make use of the function $\mathfrak{A}$ (that is one of the reasons we have deferred it until this chapter). What we shall do is introduce an operator whose only function is to make out of ***quietly*** (a member of $F_{\langle 0,0\rangle}$) an expression in $E_{\langle 2,2\rangle}$ which corresponds in meaning in the appropriate sense.

We use the symbol ***mod*** as a functor of category $\langle\langle 2,2\rangle,\langle 2,2\rangle\rangle$, $\langle 0,0\rangle\rangle$ so that the expression $\langle$***mod, quietly***$\rangle$ is in category $\langle\langle 2,2\rangle$, $\langle 2,2\rangle\rangle$. We shall require that $\mathfrak{A}(\langle$***mod, quietly***$\rangle)$ = **quietly** (just as $\mathfrak{A}$(***quietly***) = **quietly**).

In general where $\alpha \in E_{\langle 0,0\rangle}$

$$\mathfrak{A}(\langle \boldsymbol{mod}, \alpha\rangle) = \mathfrak{A}(\alpha)$$

As far as V goes:

13.4 V(***mod***) is that function $\zeta \in \mathbf{D}_{\langle\langle\langle 2,2\rangle,\langle 2,2\rangle\rangle,\langle 0,0\rangle\rangle}$ such that where $\omega \in \mathbf{D}_{\langle 0,0\rangle}$ and $\omega' \in \mathbf{D}_{\langle 2,2\rangle}$ and $\omega'' \in \mathbf{D}_2$ and $a \in \mathbf{D}_1$ then

$$(((\zeta(\omega))(\omega'))(\omega''))(a) = \omega((\omega'(\omega''))(a))$$

(Remember that $\mathbf{D}_2 = \mathbf{D}_{\langle 0,1\rangle}$ and so, since $\omega' \in \mathbf{D}_{\langle 2,2\rangle}$ and $\omega'' \in \mathbf{D}_2$, then $(\omega'(\omega'')) \in \mathbf{D}_2 = \mathbf{D}_{\langle 0,1\rangle}$. Thus, since $a \in \mathbf{D}_1$ then $\omega'(\omega''(a)) \in \mathbf{D}_0$ and so also is $\omega((\omega'(\omega'')(a))$.)

What V(***mod***) says may be illustrated in the case of ***quietly***. $\langle$***mod, quietly***$\rangle$ is of category $\langle\langle 2,2\rangle,\langle 2,2\rangle\rangle$. ***confident*** is, we suppose, of category $\langle 2,2\rangle$ so that $\langle\langle$***mod, quietly***$\rangle$, ***confident***$\rangle$ is also of category $\langle 2,2\rangle$. Consider ***man*** in F_2; then what V(***mod***) says is that for any $a \in \mathbf{D}_1$,

$$V^+(\langle\langle\langle \boldsymbol{mod}, \boldsymbol{quietly}\rangle, \boldsymbol{confident}\rangle, \boldsymbol{man}\rangle)(a) = \omega_{\boldsymbol{quietly}}((\omega_{\boldsymbol{confident}}, (\omega_{\boldsymbol{man}}))(a))$$ [273]

The other awkward case is the case of prepositional phrases which, as we noted on p. 145, can act either as adverbs or as adjectives. We try something of the same sort here and introduce a prepositional modifier which turns an adverb-forming preposition (in category $\langle\langle 0,0\rangle,1\rangle$) into an adjective-forming preposition (in category $\langle\langle 2,2\rangle,1\rangle$). We denote this modifier by ***ap*** (adjective-forming preposition). Thus as well as

(5) $\langle\lambda, x_0, \langle\langle\lambda, x_1, \langle\langle \boldsymbol{for}, x_1\rangle, x_0\rangle\rangle, \boldsymbol{Arabella}\rangle\rangle$

$\langle 0,0\rangle$ we have also

[273] If ***man*** had been in $E_{\langle 0,1\rangle}$ then ***quietly confident man*** would be analysed as $(\langle\lambda, x, \langle \boldsymbol{quietly}, \langle\langle \boldsymbol{confident}, \boldsymbol{man}\rangle, x\rangle\rangle\rangle)$, i.e. to be a quietly confident man is, on this analysis, to be quietly a confident man.

(6) $\langle \lambda, x_2, \langle \lambda, x_{\langle 0,2\rangle}, \langle\langle \lambda, x_1, \langle x_{\langle 0,2\rangle}, \langle\langle\langle \boldsymbol{ap}, \boldsymbol{for}\rangle, x_1\rangle, x_2\rangle\rangle\rangle, \boldsymbol{Arabella}\rangle\rangle\rangle$

in category $\langle 2,2\rangle$.

Since $\mathfrak{A}(\langle \boldsymbol{ap}, \alpha\rangle)$ (where α is a preposition) $= \mathfrak{A}(\alpha)$ we have both $\mathfrak{A}((5))$ and $\mathfrak{A}((6))$ as

(7) **for Arabella**

The semantic rule for ***ap*** is analogous to the rule for ***mod***:

13.5 V(***ap***) is that function $\zeta \in \mathbf{D}_{\langle\langle\langle 2,2\rangle,1\rangle,\langle\langle 0,0\rangle,1\rangle\rangle}$ such that if $\rho \in \mathbf{D}_{\langle\langle 0,0\rangle,1\rangle}$ and a, $b \in \mathbf{D}_1$ and $\omega \in \mathbf{D}_2$ then $((\zeta(\rho))(a))(\omega)(b) = (\rho(a))(\omega(b))$.

What this means is that if ω is the property of being a man and ρ is the meaning of the preposition ***in*** then $(\zeta(\rho))(a)$ means 'being in a' and $(\zeta(\rho)(a))(\omega)(b)$ means that b is a (man-in-a), which means the same as that (b is a man) in a.

Scope indicators

There are many words whose function in the shallow structure is to indicate that, of the possible deep structures from which they may be derived, only those are acceptable in which the relative scopes of the operators satisfy certain conditions. Perhaps the best-known example (to logicians at any rate) of this sort of thing is the phenomenon of ***any*** and ***every*** as noted by Quine and others.[274] Take first ***anyone*** and ***everyone*** and the two shallow structures

(1) ***Arabella does not love everyone***

and

(2) ***Arabella does not love anyone***

We shall regard the meaning of ***everyone*** and ***anyone*** in deep structure as identical (viz. the meaning of ***everyone*** as explained on p. 81). (1) and (2) can each have (at least) two deep structures:

(3) $\langle \boldsymbol{Arabella}, \langle \boldsymbol{does}, \langle \lambda, x_1, \langle \boldsymbol{not}, \langle\langle \lambda, y_1, \langle \boldsymbol{love}, x_1, y_1\rangle\rangle, \boldsymbol{everyone}\rangle\rangle\rangle\rangle\rangle$

and

(4) $\langle \boldsymbol{Arabella}, \langle \lambda, x_1, \langle\langle \boldsymbol{does}, \langle \lambda, y_1, \langle \boldsymbol{not}, \langle \boldsymbol{love}, x_1, y_1\rangle\rangle\rangle\rangle, \boldsymbol{everyone}\rangle\rangle\rangle$

are the deep structures of (1), and when ***everyone*** is replaced by ***anyone*** we get the deep structures (3′) and (4′) of (2). Since V(***everyone***) = V(***anyone***) then $V^+(3) = V^+(3')$ and $V^+(4) = V^+(4')$, But (1) and

[274] Quine [1940], p. 70 f. There is a large body of linguistic literature on the ***any/every*** situation, some of which is cited on p. 119 of Seuren [1969] and some of which has appeared since. The remarks in the text are obviously incomplete and are intended to do no more than suggest that questions of scope may turn out to be relevant even in cases in which this does not obviously seem so.

(2) do not mean the same. To see what is going on we shall omit the irrelevant complexity of the auxiliary ***does*** and shall change the word order to get

(5) $\langle \textbf{\textit{Arabella}}, \langle \lambda, x_1, \langle \textbf{\textit{not}}, \langle\langle \lambda, y_1, \langle \textbf{\textit{love}}, x_1, y_1 \rangle\rangle, \textbf{\textit{everyone}} \rangle\rangle\rangle\rangle$

(6) $\langle \textbf{\textit{Arabella}}, \langle \lambda, x_1, \langle\langle \lambda, y_1, \langle \textbf{\textit{not}}, \langle \textbf{\textit{love}}, x_1, y_1 \rangle\rangle\rangle, \textbf{\textit{everyone}} \rangle\rangle$

(5′) $\langle \textbf{\textit{Arabella}}, \langle \lambda, x_1, \langle \textbf{\textit{not}}, \langle\langle \lambda, y_1, \langle \textbf{\textit{love}}, x_1, y_1 \rangle\rangle, \textbf{\textit{anyone}} \rangle\rangle\rangle\rangle$

(6′) $\langle \textbf{\textit{Arabella}}, \langle \lambda, x_1, \langle\langle \lambda, y_1, \langle \textbf{\textit{not}}, \langle \textbf{\textit{love}}, x_1, y_1 \rangle\rangle\rangle, \textbf{\textit{anyone}} \rangle\rangle$

(5) and (5′) are synonymous and so are (6) and (6′).

We notice that in (5) and (5′) the quantifier is in the scope of ***not*** while in (6) and (6′) ***not*** is in the scope of the quantifier. Under normal circumstances (1) means (5) but (2) means (6′). This is because although ***anyone*** and ***everyone*** do not differ in meaning in the deep structure yet the acceptability principles will say that (5′) and (6) are not acceptable deep structures.[275] The precise statement of the rule is of considerable difficulty: in this case it would seem to require that a deep structure in which ***every*** is outside the scope of ***not*** is unacceptable (at least where both apply to the same verb) and a deep structure in which ***not*** is outside the scope of ***any*** is unacceptable.

The ***not*** involved in this rule need not reach the surface. Thus while

(7) **Arabella denied any knowledge**

is perfectly acceptable

(8) **Arabella claimed any knowledge**

is not.[276]

There are two ways in which we can explain this. One way is to say that the meaning of ***deny*** according to the assignment V has a 'negative flavour' and that an acceptability principle takes this into account when ruling out (8). There is nothing wrong in principle with allowing a logical deletion to be blocked on the basis of the meaning of words in the deep structure, provided that no restrictions of this kind occur which might apply to one word but not to another with the same meaning. The other way is to take seriously the role of the amalgamation function in contributing to the meaning of the surface language and

[275] ***any*** is of the same syntactical category as ***every*** and has the same deep structure semantics, viz. 9.4 on p. 136. Since the deep structures are synonymous, we must say that either the acceptability principles contribute to the meaning of these words or that the words mean the same in the surface structure. I prefer to say the former, i.e. that ***any*** and ***every*** differ in meaning in that although V(***any***) = V(***every***) yet they 'spark off' different acceptability principles. This means that the meaning of a surface word is determined by the interaction of the amalgamation and assignment functions and the acceptability principles.

[276] Seuren [1972] uses examples like these on p. 253. Cf. also Lakoff [1971a], pp. 248–51 (for a discussion of **dissuade**).

say that **deny** is a surface word represented in the deep structure by something like ***assert not***. Actually since ***assert not*** will have to be realized as **assert not** we shall need something like ***assert* not**** which will be composed of symbols whose meanings are something like those of ***assert*** and ***not***; though probably not quite the same since **deny** does not mean exactly ***assert not***. $\mathfrak{A}$ would be such that

$$\mathfrak{A}(\langle \textit{assert}^*, \textit{not}^* \rangle) = \textbf{deny}$$

Neither ***assert**** nor ***not**** would by itself be in the domain of $\mathfrak{A}$. We would probably want V(***not***) = V(***not****) and indeed ***not**** could be a common symbol for any verbs whose negative surface flavour is made explicit in the deep structure.[277]

Other cases of hidden negatives can be treated likewise. E.g., the following examples shew that the ***any/every*** rules are not merely rules of scope but rules of scope with relation to negation:

(9) **if anyone comes I'll be surprised**

(10) **if everyone comes I'll be surprised**

We shall use what are for us simpler examples:

(11) **if anyone comes Arabella runs**

(12) **if everyone comes Arabella runs**

The clue to this one is to see **if** as $\mathfrak{A}(\langle \textit{either}^*, \textit{not}^* \rangle)$ where ***either**** is a sort of disjunction (which can go in front of its arguments instead of between them) and ***not**** is the hidden negative we have just been talking about.

We have the following four deep structures:

(13) $\langle \textit{either}^*, \langle \textit{not}^*, \langle \textit{anyone}, \textit{comes} \rangle \rangle, \langle \textit{Arabella}, \textit{runs} \rangle \rangle$

(14) $\langle \textit{either}^*, \langle \lambda, x_{\langle 0,0,0 \rangle}, \langle \textit{not}^*, \langle \lambda, x_{\langle 0,0 \rangle}, \langle \textit{anyone}, \langle \lambda, x_1, \langle x_{\langle 0,0,0 \rangle}, \langle x_{\langle 0,0 \rangle}, \langle \textit{comes}, x_1 \rangle \rangle, \langle \textit{Arabella}, \textit{runs} \rangle \rangle \rangle \rangle \rangle \rangle \rangle \rangle$

(13′) $\langle \textit{either}^*, \langle \textit{not}^*, \langle \textit{everyone}, \textit{comes} \rangle \rangle, \langle \textit{Arabella}, \textit{runs} \rangle \rangle$

(14′) $\langle \textit{either}^*, \langle \lambda, x_{\langle 0,0,0 \rangle}, \langle \textit{not}^*, \langle \lambda, x_{\langle 0,0 \rangle}, \langle \textit{everyone}, \langle \lambda, x_1, \langle x_{\langle 0,0,0 \rangle}, \langle x_{\langle 0,0 \rangle}, \langle \textit{comes}, x_1 \rangle \rangle, \langle \textit{Arabella}, \textit{runs} \rangle \rangle \rangle \rangle \rangle \rangle \rangle \rangle$

In (13) and (13′) the quantifiers ***anyone*** and ***everyone*** are both clearly

[277] An explanation of this kind will not work in all cases. E.g., although **failed** can mean **did not pass**, yet **Bill failed every exam** does not mean the same as **Bill did not pass every exam**. This would suggest that **fail** at any rate is not to be analysed as ***not pass*** if the kind of ***any/every*** principles I have been illustrating are valid. Even **deny** is dubious since **he denied everything** is different from **he did not assert everything**. What this points to is that the formulation of the role of ***any*** and ***every*** in any comprehensive and precise way is going to be far more complex than the discussion in the text would lead one to believe. It need not, however, shew that the phenomenon is not one which has to do with surface indications of deep-structure scope.

within the scope of ***not***.[278] This means that by the ***any/every*** principles we have been expounding (pp. 217–19) (13) will be unacceptable since ***anyone*** is immediately within the scope of ***not****. (14) and (14′) are a little more complicated for there is the spurious sense (of p. 170) in which here too the quantifiers are both within the scope of ***not****. In this sense we may regard (14) and (14′) as versions of a more basic structure in which changes of order have been made. I.e., we might well want to say that the 'real' structures of (14) and (14′) are

$$(15)\ \langle \textbf{\textit{anyone}}, \langle \lambda, x_1, \langle \textbf{\textit{either}}^*, \langle \textbf{\textit{not}}^*, \langle \textbf{\textit{comes}}, x_1 \rangle\rangle, \langle \textbf{\textit{Arabella}}, \textbf{\textit{runs}} \rangle\rangle\rangle\rangle$$

and

$$(15')\ \langle \textbf{\textit{everyone}}, \langle \lambda, x_1, \langle \textbf{\textit{either}}^*, \langle \textbf{\textit{not}}^*, \langle \textbf{\textit{comes}}, x_1 \rangle\rangle, \langle \textbf{\textit{Arabella}}, \textbf{\textit{runs}} \rangle\rangle\rangle$$

It should be obvious that (15) converts to (14) and (15′) to (14′). In both (15) and (15′) ***not**** is within the scope of the quantifier and if we carry this over to (14) and (14′) we can rule out (14′) as unacceptable.

Thus as deep structure for (11), (13) is acceptable but not (14) and as deep structure for (12), (14′) is acceptable but not (13′). As far as the deep structures are concerned, of course, (13) and (13′) mean the same (since ***anyone*** and ***everyone*** mean the same) and (14) and (14′) mean the same. This means that (11) means the same as (13)/(13′) and (12) means the same as (14)/(14′).

There is a long discussion of the ***any/every*** problem by Pieter Seuren.[279] We have not the space here to go fully into the questions he raises but we shall take up one or two apparent difficulties in the view that ***any*** and ***every*** differ only as scope indicators. The first point we should stress is that the rule is not simply a rule about whether a quantifier should have small or large scope but rather a question about the scope of a quantifier relative to a negation. This point is important because, as Seuren notes, ***any*** sometimes behaves more like an existential quantifier than a universal quantifier. The reason for this is that when negation is involved the choice of scope may well

[278] We cannot apply the acceptability principles directly to (14) and (14′) since they are neither of them acceptable structures with **if** replacing ***either*not****. λ-convertibility is not as a rule acceptability-preserving.

[279] Seuren [1969], pp. 119–34. It should be obvious that my predisposition as a logician is to want to use scope differences to explain as much as possible rather than as little as possible. The general point of my remarks is intended to be that it is very unwise to say that scope differences are not involved merely because they do not appear in an overt way. I suspect the same is true of some of the cases discussed in Partee [1970], in which she claims that scope is not involved.

determine whether the quantifier should be existential or universal. Consider the following relations between sentences containing ***anyone***, ***everyone*** and ***someone***:

(16) $\langle$***Arabella***$, \langle\lambda, x_1, \langle\langle\lambda, y_1, \langle\langle$***loves***$, x_1, y_1\rangle,$ ***not***$\rangle\rangle,$ ***everyone***$\rangle\rangle\rangle$

(17) $\langle$***Arabella***$, \langle\lambda, x_1, \langle\langle\lambda, x_{\langle 0, \langle 0, 1\rangle\rangle}, \langle\langle\langle\lambda, y_1, \langle$***loves***$, x_1, y_1\rangle\rangle, x_{\langle 0, \langle 0, 1\rangle\rangle}\rangle,$ ***not***$\rangle\rangle,$ ***everyone***$\rangle\rangle\rangle$

(16′) $\langle$***Arabella***$, \langle\lambda, x_1, \langle\langle\lambda, y_1, \langle\langle$***loves***$, x_1, y_1\rangle,$ ***not***$\rangle\rangle,$ ***someone***$\rangle\rangle\rangle$

(17′) $\langle$***Arabella***$, \langle\lambda, x_1, \langle\langle\lambda, x_{\langle 0, \langle 0, 1\rangle\rangle}, \langle\langle\langle\lambda, y_1, \langle$***loves***$, x_1, y_1\rangle\rangle\rangle, x_{\langle 0, \langle 0, 1\rangle\rangle}\rangle,$ ***not***$\rangle\rangle,$ ***someone***$\rangle\rangle\rangle$

We may regard (17) and (17′) as converted instances of

(18) $\langle$***Arabella***$, \langle\lambda, x_1, \langle\langle\langle\lambda, y_1, \langle$***loves***$, x_1, y_1\rangle\rangle,$ ***everyone***$\rangle,$ ***not***$\rangle\rangle\rangle$

and

(19) $\langle$***Arabella***$, \langle\lambda, x_1, \langle\langle\langle\lambda, y_1, \langle$***loves***$, x_1, y_1\rangle\rangle,$ ***someone***$\rangle,$ ***not***$\rangle\rangle\rangle$

respectively. In (16) and (17) ***not*** is within the scope of the quantifier while in (18) and (19) it is not. The important thing to notice, however, is that by changing *both* the scope *and* the kind of quantifier we end up with a situation in which (16) is synonymous with (19) (and therefore with (17′)) and (17) is synonymous with (18) (and therefore with (16′)).

Suppose then that we introduce the same cases with ***anyone***:

(20) $\langle$***Arabella***$, \langle\lambda, x_1, \langle\langle\lambda, y_1, \langle\langle$***loves***$, x_1, y_1\rangle,$ ***not***$\rangle\rangle,$ ***anyone***$\rangle\rangle\rangle$

(21) $\langle$***Arabella***$, \langle\lambda, x_1, \langle\langle\lambda, x_{\langle 0, \langle 0, 1\rangle\rangle}, \langle\langle\langle\lambda, y_1, \langle$***loves***$, x_1, y_1\rangle\rangle, x_{\langle 0, \langle 0, 1\rangle\rangle}\rangle,$ ***not***$\rangle\rangle,$ ***anyone***$\rangle\rangle\rangle$

(22) $\langle$***Arabella***$, \langle\lambda, x_1, \langle\langle\langle\lambda, y_1, \langle$***loves***$, x_1, y_1\rangle\rangle,$ ***anyone***$\rangle,$ ***not***$\rangle\rangle\rangle$

((22) being the λ-converted form of (21) which reveals the 'real' scope situation).

Because of the relations between ***everyone*** and ***someone*** we can either treat ***anyone*** as a universal quantifier with wide scope and thus rule out (22) (and so (21)) as unacceptable, or treat it as an existential quantifier with narrow scope, which would rule out (20) as unacceptable. But whichever of these cases we adopt we get exactly the same result. For in the former case the shallow structure

(23) ***Arabella loves not anyone***

means the same as (16) and in the latter case (23) means the same as (17′). But as we have noted (16) and (17′) are synonymous.

Even ***someone*** can sometimes appear as a universal quantifier under rather curious circumstances. Consider the surface sentence[280]

[280] Seuren's example ([1969], p. 120) is: **if any member contributes he gets a poppy**. Our simplification involves no differences of principle. Difficulties of the kind we discuss are also alluded to in G. Lakoff [1970a], p. 243 f.

(24) **if anyone works he sleeps**

This would seem to have the deep structure

(25) $\langle$***either****, $\langle\lambda, x_{\langle 0,0,0\rangle}, \langle$***not****, $\langle\lambda, x_{\langle 0,0\rangle}, \langle$***anyone***, $\langle\lambda, x_1, \langle x_{\langle 0,0,0\rangle}, \langle x_{\langle 0,0\rangle}, \langle$***works***, $x_1\rangle\rangle, \langle\langle$***he***$^\dagger, x_1\rangle$, ***sleeps***$\rangle\rangle\rangle\rangle\rangle\rangle\rangle\rangle$

which as far as 'real' scope is concerned is

(26) $\langle$***anyone***, $\langle\lambda, x_1, \langle$***either****, $\langle$***not****, $\langle$***works***, $x_1\rangle\rangle, \langle$***sleeps***, $x_1\rangle\rangle\rangle\rangle$

It is important to realize that in a sentence like (24) the scope of the quantifier must be considered to extend throughout the whole sentence. Otherwise the pronoun ***he***† (which is clearly a bound variable pronoun in the sense of p. 178) would be left dangling and we would not have a closed sentence for the deep structure. Now (24) is equivalent to

(27) **if someone works he sleeps**

The problem here is that if we take (25) or (26) and we replace ***anyone*** by ***someone*** and still treat ***someone*** as an existential quantifier we get a structure which means that either there exists a non-worker or there exists a sleeper, which is not the normal meaning of (27). (27) in fact means exactly the same as (26) when ***anyone*** is treated as a universal quantifier. The reason for this situation is a rather complex one and it is not easy to see what is the best way of fitting it in to our scope principles. To see what is going on let us look at

(28) **if someone works Arabella sleeps**

which is also equivalent to

(29) **if anyone works Arabella sleeps**

(29) is to be treated like (24) with ***anyone*** functioning as a wide-scope universal quantifier. In (28) however ***someone***, which does not carry ***anyone***'s insistence that it dominate a ***not***, can occur in the deep structure inside the scope of ***not***. Thus the deep structures of (28) and (29) are:

(30) $\langle$***either****, $\langle$***not****, $\langle$***someone***, ***works***$\rangle\rangle, \langle$***Arabella***, ***sleeps***$\rangle\rangle$

(31) $\langle$***either***, $\langle\lambda, x_{\langle 0,0,0\rangle}, \langle$***not****, $\langle\lambda, x_{\langle 0,0\rangle}, \langle$***anyone***, $\langle\lambda, x_1, \langle x_{\langle 0,0,0\rangle}, \langle x_{\langle 0,0\rangle}, \langle$***works***, $x_1\rangle\rangle, \langle$***Arabella***, ***sleeps***$\rangle\rangle\rangle\rangle\rangle\rangle\rangle\rangle$

(30) and (31) are equivalent for the reasons we discussed above: a universal quantifier outside the scope of a negation is equivalent to an existential one inside. The reason for the choice of **someone** in (27) is presumably that it is being thought of by analogy with (28). Unfortunately the presence of **he** in (27) forces the scope of the quantifier to extend over the whole sentence; otherwise we should be left with a 'dangling' free variable. For this reason the quantifier must change into a universal by analogy with (31).

It is not clear to me how best to describe this otherwise than by some sort of *ad hoc* rule which reflects the argument just used, but it seems clear that in the deep structure of (27) and (28) there need be only two kinds of quantifiers and that questions of scope relative to ***not*** are what determine their surface form.

Other examples which Seuren brings forward in an attempt to shew that the ***any/every*** distinction is not primarily one of scope involve cases where ***any*** is selected because of a negative in an implied antecedent to a sentence. Thus the difference between

(32) **I should like to make an appointment with every man on the team**

(33) **I should like to make an appointment with any man on the team**

seems best brought out by treating (33) as something like

(34) **I should like to make an appointment with any man on the team who may desire it**

where the **who may desire it** is left unsaid. **any** in (34) works on **man in the team who may desire it** by treating it as

(35) **any *x* such that either *x* is not on the team or *x* desires an appointment**

I do not pretend to have settled these last cases and there are more that Seuren brings up. But I have yet to be convinced that the ***any/ every*** situation cannot be settled by considering the scope of the familiar universal and existential quantifiers. Seuren proposes an 'arbitrariness' operator but I see no intelligible semantics for such a thing apart from as a scope indicator.

We mentioned on p. 156 the use of ***either*** as indicating scope. Thus:

(36) ***either John runs and Arabella sleeps or Clarissa sings***

differs from

(37) ***John runs and either Arabella sleeps or Clarissa sings***

because of the scope of ***or*** in deep structure. If we regard ***either*** (when it occurs with ***or***) as an adverb having no semantic effect so that if $a \in \mathbf{D}_0$ then

$$\mathrm{V}(\textbf{\textit{either}})(a) = a,$$

then we can formulate the deep structures

(38) $\langle\langle$***either***, $\langle\langle$***John***, ***runs***$\rangle$, ***and***, $\langle$***Arabella***, ***sleeps***$\rangle\rangle\rangle$, ***or***, $\langle$***Clarissa***, ***sings***$\rangle\rangle$

(39) $\langle\langle$***either***, $\langle$***John***, ***runs***$\rangle\rangle$, ***and***, $\langle\langle$***Arabella***, ***sleeps***$\rangle$, ***or***, $\langle$***Clarissa***, ***sings***$\rangle\rangle\rangle$

Although (36) can be derived from either (38) or (39) we rule out (39) as an acceptable deep structure on the ground that the scope of ***either*** is not the whole argument of its ***or***. In general an expression beginning with ***either*** will be unacceptable if it does not form the whole of an argument of ***or***.

This principle will ensure that the acceptable deep structure of (37) is

(40) ⟨⟨***John, runs***⟩, ***and***, ⟨***either***, ⟨⟨***Arabella, sleeps***⟩, ***or***, ⟨***Clarissa, sings***⟩⟩⟩⟩

rather than

(41) ⟨⟨⟨***John, runs***⟩, ***and***, ⟨***either***, ⟨***Arabella, sleeps***⟩⟩⟩, ***or***, ⟨***Clarissa, sings***⟩⟩

Transformations

The development of Part III ought to have shewn the immense power of λ-categorial languages. One might indeed regard the difference between pure categorial languages and λ-categorial languages as akin to the difference between phrase-structure grammars and transformational grammars. Principles of λ-conversion allow us to change the order of the proper symbols, insert a functor into the middle of its argument and make many other changes in order to bring out the relation between deep and surface structure. Indeed the suspicion begins to arise that they may do too much and that any sequence of words can be seen as the representation of virtually any deep structure.

This is why we need principles of acceptability. These will tell us that certain λ-deep structures are not, under normal circumstances, acceptable inputs, via their shallow structures, for the amalgamation function. By formulating the principles at the deep structure level we can have them do two jobs at once. In the first place, if a surface sentence cannot be obtained from *any* deep structure it will be ungrammatical.[281] In the second place, a surface sentence obtainable from two or more distinct deep structures may be made unambiguous, or may have its chances of ambiguity reduced, if some of the deep structures are ruled unacceptable. For the resolution of ambiguity it must be the deep structures which are either acceptable or unacceptable.

The qualification made above about 'normal circumstances' seems necessary since, as our examples on p. 91 f shewed, in very peculiar circumstances otherwise unnatural locutions may be used. This

[281] This perhaps shews why it is so difficult in a natural language to get a clear case of ungrammaticality. Speakers with good imaginations can frequently think up *some* deep structure from which the surface sentence could be obtained.

reflects a principle which we might refer to as the overriding primacy of the semantical context. I.e., any acceptability principle may be waived in circumstances in which it is clear that the surface expression must have the meaning of an otherwise prohibited deep structure.[282]

Our approach means of course that far more deep structures will occur than will yield acceptable surface structures. Pieter Seuren has objected to a state of affairs like this, but it is not at all clear that his reasons apply in the present case.[283] One of his reasons is that the deep structure should not generate uninterpretable sentences. Now it is true that our λ-categorial deep structure may contain expressions which have no meaning because at some point a function has an argument for which it is undefined (cf. pp. 73 and 78), but Seuren rightly distinguishes between grammatical and semantic deviance. For us the semantic deviance of a deep structure expression cannot even arise unless the expression is well-formed. And any semantically non-deviant deep structure expression is semantically interpretable. The deep structure for us represents ways in which English *might* develop given a particular lexicon and meaning assingment. That it does not choose all of these ways may reflect merely the historical development of the language or may represent some universal fact about the minds of human language-users.[284] The first task is to formulate a set of principles which might apply to English; then, and perhaps only then, we can try to see what lies behind them.

The investigation of principles of acceptability would have to be, as we remarked on p. 92, a task for empirical linguistics. Those familiar with current linguistic theory will have noticed however that for all our talk of 'deep structure', 'surface structure' and the like, and for all our citing linguistic evidence to motivate our analyses, there are certain important differences between our approach and usual transformational ones.

Transformational grammar takes as basic the idea of a *phrase-marker* (*vide* p. 17) and defines a *syntactic structure* (or sometimes a

[282] Ziff [1960], p. 132, formulates this as the principle: 'Construe what is said in such a way that, with a minimum of interpretation, it is significant.'

[283] Seuren [1969], p. 52 f.

[284] Perhaps we should be considering different kinds of acceptability. For instance, a deep structure might be held to be acceptable in the sense that its surface structure could (as in the poems on p. 92) *be made* to mean what that deep structure means, but unacceptable in the sense that it does not normally mean that. The principles governing one sort of acceptability might turn out to be of a quite different kind from those governing another sort.

derivation) as a sequence

$$\langle P_1, \ldots, P_n \rangle$$

of phrase-markers, each connected with the last by a transformation rule, and satisfying certain other restrictions. It is this whole syntactic structure which represents the sentence. P_1 can be thought of as the deep structure and might be expressed in a categorial language. P_n would be the surface structure and would be represented by a phrase-marker which exhibits all the features of the sentence revealed by surface grammar.

On one view of transformational grammar the meaning of the sentence is obtained from the deep structure P_1. If this is so it is only P_1 which need be susceptible of the kind of semantic analysis proposed in this book and there is no need to require that the grammatical analysis of the other phrase-markers reflect the semantics of the sentence.

Now it may well prove that for purely linguistic purposes it is better to regard the surface structure as a phrase-marker transformationally related to a λ-categorial sentence, but for philosophical purposes it would seem desirable that the relation between deep and surface structure were made as close as possible. Further, if the arguments of Parts III and IV have carried weight then any deep structure should be at least equivalent (by λ-conversion) to one of the kind we have presented. For the immediate application of what has been said in this book to linguistics, the most desirable thing would be to find some way of generating the acceptable λ-deep structures.

It may well prove that we can here introduce transformations into the grammar in perhaps a rather different role than they have in recent transformational theory, a role, though, which may come closer to Chomsky's original insight.[285] For we might think of acceptable λ-deep structures as being derived from a set of 'kernel structures' by transformational rules. We might wish these rules to provide what might be called a general theory of grammatical acceptability. More specific rules, of the kind we discussed earlier in the chapter with regard to scope determination and so on, would rule out further structures. Perhaps rules of both kinds, or perhaps only the specific ones, might be meaning-dependent. Thus the approach (in conjunction with the amalgamation rules) need not rule out semantic syntax, though of course it does not entail it. The transformations need not be meaning-preserving since their function

[285] Chomsky [1957].

is no longer to convert deep structures into surface structures; for the semantic interpretation of each λ-categorial sentence, whether acceptable or not, is already determined.

The formulation of the 'kernel' structures is unfortunately given little help from phrase-structure grammars, which, for all their application as generators of deep structure, are still far too tied to surface grammar. This in itself of course need not be a bad thing. Such restrictions as are demanded, e.g. by the agreement principles, seem best formulated in terms of the surface structure and it may be that the task of marking out roughly the general class of 'non-bizarre' structures is most easily done in this way. Surface grammar, although an untrustworthy master, may well make a good servant. It will then be up to the particular principles of the kind we discussed earlier in the chapter to rule out the remaining unacceptable structures.

To say this of course does not really help in shewing how the enormous amount of work already accomplished towards a transformational analysis of English (a small fraction of which we have made passing references to) could be reformulated in such a way as to generate the acceptable λ-categorial sentences. Such a reformulation would certainly achieve a marriage of formal and natural languages such as many have hoped for; whether it would be regarded as a significant contribution to settling the foundations of linguistics we must leave others to judge. The present book can do no more than provide some motivation for attempting the task.

CHAPTER FOURTEEN

Meaning and Use

In our analysis of language we have said very little about the use of language. Our chapter on pragmatics did indeed have to make some reference to the utterer, time of utterance etc. of a sentence but we said nothing about what it is to utter a sentence or why one should want to do so. The purposes of language are manifold and it is not part of this book to say much about them. It may however be thought that what we have said so far has presupposed the primacy of a particular use of language, viz. its assertive use. For in concentrating our discussion on declarative sentences as opposed to imperative or interrogative sentences have we not chosen to ignore the use of language to give commands or to ask questions? It will be one of the main contentions of this chapter that the semantical analysis of language which we have been presenting is quite neutral on the question of what use the language is put to.

Meaning and truth conditions

We shall consider how our analysis of the meaning of a sentence in terms of its truth conditions (i.e. the possible worlds in which it is true) might be thought to be affected by a consideration of the uses of language. Of course this analysis was refined in at least two directions: first in Chapter Three to take care of distinct but logically equivalent propositions, and second in Chapter Eight to take care of context-dependent sentences. We shall ignore the first of these refinements here, but many of our examples will make use of context-dependent sentences.

By 'meaning' in this chapter we shall mean 'meaning' as defined in this book, i.e. in terms of a system of domains and a value assignment. This means that in the case of sentences, once a context has been specified their meaning is to be understood in terms of their truth conditions. It may be that some of what we say will not hold for other senses of 'meaning'. In particular it may be that there are senses of 'meaning' which *are* affected by the use to which a sentence is put.[286] All that we shall want to insist is that our sense is neither arbitrary nor capricious and, what is most important, does not presuppose the primacy of the 'declarative' or 'fact-stating' use of language, or indeed of any use of language.

We shall first look at ordinary indicative sentences and shall maintain that differences in the uses to which such a sentence can be put (provided they are recognized linguistic uses of the sentence in question) do not in general cause a change in its meaning. As an example, consider the sentence

(1) **the boy who is responsible will report to my office at nine o'clock tomorrow**

If this is said by a headmaster in a school assembly, it is clearly the expression of an order. Yet when repeated over morning tea in the staffroom it may well function as a prediction. It could also be a rhetorical question, a piece of day-dreaming, or a number of other things. This in itself does not prove much. What is more important is that the question of what the truth conditions of (1) are is quite independent of which of these uses it is being put to.[287] To understand what is being predicted when (1) is used as a prediction, is to understand the conditions under which it will turn out to be true. To understand what is being ordered is equally to understand the conditions under which it will turn out to be true.

[286] E.g. the theory of meaning suggested in Stenius [1967] and formalized in Åqvist [1967], in which a sentence is split into two parts, a mood and a radical. It is the value of the radical which is the meaning of the sentence in our sense. The mood tells the use to which the sentence is put.

[287] Searle [1969], pp. 22–6, adapts the terminology of Austin [1962] (particularly pp. 94–8) and distinguishes between a *propositional act* and an *illocutionary act*. Both uses of (1) would be instances of the one propositional act of predicating reporting to the office at nine o'clock on the day following the day of utterance, of the boy who is responsible (for whatever act the context supplies). They would however be different illocutionary acts and each have a different *illocutionary force*. One would be an order, the other a prediction. We shall not be taking quite the same line as Searle here but certainly some distinction of this kind is crucial.

In both cases we could imagine the comment

(2) **I know he will because none of the boys ever disobeys an order of mine**

This is just as appropriate whether it is a whispered aside to the first assistant after (1) has just occurred as an order, or whether it is a remark after (1) has occurred as a prediction at morning-tea time.

It is perhaps odd to speak of the truth condition of an imperative. We would normally speak of the imperative as being obeyed or not obeyed. But it is also odd to speak of the truth conditions of a prediction. Predictions are more naturally spoken of as coming true or being fulfilled rather than being true; in this they are like wishes, for one may speak of a wish as coming true or being fulfilled. If I ask of (1) 'Is that a wish or a hope?' there is no suggestion that I think it is ambiguous in meaning.

Perhaps an even clearer case occurs in the sentences in a story. We all of us frequently tell stories for one reason or another in which we are not trying to assert that such and such is the case but rather are inviting our hearers or readers to imagine a possible world in which things are as the story describes them. Here too it is quite in order to explicate the 'meaning' of the sentence in the story by means of its truth conditions. Knowing what the story says involves knowing what the world would have to be like for the story to be true.[288]

Explicit performatives

Probably the most common use of the sentence

(3) **I order you to run**

is to order someone to run. Sentences like (3) have been called *performatives*. The reason is that in felicitous[289] circumstances genuine tokens of them cannot be false. Actually many of those who have spoken about performatives seem to have doubted whether they could be spoken of as being true or false at all.[290] This may be because they have thought that speaking of the truth or falsity of an utterance only makes sense if the utterance is intended as an assertion of a matter of fact. Our discussion of (1) ought to have cured us of that fallacy. As

[288] In a story there are at least two possible worlds involved, the story world (i.e. the world the story-teller is describing) and the story-teller's world. (We do not say the real world for we in our world may describe a possible world in which someone is telling a story, i.e. in which he is describing a third world.)

[289] Austin [1962], p. 14, propounds the 'doctrine of *infelicities*'. Infelicities are things that can go wrong with a performative and make it fail.

[290] E.g. Austin [1962], p. 5.

we are using the term, orders can also be true or false, though to be sure we do not use this locution in describing them.

(3) has as deep structure (by the principles of pp. 169–72):

(4) $\langle \boldsymbol{I}, \langle \lambda, x_1, \langle\langle \lambda, y_1, \langle \boldsymbol{order}, x_1, y_1\rangle\rangle, \langle \boldsymbol{inf}, \langle \boldsymbol{you}, \langle \boldsymbol{to}, \boldsymbol{run}\rangle\rangle\rangle\rangle\rangle\rangle$

In order to evaluate (4) we need only have a semantic rule for ***order*** since we have already given rules for ***I*** (11.1, p. 173) and ***you*** (p. 174). A rule for ***run*** is exactly analogous to the rule for ***sleeps*** (11.2, p. 174), and the analysis of ***inf*** and ***to*** is discussed on pp. 169–73 (of course ***inf*** now behaves like the context-dependent ***that*** of 11.6 (p. 177)).

14.1 V(***order***) is that function ω in $\mathbf{D}_{\langle 0,1,1\rangle}$ such that

(i) $\langle a,b\rangle$ is in the domain of ω iff $a \in \mathbf{D}_1$ is a person and b is a proposition,

and

(ii) for any context property $\mathfrak{p}$ in the domain of $\omega(a,b)$, if $\mathfrak{p}$ specifies a time t of utterance then for any $w \in \mathbf{W}$, $w \in (\omega(a,b))(\mathfrak{p})$ iff a orders b at t in w.

This rule is of course terribly crude. For one thing, it seems plausible to think that ***order*** should be a three-place predicate involving essential reference to the person being commanded.[291] For another, we are opting out completely of the question of what it is to order or command something.[292] But rough as it is the analysis will do for what we want.

When (4) is analysed by these rules (cf. the analysis of (8), p. 175) on pp. 175–7, we find that $V^+(4)$ is the open proposition θ such that for any context property $\mathfrak{p}$ which specifies an utterer u_1, a person addressed u_2, and a time t and any $w \in \mathbf{W}$, $w \in \theta(\mathfrak{p})$ iff u_1 in w at t orders the proposition that u_2 runs at t.[293]

In felicitous circumstances a token of (3) counts as the giving of an order that the person addressed is to run. By the analysis we have just given of (4) this means that in felicitous circumstances a token of (3) cannot fail to be true. (3) is thus a performative. Whether a sentence is a performative or not is quite independent of the question of which

[291] This may point up a more general defect in our analysis of infinitives. After all, ***John orders Bill to follow Arabella*** is not synonymous with ***John orders Arabella to precede Bill.***

[292] Broadie [1972] distinguishes between orders and commands. He rightly stresses that the primary function of an analysis of imperatives is to give an understanding of what it is to 'imperate' (op. cit., p. 184).

[293] Strictly, it ought to be the proposition that u_2 runs at some time t' almost immediately after t. Perhaps the idea of futurity is conveyed by the infinitive, and this may be another respect in which our analysis of infinitives was not subtle enough. E.g., we have ***I like him singing*** but ***I would like him to sing.***

particular use of language a token of it is put to. A token of (1) may be an order but it is certainly not a performative for, however felicitous the circumstances, a genuine utterance of (1) can never guarantee its truth. On the other hand

(5) **I say that Arabella runs**

is a performative even though it is an assertion. A token of (5) would normally be used to make an emphatic assertion that Arabella runs though its truth conditions are quite different from those of

(6) **Arabella runs**

The meaning of (5) is the open proposition θ such that where $\mathfrak{p}$ is a context property which specifies an utterer u and a time of utterance t, then $\theta(\mathfrak{p})$ is true in w iff u asserts in w that Arabella runs at t. (This can be worked out given the rules 11.1, 11.5, 11.4 and 11.3.)

(5) is a performative in that in felicitous circumstances to utter it *is* to say that Arabella runs. It is perhaps a mild linguistic curiosity that one should be able to say that Arabella runs by using a sentence which does not mean that Arabella runs (for (6) does not have the same meaning as (5); (6) is false if Arabella does not run even if I say that she does, i.e. even if (5) is true.)[294] But this is no more than a slight peculiarity of the word ***say***. After all, one can hint that Arabella runs without using language at all.

One point that needs stressing is that the evaluation of (5) requires that we know the meaning of (6), and while (5) is a performative, (6) is not. The situation is similar in the case of (3). The meaning of the performative sentences (3) and (5) is dependent on the meaning of the non-performative sentences

(7) **you run**

and (6). This is a conclusive argument against the view that all sentences are concealed performatives.[295]

Implicit performatives

The sentences (3) and (5) in the last section are not only performatives but in a sense they have it written on their face. The surface structure of the sentence makes it clear. However, it has been suggested that there are sentences which are performatives although they do not

[294] *Vide* Lewis [1970], p. 60 f, and G. Lakoff [1970a], p. 166 f.

[295] Of course to every sentence there corresponds an explicit performative. Thus to (1) when functioning as an order there corresponds the sentence: **I order the boy who is responsible to report to my office at nine o'clock tomorrow** when functioning as a prediction there corresponds: **I predict that the boy who is responsible will report to my office at nine o'clock tomorrow**, and so on.

appear so. Indeed some linguists have been tempted to postulate that all sentences are performative.[296] As we shewed at the end of the last section, in our sense of 'performative' this universal claim cannot be correct. Nevertheless there may be some sentences which are implicit performatives. And indeed it turns out to be a plausible conjecture that this is so. Consider the sentence

(1) **I claim that Arabella runs because John follows**

This has the alternative deep structures

(2) $\langle \boldsymbol{I}, \langle \lambda, x_1, \langle\langle \lambda, y_1, \langle \boldsymbol{claim}, x_1, y_1 \rangle\rangle,$
$\langle \boldsymbol{that}, \langle\langle \boldsymbol{Arabella}, \boldsymbol{runs} \rangle, \boldsymbol{because}, \langle \boldsymbol{John}, \boldsymbol{follows} \rangle\rangle\rangle\rangle\rangle$

and

(3) $\langle\langle \boldsymbol{I}, \langle \lambda, x_1, \langle\langle \lambda, y_1, \langle \boldsymbol{claim}, x_1, y_1 \rangle\rangle, \langle \boldsymbol{that}, \langle \boldsymbol{Arabella}, \boldsymbol{runs} \rangle\rangle\rangle\rangle,$
$\boldsymbol{because}, \langle \boldsymbol{John}, \boldsymbol{follows} \rangle\rangle$

(2) means that John's following is the reason why Arabella is running (she may be trying to escape him). (3) means that John's following is the reason for my claim that Arabella runs. (I may not be able to see Arabella clearly but seeing John and knowing what I do about Arabella's habits I may regard John's following as a reason to suppose that she is running.)

The ambiguity in (1) is resolved by scope difference, not by a difference in the meaning of *because*. Consider now:[297]

(4) **Arabella runs because John follows**

(4′) **Arabella runs, because John follows**

(One may choose to regard (4) and (4′) as readings of a single ambiguous surface sentence rather than as two separate sentences. Nothing turns on this.) If we try to analyse these as they stand we would have to assume that *because* is ambiguous. This is undesirable for several reasons: first, because there is no reason to suppose that *because* is

[296] E.g. McCawley [1968a], pp. 155–61, G. Lakoff [1970a], pp. 165–75 and Ross [1970]. There is no need for us to deny the usefulness of these proposals. We merely point out that the sense of meaning involved in them is different from ours. Lewis [1970], pp. 54–61, wants to treat all non-declarative sentences as performatives.

[297] Cf. the following examples from Rutherford [1970], p. 97:

(a) **He's not coming to class because he's sick.**

(b) **He's not coming to class, because he just called from San Diego.**

Rutherford accepts the view of Ross [1970] that all sentences are implicit performatives. Cf. also some examples attributed in G. Lakoff [1970a], p. 172 f to R. Lakoff. Given our analysis of meaning in terms of truth conditions, most of Ross' examples seem best dealt with by what he calls the 'pragmatic analysis' (op. cit., p. 254 f). Our own policy is to invoke the performative analysis only when as in (4′) there is no satisfactory way to give a meaning to the sentence as it stands.

ambiguous in (1) and second, because an exactly analogous ambiguity arises with other words as in:[298]

(5) **he'll take his umbrella in case it rains**

(6) **he'll take his umbrella, in case you're wondering**

(4) of course has a straightforward analysis, viz.:

(7) ⟨⟨***Arabella, runs***⟩, ***because***, ⟨***John, follows***⟩⟩

But (4′) is difficult. Indeed the only analyses that suggest themselves are (3) and a deep structure for

(8) **Arabella runs and I claim that because John follows**

The point about (8) is that (4′) may be held to entail that Arabella runs while (3) clearly does not. (3) (and in part (8)) is an explicit performative so (4′) could be regarded as an implicit performative.

The question now is how to deal with this in detail. Should we claim that the deep structure contains the symbols ***I****, ***claim**** and ***that**** whose semantics are those of ***I***, ***claim*** and ***that*** but whose surface realization is null, or should we say that sentences like (4′) are not grammatical at all but represent defective performances? I have a slight preference for the latter approach, mainly because the deleted elements are not 'logical particles' but represent a wide variety of verbs; and further, which verb is involved does not seem to be recoverable from the surface structure. Thus (4′) could be obtained from any of the following:

(9) **I claim that Arabella runs because John follows**

(10) **I inform you that Arabella runs because John follows**

(11) **I know that Arabella runs because John follows**

(12) **I see that Arabella runs because John follows**

and no doubt many others depending on the context of utterance. I suppose there would be no difficulty in having 'abstract' verbs ***inform****, ***claim****, ***know****, ***see**** etc., but one wonders whether it would not be simpler to recognize that sentences like (4′) are not proper sentences, in much the same way as

(13) **the man over there**

in answer to

(14) **who ran across the road?**

is understood to be elliptical for the sentence

(15) **the man over there ran across the road**

and not to be a proper sentence in its own right.

[298] Rutherford, loc. cit.

Our examination of implicit performatives leads naturally to a consideration of imperative sentences in English. Although, as we have seen, orders can be expressed by indicative sentences, they are typically expressed by imperative sentences like

(16) **report to my office at nine o'clock tomorrow**

or

(17) **shut the door**

At least two sources have been proposed for (17). Many linguists hold that the syntactical form of imperatives in English is a second person future statement with the **you** subject deleted.[299] I.e. (17) is obtained by deletion of **you** from

(18) **you will shut the door**

This would mean that the deep structure of (17) might be

(19) $\langle \textbf{\textit{you*}}, \langle \lambda, x_1, \langle \textbf{\textit{will*}}, \langle\langle \lambda, y_1, \langle \textbf{\textit{shut}}, x_1, y_1 \rangle\rangle,$
$\langle \lambda, x_{\langle 0,1\rangle}, \langle \textbf{\textit{the}}, \textbf{\textit{door}}, x_{\langle 0,1\rangle} \rangle\rangle\rangle\rangle\rangle\rangle$

Here $V(\textbf{\textit{you*}}) = V(\textbf{\textit{you}})$ and $V(\textbf{\textit{will*}}) = V(\textbf{\textit{will}})$ but $\mathfrak{A}(\textbf{\textit{you*}}) = \varnothing$ and $\mathfrak{A}(\textbf{\textit{will*}}) = \varnothing$ (while of course $\mathfrak{A}(\textbf{\textit{you}}) =$ **you** and $\mathfrak{A}(\textbf{\textit{will}}) =$ **will.**

If we derive (17) from (19) we would need what might be called a use-dependent acceptability principle for we would want to say that (17) is acceptable for a commanding use but not acceptable for an asserting use.[300]

The other favourite[301] is to regard (17) as an implicit performative:

(20) **I order you to shut the door**

with the deep structure

(21) $\langle \textbf{\textit{I*}}, \langle \lambda, x_1, \langle\langle \lambda, y_1, \langle \textbf{\textit{order*}}, x_1, y_1 \rangle\rangle,$
$\langle \textbf{\textit{inf}}, \langle \textbf{\textit{you*}}, \langle \lambda, x_1, \langle\langle \textbf{\textit{to}}, \langle \lambda, y_1, \langle \textbf{\textit{shut}}, x_1, y_1 \rangle\rangle\rangle, \langle \lambda, x_{\langle 0,1\rangle},$
$\langle \textbf{\textit{the}}, \textbf{\textit{door}}, x_{\langle 0,1\rangle} \rangle\rangle\rangle\rangle\rangle\rangle\rangle\rangle\rangle$

inf has a null realization in any case and if ***I****, ***order**** and ***you**** do too, then (21) will give (17) as a surface sentence. I personally find the

[299] For an illuminating discussion of English imperatives *vide* Bolinger [1967a] (though Bolinger does not altogether accept the view stated in the text).

[300] The idea that acceptability principles can depend on the use to which a sentence can be put can be generalized so that such contextual features as the knowledge and beliefs of the speaker may enter into determining the deviance or acceptability of a sentence. *Vide* G. Lakoff [1971b], Fillmore [1971], pp. 380–2 and Langendoen [1971].

[301] E.g. McCawley [1968], pp. 155–61, R. Lakoff [1968], G. Lakoff [1970a], p. 166, Ross [1970]. *Vide* also Chellas [1971] and Lewis [1970]. One must of course be careful to distinguish between a *syntactic* imperative sentence and the use of a sentence to give a command. To speak as Lewis does (p. 54) of an analysis of non-declarative sentences is ambiguous. In our approach the problem of giving a meaning (in terms of truth conditions) to all sentences is quite distinct from the problem of giving an analysis of what sentences are used to do.

linguistic evidence for a decision between (19) and (21) inconclusive. (19) seems to me more elegant but since our approach can handle both alternatives the inconclusiveness is unworrying. In either case the analysis of the meaning of imperative sentences is no different from the analysis of indicative sentences.

Questions[302]

Questions could also be regarded as performatives but, in the case of yes/no questions at least, the most straightforward analysis seems to be to regard them in most cases as ordinary sentences. Thus

(1) **will you shut the door**

is derived from

(2) $\langle \textit{\textbf{will}}, \langle \textit{\textbf{you}}, \langle \lambda, x_1, \langle\langle \lambda, y_1, \langle \textit{\textbf{shut}}, x_1, y_1 \rangle\rangle, \langle \lambda, x_{\langle 0,1\rangle}, \langle \textit{\textbf{the}}, \textit{\textbf{door}}, x_{\langle 0,1\rangle} \rangle\rangle\rangle\rangle\rangle\rangle$

Here we need a use-dependent acceptability principle to say that this will only work for questions.[303] But the meaning of (1) is the same as the corresponding declarative sentence.

wh- questions are a little different. E.g., in

(3) ***who runs***

V(***who runs***) is not a proposition, for there is nothing in the domain of individuals of which it is being asked whether he runs. Rather V((3)) is the same as V(***runs***), for when a person asks (3) he can be thought of as asking for which *a* does *a* run. I.e., what is being questioned is a one-place property, where to question a one-place property is to want to know for which argument or arguments it holds. Just as in (7) on p. 232 what is being commanded is a proposition and, as we claim, it is not the business of a theory of meaning but of a theory of use to say what is being done to the proposition, so here it is not the business of a theory of meaning, as opposed to a theory of use, to tell us what is being done to a property when it is being questioned.

[302] There is quite a lot of literature on the logic of interrogatives. A bibliography and summary up to 1966 will be found in Hamblin [1967]. Our present remarks are limited to giving an indication of how we would incorporate questions into our general account of language.

[303] The way to shew that something is a part of the meaning rather than of the illocutionary force of a sentence is to look at what happens when the sentence is embedded in a larger sentence which does not have the same illocutionary force. Thus ***will he come*** becomes ***John wonders whether he will come***, which shews that the inversion of ***he*** and ***will*** is use-dependent rather than meaning-dependent. This is not an infallible guide. Sometimes, when the verb is embedded in a higher verb of saying, we may wish to report the force as well as the meaning. (This might be one way of dealing with the examples in G. Lakoff [1970a], pp. 167–70.) Cf. Cohen's arguments against Grice in Cohen [1971].

We introduce in the deep structure a symbol $\boldsymbol{who}^q$ (to distinguish it from the relative pronoun). Of course $\mathfrak{A}(\boldsymbol{who}^q) =$ **who**. $\boldsymbol{who}^q$ here is a marker which indicates that a one-place predicate is standing alone as a complete utterance. In general this can only happen in a question. $\boldsymbol{who}^q$ is therefore of category $\langle\langle 0,1\rangle,\langle 0,1\rangle\rangle$ and its semantics is:

14.2 $V(\boldsymbol{who}^q)$ is that function $\zeta \in \mathbf{D}_{\langle\langle 0,1\rangle,\langle 0,1\rangle\rangle}$ such that for any $\omega \in \mathbf{D}_{\langle 0,1\rangle}$, $\zeta(\omega) = \omega$.

The deep structure of (3) is of course

(4) $\langle \boldsymbol{who}^q, \boldsymbol{runs}\rangle$

just as the deep structure of

(5) ***who loves Arabella***

is

(6) $\langle \boldsymbol{who}^q, \langle \lambda, x_1, \langle\langle \lambda, y_1, \langle \boldsymbol{loves}, x_1, y_1\rangle\rangle, \boldsymbol{Arabella}\rangle\rangle\rangle$

Other **wh**- questions can be dealt with in the same way.

An alternative would be to have $\boldsymbol{who}^q$ in the category $\langle\langle 0,\langle 0,1\rangle\rangle, \langle 0,1\rangle\rangle$ on the ground that clauses beginning with $\boldsymbol{who}^q$ can serve as they stand as the objects of (certain) transitive verbs. E.g., it seems plausible to construe

(7) ***John knows*** $\boldsymbol{who}^q$ ***runs***

as

(8) $\langle \boldsymbol{John}, \langle \lambda, x_1, \langle\langle \lambda, y_1, \langle \boldsymbol{knows}, x_1, y_1\rangle\rangle, \langle \boldsymbol{who}^q, \boldsymbol{runs}\rangle\rangle\rangle\rangle$

If we adopt this line we would have to say that $\boldsymbol{who}^q$ makes a nominal which can stand alone as grammatically acceptable for a question. Of course, we want this nominal to be a logically proper name (in the sense of 9.3, p. 132) which picks out V(***runs***); i.e. if $V(\langle \boldsymbol{who}^q, \boldsymbol{runs}\rangle)$ is in $\mathbf{D}_{\langle 0,\langle 0,1\rangle\rangle}$ then it would be true of a property in a world iff that property held of V(***runs***) in that world.

There seem to be quite heavy restrictions on the acceptability of questions. In particular, if the question consists of $\boldsymbol{who}^q$ followed by an abstract we cannot have the variable bound by the abstract embedded in too awkward a way. Although (4) is quite acceptable,

(9) $\langle \boldsymbol{who}^q, \langle \lambda, x_1, \langle\langle \lambda, x_{\langle 0,1\rangle}, \langle\langle \boldsymbol{Arabella}, x_{\langle 0,1\rangle}\rangle, \boldsymbol{and}, \langle x_{\langle 0,1\rangle}, x_1\rangle\rangle\rangle, \boldsymbol{run}\rangle\rangle\rangle$

is not; though, curiously enough, we can say

(10) **Arabella and who run**

This probably has the deep structure

(11) $\langle\langle \lambda, x_{\langle 0,1\rangle}, \langle\langle \lambda, x_1, \langle\langle \boldsymbol{Arabella}, x_{\langle 0,1\rangle}\rangle, \boldsymbol{and}, \langle x_{\langle 0,1\rangle}, x_1\rangle\rangle\rangle, \boldsymbol{who}^q\rangle\rangle, \boldsymbol{run}\rangle$

(11) converts to

(12) $\langle\langle\lambda, x_1, \langle\langle$***Arabella, run***$\rangle$, ***and***, $\langle$***run***, $x_1\rangle\rangle\rangle$, ***who***$^q\rangle$

which is not acceptable but is perhaps more revealing.

The deep structure of **wh-** questions is a complicated subject worth a monograph in itself. But I would hope that what I have said at least indicates that questions need not be forgotten in a λ-categorial analysis of language.

Conversational meaning

In our chapter on pragmatics (especially p. 122) we discussed one way in which the context could affect the sense of what was said. But we so defined meaning that the meaning is constant though the sense may vary. Meaning in this sense is a function from contexts to senses. It is right that such an account should be called 'pragmatics' but perhaps it should be called 'semantic pragmatics'. This is because the way in which the context produces the sense is part of the meaning. Pragmatic pragmatics would then study cases where the meaning itself depended on the context. Unlike semantic pragmatics there would be no rules for getting from the context to the meaning, for if there were we could get from there to the sense and it would just be a case of semantic pragmatics.[304]

Some such theory is needed to account for cases of structural ambiguity in which the same shallow, or surface, structure can be obtained by deletion from two or more equally acceptable deep structures. Here features of the context, which can include physical properties of the utterance, such as intonation; immediately perceptible properties, like the identity of the speaker; or more general properties, such as assumed background knowledge; can make it clear in one way or another which deep structure is the intended one. By this is probably meant that one of the meanings would fit in with what had gone before while another would not; one would be a sensible thing to say and the other would not. One cannot here say more precisely what this means – if one could it could be incorporated into the semantic pragmatics – but we all know how rarely ambiguous sentences when used are taken the wrong way. One reason why newspaper headlines provide such good examples is that we usually read the headline before reading the paragraph under it and so get the sentence before we get the context and therefore sometimes take an

[304] Though Apostel [1971], pp. 4–6, appears to have in mind the possibility that, depending on the context, the very interpretation might change. (Cf. Cohen [1962], pp. 1–23.)

inappropriate meaning.[305] Ambiguities in conversation do occur but not nearly as often as the sentences we use would allow for.

The idea that context, in this vague and non-semantical way, can force a particular interpretation on what we say can be taken further than is required merely for the resolution of ambiguities. It may even force a meaning on a sentence which that sentence does not have when its deep structure is evaluated.

One might if one wished speak here about metaphorical or conversational meaning.[306] A metaphor arises when the literal meaning is not appropriate but some particular non-literal meaning is appropriate. E.g., the sentence

(1) **he's a ruthless butcher**

has a literal meaning which makes it false when said of a Minister of Railways who decides to close all the branch lines under 10 miles long and to replace all steam engines with diesel engines. But if our hearer knows whom we are talking about, knows that he is a Minister of the Crown and a lawyer and knows that we know this too, then there seems to be a sense in which in that conversational context something true may well have been said. The *conversational meaning* of (1) is more like the *literal meaning* of

(2) **his actions are unjustifiably severe**

The interesting question is how to get from (1) to (2). The answer would seem to be the same as the one given above, in terms of the most sensible thing to say in the circumstances. Since everyone knows the Minister is not a butcher in the literal sense, we search around for a proposition which has a structure analogous to (1) but is a sensible thing to say in the circumstances. The literal meaning of (1) is incompatible with a sensible contribution to the conversation and so unless we have some indication that the conversation is not a sensible one we assume that something like (2) and not (1) is meant.

When a metaphor is still a live one, as we assume (1) is, the way to obtain the meaning expressed in (2) is to obtain the literal meaning by evaluating its deep structure and *then* cast around for the nearest sensible proposition. There is nothing in this procedure which in any way affects anything we have said in the earlier parts of this book.

[305] Another reason of course is that headlines are often elliptical and can be made complete sentences in non-equivalent ways.

[306] The importance of metaphor and its role in language change is stressed in Cohen and Margalit [1970]. Leech [1969], pp. 89–93, calls this 'transferred meaning'. He postulates what he calls (p. 89 f) 'rules of transference which derive the irregular from the regular senses'. Cf. also Bloomfield [1933], p. 149 f.

Of course if (1) is used often enough in this way, it will come to have a literal meaning like (2). ***butcher*** will cease to mean only a man who cuts up and sells meat and will also mean someone who destroys things thought to be of value. This is probably the major way in which language develops. But a language in which (1) literally means (2) can only develop if there is a time at which (1) is, in the literal sense, not true, and utterances of it intend to assert things like (2).

Now it may very well be that most, or at least a great deal, of language is not to be taken literally but this does not mean that a sentence does not have a literal meaning.[307] And it does not mean that the literal meaning does not have an important part to play in arriving at the metaphorical meaning. On the contrary, if I am right, the understanding of a genuine metaphor requires us to understand the literal meaning of the sentence in which it is expressed and cast about for the nearest thing to that meaning which would be sensible to say in the circumstances. There is no reason why an analysis of language of the kind we are aiming to provide should be expected to have anything to say about what is a sensible thing to say in certain circumstances, and it is thus no criticism of our theory of meaning that we have not made room for metaphorical meaning.

Indeed our attitude to metaphor ought to please those who want to insist on the fact that language is an ever-changing and living phenomenon which cannot be tied down by formal rules. For, although we have tied down a particular synchronic description of a language by formal rules, we have, in our distinction between literal and metaphorical meaning, allowed that the things which a man may use language to express are not thereby essentially restricted.

That a formal analysis of language should impose limits on human creativity might indeed appear a melancholy conclusion, but fortunately it is one to which no account that is adequate to the facts can lead.

[307] This fact need worry us no more than the fact that most of the sentences we produce are ungrammatical need worry Chomsky (*vide* especially Chomsky [1965], pp. 3–27, for the relation between 'performance' and 'competence').

APPENDIX ONE

Some Background Notions

Set Theory

This is not an introduction to set theory for its own sake. There are many good ones available and anyone who wishes to do serious work in the philosophy of language would be well advised to buy one. Highly to be recommended are Halmos [1960] and Lemmon [1969]. Halmos is more readable (though the mathematical applications of Chapter Eleven and onward are less important for philosophers and linguists), but Lemmon uses the system of set theory which we have been presupposing, viz. that called NBG, developed by von Neumann, Bernays, and Gödel.

$x \in y$ means that x is a member of the class y. There are two ways of specifying classes. If y is finite and has as members precisely $y_1, \ldots, y_n$ then we can write $\{y_1,\ldots,y_n\}$. If y is the class of all things satisfying a certain condition then we write $\{x: --- x ---\}$. Here the $--- x ---$ is intended to stand for any sentence which can be formulated in the language. E.g. $\{x: x$ is greater than $2\}$ would be the class of everything in our domain of discourse which is greater than 2. To avoid contradictions such as Russell's paradox (Lemmon [1969], pp. 2–4, Halmos [1960], pp. 4–7) we cannot assume completely generally that every condition determines a set. In NBG we avoid Russell's contradiction by making a distinction between *sets* and *classes*. Sets are simply those classes which are members of other classes, and *proper classes* (i.e., classes which are not sets) are those classes which are not members of other classes. Things which are not classes at all (and so *a fortiori* are neither sets nor proper classes) are called *individuals*. Individuals are unlike classes in that they do not have members. They are, however, like sets in that they may be members of classes. We then have an axiom which ensures that for every condition there is exactly one class of those and only those individuals or sets which satisfy the condition. Sometimes we speak of a *family* of sets. This neutral expression refers to either a class or a set of sets.

$\varnothing$ is the class with no members. If x and y are classes, $x \cap y$, the *intersection* of x and y, is the class whose members are those things in both x and y; $x \cup y$, the *union* of x and y, the class of things in either x or y; and $x - y$ the class of things in x but not in y. x is said to be *included* in y ($x \subseteq y$) iff every member of x is also a member of y;[308] y is said in such a case to be a *subset* of x. If $x \subseteq y$ but not $y \subseteq x$ then x is a *proper* subset of y. Two classes x and y are *disjoint* iff they have no common members, i.e., iff $x \cap y = \varnothing$. A family z of sets is *pairwise disjoint* iff for any two sets x and y in z if $x \neq y$ then $x \cap y = \varnothing$.

Two classes are the same iff they have the same members. Thus $\{x,y\} = \{y,x\}$. But we sometimes want, and this is particularly important in our study of language, to speak of an *ordered class* or a *sequence*. We write $\langle x,y \rangle$ to indicate the pair consisting of x and y *in that order*.[309] If $\langle x,y \rangle = \langle u,v \rangle$ then $x = u$ and $y = v$. This is known as the *fundamental theorem on ordered pairs*. An ordered n-membered set $\langle x_1,\ldots,x_n \rangle$ is called an *n-tuple* and $\langle x_1,\ldots,x_n \rangle$ are said to be its members.

If x and y are classes then $x \times y$, the *Cartesian product* (or cross product, or sometimes just product) of x and y, is the set of all ordered pairs $\langle z,u \rangle$ where $z \in x$ and $u \in y$. $x \times x$, denoted by x^2, is the set of all ordered pairs of members of x. More generally $x_1 \times \ldots \times x_n$ is the set of all n-typles in which the first member is taken from x_1, ..., and the nth from x_n. Thus x^n is the set of all n-tuples of members of x.

For infinite sequences we need to introduce the notion of a *function*. We need such a notion in any case. Functions in set theory are a

[308] Inclusion must be distinguished from membership though sometimes in contexts where no ambiguity can arise we use 'contains' to mean 'contains as a member' or 'contains as a subset'.

[309] One can define ordered pairs and n-tuples in terms of ordinary set membership but the details do not concern us. We want, however, to have a definition of 'member of' for ordered sets which ensures that $\langle x,y,z \rangle$ has three members, x, y and z in that order, while $\langle\langle x,y \rangle,z \rangle$ and $\langle x,\langle y,z \rangle\rangle$ have only two. Further, that the two members of $\langle\langle x,y, \rangle,z \rangle$ and $\langle x,y \rangle$ and z and the two members of $\langle x,\langle y,z \rangle\rangle$ are x and $\langle y,z \rangle$. It is important for us to insist that $\langle x,y,z \rangle$, $\langle\langle x,y \rangle,z \rangle$ and $\langle x,y,\langle z \rangle\rangle$ are three distinct ordered sets. (Perhaps we should distinguish between an ordered pair as used in the definition of a relation and a 2-tuple or two-membered sequence. Our notation is ambiguous here.)

special kind of relation and a relation is a special kind of class. A relation is a class of ordered pairs.[310] The idea is quite simply that x is related to y by r iff $\langle x,y\rangle \in r$. Every relation has a *domain* and a *range*. The domain of r is the class of all x's which are related by r to something. More formally:

$$\{x\text{: For some } y, \langle x,y\rangle \in r\}$$

The range of r is the class of all y's to which something is related by r:

$$\{y\text{: For some } x, \langle x,y\rangle \in r\}$$

A function is a relation such that for every x in its domain there is *exactly one* y to which x is related. I.e., r is a function iff for any x, y, and z, if $\langle x,y\rangle \in r$ and $\langle x,z\rangle \in r$ then $y = z$. When we are speaking of functions we frequently use 'f' instead of 'r'. So if $\langle x,y\rangle \in f$ and $\langle x,z\rangle \in f$ then $y = z$. Since f associates only one thing with x we can use the notation $f(x)$ to indicate the unique y such that $\langle x,y\rangle \in f$. $f(x)$ is called the *value of the function f for the argument* x. Occasionally $f(x)$ is written f_x. This is most often done when we want to speak of a series of things $f_1, \ldots, f_n$, say. Here f can be regarded as a function which gives a series of values $f_1, \ldots, f_n$ for the numbers 1 to n. (1 to n here form what is sometimes called an *index* set.) We also speak of the function f *applied* to x to give $f(x)$.

Note that there is no reason why the range of values of a function should not be included in, or be the same as, its domain, and there is no reason why a function applied to x should not have x as its value. Both these points can be illustrated by the case of what are called truth functions (and here I do not mean the symbols, which I would call truth functors, but the functions these symbols represent). The domain of truth functions is the set $\{1,0\}$ and the range is also $\{1,0\}$. There are four (one-place) truth functions, viz.:

$$f_1 = \{\langle 1,1\rangle, \langle 0,1\rangle\}$$
$$f_2 = \{\langle 1,1\rangle, \langle 0,0\rangle\}$$
$$f_3 = \{\langle 1,0\rangle, \langle 0,1\rangle\}$$
$$f_4 = \{\langle 1,0\rangle, \langle 0,0\rangle\}$$

Thus, e.g., $f_2(1) = 1, f_2(0) = 0, f_3(1) = 0, f_3(0) = 1$. In the case of f_2 the value is always the same as the argument, in the case of f_1 and f_4 sometimes, while in the case of f_3 never, though if f_3 is applied twice we have $f_3(f_3(x)) = x$ for both 1 and 0. The important thing to note here is that the things which can be the values of the functions are exactly

[310] That is, a two-place (or *binary*, or *dyadic*) relation is a class of ordered pairs. An n-place relation is a class of n-tuples. But some authors use the word 'relation' only to mean a two-place relation.

the same as the things which are its arguments. There is a tendency to think of, say, $f_1(1)$ as somehow a more complicated thing than 1, but this is misleading for $f_1(1)$ just *is* 1.

We sometimes wish to speak, if we have two classes x and y, of the set of all functions whose domain is y and whose range is included in x. We use the notation x^y for this purpose. Sometimes a function is called a *mapping*. We speak of a class x as being *mapped into* a class y iff there is a function f whose domain is x and whose range is included in y. Where the range of f is the whole of y (i.e., where every member of y is the value of f of something in x) we say that x is mapped *onto* y. A special kind of function or mapping is a $1-1$ function. f is a $1-1$ function iff no two arguments have the same value. This need not be true of functions in general. E.g., in our f_1 above we have both $f_1(1) = 1$ and $f_1(0) = 1$, and so f_1 is not $1-1$. f_2 and f_3 are, however. Put more formally, f is $1-1$ iff f is a function and if $f(x) = f(y)$ then $x = y$. Intuitively we can think of a $1-1$ function (or $1-1$ correspondence, as it is sometimes called) as a function which pairs off the members of two classes so that each member of the one is associated with one and only one member of the other.

The functions we have discussed so far have all taken a single argument and associated a value with it. There is no difficulty in thinking of a function which takes two or more arguments. An example from arithmetic is $+$. $x + y$ denotes a unique number given x and y. Conventionally we write '$+$' between the names of its arguments, but we could equally write '$+(x,y)$' and in any case the sign '$+$' is not the function itself but merely the sign we use to refer to the operation of adding two numbers together. We can always treat an n-place function as a 1-place function by collecting together the n arguments into an n-tuple and applying the function to that n-tuple. Thus whether we write $f(x_1,\ldots,x_n)$ or $f(\langle x_1,\ldots,x_n\rangle)$ the difference is, for most practical purposes, negligible. Sometimes the word 'function' is reserved for one-place functions, and a two-place function like $+$ is called an *operation*. We shall use both terms. We shall frequently use the letter 'ω', sometimes indexed by an appropriate index set, to refer to operations. The word 'operation' is most often used when the range of the function is included in its domain.

A *sequence* is a function from the natural numbers 1, 2, ... etc. If σ is a sequence, then $\sigma(1)$, often written σ_1, is its first member, σ_2 is its second, and so on. The important thing here is to divorce entirely from one's mind the idea that the *order of representation* has anything to do with the order of the sequence. σ_3 does not precede σ_4 in the sequence σ because the sign for σ_3 (viz. 'σ_3') is written to the left of the sign for σ_4 (viz. 'σ_4'); it precedes it because 3 precedes 4 in the standard ordering of the natural numbers and σ_3 is the value of σ for 3 while σ_4 is the value of σ for 4.

We shall frequently have occasion to speak of a function f from some index set I whose values are all sets. If we want to speak of the union of all the sets in the range of f then we shall, unless this would cause ambiguity, denote this by f^+. I.e., $x \in f^+$ iff for some $i \in \mathrm{I}$, $x \in f_i$. An example of this is the class Δ^+ of symbols of a propositional language as defined on p. 13. $\delta \in \Delta^+$ iff for some number n, $\delta \in \Delta_n$. This convention is our own and requires contexts in which no confusion can arise. Some such notation as $\bigcup_{i \in \mathrm{I}} f_i$ is much more suitable for the general case but proves cumbersome when there is only one i involved. It should also be noted that we use $+$ in slightly different ways on other occasions (as in V^+ on p. 19 and π^+ on p. 74). These other usages are explained.

Language and Metalanguage

It is perhaps odd that we should have relegated explicit discussion of the relation between language and metalanguage to an appendix. Yet explicit discussion of this relation in a treatise on language can, paradoxically, induce confusion over matters which are otherwise clearly understood. I would hope that the discussion in the text reads well enough to shew what is happening without explanation, and the present explanation is for those who already have some idea of the issues and want to be reassured that I am clear about what is going on.

When we talk about a language we must do so in a language. This language might be the same as the language we are talking about, as when we say

(1) The word 'dog' in English is often used to refer to an animal

or even

(2) The word 'dog' is normally used to refer to dogs though it can be used to refer to people, whereas the word 'people' is seldom used to refer to anything but people.

But one can also say

(3) The word 'chien' in French is normally used to refer to dogs.

In case (3) the language we are talking about, the *object language*, is French, while the language in which we are talking about it, the *metalanguage*, is English.

The present book talks about languages. Many of the languages it talks about are formal or artificial languages and frequently it talks about classes of languages. In technical jargon one would say that these languages and the words in them are *mentioned*, just as the words 'dog', 'people', and 'chien' were mentioned in the examples above. Of these, the words 'dog' and 'people' are also being *used*, in the metalanguage. If the word 'dog' is mentioned this means we are talking about the word 'dog'. If the word 'dog' is being used (in English) then we are talking about dogs. Probably no one would be confused when the languages are ordinary languages; but the same distinctions apply when we are talking about formal languages – and perhaps the most confusing situation of all is when the metalanguage *uses* symbols from, say, mathematical or set-theoretical vocabulary. This confusion is particularly acute when the same symbol is mentioned (as a part of the object language) and used in the metalanguage; e.g. one might say, when explaining the role of the sign '=' in the object language, that the sentence '$x = y$' is true iff $x = y$. Yet this is really no worse than "'dogs' refers to dogs".

Earlier in this appendix we were using signs like '$f(x)$' and so on to refer to the value of the function f for the argument x. This is why we could say that $f(x)$ might be x; though of course the complex expression '$f(x)$' is clearly distinct from the symbol 'x'. Thus '$f(x) = x$' will be a true sentence, if $f(x)$ is indeed x, though "'$f(x)$' = 'x'" is clearly not true since '$f(x)$' and 'x' are different (linguistic) entities.

When we say as we do in 1.2 that where δ is a symbol of a certain kind and where $\alpha_1, \ldots, \alpha_n$ are symbols of a certain kind then $\langle\delta,\alpha_1,\ldots,\alpha_n\rangle$ is a sentence, the signs 'δ', 'α_1', ..., 'α_n' are part of a metalanguage which is basically English but also contains other symbols, e.g. Greek letters. This is the metalanguage in which this book is written. 'δ', i.e., refers to an entity of the object language and is used in the metalanguage to refer to that entity. Actually 'δ' is a *metavariable* since we do not have a particular entity in mind but are talking indifferently about many members of a class; just as we do when we say 'A car to me is simply a means of getting from A to B.' We say in the text what sort of thing δ can be (our conditions are almost unlimited). Similarly the complex sign '$\langle\delta,\alpha_1,\ldots,\alpha_n\rangle$' (strictly '$\langle$' to the left of '$\delta$' to the left of ',' and so on) is the symbol of our enriched metalanguage which designates the ordered $n+1$-tuple whose first member is δ (*not* 'δ' and *certainly* not '$\langle$'), whose second is α_1, and so on. This is a set-theoretical entity of the kind we have described earlier in this appendix: the brackets and the left-to-right juxtaposition are merely the way in which our enriched English metalanguage talks about it. The sign '$\langle\delta,\alpha_1,\ldots,\alpha_n\rangle$' is very rarely mentioned in the text but frequently used.

Or when, e.g., we say $V(x) = u$, the letter 'V' in the metalanguage denotes a value assignment, 'x' denotes a symbol of the object language and 'u' a member of the domain of values. It is important to realize that 'u' is just as much a metavariable as 'x' is in the sense that both 'x' and 'u' occur as variables in the metalanguage; though there is of course a sense in which 'x' is a metavariable while 'u' is not, for 'x' is a variable in the metalanguage ranging over certain linguistic entities in the object language while 'u', though a variable in the metalanguage, has as its range not linguistic entities but the values (whatever they are) of those linguistic entities.

'=' is always in the metalanguage except in Chapter Two. Thus $\alpha = \beta$ is a completely metalinguistic assertion (just like $x = y$) saying that α and β are the same expression. Our use of quotation marks in the metalanguage is intended to be careful philosophical usage. We discuss a general theory of quotation on pp. 104–8.

Some more remarks about the language/metalanguage distinction are made in Chapter Four, where they are needed to correct certain misconceptions about the nature of the study of semantics.

APPENDIX TWO

A Uniqueness Theorem

From time to time in Parts I and II, particularly in Chapters Five and Six, we have been concerned to shew the uniqueness of various sets of complex entities constructed in certain ways out of initially given sets of simply entities. The object of this appendix is to shew how this may be proved. We shall first prove the uniqueness of the set *Syn* of syntactical categories as defined on p. 71.

The definition given there is a little loose. More properly Syn is the intersection of all sets Σ such that

A1 $\text{Nat} \subseteq \Sigma$
A2 If $\tau, \sigma_1, \ldots, \sigma_n \in \Sigma$ then $\langle \tau, \sigma_1, \ldots, \sigma_n \rangle \in \Sigma$

This gives us the sense in which Syn is the *smallest* set satisfying A1 and A2. Since if any Σ satisfies A1 and A2 then $\text{Syn} \subseteq \Sigma$. We assume that there are sets satisfying A1 and A2 (it should be clear that the universe class of NBG satisfies A1 and A2). Given that there are, then obviously Syn is unique by this definition but it is necessary to prove that Syn satisfies A1 and A2. We shew that if X is a family of sets all satisfying A1 and A2 then $\cap X$ satisfies A1 and A2.

For A1 if $\text{Nat} \subseteq \Sigma$ for every $\Sigma \in X$ then obviously $\text{Nat} \subseteq \cap X$.

For A2 suppose that $\tau, \sigma_1, \ldots, \sigma_n \in \cap X$; then for every $\Sigma \in X$, $\tau, \sigma_1, \ldots, \sigma_n \in \Sigma$. But Σ satisfies A2, so $\langle \tau, \sigma_1, \ldots, \sigma_n \rangle \in \Sigma$. Thus $\langle \tau, \sigma_1, \ldots, \sigma_n \rangle$ is in every member of X, whence $\langle \tau, \sigma_1, \ldots, \sigma_n \rangle \in \cap X$ and so $\cap X$ satisfies A2. In particular Syn satisfies A1 and A2.

We now establish the uniqueness of the function E defined on p. 72. The proof of this theorem will in fact indicate how the proofs of all the other uniqueness theorems of this type will go. E is defined in the text as that function from Syn whose range is the system of smallest sets satisfying

5.13 $F_\sigma \subseteq E_\sigma$

5.14 If $\alpha_1, \ldots, \alpha_n \in E_{\sigma_1}, \ldots, E_{\sigma_n}$ respectively and $\delta \in E_{\langle\tau,\sigma_1,\ldots,\sigma_n\rangle}$ then $\langle\delta,\alpha_1,\ldots,\alpha_n\rangle \in E_\tau$.

Since relations can be regarded as sets of ordered pairs we first define Θ^- to be that unique set which is included in all sets Θ of ordered pairs which satisfy

A3 For any $\sigma \in$ Syn, if $\alpha \in F_\sigma$ then $\langle\sigma,\alpha\rangle \in \Theta$

A4 If $\langle\sigma_1,\alpha_1\rangle, \ldots, \langle\sigma_n,\alpha_n\rangle, \langle\langle\tau,\sigma_1,\ldots,\sigma_n\rangle, \delta\rangle \in \Theta$ then $\langle\tau,\langle\delta,\alpha_1, \ldots,\alpha_n\rangle\rangle \in \Theta$.

Θ^- will in fact be the intersection of all sets satisfying A3 and A4. It is sufficient to prove that if every member of a set Y satisfies A3 and A4 then $\cap$Y satisfies A3 and A4. Obviously if every $\Theta \in$ Y satisfies A3 then $\cap$Y satisfies A3. Suppose that for every $\Theta \in$ Y, $\langle\sigma_1,\alpha_1\rangle, \ldots, \langle\sigma_n,\alpha_n\rangle, \langle\langle\tau,\sigma_1,\ldots,\sigma_n\rangle,\delta\rangle \in \Theta$, then since Θ satisfies A4, $\langle\tau,\langle\delta,\alpha_1,\ldots,\alpha_n\rangle\rangle \in \Theta$. Thus $\langle\tau,\langle\delta,\alpha_1,\ldots,\alpha_n\rangle\rangle$ is in every $\Theta \in$ Y and thus in $\cap$Y. Given a unique Θ^- as so defined, we define E as the function from Syn such that for any $\sigma \in$ Syn, $E_\sigma = \{\alpha: \langle\sigma,\alpha\rangle \in \Theta^-\}$.

In fact, given any Θ satisfying A3 and A4 we may define a function based on it in just the way E is based on Θ^-. We shall call this function E(Θ). I.e. for any $\sigma \in$ Syn

$$(E(\Theta))_\sigma = \{\alpha: \langle\sigma,\alpha\rangle \in \Theta\}$$

Each E(Θ) will satisfy 5.13 and 5.14 and further

$$E_\sigma \subseteq (E(\Theta))_\sigma$$

so that E will be the system of smallest sets satisfying 5.13 and 5.14.

It will also be the case that, provided $\mathscr{L}$ is grounded, no expression will belong to more than one syntactic category. The proof of this requires a rather more complicated proof of the uniqueness of E than we have given and will therefore be omitted.

Other uniqueness theorems, e.g. the extension of $\mathscr{L}$ to $\mathscr{L}^\lambda$, as described on p. 85, will follow much the same pattern as the one we have outlined.

Bibliography

After each item will be found a list of the numbers of the footnotes in which reference to the item in question is made.

Abbreviations

FL	*Foundations of Language*. Dordrecht, Reidel.
JSL	*The Journal of Symbolic Logic*. Providence, Rhode Island. Association for Symbolic Logic.
LA	*Logique et Analyse*. Louvain, E. Nauwelearts.
PNL	*Pragmatics of Natural Languages* (ed. Y. Bar Hillel). Dordrecht, Reidel, 1971.
PPL	*Philosophical Problems in Logic* (ed. K. Lambert). Dordrecht, Reidel, 1970.
RTG	*Readings in English Transformational Grammar* (ed. R. A. Jacobs and P. S. Rosenbaum). Waltham, Mass., Ginn and Co., 1970.
ULT	*Universals in Linguistic Theory* (ed. E. Bach and R. T. Harms). New York, Holt, Rinehart and Winston, 1968.
ZML	*Zeitschrift für mathematische Logik und Grundlagen der Mathematik*. Berlin, VEB Deutscher Verlag der Wissenschaften.
ΦΛΨ	*Semantics*, *An Interdisciplinary Reader in Philosophy*, *Linguistics and Psychology* (ed. D. Steinberg and L. A. Jakobovits). Cambridge, Cambridge University Press, 1971.

ADJUKIEWICZ, K.

[1935] Syntactic connection. *Polish Logic* (ed. S. McCall). Oxford, Oxford University Press, 1967, pp. 207–31. (English translation of 'Die syntaktische Konnexität' *Studia Philosophica*, Vol. 1 (1935) pp. 1–27.) (**11**, **21**)

APOSTEL, L.

[1971] Further remarks on the pragmatics of natural languages. *PNL* pp. 1–34. (**304**)

ÅQVIST, L.

[1967] Semantic and pragmatic characterizability of linguistic usage. *Synthese* Vol. 17 (1967) pp. 281–91. (**286**)

AUSTIN, J. L.

[1962] *How to do things with Words*. Oxford, Oxford University Press, 1962. (**79**, **287**, **289**, **290**)

BACH, E.

[1968] Nouns and noun phrases. *ULT* pp. 91–122. (**170**, **185**, **199**, **206**, **224**)

BAMBROUGH, R.

[1971] Objectivity and objects. *Proceedings of the Aristotelian Society* (N.S.) Vol. 72 (1971/72) pp. 65–81. (**243**)

BAR HILLEL, Y.

[1963] Can indexical sentences stand in logical relations? *Philosophical Studies* Vol. 14 (1963) pp. 89–90. (**145**)

[1964] *Language and Information*. New York, Addison-Wesley, 1964. (**21**, **22**, **89**)

BARCAN MARCUS, R. C.

[1962] Interpreting quantification. *Inquiry* Vol. 5 (1962) pp. 252–9. (**47**)

BLOOMFIELD, L.

[1933] *Language*, New York, Holt, 1933. (**173**, **204**, **306**)

[1936] Review of A. F. Bentley. *Language* Vol. 12 (1936) pp. 137–41. (Reprinted in *A Leonard Bloomfield Anthology* (ed. C. F. Hockett). Bloomington, Indiana University Press, 1970, pp. 328–32.) (**3**)

BOLINGER, D. L.

[1967a] The imperative in English. *To Honor Roman Jakobson*. The Hague, Mouton and Co., 1967. Vol. I pp. 335–62. (**299**)

[1967b] Adjectives in English: attribution and predication. *Lingua* Vol. 18 (1967) pp. 1–34. (**242**)

BORKOWSKI, L.
[1958] The reduction of arithmetic to logic based on the theory of types without the axiom of infinity or the typical ambiguity of arithmetical constants. *Studia Logica* Vol. 8 (1958) pp. 283–95. (**173**)

BRESNAN, J. W.
[1970] On complementizers: toward a syntactic theory of complement types. *FL* Vol. 6 (1970) pp. 297–321. (**222**)

BROADIE, A.
[1972] Imperatives. *Mind* Vol. 81 (1972) pp. 179–90. (**292**)

CARNAP, R.
[1942] *Introduction to Semantics*. Cambridge, Mass., Harvard University Press, 1942. (**4**)
[1947] *Meaning and Necessity*. Chicago, University of Chicago Press, 1947 (2nd ed. 1956). (**6, 9, 49, 57**)
[1950] *Logical Foundations of Probability*. Chicago, University of Chicago Press, 1950 (2nd ed. 1962). (**6**)

CHELLAS, B. F.
[1971] Imperatives. *Theoria* Vol. 37 (1971) pp. 114–28. (**301**)

CHOMSKY, A. N.
[1957] *Syntactic Structures*. The Hague, Mouton and Co., 1957. (**4, 15, 21, 102, 107, 285**)
[1965] *Aspects of the Theory of Syntax*. Cambridge, Mass., M.I.T. Press, 1965. (**162, 199, 307**)
[1968] *Language and Mind*. New York, Harcourt, Brace, 1968. (**184, 234, 265**)
[1970] Remarks on Nominalization. *RTG* pp. 184–221. (**261**)
[1971] Deep structure, surface structure and semantic interpretation. *ΦΛΨ* pp. 183–216. (**259**)

CHURCH, A.
[1940] A formulation of the simple theory of types. *JSL* Vol. 5 (1940) pp. 56–68. (**22, 109**)
[1941] *The Calculi of Lambda Conversion*. Princeton, Princeton University Press, 1941. (**112**)
[1956] *Introduction to Mathematical Logic Vol. I*. Princeton, Princeton University Press, 1956. (**40, 97**)

COCCHIARELLA, N. B.
[1969] Existence entailing attributes, modes of copulation and modes of being in second-order logic. *Nous* Vol. 3 (1969) pp. 33–48. (**117**)

COHEN, L. J.

[1962] *The Diversity of Meaning*. London, Methuen, 1962. (**304**)

[1971] Some remarks on Grice's views about the logical particles of natural languages. *PNL* pp. 50–68. (**303**)

COHEN, L. J. and MARGALIT, A.

[1970] The role of inductive reasoning in the interpretation of metaphor. *Synthese* Vol. 21 (1970) pp. 469–87. (**306**)

COHN, P. M.

[1965] *Universal Algebra*. New York, Harper and Row, 1965. (**67**)

CRAIG, W.

[1953] On axiomatizability within a system. *JSL* Vol. 18 (1953) pp. 30–3. (**44**)

CRESSWELL, M. J.

[1966a] The completeness of SO.5. *LA* No. 34 (1966) pp. 263–6. (**98**)

[1966b] Functions of propositions. *JSL* Vol. 31 (1966) pp. 545–60. (**28**)

[1967] Propositional identity. *LA* No. 39–40 (1967) pp. 283–92. (**28**)

[1968] The representation of intensional logics. *ZML* Vol. 14 (1968) pp. 289–98. (**16**)

[1970] Classical intensional logics. *Theoria* Vol. 36 (1970) pp. 347–72. (**36, 43, 53, 55, 98**)

[1972a] Intensional logics and logical truth. *Journal of Philosophical Logic* Vol. 1 (1972) pp. 2–15. (**36, 38, 43, 53, 61**)

[1972b] The world is everything that is the case. *Australasian Journal of Philosophy* Vol. 50 (1972) pp. 1–13. (**48, 84, 143, 152**)

[1972c] Second order intensional logic. *ZML* Vol. 18 (1972) pp. 297–320. (**64, 113**)

DAVIDSON, D.

[1967] Truth and meaning. *Synthese* Vol. 17 (1967) pp. 304–23. (**23**)

DELMORE, E. and DOUGHERTY, R. C.

[1972] Appositive NP constructions. *FL* Vol. 8 (1972) pp. 2–29. (**206**)

DONELLAN, K. S.

[1966] Reference and definite descriptions. *The Philosophical Review* Vol. 75 (1966) pp. 281–304. (Reprinted in *ΦΛΨ* pp. 100–14.) (**158**)

[1970] Proper names and identifying descriptions. *Synthese* Vol. 21 (1970) pp. 335–58. (**158**)

DOUGHERTY, R. C.

[1970] A grammar of coordinate conjoined structures: I. *Language* Vol. 46 (1970) pp. 850–98. (**206, 213**)

FEYS, R.

[1946] Logique combinatoire. *Revue Philosophique de Louvain* Vol. 44 (1946) pp. 74–103, 237–70. (**109**)

FILLMORE, C. J.

[1968] The case for case. *ULT* pp. 1–88. (**191, 271**)

[1971] Types of lexical information. *ΦΛΨ* pp. 370–92. (**300**)

FØLLESDAL, D.

[1966] *Referential Opacity and Modal Logic*. Oslo, Universitets forlaget, 1966. (**194**)

FRAASSEN, B. C. VAN

[1970] Inference and self reference. *Synthese* Vol. 21 (1970) pp. 425–38. (**125**)

FREGE, G.

[1892] Über Sinn und Bedeutung. *Zeitschrift für Philosophie und philosophische Kritik* (N.S.) Vol. 100 (1892) pp. 25–50 (translated in Frege [1952] pp. 56–78 as 'On sense and reference'). (**97**)

[1952] *Translations from the Philosophical Writings of Gottlob Frege*. Trsl. P. T. Geach and M. Black. Oxford, Blackwell, 1952. (**97**)

GEACH, P. T.

[1970] A program for syntax. *Synthese* Vol. 22 (1970) pp. 3–17. (**21, 189**)

GLEASON, H. A.

[1961] *An Introduction to Descriptive Linguistics*. (Revised edition) New York, Holt, Rinehart and Winston, 1961. (**210, 248, 264**)

GODDARD, L. and ROUTLEY, F. R.

[1966] Use, mention and quotation. *Australasian Journal of Philosophy* Vol. 44 (1966) pp. 1–49. (**133, 160**)

GOGUEN, J. A.

[1969] The logic of inexact concepts. *Synthese* Vol. 19 (1969) pp. 325–73. (**80**)

GOODMAN, N.

[1951] *The Structure of Appearance*. Cambridge, Mass., Harvard University Press, 1951. (**181**)

[1954] *Fact, Fiction and Forecast*. London, The Athlone Press, 1954. (**63**)

GRICE, H. P.

[1968] Utterer's meaning, sentence-meaning and word-meaning. *FL Vol.* 4 (1968) pp. 1–18 (reprinted in Searle [1971]). (**5**)

HALLIDAY, M. A. K.

[1970] Functional diversity in language as seen from a consideration of modality and mood in English. *FL* Vol. 6 (1970) pp. 322–61. (**5**)

HALMOS, P. R.

[1960] *Naive Set Theory*. Princeton, Van Nostrand, 1960.

HAMBLIN, C. L.

[1967] Questions. *The Encyclopedia of Philosophy* New York, Macmillan, 1967, Vol. 7 pp. 49–53. (**302**)

HARMAN, G. H.

[1970] Deep structure as logical form. *Synthese* Vol. 21 (1970) pp. 275–97. (**167, 235**)

[1971] Three levels of meaning. *ΦΛΨ* pp. 66–75. (**4**)

HERMES, H.

[1965] *Enumerability, Decidability, Computability*. Berlin, Springer Verlag, 1965 (2nd ed. 1969). (**44, 45**)

HINTIKKA, K. J. J.

[1962] *Knowledge and Belief*. Ithaca, Cornell University Press, 1962. (**61**)

[1969] *Models for Modalities*. Dordrecht, Reidel, 1969. (**116, 117**)

[1970] The semantics of modal notions and the indeterminacy of ontology. *Synthese* Vol. 21 (1970) pp. 408–24. (**117**)

HUGHES, G. E. and CRESSWELL, M. J.

[1968] *An Introduction to Modal Logic*. London, Methuen, 1968. (**30, 35, 41, 42, 85, 86**)

JACKENDOFF, R. S.

[1968] Quantifiers in English. *FL* Vol. 4 (1968) pp. 422–42. (**173, 190**)

JACOBS, R. A. and ROSENBAUM, P. S.

[1968] *English Transformational Grammar*. Waltham, Mass., Blaisdell, 1968. (**216, 223**)

JOURDAIN, P. E. B.

[1918] *The Philosophy of Mr B*rtr*nd R*ss*ll*. London, George Allen and Unwin, 1918. (**231**)

KARTTUNEN, L.

[1971] Definite descriptions with crossing co-reference. *FL* Vol. 7 (1971) pp. 157–82. (**235**)

KASHER, A.

[1971] A step toward a theory of linguistic performance. *PNL* pp. 84–93. (**145**)

KATZ, J. J.

[1966] *The Philosophy of Language*. New York, Harper and Row, 1966. (**1, 75, 77, 104**)

[1967] Recent issues in semantic theory. *FL* Vol. 3 (1967) pp. 124–94. (**104**)

KATZ, J. J. and FODOR, J. A.

[1963] The structure of a semantic theory. *Language* Vol. 39 (1963) pp. 170–210 (reprinted in *The Structure of Language* (ed. J. A. Fodor and J. J. Katz) Englewood Cliffs, N.J., Prentice-Hall, 1964). (**75, 104**)

KATZ, J. J. and POSTAL, P. M.

[1964] *An Integrated Theory of Linguistic Descriptions*. Cambridge, Mass., M.I.T. Press, 1964. (**75, 77, 104**)

KEENAN, E. L.

[1971] Quantifier Structures in English. *FL* Vol. 7 (1971) pp. 255–84. (**21**)

KIPARSKY, P. and KIPARSKY, C.

[1971] Fact. *ΦΛΨ* pp. 345–69. (**222**)

KNEALE, W. C.

[1972] Propositions and truth in natural languages. *Mind* Vol. 81 (1972) pp. 225–43. (**218**)

KRIPKE, S. A.

[1963a] Semantical analysis of modal logic I, normal modal propositional calculi. *ZML* Vol. 9 (1963) pp. 67–96. (**35**)

[1963b] Semantical considerations on modal logics. *Acta Philosophica Fennica* (1963) *Modal and Many-valued Logics* pp. 83–94. (**35**)

LAKOFF, G.

[1968] Instrumental adverbs and the concept of deep structure. *FL* Vol. 4 (1968) pp. 4–29. (**191, 192**)

[1970a] Linguistics and natural logic. *Synthese* Vol. 22 (1970, pp. 151–271. (**2, 183, 192, 212, 220, 224, 280, 294, 296, 297, 301, 303**)

[1970b] Pronominalization, negation, and the analysis of adverbs. *RTG* pp. 145–65. (**234**)

[1971a] On generative semantics. *ΦΛΨ* pp. 232–96. (**115, 162, 202, 276**)

[1971b] Presupposition and relative well-formedness. *ΦΛΨ* pp. 329–40. (**300**)

LAKOFF, R.

[1968] *Abstract Syntax and Latin Complementation*. Cambridge, Mass., M.I.T. Press, 1968. (**301**)

[1970] Tense and its relation to participants. *Language* Vol. 46 (1970) pp. 838–49. (**252**)

LAMBERT, K. and FRAASSEN, B. C. VAN

[1970] Meaning relations, possible objects and possible worlds. *PPL* pp. 1–19. (**117**)

LANGENDOEN, D. T.

[1971] Presupposition and assertion in the semantic analysis of nouns and verbs in English. *ΦΛΨ* pp. 334–44. (**300**)

LEBLANC, H. and MEYER, R. K.

[1970] Truth value semantics for the theory of types. *PPL* pp. 77–101. (**47**)

LEE, D. A.

[1971] Quantifiers and identity in relativization. *Lingua* Vol. 27 (1971) pp. 1–19. (**190**)

LEECH, G. N.

[1969] *Towards a Semantic Description of English*. Harlow, Longmans, 1969. (**306**)

LEES, R. B.

[1960] *The Grammar of English Nominalizations*. The Hague, Mouton and Co., 1960. (**260**)

LEMMON, E. J.

[1969] *Introduction to Axiomatic Set Theory*. London, Routledge and Kegan Paul, 1969. (**123, 124**)

LEWIS, D. K.

[1968] Counterpart theory and quantified modal logic. *Journal of Philosophy* Vol. 65 (1968) pp. 113–26. (**116**)

[1970] General Semantics. *Synthese* Vol. 22 (1970) pp. 18–67. (**10, 15, 21, 23, 46, 57, 58, 59, 60, 62, 69, 70, 76, 80, 89, 142, 169, 176, 177, 188, 226, 235, 268, 272, 294, 296, 301**)

ŁUKASIEWICZ, J.

[1929] *Elementy logiki matematcznej.* Warsaw, 1929. (**103**).

LYONS, J.

[1966] Towards a 'notional' theory of the parts of speech. *Journal of Linguistics* Vol. 2 (1966) pp. 209–36. (**21**)

[1967] A note on possessive, existential and locative sentences. *FL* Vol. 4 (1967) pp. 390–6. (**240**)

[1969] *Introduction to Theoretical Linguistics.* Cambridge, Cambridge University Press, 1969. (**15, 18, 21, 185, 240, 258, 259**)

MCCAWLEY, J. D.

[1968a] The role of semantics in a grammar. *ULT* pp. 125–69. (**199, 213, 214, 215, 296, 301**)

[1968b] Concerning the base component of a transformational grammar. *FL* Vol. 3 (1968) pp. 243–69. (**21**)

[1971] Where do noun phrases come from? *ΦΛΨ* pp. 217–31. (**2, 199, 235**)

MARTIN, R. L.

[1971] Some thoughts on the formal approach to the philosophy of language. *PNL* pp. 120–44. (**7**)

MONTAGUE, R.

[1968] Pragmatics. *Contemporary Philosophy* (ed. R. Klibansky). Florence, La Nuova Italia Editrice, 1968, pp. 102–21. (**36**)

[1969] On the nature of certain philosophical entities. *The Monist* Vol. 35 (1969) pp. 159–94. (**46, 120**)

[1970a] Universal grammar. *Theoria* Vol. 36 (1970) pp. 373–98. (**10, 21, 23, 29, 34, 38, 53, 89, 92, 110, 136, 138, 142, 143, 183, 266**)

[1970b] Pragmatics and intensional logic. *Synthese* Vol. 22 (1970) pp. 68–94. (**23, 29, 140, 255**)

[1973] The proper treatment of quantification in ordinary English. *Approaches to Natural Language* (ed. K. J. J. Hintikka, J. M. E. Moravcsik and P. Suppes). Dordrecht, Reidel, 1973, pp. 221–42. (**106, 225, 227, 272**)

PARSONS, T.

[1970a] Some problems concerning the logic of grammatical modifiers. *Synthese* Vol. 21 (1970) pp. 320–34. (**183**, **189**)

[1970b] An analysis of mass and amount terms. *FL* Vol. 6 (1970) pp. 362–88. (**176**, **180**, **182**)

PARTEE, B. H.

[1970] Opacity, co-reference and pronouns. *Synthese* Vol. 21 (1970) pp. 359–85. (**227**, **279**)

POSTAL, P. M.

[1970] On so-called pronouns in English. *RTG* pp. 56–82. (**247**)

PRIOR, A. N.

[1957] *Time and Modality*. Oxford, Oxford University Press, 1957. (**33**)

[1963] Is the concept of referential opacity really necessary? *Acta Philosophica Fennica* (1963) *Modal and Many-valued Logics* pp. 189–89. (**71**)

[1967] *Past, Present and Future*. Oxford, Oxford University Press, 1967. (**33**, **252**)

[1968] *Papers on Time and Tense*. Oxford, Oxford University Press, 1968. (**33**)

[1971] *Objects of Thought* (ed. P. T. Geach and A. J. P. Kenny). Oxford, Oxford University Press, 1971. (**90**, **109**)

QUINE, W. V.

[1940] *Mathematical Logic*. Cambridge, Mass., Harvard University Press, 1940 (2nd ed. 1957). (**39**, **130**, **131**, **134**, **274**)

[1953] *From a Logical Point of View*. Cambridge, Mass., Harvard University Press, 1953. (**38**, **82**, **132**)

[1960] *Word and Object*. Cambridge, Mass., M.I.T. Press, 1960. (**20**, **81**, **180**, **182**, **246**, **257**)

[1969] *Ontological Relativity and Other Essays*. New York, Columbia University Press, 1969. (**47**, **51**, **52**, **63**)

[1970] Methodological reflections on current linguistic theory. *Synthese* Vol. 21 (1970) pp. 387–98. (**257**)

RASIOWA, H. and SIKORSKI, R.

[1963] *The Mathematics of Metamathematics*. Warsaw, P.W.N., 1963 (2nd ed. 1968). (**66**)

REICHENBACH, H.

[1947] *Elements of Symbolic Logic*. New York, Macmillan, 1947. (**183**)

RENNIE, M. K.

[1971] Completeness in the logic of predicate modifiers. *LA* No. 55 (1971) pp. 627–43. (**183**)

ROBBINS, B. L.

[1968] *The Definite Article in English Transformations.* The Hague, Mouton and Co., 1968. (**239**)

ROSS, J. R.

[1967] On the cyclic nature of English pronominalization. *To Honor Roman Jakobson*, The Hague, Mouton and Co., 1967. Vol. III, pp. 1669–82. (**234**)

[1970] On declarative sentences. *RTG* pp. 222–72. (**296, 297, 301**)

ROUTLEY, F. R.

[1971] Domainless semantics for free, quantification and significance logics. *LA* No. 55 (1971) pp. 603–26. (**54, 121**)

RUTHERFORD, W. E.

[1970] Some observations concerning subordinate clauses in English. *Language* Vol. 46 (1970) pp. 97–115. (**297, 298**)

SCOTT, D. S.

[1970] Advice on modal logic. *PPL* pp. 143–73. (**36, 41, 86, 87, 97, 116, 117, 118, 142, 255**)

SEARLE, J. R.

[1969] *Speech Acts.* Cambridge, Cambridge University Press, 1969. (**287**)

[1971] *The Philosophy of Language* (ed.). Oxford, Oxford University Press, 1971. (**63**)

SEGERBERG, K.

[1972] *An Essay in Classical Modal Logic.* 3 Vols. Uppsala, Philosophical Studies, 1972. (**36, 41**)

SEUREN, P. A. M.

[1969] *Operators and Nucleus.* Cambridge, Cambridge University Press, 1969. (**274, 279, 280, 283**)

[1972] Autonomous versus semantic syntax. *FL* Vol. 8 (1972) pp. 237–65. (**276**)

SMULLYAN, A. F.

[1948] Modality and description. *JSL* Vol. 13 (1948) pp. 31–7. (**194**)

SOBOCIŃSKI, B.

[1955] Studies in Leśniewski's mereology. *Polish Society of Arts and Sciences Abroad Yearbook for 1954–55* pp. 34–43. (**181**)

SPIEGL, F.

[1965] *What the Papers Didn't mean to Say*. Liverpool, Scouse Press, 1965. (**100**)

STAAL, J. F.

[1967] Some semantic relations between sentoids. *FL* Vol. 3 (1967) pp. 66–88. (**271**)

[1969] Formal logic and natural languages (ed.). *FL* Vol. 5 (1969) pp. 256–84. (**145**)

STALNAKER, R. C.

[1970] Pragmatics. *Synthese* Vol. 22 (1970) pp. 272–89. (**46**)

STENIUS, E.

[1967] Mood and language game. *Synthese* Vol. 17 (1967) pp. 254–74. (**286**)

STRAWSON, P. F.

[1950] On referring. *Mind* (N.S.) Vol. 59 (1950) pp. 320–44. (**154**)

[1959] *Individuals*. London, Methuen, 1959. (**13**, **119**)

SUPPES, P.

[1960] *Axiomatic Set Theory*. Princeton, Van Nostrand, 1960. (**123**)

TARSKI, A.

[1935] Der Wahreitsbegriff in den formalisierten Sprachen. *Studia Philosophica* Vol. 1, pp. 261–405. (**23**, **128**)

[1956] *Logic Semantics and Metamathematics* (translated by J. H. Woodger). Oxford, Oxford University Press, 1956. (**128**, **130**)

THOMASON, R. H. and STALNAKER, R. C.

[1968] Modality and reference. *Nous* Vol. 2 (1968) pp. 359–72. (**194**)

TICHÝ, P.

[1971] An approach to intensional analysis. *Nous* Vol. 5 (1971) pp. 273–97. (**109**)

[1972] Plantinga on essence: a few questions. *The Philosophical Review* Vol. 81 (1972) pp. 82–93. (**31**)

URMSON, J. O.

[1956] *Philosophical Analysis*. Oxford, Oxford University Press, 1956. (**49**)

VENDLER, Z.

[1967] *Linguistics in Philosophy*. Ithaca, N.Y., Cornell University Press, 1967 (Chapter 2 is reprinted as 'Singular terms' in *ΦΛΨ* pp. 33–69). (**184**, **212**, **222**, **239**, **256**, **265**)

WASOW, T. and ROEPER, T.

[1972] On the subject of gerunds. *FL* Vol. 8 (1972) pp. 44–61. (**261**)

WHITEHEAD, A. N. and RUSSELL, B. A. W.

[1910] *Principia Mathematica*. Cambridge, Cambridge University Press, 3 Vols., first edition 1910–1913, second edition 1923–1927. (**166, 194**)

WIGGINS, D.

[1971] On sentence-sense, word-sense and a difference of word-sense. Towards a philosophical theory of dictionaries. *ΦΛΨ* pp. 14–34. (7)

WITTGENSTEIN, L.

[1922] *Tractatus Logico-philosophicus*. First published, London, Kegan Paul, 1922. (8)

WOODRUFF, P. W.

[1970] Logic and truth-value gaps. *PPL* pp. 121–42. (**154**)

ZIFF, P.

[1960] *Semantics Analysis*. Ithaca, N.Y., Cornell University Press, 1960. (**184, 282**)

Author Index

Subject Index

Lexicon

This lexicon contains only symbols which are referred to as separate entities in the deep or surface structures of a λ-categorial language. Page references indicate where a word is introduced or discussed. An italicized page number indicates a semantic rule for the word.